WORLD FOLKTALES

A Scribner Resource Collection

WORLD FOLKTALES

A SCRIBNER RESOURCE COLLECTION

ATELIA CLARKSON
& GILBERT B. CROSS

Charles Scribner's Sons · New York

To Peggy and Charles and four young sons:
Derek, John, Gavin, and Robert

Library of Congress Cataloging in Publication Data

Main entry under title:

World folktales.
  "A Scribner resource collection."
  Bibliography: p.
  Includes indexes.
  1. Tales. 2. Tales—Classification. I. Clarkson,
Atelia. II. Cross, Gilbert B.
GR74.W67   398.2   79–20921
ISBN 0–684–16290–3

1 3 5 7 9 11 13 15 17 19 F/C 20 18 16 14 12 10 8 6 4 2

Printed in the United States of America

Preface

There is no "correct" version of a tale; nor is there any one correct approach to folktale study. Certainly no single standard reference work has heretofore been suitable for students, folklore enthusiasts, potential folklore enthusiasts, and all lovers of good tales. Any such handbook would need to depart drastically from the format of traditional folktale anthologies. We hope that *World Folktales* does just that. The purpose of this resource collection is to present a single volume that explains one way to approach the complex study of the folk narrative, offers a representative sampling of tales from all over the world, and finally, demonstrates and suggests how to use the material in a classroom, a library, or in front of a good fire.

Collections of folktales have traditionally fallen into two basic categories: those that limit themselves to tales from a certain geographical area and those that are restricted to the work of a particular collector, some more scrupulous in their treatment of materials than others. Children's literature anthologies and editions constitute still another repository of printed folktales. Such books generally reprint tales without supplying any scholarly apparatus and with scant regard for the authenticity of the text itself. *World Folktales* is an attempt to mend the rift that has grown between the scholars and the children, between those who would study the tales and those who would enjoy them.

Because we believe that there is a middle ground where specialists and

v

enthusiasts can both be comfortable, we have divided this resource collection into two parts. The first part is concerned with those research tools needed for any comprehensive study of the folktale. Folktales are fun; their study should not be drudgery. Therefore, we have attempted to soothe unnecessary fears about the seemingly complicated and highly abbreviated folklore indexes. Such basic works as the Aarne-Thompson *Type Index,* Thompson's *Motif Index,* and Baughman's *Type and Motif Index of the Folktales of England and North America* are invaluable tools and need not intimidate the unwary or those without an advanced degree in folklore. We also discuss and explain other indexes designed to help teachers and storytellers locate folktales in collections that are less scholarly in nature.

The main section of the book is, of course, the tales themselves and their annotations. We have carefully selected tales representative of the major geographical, ethnic, and cultural regions of the world. Thus, we have chosen fifteen tales from North America, thirteen from the British Isles, ten from Scandinavia, eight from Central Europe, and eight from the Far East. The Hispanic cultures are represented by four tales, the Near East by four tales, Africa by four tales, and Australasia by one.

Within the North America tale group we have selected tales from southern whites, black Americans, American Indians, Cajun Americans, Jewish Americans, Canadians, and Canadian Indians. The British Isles are represented by tales from England, Scotland, Ireland, Wales, and the Isle of Man. The Scandinavian storytelling tradition is expressed in tales from Iceland, Finland, Norway, Denmark and Sweden. Central Europe is represented by France, Germany, Italy, Czechslovakia, and Poland. China, Russia, Japan, Cambodia, Korea and Tibet speak for the folktale tradition in the Far East. And so on. Wherever possible, we have selected either tales not frequently anthologized or at least have chosen a less familiar version of a more familiar tale.

A similar balance, but one more difficult to manage, is attempted between folktale collectors from the nineteenth century—those great pioneers in the field—and contemporary folktale scholars of the highest caliber. Thus we have assembled twenty-one tales from such early collectors as Grimm, Asbjørnsen, Croker, Hunt, Halliwell, and Crane, as well as tales from that first popularizer, Joseph Jacobs. Another twenty-one tales reflect the collection of modern folktale scholars such as Richard Dorson, Katharine Briggs, Leonard Roberts, Marie Campbell, J. Mason Brewer, and Harold Courlander, as well as another well-known popularizer of this century, Richard Chase. Two field collections come directly from our student archives at Eastern Michigan University.

But this book is not intended for folklorists only, and we have selected some tales from the other side of the folklore/children's literature barrier. Two tales represent some of the best names in the literary storytelling tradition—Charles Perrault and Walter de la Mare. Additionally, storytellers whose publications were landmarks in the historical development of children's literature are represented by the *St. Nicholas* magazine, and other such well-known names in children's literature as Virginia Tashjian, Parker Fillmore, Sara Cone Bryant and Kate Wiggin.

A collection of tales, however, no matter how balanced or versatile, serves little purpose without suitable annotations. We have therefore provided background information on each tale. Notes contain most or all of the following: the tale's pedigree, history, and dispersion; a comparison with variants, literary versions, and similar tales; explanations of cultural and historical references; reasons for the tale's appeal; and considerations relative to children's literature. Each annotation also includes all technical information necessary for scholarly comparison—type number, principal motifs, and a list of parallel versions. In short, the annotations are informative essays designed to help the reader understand the nature of traditional literature.

We attempt another balance in the classification of the tales themselves. In order to avoid the greatest pitfall of all—the abuse of classification —we have chosen to depart from some of the anachronistic folktale categories, and to flee forever from the popularizers who would label all folktales "fairy tales." Instead we have settled on ten divisions of folktales and legends which we believe will assist the reader in understanding the nature of a particular kind of tale by focusing on the most obvious similarities and apparent relationships. Nothing in the world is ever going to prevent a trickster like Anansi from jumping out of his category, running up and down the Roman numerals of our careful classification system, and appearing in a Formula Tale, just for the mischief of it all. Such is the vital and elusive nature of a folktale tradition that is alive and well and inhabited by human narrators who either get mixed up or like the story better that way. Nevertheless, the choice may well be to study the nature of classification at that point or move on to the nature of traditional narrative within general and logical classifications.

Clearly we have opted for the latter, for our three decades of teaching children's literature and folklore have convinced us that there are two essential goals for all who wish to achieve proficiency in the study of the folktale. First, they must read a wide selection of tales in a variety of tellings: literary versions of folktales, field collections of folktales, regional dialect collections of folktales, and some masterful retellings of folktales by talented storytellers. Then they should study one tale in depth. Only by reading several versions of the same tale, comparing both structure and plot, and finally drawing conclusions about the patchwork relationship of motif to tale to character to idiosyncracy of narrator—only then can they begin to understand the nature of traditional material. When they discover the long and elaborate matrix of plot and digression and good/bad/forgetful narrators and tales wandering from one country to the next, they gain insights into all those fascinating byways that make the study of traditional material so rewarding.

To assist in the comparative study of folktales, two appendices follow the major divisions of the book and deal specifically with folktales in the college and elementary classroom. In both instances our approach to the study of the folktale remains two-pronged. Whether this book is used as an anthology in a children's literature survey class, as a text in a folklore class, or as a source for storytellers and elementary school teachers and librarians, we still suggest that all be encouraged to concentrate on reading a variety of tales and on studying one tale in depth by comparison and contrast.

For the elementary classroom, we describe the comparative folktale unit as it was presented in one fourth-grade class, together with instructions for writing a paper and a sample paper written by a fourth grader. Additionally, we offer a variety of suggestions for combining folklore with the more traditional subjects—art, literature, dramatics, creative writing, and social studies—as well as for library use.

For the college classroom spending two to three weeks on a folktale unit, we present detailed aims and objectives of the comparison paper, give directions for researching and writing such a paper, demonstrate the use of tabular worksheets, offer advice to the weary student as well as the overeager, and finally print a sample comparison paper of a familiar folktale. In so doing, we have, we hope, opened the door to this fascinating area of scholarship on hinges strong enough to carry the load of the heaviest objections or the weight of the unenthusiastic. The tales themselves will do the rest.

The bibliography contains all books mentioned in the text and itself constitutes a resource. A popular title index, tale type index, and motif index are provided for easy reference. The poplar title index contains a listing of many of the more common titles by which familar folktales are known. This list is designed more to be helpful than exhaustive, but perhaps it will be useful to a storyteller looking for another version of a tale known only by common title.

The motif index and tale-type index, on the other hand, offer a more technical system for locating and identifying those specific motifs and tale types included in *World Folktales*. A general explanation of this system, for newcomers, is offered in the section entitled "Research Tools."

Since our belief in the value of the comparative paper is based on the reactions and comments of students over the years, we have emphasized throughout the simplicity rather than the complexity of the study of traditional literature. We have attempted to do much of the work by locating texts for comparison and by listing parallels from as broad a range as possible in order to accommodate even the small library with limited folklore holdings. We have tried to be sufficiently versatile in order to fill as many needs as possible for a reliable folktale text with scholarly annotations designed for student and enthusiast alike. If we have contributed, in some small way, to a deeper appreciation of folktales, we are content.

Contents

Preface   *v*

One. *An Introduction to the Study of the Folk-tale*   *1*

First Words   *3*
Research Tools   *5*

Two. *Tale Texts and Annotations*   *15*

A. *WHERE DREAMS COME TRUE: TALES OF MAGIC*

   1. Koshalki-Opalki   (Polish)   *19*
   2. The Gold in the Chimley   (American)   *26*
   3. Mighty Mikko   (Finnish)   *33*

4. The Indian Cinderella   (Canadian Indian)   43
5. The Do-All Ax   (Black American)   49
6. Molly Whuppie   (English)   54
7. The Toad-Bridegroom   (Korean)   59

B. TALES THAT MIGHT HAVE BEEN: REALISTIC TALES

8. The Cow on the Roof   (Welsh)   67
9. Crab   (Italian)   71
10. Gudbrand on the Hill-side   (Norwegian)   75
11. The Story of Kunz and His Shepherd   (Jewish)   81
12. The Most Obedient Wife   (Danish)   86
13. Clever Manka   (Czechoslovakian)   93

C. FAIRIES, PIXIES, AND OTHER WEE FOLK: FAIRY
    TALES

14. Rumpelstiltskin   (German)   103
15. The Fairy Dwelling on Selena Moor   (English)   109
16. Field of Boliauns   (Irish)   115
17. The Brownie of Blednock   (Scottish)   121
18. The Adventure of Cherry of Zennor   (English)   129
19. The Seal's Skin   (Icelandic)   136
20. Te Kanawa and the Fairies   (New Zealand)   140

D. FUR AND FEATHER: ANIMAL TALES

21. Buh Fox's Number Nine Shoes   (Black American)   145
22. The Three Billy-Goats Gruff   (Norwegian)   150
23. The Cat that Went a-Traveling   (American)   154
24. The Three Hares   (Turkish)   159
25. The Hare and the Hedgehog   (English)   164

E. BROOMSTICKS AND NIGHT RIDE: STORIES OF
    WITCHES AND DEVILS

26. The Witches' Ride   (Costa Rican)   173
27. The Baba Yaga   (Russian)   179
28. The Toad Witch   (Polish)   185

29. *The Tinker and the Ghost* *(Spanish)* 188
30. *The Golden Arm* *(English)* 194
31. *The Coffin-Lid* *(Russian)* 197
32. *The Wolf-Child* *(Portugese)* 202
33. *The King o' the Cats* *(English)* 210
34. *The Shrove Tuesday Visitor* *(Canadian)* 214

F. PATTERN AND RHYTHM: FORMULA TALES

35. *The Cat and the Parrot* *(Indian)* 223
36. *Talk* *(African)* 229
37. *Plop!* *(Tibetan)* 233
38. *The Cat and the Mouse* *(English)* 237
39. *The Gingerbread Boy* *(American)* 242
40. a. *An Endless Story* *(Japanese)* 247
    b. *A Dark and Stormy Night* *(American)* 249
41. *The Travels of a Fox* *(American)* 251

G. A CLEVER FELLOW BY ANY OTHER NAME: TRICK-STER TALES

42. *Anansi Plays Dead* *(African)* 259
43. *Jack and the Varmints* *(American)* 264
44. *Sheer Crops* *(Black American)* 272
45. *Boots and His Brothers* *(Norwegian)* 277
46. *Coyote Tricks the White Man* *(American Indian)* 283
47. *Baby in the Crib* *(Black American)* 286
48. *Nasr-ed-Din Hodja in the Pulpit* *(Turkish)* 289
49. *Pedro de Urdemalas* *(Chilean)* 293

H. WISDOM OF THE AGES: MORALITY TALES

50. *The Honey Gatherer's Three Sons* *(African)* 301
51. *The Ridiculous Wishes* *(French)* 305
52. *The Man Who Knew How to Cure a Snakebite* *(Cambodian)* 309
53. *The Tale of Ivan* *(Welsh)* 314
54. *The Foolish Man* *(Armenian)* 319
55. *The Old Man and His Grandson* *(German)* 324

I. BEGINNINGS: POURQUOI TALES

56. How the Manx Cat Lost Her Tail   (Isle of Man)   329
57. Compair Lapin and Madame Carencro   (Cajun
       American)   332
58. Why the Sea Is Salt   (Norwegian)   336
59. The Tortoise and the Osprey   (African)   342

J. NOODLES AND SIMPLETONS FROM ALL OVER: DROLL TALES

60. Lazy Jack   (English)   351
61. The Story of Brave Kong   (Cambodian)   356
62. Bastianelo   (Italian)   362
63. The Mirror   (Chinese)   367
64. The Old Woman and the Tramp   (Swedish)   370
65. Now I Should Laugh, If I Were Not Dead   (Norwegian) 377
66. The Pig-Headed Wife   (Finnish)   381

APPENDIXES

I. Folktales in the Elementary Classroom   385
II. Folktales in the College Classroom   399
III. Popular Title Index   413
IV. Index of Motifs   420
V. Index of Tale Types   431

SELECTED BIBLIOGRAPHY

434

ONE

An Introduction to the Study of the Folktale

First Words

Before any kind of meaningful analysis of individual tales can be attempted, folktales must be collected, classified, and indexed. Scholars must first hear and write down the tales, then identify those tales with similar plots by some system of classification, and finally index the tales so that others who come later can locate individual tales for study. This chapter will discuss those indexes, catalogues, dictionaries, and summary studies that have become "tools of the trade" in folktale scholarship.

The active collecting of folktales was begun in earnest in the nineteenth century, flourished in the latter half of that century, and continues today, although interests of modern folklorists have shifted more toward context than text. The classification of tales by type or similarity of plot structure was also completed in one form as early as 1928, and now scholars all over the world generally refer to similar types of tales by number. Although treated with great deference, these numbers themselves are not magic numbers. Rather they represent a convenient point of reference for identifying tales with similar plots that have an independent existence. These numbers have, as a matter of fact, been revised and expanded over the years, challenged by new systems of classification from time to time, and praised as well as damned. Nevertheless, the use of Aarne-Thompson Tale Type Numbers, as they are known, in the annotations to *World Folktales,* as well as the later Christiansen Migratory Legend Numbers, supplies the reader with the standard system of classification of folktales in current folktale scholarship.

Classification of smaller elements within tales—the motifs—has also been accomplished and is now a basic part of folktale scholarship. The motifs (defined as the smallest element of a tale having the power to persist in tradition) of individual tales are also listed in *World Folktales* annotations and provide the reader with the means of analyzing the components of an individual tale by examining its constituent smallest parts.

Folktale indexes are the bread-and-butter of comparative scholarship, and no comparative study would be possible without some system of locating tale texts in individual collections. Several landmark indexes exist, most having been written in the early part of the twentieth century, and are discussed below. Computer technology is currently being employed by innovative scholars, and even more comprehensive data is expected with electronic classification and cross-classification.

Meaningful analysis and interpretation of folktales follow in sequence after collection and classification have been accomplished. The direction of such analysis can be historical, anthropological, psychological, sociological, psychoanalytical, contextual, or structural—all current valid approaches to the study of the folktale by professional folklorists. The beginner is not limited in the direction of his interpretation but rather greatly assisted by *first* employing the comparative method of the study of folktales described in *World Folktales*.

For individual comparative study, the annotations to the tale texts in *World Folktales* are designed to facilitate much of the basic research required. These annotations list a wide sampling of parallel versions (or variants) of each tale in the text in order to give the reader ready access to comparative tales as well as to eliminate any frustration that might come from working with international indexes which list tales in many different languages in highly abbreviated form. *World Folktales* references are given in standard short-form abbreviations, and confirmation of the abbreviation is indicated in the bibliography by italics. Wherever possible, reference is to a tale number in a collection and not to a page number. Such reference permits easier tracing of a tale through revisions and reprints of a collection.

Teachers, storytellers, and general readers may be content with the information contained in the annotations when coupled with the summary of folktale scholarship described in this chapter. College students, on the other hand, will be expected to become familiar, firsthand, with the tools of comparative folktale research, using them according to the guidelines given in the "how to research" section of Appendix II, "Folktales in the College Classroom." The discussion of the following basic research tools will provide an introduction to their contents for the college student as well as assist that reader who wishes to pursue his study of traditional literature more extensively.

Research Tools

1. *The Types of the Folktale: A Classification and Bibliography* (second rev. 1961) by Antti Aarne and Stith Thompson, Helsinki: 1961. Folk Lore Fellows Communications #184.

Because folktales contain a limited number of basic forms, early scholars sought a means of identifying and classifying tales with similar plots. At first short titles were used—"Cinderella," "Tom Tit Tot," "Rumpelstiltskin"— but as the number of collected variants grew, it became clear that some better system was needed to indicate that "Tom Tit Tot" and "Rumpelstilt-skin" were variants of the same tale.

A comprehensive classification, an accepted international method of cataloging tales of similar plots from different countries, was needed. In 1910 a Finnish scholar, Antti Aarne, devised such a catalog of tale types (a recognizable tale for which variants are known), and his work was translated and enlarged by Stith Thompson of Indiana University in 1928, later revised in 1961. In this basic reference work some 2,499 tale types are given numbers and categorized within five basic divisions of tales: Animal Tales, Ordinary Folktales, Jokes and Anecdotes, Formula Tales, and Un-classified Tales.

A researcher can find the tale type number of "Rumpelstiltskin" by looking up that title in the index of the *Type-Index*. Additional references can also be found under such topics as "Helpers"; "Spinning Women"; "Name—of Helper discovered"; "Task, because of mother's foolish boast";

and even under a variant title—"Tom Tit Tot." The story about a magic
helper who performs extraordinary tasks for a woman who must guess his
name is identified in any one of these index entries as Tale Type 500: The
Name of the Helper.

A typical page from the *Type-Index* is reprinted below.

500   *The Name of the Helper* (Titeliture, Rumpelstilzchen, Tom-Tit-Tot).
The maiden learns the name of her supernatural helper.

I. *Impossible Task.* (a) A girl wedded to prince is compelled (to
fulfill her mother's false boasting) to spin an impossible amount of yarn
or (b) to spin gold. Cf. Type 501.

II. *Bargain with the Helper.* (a) A supernatural being agrees to help
the girl (b) or to reward a man (c) but she must give him her child or
(d) herself, (e) if she cannot within a certain time guess his name or (f)
his age.

III. *The Helper Overcome.* (a) By chance the name (age) is discovered, (b) the name is pronounced, and the helper vanishes.

Motifs:

I. H914. Tasks assigned because of mother's foolish boasting.
H1092. Task: spinning impossible amount in one night. H1021.8. Task:
spinning gold.

II. D2183. Magic spinning. Usually performed by a supernatural
helper. S222. Man promises (sells) child in order to save himself from
danger or death. S222.1. Woman promises her unborn child to appease
offended witch. H512. Guessing with life as wager. H521. Test: guessing
unknown propounder's name. H521.1. Test: guessing unknown propounder's age.

III. N475. Secret name overheard by eavesdropper. C432.1. Guessing name of supernatural creature gives power over him.

**Clodd *Tom-Tit-Tot;* **Polívka Zs. f. Vksk. X 254–272, 325, 382–
396, 438f.; **von Sydow *Två Spinnsagor;* Liungman *Rig* (1941) 89ff.,
and *Folkminnen och Folktankar* (1943) 94ff.; Hartmann *Trollvorstellun-
gen* 170; Boberg FFC CLI 10ff.; Coffin *3;* *BP I 490 (Grimm No. 55).
—Finnish *70;* Finnish-Swedish *3;* Estonian *16;* Lithuanian *8;* Swedish
47 (Uppsala *13,* Stockholm *5,* Göteborg *12,* Lund *4,* Liungman *3,* misc.
10); Norwegian *4,* Solheim *2;* Danish *90,* Grundtvig No. 50A; Icelandic
4; Irish *171,* Beal I 301f., III 467f. No. 10, V 221, VII 105, VIII 150,
X 44ff., XII 165; English *3;* Basque *2;* French *39;* Spanish *1;* Flemish
4; German: Ranke *96;* Austrian: Haiding No. 46; Italian *3* (Tuscan [908]
1, Sicilian *2,* Gonzenbach No. 84); Hungarian *6;* Czech: Tille Soupis II
(2) 129–131 *4;* Slovenian *5;* Serbocroatian *2;* Polish *3;* Russian: An-
drejev; Turkish: Eberhard-Boratav Anlage A c *4.*—Franco-American
9; Spanish-American: Hansen (Puerto Rico) *2;* West Indies (Negro) *26.*

The first entry is always the type number followed by a short descriptive title. Next comes a summary of the plot of the narrative.

If the tale is long enough, it is divided into basic episodes. In this instance, there are three plot divisions, each indicated by a Roman numeral and summarized. Complex episodes are subdivided by the use of lowercase letters. In some instances the letters indicate possible variations found in different versions. Taken as a whole, these subdivisions represent the most predominant plot variations to be found in the larger body of European tales.

The tale is now broken down into motifs, defined by Thompson as a single narrative element, the smallest that can persist in tradition. These motifs follow the numbering system used in the *Motif-Index* (described later) and coordinate the plot analysis of the *Type-Index* with the more compehensive worldwide motif cataloging system.

The final section gives abbreviated bibliographic references and an approximate inventory in italics of the number of variants to be found at each location. Items marked with asterisks indicate major works or studies. By examining this section carefully, the researcher can learn that "Rumpelstiltskin" is number 55 in the Grimm canon, and that the German folklorist Ranke has collected 96 versions, the Finns 70 versions, and the Danes 90 versions. Based on that information a researcher could conclude that the tale is highly popular in Northern European countries but absolutely beloved by the Irish who have cataloged a total of 171 versions of the tale.

Complete bibliographical references for each abbreviated item are listed in the first few pages of the *Type-Index* itself. As might be expected of a reference tool of international scope, the majority of the references are to materials not found in the average college library. The American Folklore Society is currently in the process of revising the entire *Type-Index,* however, and additional attention will soon be paid to the many recent English language texts that are more readily available to American college students.

As editors we have used the Aarne-Thompson tale type numbers throughout, since they are internationally recognized by scholars of the folk narrative. Classification of tales, however, underwent considerable modification in our presentation, especially in those areas omitted by Aarne and Thompson. Our categories group tales according to the *kind* of narrative they are, and while some correspond to the *Type-Index* (animal, magic, formula), others have been created to suit the particular emphasis of this book. The Index of Tale Types in the back of *World Folktales* (Appendix V) is based on the Aarne-Thompson system and refers to those tale texts reprinted in this volume.

2. *The Motif-Index of Folk-Literature* (6 vols., revised ed.) by Stith
Thompson. Bloomington, Ind.: Indiana University Press, 1955–58.

Beginning students frequently confuse the *Type-Index* and the *Motif-Index,*
both by the same author. It is helpful to remember that the *Type-Index*
deals with entire tales; the *Motif-Index,* a bigger six-volume encyclopedic
work, deals with smaller elements of those tales. Thompson defines the
motif as "the smallest element that persists in tradition"; in actual practice
this element can be a character, a formula, a concept, an activity, or any
one of the multitude of details found in folktales.

The *Motif-Index* arranges in a single logical classification the elements that make up traditional narrative literature throughout the
world. There are twenty-three divisions (chapters) in Volumes 1–5, each
of which classifies motifs dealing with the same general subject. Thus
Chapter A is concerned with mythological motifs—creation, gods, the
beginning of life, the establishment of the animal and vegetable worlds.
Chapter B deals with Animals, C with Tabu, D with Magic, and so on.
Each chapter is further divided by a numbering system somewhat similar to the Dewey Decimal system. The general idea of the grand division is treated first, followed by the more specific material, and finally
the miscellaneous.

Thus in Chapter F, Marvels, numbers 400–499 are assigned to "Spirits
and Demons," including F480 "House-spirits" and F482 "Brownie." The
use of "points" produces subdivisions and additional motif numbers:

F482.1   Appearance of brownie
    .2   Clothing of brownie
    .3   Home of brownie
    .4   Possessions of brownie
    .5   Deeds of brownie

Additional "pointing" produces:

F482.5.1   Brownies dance
      .2   Brownies sew by moonlight
      .3   Brownies tease
      .4   Helpful deeds of brownies or other household spirits

Occasionally "pointing" produces a reference number of alarming propor-
tions, but the system remains logical throughout.

Volume six constitutes an index to the previous five volumes.

The Index of Motifs to be found in the back of *World Folktales*

(Appendix IV) catalogues all the motifs discovered in each tale type reprinted in this collection.

3. *Type and Motif-Index of the Folktales of England and North America* by Ernest Baughman. The Hague, Holland: Mouton and Co., 1966.

Baughman's *Index* is modeled on the *Indexes* of Thompson but deals exclusively with English language folktales found in the British Isles and North America. With his listing of 1,652 variants of 371 tale types, Baughman's *Index* is particularly valuable in locating English language examples of tale types and is a favorite of college students doing the comparative paper because they can locate most of the tale variants listed. Most entries include a summary of the type, a list of variants, their sources (with full details in the "Bibliography and Abbreviation" section), and comments about the particular type.

The second part of the index, the "Motif-Index" (ten times the length of the first part), employs the arrangement of Thompson's *Motif-Index,* adds motifs where needed, and lists comprehensive references for most motifs. It is important to note that many of the books indexed in Baughman are available in most libraries.

4. *Migratory Legends: A Proposed List of Types with a Systematic Catalogue of the Norwegian Variants* by Reidar Christiansen. Helsinki: 1958. Folklore Fellows Communication #175.

This useful index continues the numbering system of the *Type-Index* but Christiansen begins with the number 3,000, uses multiples of 5 in his coding, and only includes migratory legends, i.e., those tales believed to be true that have passed from one country to another. His system uses eight basic divisions. Readers will find the following most significant:

3030–3080	Witches and witchcraft
4000–4050	Legends of the Human Soul, of Ghosts and Revenants
5050–6070	The Fairies

Each main division is subdivided—for example, all legends dealing with a mortal who becomes a midwife to the fairies are numbered 5070.

The narrative content of the legends is summarized, and the localities and sources in Norway of archive variants are listed. In other reference works the initials ML generally precede Christiansen's four-digit number.

5. *A Dictionary of British Folk-Tales in the English Language* by Katharine Briggs. London: Routledge and Kegan Paul, 1970–71.

This work is not primarily an index, but a dictionary containing the tales themselves (or summaries) in alphabetical order. Part A (2 volumes) deals with Folk Narratives, and Part B (2 volumes) with Folk Legends.

The first volume of each part contains two indexes. The first classifies tales according to type and gives a short title for the story with a reference to the Part and section of the *Dictionary* where it is located.

The second index is to the short title. Thus, if a researcher knows a tale or legend type, he can consult the tale type index and learn the titles of all tales in the *Dictionary* with that type number. If he knows only a title, there is still a good chance he can locate the tale itself via the title index. Once he does so, he will find the type number given after the story, along with the source of each tale, the principal motifs, and possibly a scholarly note or a cross reference to other tales.

6. *The Folktale* by Stith Thompson. New York: Dryden Press, 1951.

Thompson's book remains the best introduction to the folktale available. Although the bibliography is somewhat dated, the work is written in a pleasant, informal manner. Over five hundred tale types are discussed. Any serious student of the genre should consult *The Folktale* before beginning a major research project.

7. *The Classic Fairy Tales* by Iona and Peter Opie. London: Oxford University Press, 1974.

An edition of twenty-four of the "best-known" tales, emphasizing versions as they were first printed in English. Following a general introduction, each tale is preceded by a discussion of its history and textual points of interest. With its many fine illustrations, this work is designed more for the general reader than for the scholar, but it contains some interesting information about the early history of the printed tale.

B. Indexes to Children's Versions of Folktales

1. *Index to Fairy Tales and Legends* (second ed.) by Mary Huse Eastman. Boston: F. W. Faxon, 1926.

In 1915 Mary Eastman published the first of four books designed to help teachers find "at a glance the source of an asked-for story." The difficulty Ms. Eastman faced was that different versions of the same story had titles that bore little or no resemblance to each other. It was this problem that had led Antti Aarne to use type numbers as a means of identifying tales and their variants. Her solution was different, however.

Since inquiries for stories are mainly by title, Eastman's *Index* is first of all a title index. When the same story appears under several titles, it is indexed under the best-known one or the one that seems most descriptive of the story. Thus such titles as "Chicken-diddle" and "Chicken-Licken" are referenced to "Chicken Little," under which heading thirty-seven books are listed. The title as given in a particular book, when it differs from the one under which it is indexed, is given in parentheses at the end of the entry.

Cross references are given from one story to another so that if a particular story cannot be located, a similar one can be. The cross references from subjects are intended to help a teacher find tales when the inquirer has forgotten the title and asks for the story by subject or contents. An asterisk is used to indicate tales suitable for smaller children.

The Eastman *Index* was revised in 1926, and supplements were issued in 1937 and 1952.

2. *Index to Fairy Tales 1949–1972* by Norma Olin Ireland. Westwood, Mass.: F. W. Faxon, 1973.

The second supplement to the Eastman *Index* did not list any tales printed after 1948. A new index, prepared by Norma Olin Ireland, was issued for tales published between 1949 and 1972. Four hundred and six books were indexed under title and subject. Only tales in *collections* were included; books that contain only one story were not listed. (See Zeigler below.)

Several important modifications were made in this index. The sketchy subject indexes of the four previous books were replaced by a very comprehensive subject index. The limited author and geographic indexes were interfiled with the main index.

The procedure is simplicity itself. If a student wishes to find stories about "Henny Penny," he simply consults the index. There he will find two versions of the tale listed alphabetically by author/editor.

Henny Penny
ARBUTHNOT—TIME p12–13
MONTGOMERIE—25 p24–25

In this example, "Arbuthnot" and "Montgomerie" refer to the authors, and "Time" and "25" to the works. Full bibliographical information is available in another section of the Ireland book, but short titles such as these are essential in such an extensive index.

3. *Annotated Bibliography and Index to Single Editions* by Elsie Zeigler. Westwood, Mass.: F. W. Faxon, 1973.

Because the Ireland *Index* did not include books consisting of only one tale, an index was prepared by Elsie Zeigler to fill this gap. Her book is divided into six sections: Part I, Annotated Bibliography; Part II, Subject Index; Part III, Motif Index; Part IV, Country Index; Part V, Type of Folklore Index; Part VI, Illustrator Index. The first two are the most important.

Supposing we look up "Chicken Little." Under this heading are two books about Henny Penny.

0503 CHICKEN LITTLE

0278 Henny Penny

Reteller, Paul Galdone
Illus. Paul Galdone
New York, The Seabury Press, 1968. unp.

Henny Penny is struck by an acorn and thinks the sky is falling. On her way to tell the king, she and her friends are tricked by the fox who offers them a shortcut and they are never seen again.

SUBJECTS	— Cumulative Tale	COUNTRY	— United
	Chain Tale		Kingdom
	Animals with		
	Strange Names		
	Acorn (Hits		
	Chicken's Head)		
	Formula Tale		

MOTIFS	— Humor	TYPE OF	
	Talking Animals	FOLKLORE	— Folk Tales

The first entry shows that the book was retold and illustrated by Paul Galdone and gives the publishing information. Then follows a summary of the plot. The tale itself is next indexed under four headings. The first of these gives five subject headings under which the tale is listed. If a child could only remember that an acorn fell on a chicken's head, that information is enough to locate "Henny Penny." If a teacher wanted to demonstrate a formula tale, the main index would point to several formula tales including this one. The so-called "motif index" is an index employing sixteen large areas of motifs such as humor, magic objects, wishes, talking animals, trickery and so forth.

The country index gives the country of origin (United Kingdom, for example), and the "type of folklore" index presents the many facets of folklore in eight basic categories: epics, fables, folksongs, ballads, folktales, legends, myths, and nursery rhymes.

It must be pointed out that the Eastman, Ireland, and Ziegler indexes are most useful to the storyteller, elementary teacher, or casual reader who is looking for a tale by title. The comparative researcher should be warned that much of the material included in the "children's version" indexes is unsifted and vague, more "rewritten" than traditional. Nevertheless, much of the material is valuable and often not available in other forms or in other more scholarly indexes.

TWO

Tale Texts
and Annotations

A

Where Dreams Come True:
TALES OF MAGIC

Enchantment and the supernatural play an important role in these familiar stories where the lowly protagonist confronts great danger, accomplishes impossible tasks, marries a prince or princess, and lives happily ever after. These magic tales (called märchen by scholars) have been retold and refashioned a thousand times and represent for most readers the core of traditional narrative.

1. *KOSHALKI-OPALKI*   19
   TT 563—*The Table, the Ass, and the Stick*
   Also known as *The Lad Who Went to the North Wind*

2. *THE GOLD IN THE CHIMLEY*   26
   TT480—*The Spinning-Women by the Spring, The Kind and Unkind Girls*
   Also known as *Mother Holle, Old Gallymander*

3. *MIGHTY MIKKO*   33
   TT 545B—*Puss in Boots*
   Also known as *The Master Cat, The Count of Carabas*

4.   *THE INDIAN CINDERELLA*   43
TT 510A—*Cinderella*
Also known as *Little Burnt Face, Cinderella and the
Strong Wind*

5.   *THE DO-ALL AX*   49
TT 325*—*Apprentice and Ghost*
Also known as *Sorcerer's Apprentice, Magician and
the Pupil*

6.   *MOLLY WHUPPIE*   54
TT 327—*The Children and The Ogre*
TT 1119—*The Ogre Kill his Own Children*
Also known as *The Brave Girl and the Giant*

7.   *THE TOAD-BRIDEGROOM*   59
TT 440—*The Frog King or Iron Henry*
Also known as *The Frog Prince, The Enchanted
Prince*

1

Koshalki-Opalki

or How A Simpleton Became King*

Who would believe that even a simpleton might become king? But once it did happen; true it was many years ago. Just listen.

One bright day a peasant was cutting trees in the woods. Suddenly he heard someone calling for help; he looked around and saw a nobleman with his horses and wagon stuck in the mire.

The peasant took a deep breath and, using all his strength, raised the wagon out of the mud.

The nobleman wished to show his gratitude to the peasant and said: "Tell me what you desire and you shall have it."

The peasant was so stupid that he did not even know what to ask for. So the nobleman, who really was a famous wizard, did not wait for an answer, thinking to himself:

"You are so simple that there is no use talking to you." So he gave him a ram and said: "Here is a ram. Every time you shake it, you will have gold."

The peasant, very happy, went home with the ram. On his way an old woman who lived in the same village came out to meet him and said:

---

*From *The Jolly Tailor and Other Fairy Tales Translated From the Polish* by Lucia Borski and Kate Miller (New York: Longmans, Green and Co., 1928), pp. 41–48. Copyright © 1928 by Lucia Borski and Kate Miller. Reprinted by permission of the David McKay Company, Inc.

"I have heard of your good luck, neighbor, and you must have a drink of good wine. Let me give you some."

"Surely," agreed the simpleton. "I am not easily fooled; a good drink will do me no harm."

And so he drank.

When the peasant fell asleep, the old woman took the miraculous ram from him and cunningly put another in its place.

The peasant slept well and long and when he awoke, he shook the ram so that he might have some gold coins. He shook and shook, but in vain, for, as you know, from an ordinary ram no man will ever gather gold coins. The most he can expect is but a little wool for a sheepskin coat or some meat for roast mutton.

Hm . . . He grew sad, and after thinking awhile he went to the woods.

"Because," he thought, "who knows what will happen if I meet again the man whom I have raised out of the mire? Maybe he will help me."

The peasant was not disappointed, because the wizard did help, for he had great power. This time he gave him a hen, saying:

"If you call her and say, *My hen, my hen, give me a golden egg!* right on the spot she will lay a golden egg."

The peasant thanked him, took the hen under his arm, and returned home. The same old woman awaited him and said:

"I honor you, my neighbor, for you have good common sense. I have some good whiskey. Won't you have a glass?"

"Surely, I will have one," he said. "Good whiskey is always worth drinking, especially when one has a hen that lays golden eggs whenever asked."

The simpleton had sense of a kind, but he did not see that the woman changed his hen for another. He went home. Pretty soon he called, saying:

"My hen, my hen, give me a golden egg."

He coaxed and petted her, but she did not lay the golden egg. So he thought to himself:

"There is nothing to do in this misfortune but to try my luck again and go to the woods. I may have luck," he said, "may I not?"

And indeed he did, for he met the wizard, who this time gave him a magic table-cloth, saying, "If you lay it out and say, *Table-cloth, table-cloth, spread yourself,* at that very moment the table-cloth will spread itself, and there will be plenty to eat and drink on it; everything that one might desire."

The peasant, very curious, ordered the table-cloth to spread itself out in the woods. After having eaten well, he began to try all the different kinds of drinks. He tried this one and he tried that one, until he fell asleep. In his dreams he was only too sorry not to have invited his friend, the old woman, to sup with him. But the old hag was not far off. She had watched him, and when he lay there dead asleep, like a log of wood, she stole the magic table-cloth, and gave him another, a plain one.

The peasant woke up and saw that, although he was not easily deceived, the old woman's brains worked better than his. So again he looked for his friend the wizard, and when he found him, he said:

"Why should a woman have more sense than we? Why is it so?"

"But it is true," the wizard answered, "and there is nothing to do but beat her, and then she will become less cunning."

The wizard gave the simpleton a basket full of beech and oak sticks and taught him to say:

"Koshalki-opalki, out of my basket."

At this command, he said, the sticks would do their work. He demonstrated it on the peasant's back, for he believed that even a peasant needs a beating sometimes.

Although the beating hurt his back, the peasant was glad to have a medicine that would end the old woman's rule over him, and so he took the basket on his back and smilingly went to see the hag.

She welcomed him, for she thought he surely had something in his basket that might be a help to her. She took a glass of wine and drank to his health. Just at this point he shouted:

"Koshalki-opalki, out of my basket!" and all the beech and oak sticks began to beat the hag, and they beat as hard as ever they could.

The hag swore she would return all his things and give him still more, if he would only let her go. But he said: "I am beating you because I must beat you. I need none of your things, you wretched hag. You are a wrong doer; therefore you shall die." And he let her be beaten to death.

Then he ordered the sticks to get back into the basket, put the basket on his back, took the ram and the hen and the table-cloth, and off he went into the world. Having all these things, he desired to be a great ruler.

"I have a ram that gives me gold ducats when I shake it, a hen that lays golden eggs, a table-cloth that always provides plenty of food and drink, and a basket with sticks for defense. Why should I not become King?"

Thus he spoke to himself.

Almost immediately he joined the army of a King who was at war with an ancient enemy. The peasant beat the enemy's army in a short time with his oak and beech sticks, and as reward he received the King's beautiful daughter for his wife, and after the old King's death, he took the throne and reigned very wisely over his people.

No wonder, for he had a ram that scattered gold ducats for him, a hen that laid golden eggs, a tablecloth spread with food and drink, and a basket with beech and oak sticks that could beat not only a whole army but also the shrewdest hag, when there was such need.

Such is, as you have seen, the story of the simpleton who, more because of good luck than good judgment, became a king.

Notes and Comments

Many collections of folktales contain a tale of a lad who acquires a number of magic objects with supernatural assistance. The universal appeal of the Tale Type popularly known as "The Lad Who Went to The North Wind" is accounted for, in large measure, by the hero's acquisition of those things so many of us have coveted—inexhaustible food, infinite riches, and most important, limitless power. Usually there are three objects, two of which are lost or stolen, and a third that is used to recover the first two. There is always an unfortunate hero—stupid, poor, or young—who inevitably triumphs and lives happily ever after.

Naturally, tales of magic should provide the ultimate experience in wish-fulfillment. The magic objects in these tales are designed to provide in simple and direct ways for man's most basic needs. In many variants the food-producing object is a standard item received by the hero. Often it is a tablecloth that will provide a sumptuous meal when the command is given. In a German variant the owner of a magic wallet cries, "Three men out of the bag! Lay the table; get food and drink." A more unusual incident is found in a Jamaican tale where a magic Packey found only on a calabash tree responds to outrageous flattery. When told "My! there's a han'some packey!" he replies, "I han'some an' I can do han'some work." When the master says, "Do it, let I see!" the Packey not only provides a large table "full of nice eatables" but cleans up after the meal.

Another magic object found in these stories provides great wealth for the hero, generally by producing gold in large quantities. In one story Jack has a rooster, and all he has to do is hold his hat under it and say "Come, gold! come," and the rooster will lay a hat full of golden eggs. A Turkish noodle has a donkey that responds to the command "Whoa donkey, whoa!" by raising its tail and dropping a hatful of gold pieces.

Ultimately, the hero of the tale manages to lose all but one of his magic objects. Either they are stolen by an unscrupulous innkeeper, a jealous relative, some rough boys in the neighborhood, or, in an unusually cruel

French version, by the stepparents of two rejected children. At this point the final magic object redresses the balance of justice by providing the hero with all the power he needs. Either he has a stick that will respond to the command "Stick, stick, lay on" and beat the innkeeper until he returns the stolen objects, or he has a harmonica which plays such compelling music that all who hear it must dance until they will agree to anything just to rest their weary feet.

Major variations in the tale type are generally placed at the beginning and conclusion of the story. For example, the reason for the lad's search for help varies. In an Appalachian Jack tale, the Northwest Wind has been blowing through the old rickety house on top of a hill for so long that Jack resolves to go and find the place where the wind blows out his breath. Jack takes his old hat and plugs it right into the hole. Other variants omit the wind motif entirely. An Israeli tale begins with a poor woodcutter being accosted by a black man who demands, "Why do you cut my head every day?" The amazed woodcutter is given the three magic objects on condition he won't chop wood. In a Turkish variant the hoopoe bird gives the magic object when the crazy brother begins cutting down the tree upon which he is perched.

Endings vary too. The Appalachian version is chatty and informative:

> And [Jack] and his mother were both doin' pretty well, last time I saw 'em. They had that old rickety house fixed up tight against the Wind, too.
>
> (Chase, *Jack,* 57)

The Jamaican tale mentioned above tacks an explanatory motif onto the end of the tale. When the Packey produces a cow whip and begins to lash Anansi's wife and children "right and left,"

> some tumble down, some get into the shingle hide themselves all around in the crevice. Jack man dora! That's the reason why you see Anansi live in the crevice!
>
> (Beckwith, *Jamaica Anansi,* p. 32)

Finally, no matter what the motivation of the hero, the despicable actions of the villains, or the problems encountered throughout the tale, the hero lives happily ever after—either married to the princess, in comfort with his wife and family, or warm and cozy against the chill cuts of the north wind. Such a tale of wish-fulfillment is bound to be popular with many narrators, and Thompson in *The Folktale,* says that this particular tale can be found in almost every collection of stories in Europe and Asia. It is told in Africa as well as in North and South America. He adds,

> there is indication that a tale with most of its essentials was current at least as early as the sixth century after Christ, since it appears in a collection of Chinese Buddhistic legends. (p. 72)

Ranke points out that tales of objects fulfilling wishes are as old "as the human pleasure of inventing stories." He cites the Book of Kings' tale of the inexhaustible flour box and cruse of oil of the widow of Zarpath as well as the gold-producing animals in the *Panchatantra* (Ranke, *Germany,* p. 215). By beginning this magic section with the story of the simpleton who became king, we are beginning in the very heart of the enchanted land where all things are possible for those who only wish hard enough.

Tale Type 563   The Table, the Ass, and the Stick

Principal Motifs:

B103.0.3	Gold-producing ram
D861	Magic object stolen
D881.2	Recovery of magic object by use of magic cudgel
D1254	Magic stick
D1401.1	Magic club beats person
D1472.1.8	Magic table cloth supplies food and drink
J2355.1	Fool loses magic objects by talking about them

Parallel Stories in:

Asbjørnsen, #34
Barker, *West African,* pp. 39–44
Beckwith, *Jamaica Anansi,* #25 (2 variants)
Carrière, *Missouri,* #26, #40 (summaries in English)
Carter, *Mountain White,* #12
Chase, *Jack,* #5, p. 191 (references)
Crane, *Italian,* #32 (reprinted in Thompson, *One,* #53)
Dobie, *Texas Household,* pp. 45–47
Dorson, *World,* pp. 138–44
Fauset, *Nova Scotia,* #16
Jacobs, *English,* #39
Kennedy, *Fireside,* pp. 25–30
Massignon, *France,* #51

Musick, *Green Hills,* #34
Noy, *Israel,* #21
Parsons, *Bahamas,* #92
Protter, *Celtic,* #14
Ranke, *Germany,* #41
Roberts, *South,* #23a
Sherlock, *Anansi,* pp. 13–19

2

The Gold in the Chimley*

Once upon a time there was two girls. They were sisters, and one went to a witch's house to get a place to stay. Well, the witch said, "All right, you can stay." Said, "I'm goin to the store and don't you look up the chimley while I'm gone."

While she was gone she looked up the chimley. There hung a bag of gold. She got this gold and started, and come to a cow. The cow says, "Please milk me, little girl, I hain't been milked in several long years."

She says, "I hain't got time."

She went to a sheep and the sheep said, "Please shear me, little girl, I hain't been sheared in several long years."

She says, "I hain't got time."

She went on to a horse, and the horse said, "Please ride me, little girl, I hain't been rode in several long years."

She said, "I hain't got time."

She went on and come to a mill. The mill said, "Please turn me, little girl, I hain't been turned in several long years."

*Collected by Leonard Roberts. *Midwest Folklore* 6, no. 2 (Summer 1956): 76–78. Reprinted by kind permission, Leonard Roberts.

The little girl said, "I hain't got time." She went over and laid down behind the door and went to sleep.

Well, the old witch come back, and her gold was gone. She started out and come to the cow and said,

> Cowel o mine, cowel o mine,
> Have you ever seen a maid o mine,
> With a wig and a wag and a long leather bag,
> Who stold all the money I ever had?

She said, "Yeau, she just passed."
Went on to the sheep, said,

> Sheep o mine, sheep o mine,
> Have you ever seen a maid o mine,
> With a wig and a wag and a long leather bag,
> Who stold all the money I ever had?

She said, "Yeau, she just passed."
She went on to the horse and said,

> Horse o mine, horse o mine,
> Have you ever seen a maid o mine,
> With a wig and a wag and a long leather bag,
> Who stold all the money I ever had?

The horse said, "Yeau, she just passed."
She went on to the mill and said,

> Mill o mine, mill o mine,
> Have you ever seen a maid o mine,
> With a wig and a wag and a long leather bag,
> Who stold all the money I ever had?

It said, "She's layin over there behind the door."
She went over there and turned her into a stone. She got her gold and went on back home.

Well, the next girl come along and said, "Can I get to stay here?"
She said, "Yeau, but I'm going to the store," and said, "don't look up the chimley while I'm gone."

When she got gone she looked up the chimley. There hung this bag of gold. She got it and started. Come to this cow, and the cow said, "Please milk me, little girl, I hain't been milked in several long years."

She milked the cow. Went on to the sheep. The sheep said, "Please shear me, little girl, I hain't been sheared in several long years."

She sheared the sheep. Went on to the horse. The horse said, "Please ride me, little girl, I hain't been rode in several long years."

So she rode the horse. Come to the mill. The mill says, "Please turn me, little girl, I hain't been turned in several long years."

She turned the mill.

Well, the old witch come back, and her gold was gone. She started. She come to the cow and said,

> Cowel o mine, cowel o mine
> Have you ever seen a maid o mine,
> With a wig and a wag and a long leather bag,
> Who stold all the money I ever had?

She said, "No."
She went to the sheep—

> Sheep o mine, sheep o mine,
> Have you ever seen a maid o mine,
> With a wig and a wag and a long leather bag,
> Who stold all the money I ever had?

Said, "No, I hain't never seen her."
Went on to the horse and said,

> Horse o mine, horse o mine,
> Have you ever seen a maid o mine,
> With a wig and a wag and a long leather bag,
> Who stold all the money I ever had?

Said, "No, I hain't never seen her."
She went on to the mill and said,

> Mill o mine, mill o mine,
> Have you ever seen a maid o mine,
> With a wig and a wag and a long leather bag,
> Who stold all the money I ever had?

It said, "Get up in my hopper, I can't hear good."
She got up in the hopper and said,

MILL O MINE, MILL O MINE,
HAVE YOU EVER SEEN A MAID O MINE
WITH A WIG AND A WAG AND A LONG LEATHER BAG,
WHO STOLD ALL THE MONEY I EVER HAD?

The mill started grinding and ground her up.

The little girl she got up, turned the stone back into her sister and they lived happy ever after.

Notes and Comments

This version of a well-known international tale studied extensively by Warren E. Roberts in *The Tale of the Kind and Unkind Girls* is included here because it is a fine example of the "cante fable" or singing story recently discovered to be alive and well in American folk tradition. The singing story is one told partly in prose and partly in verse. Sometimes the verse parts are sung to a recognizable tune; sometimes they are chanted in a rhythmic or dramatic display. According to Leonard Roberts who has observed many of the cante fables in performance, whatever the form used, the storyteller seems to distinguish his "singing" part from the prose part. The storyteller takes pride in his ability to chant rapidly in formula tales or dramatically in magic tales.

The cante fable is an ancient and distinguished method of storytelling. The ancient epics were certainly sung, perhaps even with instrumental accompaniment. Some scholars suggest that all stories were at one time sung or chanted, with occasional interspersed passages of explanatory prose. Roberts theorizes that in oral transmission the two parts, song and prose, became separated, thus giving us on the one hand rhymes, riddles, and ballads; on the other, short magic stories and anecdotes.

The cante fable form of this story, known universally as Tale Type 480 is, however, less frequently collected than other variant forms. Thompson reports that this tale is one of the most popular of oral tales, being distributed over nearly the whole world. (*Folktale,* p. 126). Distribution is concentrated in northern Europe, with Finland, Estonia, and Sweden each reporting over one hundred texts. When Dr. Roberts did his major study of the tale, he consulted over nine hundred variants; many others have been collected and archived since.

In the *Type-Index,* Aarne and Thompson divide the tale into eight basic plot sections. While many tales have all eight major elements or scene divisions, others seem to follow the prototype of Grimm's "Mother Holle," or the shortened form frequently collected in America and reprinted here as "The Gold in the Chimley."

The first group, the spindle and well tales, seems to be the more complex and complete, focusing alternately on the girl's experiences at the well, the reason for the journey, her encounters en route to the witch's house, and on her experiences in the house itself. Both have the kind/unkind repetition for the second sister. Stories of the "Mother Holle" type have a long literary history in England, and the versions in Jacobs and Hartland are actually reprints of chapbook editions. Basile's *Pentamerone* and Perrault's *Tales of My Mother Goose* also have treatments of this type.

The second group, the form typified by "The Gold in the Chimley," is generally a shorter version, often telescoping the entire journey into one sentence: "They were sisters, and one went to a witch's house to get a place to stay." These stories of "the long leather bag" form may tell of encounters along the way with a cow, a sheep, a horse, a tree, an oven, or a mill, for example, all of which provide opportunities to demonstrate the "kind/unkind" natures of the two girls. The same animals or objects who point out the way of escape of the "unkind" girl are the very ones who conceal the "kind" girl and deceive the old witch.

For most storytellers, the cante fable refrain is the most appealing part of the entire story and variation here occurs primarily in the second line of the stanza. Variations range from:

> Pray, fence, have you seen ary gal here,
> With a wig wig wag [and a great big bag.] . . .

>> Roberts, *Cante* (p. 79)

to a male version of the "Man with a Long Nose":

> Did you see a maid running zigzag,
> And in her hand a long leather bag
> With all the gold that e'er I won, since the time I was a boy yet?

> > (Briggs, *Dictionary*, A, 1, p. 409)

and an American old woman who shrieks:

> Gallymanders! Gallymanders!
> All my gold and silver's gone!
> My great long moneypurse

and runs along the road crying:

> Seen a little gal go by here,
> with a jig and a jag
> and a long leather bag
> and all my gold and silver?

(Chase, *Grandfather* #2)

This phrase of the "long leather bag" seems as ubiquitous as the one in jingles and jump-rope rhymes calling for "the lady with the alligator purse." The fact that Tale Type 480 undergoes extensive change and variation while this cante fable refrain remains fairly constant attests to the popularity of this form with storytellers of all ages.

Finally, because of the complexity of the tale, with no fewer than eight major scenes or plot divisions; because of the polarity of the tales in English which tend to cluster about one of the scenes described to the exclusion of the rest; and because all these tales of *The Kind and Unkind Girls* are indexed under Type 480, a comparative study by a beginning student is somewhat difficult unless versions selected are naturally compatible with the grouping suggested below.

Tale Type 480   The Spinning Women by the Spring, or
The Kind and Unkind Girls

Principal Motifs:

C337	Tabu: looking into a chimney
B412	Helpful sheep
B394	Cow grateful for being milked
B401	Helpful Horse
Q469.3	Punishment: grinding up in a mill

Parallel Stories "Leather Bag" type *in:*

Botkin, *American,* pp. 676–78 (reprinted from Fortier, *Louisiana,* 2:117–19)
Briggs, *Dictionary,* A(1) (10 variants)
Carter, *Mountain White,* #15
Chase, *Grandfather,* #2
Conant, *English,* 143–44
Dobie, *Texas Household,* 42–45
Gardner, *Schoharie,* pp. 123–28 (variant) references given

Jacobs, *More English,* #64
MacManus, *Donegal,* pp. 233–56
O'Suilleabhain, *Handbook,* #34 (summary), p. 619
Roberts, *Kind and Unkind* (major study)

Parallel Stories: "Spindle and Well" Type:

Asbjørnsen, *Norse,* #17
Briggs, *Dictionary,* A (1), pp. 167, 517, 551
Grimm, #24
Halliwell, *Nursery,* 38–42 (reprinted with minor changes in Jacobs, *English,* #43)
Kennedy, *Fireside,* pp. 33–37
Perrault, "Les Fées"
Roberts, *South,* #16c

3

Mighty Mikko*

There was once an old woodsman and his wife who had an only son named Mikko. As the mother lay dying the young man wept bitterly.

"When you are gone, my dear mother," he said, "there will be no one left to think of me."

The poor woman comforted him as best she could and said to him: "You will still have your father."

Shortly after the woman's death, the old man, too, was taken ill.

"Now, indeed, I shall be left desolate and alone," Mikko thought, as he sat beside his father's bedside and saw him grow weaker and weaker.

"My boy," the old man said just before he died, "I have nothing to leave you but the three snares with which these many years I have caught wild animals. Those snares now belong to you. When I am dead go into the woods and if you find a wild creature caught in any of them, free it gently and bring it home alive."

After his father's death, Mikko remembered the snares and went out to the woods to see them. The first was empty and also the second, but in

*From *The Shepherd's Nosegay: Stories From Finland and Czechoslovakia* by Parker Fillmore, edited by Katherine Love. Copyright 1922 by Parker Fillmore; copyright 1950 by Louise Fillmore. Reprinted by permission of Harcourt Brace Jovanovich, Inc.

the third he found a little red Fox. He carefully lifted the spring that had shut down on one of the Fox's feet and then carried the little creature home in his arms. He shared his supper with it and when he lay down to sleep the Fox curled up at his feet. They lived together some time until they became close friends.

"Mikko," said the Fox one day, "why are you so sad?"

"Because I'm lonely."

"Pooh!" said the Fox. "That's no way for a young man to talk! You ought to get married! Then you wouldn't feel lonely!"

"Married!" Mikko repeated. "How can I get married? I can't marry a poor girl because I'm too poor myself and a rich girl wouldn't marry me."

"Nonsense!" said the Fox. "You're a fine well set up young man and you're kind and gentle. What more could a princess ask?"

Mikko laughed to think of a princess wanting him for a husband.

"I mean what I say!" the Fox insisted. "Take our own Princess now. What would you think of marrying her?"

Mikko laughed louder than before.

"I have heard," he said, "that she is the most beautiful princess in the world! Any man would be happy to marry her!"

"Very well," the Fox said, "if you feel that way about her then I'll arrange the wedding for you."

With that the little Fox actually did trot off to the royal castle and gain audience with the King.

"My master sends you greetings," the Fox said, "and he begs you to loan him your bushel measure."

"My bushel measure!" the King repeated in surprise. "Who is your master and why does he want my bushel measure?"

"Ssh!" the Fox whispered as though he didn't want the courtiers to hear what he was saying. Then slipping up quite close to the King he murmured in his ear:

"Surely you have heard of Mikko, haven't you?—Mighty Mikko as he's called."

The King had never heard of any Mikko who was known as Mighty Mikko but, thinking that perhaps he should have heard of him, he shook his head and murmured:

"H'm! Mikko! Mighty Mikko! Oh, to be sure! Yes, yes, of course!"

"My master is about to start off on a journey and he needs a bushel measure for a very particular reason."

"I understand! I understand!" the King said, although he didn't understand at all, and he gave orders that the bushel measure which they used in the storeroom of the castle be brought in and given to the Fox.

The Fox carried off the measure and hid it in the woods. Then he scurried about to all sorts of little out of the way nooks and crannies where people had hidden their savings and he dug up a gold piece here and a silver piece there until he had a handful. Then he went back to the woods and stuck the various coins in the cracks of the measure. The next day he returned to the King.

"My master, Mighty Mikko," he said, "sends you thanks, O King, for the use of your bushel measure."

The King held out his hand and when the Fox gave him the measure he peeped inside to see if by chance it contained any trace of what had recently been measured. His eye of course at once caught the glint of the gold and silver coins lodged in the cracks.

"Ah!" he said, thinking Mikko must be a very mighty lord indeed to be so careless of his wealth; "I should like to meet your master. Won't you and he come and visit me?"

This was what the Fox wanted the King to say but he pretended to hesitate.

"I thank your Majesty for the kind invitation," he said, "but I fear my master can't accept it just now. He wants to get married soon and we are about to start off on a long journey to inspect a number of foreign princesses."

This made the King all the more anxious to have Mikko visit him at once for he thought that if Mikko should see his daughter before he saw those foreign princesses he might fall in love with her and marry her. So he said to the Fox:

"My dear fellow, you must prevail on your master to make me a visit before he starts out on his travels! You will, won't you?"

The Fox looked this way and that as if he were too embarrassed to speak.

"Your Majesty," he said at last, "I pray you pardon my frankness. The truth is you are not rich enough to entertain my master and your castle isn't big enough to house the immense retinue that always attends him."

The King, who by this time was frantic to see Mikko, lost his head completely.

"My dear Fox," he said, "I'll give you anything in the world if you prevail upon your master to visit me at once! Couldn't you suggest to him to travel with a modest retinue this time?"

The Fox shook his head.

"No. His rule is either to travel with a great retinue or to go on foot disguised as a poor woodsman attended only by me."

"Couldn't you prevail on him to come to me disguised as a poor woodsman?" the King begged. "Once he was here, I could place gorgeous clothes at his disposal."

But still the Fox shook his head.

"I fear Your Majesty's wardrobe doesn't contain the kind of clothes my master is accustomed to."

"I assure you I've got some very good clothes," the King said. "Come along this minute and we'll go through them and I'm sure you'll find some that your master would wear."

So they went to a room which was like a big wardrobe with hundreds and hundreds of hooks upon which were hung hundreds of coats and breeches and embroidered shirts. The King ordered his attendants to bring the costumes down one by one and place them before the Fox.

They began with the plainer clothes.

"Good enough for most people," the Fox said, "but not for my master."

Then they took down garments of a finer grade.

"I'm afraid you're going to all this trouble for nothing," the Fox said. "Frankly now, don't you realize that my master couldn't possibly put on any of these things!"

The King, who had hoped to keep for his own use his most gorgeous clothes of all, now ordered these to be shown.

The Fox looked at them sideways, sniffed them critically, and at last said:

"Well, perhaps my master would consent to wear these for a few days. They are not what he is accustomed to wear but I will say this for him: he is not proud."

The King was overjoyed.

"Very well, my dear Fox, I'll have the guest chambers put in readiness for your master's visit and I'll have all these, my finest clothes, laid out for him. You won't disappoint me, will you?"

"I'll do my best," the Fox promised.

With that he bade the King a civil good day and ran home to Mikko.

The next day as the Princess was peeping out of an upper window of the castle, she saw a young woodsman approaching accompanied by a Fox. He was a fine stalwart youth and the Princess, who knew from the presence of the Fox that he must be Mikko, gave a long sigh and confided to her serving maid:

"I think I could fall in love with that young man if he really were only a woodsman!"

Later when she saw him arrayed in her father's finest clothes—which looked so well on Mikko that no one even recognized them as the King's —she lost her heart completely and when Mikko was presented to her she blushed and trembled just as any ordinary girl might before a handsome young man.

All the Court was equally delighted with Mikko. The ladies went into ecstasies over his modest manners, his fine figure, and the gorgeousness of his clothes, and the old graybeard Councilors, nodding their heads in approval, said to each other:

"Nothing of the coxcomb about this young fellow! In spite of his great wealth see how politely he listens to us when we talk!"

The next day the Fox went privately to the King, and said:

"My master is a man of few words and quick judgment. He bids me tell you that your daughter, the Princess, pleases him mightily and that, with your approval, he will make his addresses to her at once."

The King was greatly agitated and began:

"My dear Fox—"

But the Fox interrupted him to say:

"Think the matter over carefully and give me your decision to-morrow."

So the King consulted with the Princess and with his Councilors and in a short time the marriage was arranged and the wedding ceremony actually performed!

"Didn't I tell you?" the Fox said, when he and Mikko were alone after the wedding.

"Yes," Mikko acknowledged, "you did promise that I should marry the Princess. But, tell me, now that I am married what am I to do? I can't live on here forever with my wife."

"Put your mind at rest," the Fox said. "I've thought of everything. Just do as I tell you and you'll have nothing to regret. To-night say to the King: 'It is now only fitting that you should visit me and see for yourself the sort of castle over which your daughter is hereafter to be mistress!' "

When Mikko said this to the King, the King was overjoyed for now that the marriage had actually taken place he was wondering whether he hadn't perhaps been a little hasty. Mikko's words reassured him and he eagerly accepted the invitation.

On the morrow the Fox said to Mikko:

"Now I'll run on ahead and get things ready for you."

"But where are you going?" Mikko said, frightened at the thought of being deserted by his little friend.

The Fox drew Mikko aside and whispered softly:

"A few days' march from here there is a very gorgeous castle belonging to a wicked old dragon who is known as the Worm. I think the Worm's castle would just about suit you."

"I'm sure it would," Mikko agreed. "But how are we to get it away from the Worm?"

"Trust me," the Fox said. "All you need do is this: lead the King and his courtiers along the main highway until by noon to-morrow you reach a crossroads. Turn there to the left and go straight on until you see the tower of the Worm's castle. If you meet any men by the wayside, shepherds or the like, ask them whose men they are and show no surprise at their answer. So now, dear master, farewell until we meet again at your beautiful castle."

The little Fox trotted off at a smart pace and Mikko and the Princess and the King attended by the whole Court followed in more leisurely fashion.

The little Fox, when he had left the main highway at the crossroads, soon met ten woodsmen with axes over their shoulders. They were all dressed in blue smocks of the same cut.

"Good day," the Fox said politely. "Whose men are you?"

"Our master is known as the Worm," the woodsmen told him.

"My poor, poor lads!" the Fox said, shaking his head sadly.

"What's the matter?" the woodsmen asked.

For a few moments the Fox pretended to be too overcome with emotion to speak. Then he said:

"My poor lads, don't you know that the King is coming with a great force to destroy the Worm and all his people?"

The woodsmen were simple fellows and this news threw them into great consternation.

"Is there no way for us to escape?" they asked.

The Fox put his paw to his head and thought.

"Well," he said at last, "there is one way you might escape and that is by telling every one who asks you that you are the Mighty Mikko's men. But if you value your lives never again say that your master is the Worm."

"We are Mighty Mikko's men!" the woodsmen at once began repeating over and over. "We are Mighty Mikko's men!"

A little farther on the road the Fox met twenty grooms, dressed in the same blue smocks, who were tending a hundred beautiful horses. The Fox talked to the twenty grooms as he had talked to the woodsmen and before he left them they, too, were shouting:

"We are Mighty Mikko's men!"

Next the Fox came to a huge flock of a thousand sheep tended by thirty shepherds all dressed in the Worm's blue smocks. He stopped and talked to them until he had them roaring out:

"We are Mighty Mikko's men!"

Then the Fox trotted on until he reached the castle of the Worm. He found the Worm himself inside lolling lazily about. He was a huge dragon and had been a great warrior in his day. In fact his castle and his lands and his servants and his possessions had all been won in battle. But now for many years no one had cared to fight him and he had grown fat and lazy.

"Good day," the Fox said, pretending to be very breathless and frightened. "You're the Worm, aren't you?"

"Yes," the dragon said, boastfully, "I am the great Worm!"

The Fox pretended to grow more agitated.

"My poor fellow, I am sorry for you! But of course none of us can expect to live forever. Well, I must hurry along. I thought I would just stop and say good-by."

Made uneasy by the Fox's words, the Worm cried out:

"Wait just a minute! What's the matter?"

The Fox was already at the door but at the Worm's entreaty he paused and said over his shoulder:

"Why, my poor fellow, you surely know, don't you? that the King with a great force is coming to destroy you and all your people!"

"What!" the Worm gasped, turning a sickly green with fright. He knew he was fat and helpless and could never again fight as in the years gone by.

"Don't go just yet!" he begged the Fox. "When is the King coming?"

"He's on the highway now! That's why I must be going! Good-by!"

"My dear Fox, stay just a moment and I'll reward you richly! Help me to hide so that the King won't find me! What about the shed where the linen is stored? I could crawl under the linen and then if you locked the door from the outside the King could never find me."

"Very well," the Fox agreed, "but we must hurry!"

So they ran outside to the shed where the linen was kept and the Worm hid himself under the linen. The Fox locked the door, then set fire to the shed, and soon there was nothing left of that wicked old dragon, the Worm, but a handful of ashes.

The Fox now called together the dragon's household and talked them over to Mikko as he had the woodsmen and the grooms and the shepherds.

Meanwhile the King and his party were slowly covering the ground over which the Fox had sped so quickly. When they came to the ten woodsmen in blue smocks, the King said:

"I wonder whose woodsmen those are."

One of his attendants asked the woodsmen and the ten of them shouted out at the top of their voices:

"We are Mighty Mikko's men!"

Mikko said nothing and the King and all the Court were impressed anew with his modesty.

A little farther on they met the twenty grooms with their hundred prancing horses. When the grooms were questioned, they answered with a shout:

"We are Mighty Mikko's men!"

"The Fox certainly spoke the truth," the King thought to himself, "when he told me of Mikko's riches!"

A little later the thirty shepherds when they were questioned made answer in a chorus that was deafening to hear:

"We are Mighty Mikko's men!"

The sight of the thousand sheep that belonged to his son-in-law made the King feel poor and humble in comparison and the courtiers whispered among themselves:

"For all his simple manner, Mighty Mikko must be a richer, more powerful lord than the King himself! In fact it is only a very great lord indeed who could be so simple!"

At last they reached the castle which from the blue smocked soldiers that guarded the gateway they knew to be Mikko's. The Fox came out to welcome the King's party and behind him in two rows all the household servants. These, at a signal from the Fox, cried out in one voice:

"We are Mighty Mikko's men!"

Then Mikko in the same simple manner that he would have used in his father's mean little hut in the woods bade the King and his followers welcome and they all entered the castle where they found a great feast already prepared and waiting.

The King stayed on for several days and the more he saw of Mikko the better pleased he was that he had him for a son-in-law.

When he was leaving he said to Mikko:

"Your castle is so much grander than mine that I hesitate ever asking you back for a visit."

But Mikko reassured the King by saying earnestly:

"My dear father-in-law, when first I entered your castle I thought it was the most beautiful castle in the world!"

The King was flattered and the courtiers whispered among themselves:

"How affable of him to say that when he knows very well how much grander his own castle is!"

When the King and his followers were safely gone, the little red Fox came to Mikko and said:

"Now, my master, you have no reason to feel sad and lonely. You are lord of the most beautiful castle in the world and you have for wife a sweet and lovely Princess. You have no longer any need of me, so I am going to bid you farewell."

Mikko thanked the little Fox for all he had done and the little Fox trotted off to the woods.

So you see that Mikko's poor old father, although he had no wealth to leave his son, was really the cause of all Mikko's good fortune, for it was he who told Mikko in the first place to carry home alive anything he might find caught in the snares.

Notes and Comments

Though it is not generally recognized, there are probably more tales in which animals act as helpers than those in which supernatural helpers appear. In some tales, the central focus is upon the role played by the animal rather than upon the fortunes of the hero. The best known story of an animal helper is undoubtedly Type 545B *Puss in Boots*. For all its extraordinary popularity, this tale does not appear extensively in the oral tradition of Britain and the United States. Even in France, oral versions of Type 545B are rare. Nevertheless, versions have been found very far afield. A Filipino tale "The Monkey and Juan Puson Tambi-Tambi" begins with the tarbaby story, and becomes Type 545B when the thieving monkey has been caught and set free upon his promise to help Juan marry the king's daughter.

In German, French, English and Scandinavian versions the helpful animal is a cat. In Greek, Russian and Eastern European tales, it is regularly a fox. In all instances the animal is a common one to all outward appearances, easily obtained by even the poorest peasant. Thus, in this magic world of wish fulfillment, anyone could imagine himself married to the princess and living in a big castle, if he could only find the right kind of cat or fox.

Perhaps Type 545B is so widely known and so infrequently collected in the field because of the strong literary influence on the tale from Charles Perrault. This French academician published a collection of tales in 1697 entitled *Histories and Tales of Long Ago with Morals.* One of the tales he included was "Chat Botté," generally known in English as "Puss in Boots."

While Perrault based his tales upon the stories he heard in the nurseries and kitchens and by the hearth, he wrote them down with certain discernible literary touches. Scholars generally refer to this hybrid form of a folktale as a literary revision, and among early writers of literary "folktales" this tale type has always been a favorite. It appears in the collections of such

Italian masters as Straparola and Basile, but Perrault's version has been a primary influence on the tale's tradition.

Tale Type 545B   Puss in Boots

Principal Motifs:

B422   Helpful fox
B580   Animal helps man to wealth and greatness
B582.1.1   Animal wins wife for his master (Puss in Boots)
K1954.1   Helpful cat [fox] borrows measure for his master's wealth

Parallel Stories in:

Afanas'ev, pp. 168–70
Asbjørnsen, #42 (also in Thompson, *One*, #48)
Crane, *Italian*, #33 (a translation of Straparola 11 [1] is included pp. 348–50)
Fansler, *Filipino*, #48(a) (with tarbaby motif)
Grimm, #106
Massignon, *France*, #25

(Literary)
Basile, *Pentamerone* 2 (4)
Perrault,"Le Maistre Chat ou Le Chat Botté"

PICTURE BOOKS:

Puss in Boots. Illustrated by Barry Wilkinson. New York: World, 1969.
Puss in Boots. Illustrated by Marcia Brown. New York: Charles Scribner's Sons, 1952.
Puss in Boots. Retold and illustrated by Hans Fischer. New York: Harcourt, Brace & World, 1959.

4

The Indian Cinderella*

O n the shores of a wide bay on the Atlantic coast there dwelt
in old times a great Indian warrior. It was said that he had been
one of Glooskap's best helpers and friends, and that he had done for him
many wonderful deeds. But that, no man knows. He had, however, a very
wonderful and strange power; he could make himself invisible; he could
thus mingle unseen with his enemies and listen to their plots. He was known
among the people as Strong Wind, the Invisible. He dwelt with his sister
in a tent near the sea, and his sister helped him greatly in his work. Many
maidens would have been glad to marry him, and he was much sought after
because of his mighty deeds; and it was known that Strong Wind would
marry the first maiden who could see him as he came home at night. Many
made the trial, but it was a long time before one succeeded.

Strong Wind used a clever trick to test the truthfulness of all who
sought to win him. Each evening as the day went down, his sister walked
on the beach with any girl who wished to make the trial. His sister could
always see him, but no one else could see him. And as he came home from
work in the twilight, his sister as she saw him drawing near would ask the

*From *Canadian Wonder Tales* by Cyrus Macmillan (London: John Lane Company, 1920),
pp. 116–19. Reprinted by permission of The Bodley Head.

girl who sought him, "Do you see him?" And each girl would falsely answer "Yes." And his sister would ask, "With what does he draw his sled?" And each girl would answer, "With the hide of a moose," or "With a pole," or "With a great cord." And then his sister would know that they all had lied, for their answers were mere guesses. And many tried and lied and failed, for Strong Wind would not marry any who were untruthful.

There lived in the village a great chief who had three daughters. Their mother had long been dead. One of these was much younger than the others. She was very beautiful and gentle and well beloved by all, and for that reason her older sisters were very jealous of her charms and treated her very cruelly. They clothed her in rags that she might be ugly; and they cut off her long black hair; and they burned her face with coals from the fire that she might be scarred and disfigured. And they lied to their father, telling him that she had done these things herself. But the young girl was patient and kept her gentle heart and went gladly about her work.

Like other girls, the chief's two eldest daughters tried to win Strong Wind. One evening, as the day went down, they walked on the shore with Strong Wind's sister and waited for his coming. Soon he came home from his day's work, drawing his sled. And his sister asked as usual, "Do you see him?" And each one, lying, answered "Yes." And she asked, "Of what is his shoulder strap made?" And each, guessing, said "Of rawhide." Then they entered the tent where they hoped to see Strong Wind eating his supper; and when he took off his coat and his moccasins they could see them, but more than these they saw nothing. And Strong Wind knew that they had lied, and he kept himself from their sight, and they went home dismayed.

One day the chief's youngest daughter with her rags and her burnt face resolved to seek Strong Wind. She patched her clothes with bits of birch bark from the trees, and put on the few little ornaments she possessed, and went forth to try to see the Invisible One as all the other girls of the village had done before. And her sisters laughed at her and called her "fool"; and as she passed along the road all the people laughed at her because of her tattered frock and her burnt face, but silently she went her way.

Strong Wind's sister received the little girl kindly, and at twilight she took her to the beach. Soon Strong Wind came home drawing his sled. And his sister asked, "Do you see him?" And the girl answered "No," and his sister wondered greatly because she spoke the truth. And again she asked, "Do you see him now?" And the girl answered, "Yes, and he is very wonderful." And she asked, "With what does he draw his sled?" And the girl answered, "With the Rainbow," and she was much afraid. And she asked further, "Of what is his bowstring?" And the girl answered, "His bowstring is the Milky Way."

Then Strong Wind's sister knew that because the girl had spoken the truth at first her brother had made himself visible to her. And she said, "Truly, you have seen him." And she took her home and bathed her, and all the scars disappeared from her face and body; and her hair grew long and black again like the raven's wing; and she gave her fine clothes to wear and many rich ornaments. Then she bade her take the wife's seat in the tent. Soon Strong Wind entered and sat beside her, and called her his bride. The very next day she became his wife, and ever afterwards she helped him to do great deeds. The girl's two elder sisters were very cross and they wondered greatly at what had taken place. But Strong Wind, who knew of their cruelty, resolved to punish them. Using his great power, he changed them both into aspen trees and rooted them in the earth. And since that day the leaves of the aspen have always trembled, and they shiver in fear at the approach of Strong Wind, it matters not how softly he comes, for they are still mindful of his great power and anger because of their lies and their cruelty to their sister long ago.

Notes and Comments

"Cinderella" may well be the world's best known folktale, and the rags to riches theme of the lowly heroine marrying her prince has frequently been employed in works as single-minded as the novels of Horatio Alger or the plays of Victorian England or by more sophisticated writers such as Jane Austen and Charlotte Bronte. The many uses of this theme suggest that it is one of universal significance.

There have been ten major analyses and compilations of the Cinderella cycle and two exhaustive book-length studies. Miriam Cox's 1893 study was the first extensive investigation ever made of a folktale. She analyzed 345 versions of the tale. In 1951 a second examination of the cycle took place when Anna Rooth studied 900 versions from Europe and Asia in *The Cinderella Cycle* (1951).

The tale is very old; elements of the story have been found in Chinese texts of the seventh century, but it seems that the tale may have originated somewhere in the Middle East and spread both east and west from there. However, the relationship of the various traditions still remains to be clarified. What is clear is that variants have adapted to the cultures in which they have taken root. American tellers relating adventures of lowly heroines they named "Ashpet" dropped the coach and white horses for "the finest little pied-ed mare you ever saw: pretty new saddle and bridle on it." The fabulous ball gown and glass slippers become "a pretty red dress stretched out on the coverlet, and under the bed . . . the prettiest red slippers." (Chase, *Grandfather,* p. 119). Nevertheless, the mountain tradition did not abandon all the old world fantasy. The young lovers were married at the church house, but Ashpet still found a prince.

In a Japanese variant there are only two sisters, and they wish to go to the Kabuki theater rather than to a ball. Later the famous "slipper test" is replaced by another test—to compose a classical song extemporaneously. To begin the test the lord takes a plate and puts it on a tray, then piles salt on the plate and sticks a pine needle in it. The stepsister, Kakezara (Broken Dish), can only manage in a loud voice:

> Put a plate on a tray
> Put some salt on the plate
> Stick a pine needle in the salt;
> It'll soon fall over.

Knowing the verdict in advance (she fails miserably to follow any of the rigid rules of meter), Broken Dish flees, stopping only to hit the lord on the head. Benizara (Crimson Dish) manages both the meter and metaphor adroitly:

> A tray and plate, oh!
> A mountain rises from the plate,
> On it, snow had fallen.
> Rooted deep into the snow,
> A lonely pine tree grows.

Poor Broken Dish and her mother are in despair. They are going to the palace anyway when Broken Dish falls over a precipice. The Japanese were severe on poetasters; all cultures have been severe on wicked stepsisters.

The version of Cinderella printed here is a distant cousin of other worldwide variants, sharing with them the family situation of three sisters, an abused youngest daughter, and marriage to a prince. The outward appearance of the Indian Cinderella, her dress of rags, her shorn hair, her ashes-scarred face was probably much like that of her equally unfortunate European or Asian sister. The test for the true princess in this version is closer to the Asian test of true intellectual ability than is the test of the smallest foot, for truthfulness and intellectual honesty are the distinguishing characteristics of the truly worthy Indian maiden.

Elements of mythology are present with the Strong Wind as the central character and the two ugly sisters turned into quaking aspen trees in the end. Strong Wind draws his sled with the Rainbow and sets his bow with the string of the Milky Way, and the reader is reminded of the mystical power of the unseen wind as celebrated in Christina Rosetti's poem:

Who has seen the wind?
Neither I nor You;
But when the leaves hang trembling,
The wind is passing through.

Who has seen the wind?
Neither you nor I;
But when the trees
Bow down their heads,
The wind is passing by.

Tale Type 510A   Cinderella

Principal Motifs:

A2762.1	Why aspen leaves tremble
D1981	Certain persons invisible
K1911.3.3.2	False bride fails when magician tests her
K2212	Treacherous sister
L52	Abused youngest daughter
L102	Unpromising heroine
L162	Lowly heroine marries prince

Parallel Stories in:

Afanas'ev, pp. 439–47
Boucher, *Moondaughter*, pp. 146–52
Briggs, *Dictionary*, A (1) (16 versions)
Campbell, *West Highlands* 1:#14
Chase, *Grandfather*, #11
Cox, *Cinderella* (major study)
Crane, *Italian*, #9
Curtin, *Myths and Folklore*, pp. 78–92
Dawkins, *Modern Greek*, #21 (references)
Dorson, *World*, pp. 57–59 (from Massignon, *France*, #43)
Fansler, *Filipino*, #45
Gardner, *Schoharie*, pp. 128–31, 131–37 (references)

Grimm, #21
Jacobs, *More English,* #56
Marwick, *Orkney,* pp. 164–70 (in dialect)
Massignon, *France,* #43
Parsons, *Bahamas,* #17
Pedroso, *Portuguese,* pp. 75–79
Perrault, "Cendrillon"
Saucier, *Louisiana,* #2
Seki, *Japan,* #38
Thompson, *One,* #40 (from Pedroso)

PICTURE BOOKS:

Cinderella. Retold and illustrated by Beni Montresor. New York: Alfred Knopf, 1965.
Cinderella or The Little Glass Slipper. Marcia Brown. New York: Scribners, 1954.
Vasilisa the Beautiful. Retold by Thomas Whitney and illustrated by Nonny Hogrogian. New York: Macmillan, 1970. (Has Baba Yaga character)

5

*The Do-All Ax**

No, don't know as I can tell you anything with magic in it. How you expect I can tell you about magic when they ain't no such thing? Of course, there's two-three exceptions, like those flyin' slaves in the old days. Folks say there was a couple of field hands down around Johnson's Landing who didn't like the way they was bein' treated as slaves, and they just flapped their arms and took off. When last seen they was over the water headed east like a ball of fire.

Then there was that do-all ax. It sure got magic in it, what I mean.

The way it was, in the old days there was a man who had this do-all ax. When it was time to clear the trees off the ground to do some plantin', this man'd take his ax and his rockin' chair and go out and sit down in the shade. Then he'd sing a kind of song:

Bo kee meeny, dah ko dee,
Field need plantin', get off my knee.

That ax would just jump off his knee and start choppin' wood without no one holdin' onto the handle or anything. All by itself it went around

*From *Terrapin's Pot of Sense* by Harold Courlander (New York: Henry Holt and Company, 1957), pp. 80–83. Reprinted by permission of Harold Courlander.

cuttin' down the timber till the field was cleared. Then it chopped up the trees into stovewood lengths and threw 'em in a pile in the barnyard.

And next thing you know, this ax turn itself into a plow and went to plowin' up the field to make ready for plantin'. And when that's done, the plow turn into a corn planter and plant the corn.

All the time this man who owned it was rockin' back and forth in the shade, fannin' himself with a leaf. Well, that corn was sure-enough magic corn, grew up almost as fast as it went in the ground; little sprouts start to pop out 'fore the sun went down.

'Bout this time the man sing another song:

> Kah bo denny, brukko bay
> Time for dinner, quit this play.

Then the corn planter turned itself back into an ax and stopped workin'.

Well, three-four days later that corn was tall and ready for hoein'. Man went out with his ax, and it turned into a hoe. It went up and down the rows by itself, hoein' corn till the whole field was done. Next week the man came back and the hoe turn itself into a corn knife to cut all them stalks down. You see, the whole job was done just by this here magic ax.

Other folks used to come around and watch all these goin's-on. Everybody figure if they only had an ax like that, life would be a powerful lot better for them.

There was one man named Kwako who wanted that ax more'n anyone else. Said he reckoned he'd about die if he didn't get that ax. And when there wasn't nobody home one time, this Kwako went in and took it. Figured he'd get his own work done and then bring the ax back and wouldn't nobody know the difference.

He ran home and got his own rockin' chair and went out in the field. Laid the ax across his lap and sang like the other man did:

> Bo kee meeny, dah ko dee,
> Field need plantin', get off my knee.

Man, that ax went to work. Chopped down all the trees, cut the wood up in stovewood lengths, and stacked it by the house. Then it turned itself to a plow and plowed the ground. Then it turned to a corn planter and planted corn. 'Bout the time it was done plantin', the corn sprouts was already pokin' through the ground.

Kwako he was mighty pleased when he see all that. He sat rockin' back and forth in the shade enjoyin' himself real good. So when the corn was all planted he hollered, "That's enough for now, come on home." But corn planter didn't pay no attention, just kept jumpin' all around. Kwako hollered, "Didn't you hear what I said? Quit all this foolishness and come on home." Trouble was, he didn't know the song to stop it. He should have said:

Kah bo denny, brukko bay,
Time for dinner, quit this play.

But he didn't know the words, and he just kept hollerin', and the corn planter just kept jumpin' around, plantin' corn every-which-way till the seed was all gone. Then it turned into a hoe and started hoein' up the field. Now, that corn wasn't tall enough to be hoed, and it got all chopped to little pieces. Man, that field was a mess. Kwako he ran back and forth tryin' to catch the hoe, but he couldn't make it, hoe moved around too fast. Next thing you know, the hoe turned into a corn knife and started cuttin' in the air. But wasn't no corn to cut. So it went over in the cotton field and started cuttin' down the cotton. Just laid that cotton field low. And then it moved west, cuttin' down everything in the way. And when last seen it was followin' the settin' sun. After that it was gone for good.

Since that time there hasn't ever been a magic do-all ax in this part of the world, and folks has to do their farmin' the hard way.

But get it out of your head that there's magic things roundabout. What I told you is true, but it's an *exception.*

Notes and Comments

The general theme of a protagonist unable to stop a magical device is widely known in Europe. Tale Type 325*, *Apprentice and Ghost,* is more closely related to "The Do-All Ax" than the more inclusive Type 325 *The Magician and His Pupil.*

Several features of witch lore are illustrated in this tale. Flying slaves are commonly mentioned in black folklore since wind was often associated with witches in books of magic. Prominent wizards often kept their books chained to prevent them from flying away. J. Mason Brewer was once told about flying people by an informant who issued a disclaimer that would have done credit to the teller of "The Do-All Ax":

He got tuh whip um, Mr. Blue; he ain' hab no choice. Anyways, he whip um good an' dey gits tuhgedder an' stick duh hoe in duh fiel' an' den say

'Quack, quack, quack,' an' dey riz in duh sky an' tun desef intuh buzzards an' fly right back tuh Africa. . . .

No, ma'am, I ain' seen um, . . . but I know'd plenty wut did see um, planty wut was right deah in duh fiel' wid um an see de hoe wut dey lef' stickin' up attuh dey done fly away.

(American Negro Folklore, p. 309)

The basic theme of a sorcerer's apprentice who unleashes powers he cannot control is analogous to the story of the unfortunate Kwako. In the latter's case it was merely an ax that went berserk; other apprentices have been less fortunate. Some have accidentally summoned the devil himself. Only quick thinking can avert disaster in such cases. The devil must be given tasks he cannot perform—making a rope of sand that must be washed, or counting the letters of the Bible. Obviously the magic rope won't stand water, and the devil cannot bear to look on the Holy Writ.

The mystique of incantation is here reduced to gibberish:

Bo kee meeny, dah ko dee,
Field need plantin', get off my knee.

But incantations and spells played a very serious role in witch lore. The devil could be summoned by saying the Lord's Prayer backwards. Other spells could be broken either by saying the words backwards or by knowing a counter spell. Unfortunately for Kwako he forgot the equally important rhyme for stopping the ax. This motif is almost universal in Tale Type 325.

The attitude of the storyteller is an interesting one. He begins by denying that there is such a thing as magic except in very rare stories, one of which, not surprisingly, is the tale he is about to tell. His insistence that he doesn't believe in magic is an old persuasive technique that lends credence to a narrative. He frames his story not only with denials of the existence of magic but with such phrases as "folks say" and, "in the old days." These devices differ little from their European counterparts of "once upon a time" and "a long time ago." All serve the same purpose—to preserve the credibility of the storyteller while not pinning him down to anything that could be easily disproved by the skeptical.

Tale Type 325* Apprentice and Ghost

Principal Motifs:

D806   Magic object effective only when exact instructions for its use are followed

D1601.14   Self-chopping ax
D1711.0.1   Magician's apprentice
J2411.4   Imitation of magician unsuccessful; person does self injury

Parallel Stories in:

Briggs, *Dictionary,* A (1), pp. 411–12; B (2), pp. 614–15
Carrière, *Missouri,* #18 (summary in English)
Courlander, *Hat-Shaking,* pp. 86–87
Dorson, *American Negro,* #45
Rattray, *Akan-Ashanti,* #12
Writers' Project, Georgia, *Drums,* pp. 110–11

6

Molly Whuppie*

Once upon a time there was a man and a wife had too many children, and they could not get meat for them, so they took the three youngest and left them in a wood. They travelled and travelled and could see never a house. It began to be dark, and they were hungry. At last they saw a light and made for it; it turned out to be a house. They knocked at the door, and a woman came to it, who said: "What do you want?" They said: "Please let us in and give us something to eat." The woman said: "I can't do that, as my man is a giant, and he would kill you if he comes home." They begged hard. "Let us stop for a little while," said they, "and we will go away before he comes." So she took them in, and set them down before the fire, and gave them milk and bread; but just as they had begun to eat, a great knock came to the door, and a dreadful voice said:

Fee, fie, fo, fum,
I smell the blood of some earthly one.

"Who have you there, wife?" "Eh," said the wife, "it's three poor lassies cold and hungry, and they will go away. Ye won't touch 'em, man." He said

*From *English Fairy Tales* collected by Joseph Jacobs (London: David Nutt, 1898), pp. 130–35.

nothing, but ate up a big supper, and ordered them to stay all night. Now he had three lassies of his own, and they were to sleep in the same bed with the three strangers. The youngest of the three strange lassies was called Molly Whuppie, and she was very clever. She noticed that before they went to bed the giant put straw ropes round her neck and her sisters', and round his own lassies' necks, he put gold chains. So Molly took care and did not fall asleep, but waited till she was sure every one was sleeping sound. Then she slipped out of the bed, and took the straw ropes off her own and her sisters' necks, and took the gold chains off the giant's lassies. She then put the straw ropes on the giant's lassies and the gold on herself and her sisters, and lay down. And in the middle of the night up rose the giant, armed with a great club, and felt for the necks with the straw. It was dark. He took his own lassies out of bed on to the floor, and battered them until they were dead, and then lay down again, thinking he had managed finely. Molly thought it time she and her sisters were off and away, so she wakened them and told them to be quiet, and they slipped out of the house. They all got out safe, and they ran and ran, and never stopped until morning, when they saw a grand house before them. It turned out to be a king's house: so Molly went in, and told her story to the king. He said: "Well, Molly, you are a clever girl, and you have managed well; but, if you would manage better, and go back and steal the giant's sword that hangs on the back of his bed, I would give your eldest sister my eldest son to marry." Molly said she would try. So she went back, and managed to slip into the giant's house, and crept in below the bed. The giant came home, and ate up a great supper, and went to bed. Molly waited until he was snoring, and she crept out, and reached over the giant and got down the sword; but just as she got it out over the bed it gave a rattle, and up jumped the giant, and Molly ran out at the door and the sword with her; and she ran, and he ran, till they came to the "Bridge of one hair"; and she got over, but he couldn't, and he says, "Woe worth ye, Molly Whuppie! never ye come again." And she says: "Twice yet, carle," quoth she, "I'll come to Spain." So Molly took the sword to the king, and her sister was married to his son.

Well, the king he says: "Ye've managed well, Molly; but if ye would manage better, and steal the purse that lies below the giant's pillow, I would marry your second sister to my second son." And Molly said she would try. So she set out for the giant's house, and slipped in, and hid again below the bed, and waited till the giant had eaten his supper, and was snoring sound asleep. She slipped out and slipped her hand below the pillow, and got out the purse; but just as she was going out the giant wakened, and ran after her; and she ran, and he ran, till they came to the "Bridge of one hair," and she got over, but he couldn't, and he said, "Woe worth ye, Molly Whuppie! never you come again." "Once yet, carle," quoth she, "I'll come to Spain."

So Molly took the purse to the king, and her second sister was married to the king's second son.

After that the king says to Molly: "Molly, you are a clever girl, but if you would do better yet, and steal the giant's ring that he wears on his finger, I will give you my youngest son for yourself." Molly said she would try. So back she goes to the giant's house, and hides herself below the bed. The giant wasn't long ere he came home, and, after he had eaten a great big supper, he went to his bed, and shortly was snoring loud. Molly crept out and reached over the bed, and got hold of the giant's hand, and she pulled and she pulled until she got off the ring; but just as she got it off the giant got up, and gripped her by the hand and he says. "Now I have caught you, Molly Whuppie, and, if I had done as much ill to you as ye have done to me, what would ye do to me?"

Molly says: "I would put you into a sack, and I'd put the cat inside wi' you, and the dog aside you, and a needle and thread and a shears, and I'd hang you up upon the wall, and I'd go to the wood, and choose the thickest stick I could get, and I would come home, and take you down, and bang you till you were dead."

"Well, Molly," says the giant, "I'll just do that to you."

So he gets a sack, and puts Molly into it, and the cat and the dog beside her, and a needle and thread and shears, and hangs her up upon the wall, and goes to the wood to choose a stick.

Molly she sings out: "Oh, if ye saw what I see."

"Oh," says the giant's wife, "what do ye see, Molly?"

But Molly never said a word but, "Oh, if ye saw what I see!"

The giant's wife begged that Molly would take her up into the sack till she would see what Molly saw. So Molly took the shears and cut a hole in the sack, and took out the needle and thread with her, and jumped down and helped the giant's wife up into the sack, and sewed up the hole.

The giant's wife saw nothing, and began to ask to get down again; but Molly never minded, but hid herself at the back of the door. Home came the giant, and a great big tree in his hand, and he took down the sack, and began to batter it. His wife cried, "It's me, man"; but the dog barked and the cat mewed, and he did not know his wife's voice. But Molly came out from the back of the door, and the giant saw her and he after her; and he ran, and she ran, till they came to the "Bridge of one hair," and she got over but he couldn't; and he said, "Woe worth you, Molly Whuppie! never you come again." "Never more, carle," quoth she, "will I come again to Spain."

So Molly took the ring to the king, and she was married to his youngest son, and she never saw the giant again.

Notes and Comments

It is most fortunate for the heroes of traditional literature that ogres and giants do not have intellects to match their size or acute sense of smell. Like the dull Cyclops, Polyphemus, who lost his one eye to Odysseus, or the giant and his wife in this tale, most ogres are easy prey for the witty hero. Consequently the teller must be careful to preserve just the right tone, or the excitement of tales like "Molly Whuppie" will be lost. The listener must shudder (if only slightly) at the ominous rumble of

Fee, fie, fo, fum,
I smell the blood of some earthly one.

Richard Chase, who heard the tale in Virginia, remarks that "Mr. Rasnik boomed out the old giant's voice most terrifyingly and had Mutsmeg (the heroine) answer him in tiny piping tones" (*Grandfather Tales,* p. 235).

The presence of a giant (or sometimes a witch) and the stealing motif are two of the few constant features of Tale Type 327. Thompson divided Type 327 *The Children and the Ogre* into seven categories, but none of the subdivisions adequately describes "Molly Whuppie." To help clear away some of the confusion, we have listed only those parallel versions that have a female heroine deceiving an ogre, a flight and pursuit, and a scolding match.

An especially interesting feature of the pursuit and scolding match is the reference to the "Bridge of one hair." The Norse gods rode over Bifrost to reach Asgard, their home, and this bridge could not be traversed by their deadly enemies, the giants. There is also a bridge, as fine as a hair, over which Moslems pass on their way to heaven. John Campbell records a Scottish variant, "Maol a Chliobain" in which the heroine plucks a hair from her head and escapes, using it as a bridge. There was a prevalent belief in Scotland that witches could ride on a bridge made from a single hair.

There is more to this tale, however, than an unequal battle of wits. It is a very satisfying tale, especially for children, for though it begins tragically enough with three girls being abandoned by their destitute parents, it shows at least one of them summoning her inner resources to overcome terror and to learn to manage well in the world. Molly is especially noteworthy in that she is a female heroine—one of the few heroines in magic tales who takes an active part in tricking an ogre. Having escaped the giant's first attempt to kill her, Molly has every reason to lie low, but heroes (and heroines) are made of much sterner stuff. She undertakes the formulaic three tasks, each more dangerous than the previous one, and every success is crowned by a royal marriage, the last one being her own.

Tale Types: *327* The Children and the Ogre;
1119 The Ogre Kills His Own Children

Principal Motifs:

G84   Fee fi fo fum
G519.1   Ogre's wife killed through other tricks
G610.2   Stealing from ogre to help friendly king
K526   Captor's bag filled with animals or objects while captives escape
K1611   Substituted caps cause ogre to kill his own children
K842   Dupe persuaded to take prisoner's place in sack; killed

Parallel Stories in:

Briggs, *Dictionary,* A (1), pp. 154–55, 400–403
Campbell, *West Highlands,* 1: #17 (4 versions)
Chase, *Grandfather,* #4
Kennedy, *Fireside,* pp. 3–9
Roberts, *Sang Branch,* #108

Literary Retelling:

De La Mare, Walter. *Told Again,* pp. 193–200.

PICTURE BOOK:

Molly Whuppie. Joseph Jacobs. Illustrated by Pelagie Doane. New York: Oxford University Press, n.d. (Set in England)

7

The Toad-Bridegroom*

L ong ago there lived a poor fisherman in a certain village. One day
he went fishing in the lake as usual, but found he could not catch
as many fish as he was accustomed to. And on each of the following days
he found his catch growing smaller and smaller. He tried new baits, and
bought new hooks, but all to no avail. At last even the water of the lake
began to disappear, until in the end it became too shallow for fishing. One
afternoon in the late summer the bottom of the lake was exposed to view,
and a big toad came out from it. The fisherman immediately thought that
it must have eaten up all the fish and angrily cursed the *samzog* or three
families of the frog, its parents, brothers, wife and children, for it is popularly believed that the toad is a relative of the frog. Then the toad spoke to
him gently, rolling its eyes, "Do not be angry, for one day I shall bring you
good fortune. I wish to live in your house, so please let me go with you."
But the fisherman was annoyed that a toad should make such a request and
hastened home without it.

That evening the toad came to his house. His wife, who had already

*From *Folk Tales from Korea* collected and translated by Zong In-Sob (London: Routledge
& Kegan Paul Ltd., 1952), pp. 175–78. Reprinted by permission of Routledge & Kegan Paul
Ltd.

heard about it from her husband, received it kindly, and made a bed for it in a corner of the kitchen. Then she brought it worms and scraps to eat. The couple had no children of their own, and decided to keep the toad as a pet. It grew to be as big as a boy, and they came to love it as if it were their son.

Nearby there lived a rich man who had three daughters. One day the toad told the fisherman and his wife that it would like to marry one of the three daughters. They were most alarmed at this most unreasonable request and earnestly advised it to forget such an impossible ambition. "It is utterly absurd," they said. "How can poor people like us propose marriage to such a great family? And you are not even a human being."

So the toad replied, "I don't care what the rank of the family is. The parents may object, but yet one of the daughters may be willing to accept me. Who knows? Please go and ask, and let me know what answer you receive."

So the fisherman's wife went and called on the mistress of the rich man's house and told her what her toad-son had asked. The lady was greatly displeased and went and told her husband. He was furiously angry at such a preposterous suggestion and ordered his servant to beat the toad's foster-mother. So the poor woman returned home and told the toad of her painful experience.

"I'm very sorry that you have been treated like that, Mother," the toad said to her, "but don't let it worry you too much. Just wait and see what will happen." Then he went out and caught a hawk and brought it home. Late that night he tied a lighted lantern to its foot, and crept stealthily to the rich man's house. He tied a long string to the hawk's foot and then climbed a tall persimmon tree which stood by the house. Then he held the end of the string in his hand and released the hawk to fly over the house. As it flew into the air he solemnly declared in a loud voice, "The master of this house shall listen to my words, for I have been dispatched by the Heavenly King. To-day you rejected a proposal of marriage, and now you shall be punished for your arrogance. I shall give you one day to reconsider your decision. I advise you to accept the toad's proposal, for if you do not, you, your brothers, and your children shall be utterly destroyed."

The people in the house were startled by this nocturnal proclamation from the sky, and they opened the windows to see what was going on. When they looked up into the sky they saw a dim light hovering overhead. The master of the house went out into the garden and kneeled humbly on the ground looking up into the sky. Then the toad let go of the string he held in his hand, and the hawk soared skywards with the lantern still tied to its foot. The rich man was now convinced that what he had heard was spoken by a messenger from Heaven, and at once resolved to consent to the toad's marriage to one of his daughters.

Next morning the rich man went and called on the toad's foster-parents, and apologized humbly for his discourteous refusal on the previous day. He said now that he would gladly accept the toad as his son-in-law. Then he returned home and asked his eldest daughter to marry the toad, but she rushed from the room in fury and humiliation. Then he called his second daughter, and suggested that she be the toad's wife, but she too rushed from the room without a word. So he called his youngest daughter and explained to her that if she refused she would place the whole family in a most difficult position indeed, so stern had been the warning from Heaven. But the youngest daughter agreed to marry the toad without the slightest hesitation.

The wedding took place on the following day, and a great crowd of guests attended consumed by curiosity at such an unusual happening. That night, when they retired, the toad asked his bride to bring him a pair of scissors. She went and got a pair, and then he asked her to cut the skin off his back. This strange request startled her greatly, but he insisted that she do so without delay, and so she made a long cut in his back. Then, lo and behold, there stepped forth from the skin a handsome young man.

In the morning the bridegroom put on his toad skin again, so that nobody noticed any difference. Her two sisters sneered contemptuously at the bride with her repulsive husband, but she took no notice of them. At noon all the men of the household went out on horseback with bows and arrows to hunt. The toad accompanied them on foot and unarmed. But the party had no success in the hunt and had to return empty-handed. The bridegroom stripped off his toad skin and became a man when they had gone, and waved his hand in the air. Then a white haired old man appeared and he bade him bring one hundred deer. When the deer came he drove them homeward, once more wearing his toad skin. Everyone was most surprised to see all the deer, and then he suddenly stripped off the toad skin and revealed himself as a handsome young man, at which their astonishment knew no bounds. Then he released all the deer and rose up to Heaven, carrying his bride on his back and his parents on his arms.

Notes and Comments

When the Grimm Brothers published the first volume of their famous collection, *Kinder-und Hausmärchen,* in 1812, they chose "The Frog

Prince" for their first tale. The Frog Prince or Frog King (sometimes known as Iron Henry because of the famous bands around his servant's heart which keep it from breaking while his master is under enchantment) is a much-traveled story. Widely collected in Europe, Scandinavia, and Russia, it has also made its way into the Far East repertory, as evidenced by this unusual Korean version, "The Toad-Bridegroom."

Sir Walter Scott, in commenting on a version of Type 440 printed in James Halliwell's *Popular Rhymes and Nursery Tales,* says, "These enchanted frogs have migrated from afar, and we suspect they were originally crocodiles; we trace them in a tale . . . of the Calmuck Tartars" (p. 42n). While there is no way of proving Scott's theory, it would not be too surprising. Even the fabled Minotaur of Crete, though described as half man, half beast, is thought by some to have been a crocodile. Psychologists would even say that as long as the animal is either repulsive or fearsome, it would be appropriate in the context of the Frog King.

Like many of the magic tales, Type 440 is interrelated with other types. It stands somewhere between Type 425 *The Search for the Lost Husband* or Cupid and Psyche, and Type 480 *The Spinning-Women by the Spring* or Mother Holle. In the first type there is a tabu that must not be broken by the girl. The animal husband in his most grotesque form must be loved for his inner qualities or the wife must not look at him. She, however, cannot wait to see what the monster is like without his skin, and her violation of the tabu leads to a long and strenuous separation before the two are reunited.

The connection between 440 and 480 is not quite so complicated, for Type 440 is used only as an introduction to the longer tale. In Type 480 the girl is often sent to a well to carry out an impossible task—usually to gather water in a container that will not hold water. A frog offers advice to a kind girl who is then able to complete her assigned task. For his help, the frog gains the right to sleep before the girl's door, at the foot of her bed, and finally by her side. The frog, who is always under enchantment, is restored to his former shape by a kiss, or by sleeping on her pillow all night long, or more violently, by having his head cut off, being thrown against a wall, or by having his skin burned off. In the Korean version printed here, the frog has the power to remove his skin at will and appears to have taken the form of a frog from choice.

This story reveals dramatically the kinds of cultural and social changes that a folktale may undergo as it finds new settings and ways of life. (A Filipino variant employs a monkey in place of the toad.) Nevertheless, the major theme of the triumph of love over physical deformity persists. In this tale, the Korean toad outdoes his European counterparts. He not only gains admittance to a house but becomes a son. Interestingly enough the major objections to the toad are not to his physical appearance as much as to his social status. This same theme is presented at its most humorous in Kenneth Graham's *Wind in the Willows* where the imprisoned Toad finds the gaoler's daughter a comely lass and "could not help half regretting that the social gulf between them was so very wide." (Ch. 8)

Korean cultural variations are also apparent in the rich man's reaction to the marriage proposal. The father is so affronted by the difference in rank that Toad's adopted mother is vigorously beaten for her presumption in suggesting such a match. Even more interesting, however, is the fact that later, Toad's prowess as a hunter is almost as significant in this culture as his ability to step in and out of his toad skin at will.

The story ends with a variation of the traditional "they lived happily ever after" as the protagonists ascend up to heaven.

Tale Type 440   The Frog King or Iron Henry

Principal Motifs:

B211.7.2   Speaking toad
B655   Marriage to amphibia in human form
D395   Transformation: frog to person
D721.3   Disenchantment by destroying skin

Parallel Stories in:

Afanas'ev, pp. 119–23
Briggs, *Dictionary,* A (1), pp. 258–61
Campbell, *West Highlands,* 2: #33
Fansler, *Filipino,* #29 (variant)
Grimm, #1
Halliwell, *Nursery,* pp. 42–45
Jacobs, *English,* #41
Jones, *Magyars,* pp. 404–5n
O'Suilleabhain, *Handbook,* p. 563 (summary)
Thompson, *One,* #29 (from Grimm)

B

Tales that Might Have Been:
REALISTIC TALES

These humorous domestic dramas deal with the virtues of cleverness, patience, and endurance in the lives of ordinary people who have naught to do with magic or enchantment. While peasant girls may occasionally marry lords, they must first impress them with their extraordinary wit and intelligence.

8. *THE COW ON THE ROOF*   67
    TT 1408—*The Man who Does his Wife's Work*
    Also known as *The Husband Who Was to Mind the House*

9. *CRAB*   71
    TT 1641—*Doctor Know-All*
    Also known as *Cricket; "You've Got the Old Coon Now"*

10. *GUDBRAND ON THE HILL-SIDE*   75
    TT 1415—*Lucky Hans*
    Also known as *A Swapping Story, Wager on the Faithful Wife*

11. *THE STORY OF KUNZ AND HIS SHEPHERD*   81
     TT 922—*The Shepherd Substituting for the Priest
     Answers the King's Questions*
     Also known as *The King and the Abbot*

12. *THE MOST OBEDIENT WIFE*   86
     TT 901—*Taming of the Shrew*
     Also known as *You Haven't Carried the Saddle*

13. *CLEVER MANKA*   93
     TT 875—*The Clever Peasant Girl*
     Also known as *A Riddle Story, The Most Precious
     Thing in the World*

8

The Cow on the Roof*

Siôn Dafydd always grumbled that his wife could do nothing properly in the house. Neither a meal nor anything else ever pleased
him. At last his wife got tired of his grumbling and one day told him she
would go to weed turnips and that he should stay to take care of the baby
and the house, to make dinner, and some other things which she used to
do. Siôn readily agreed, so that she might have an example.

In setting out to the field, the wife said: "Now, you take care of the
baby, feed the hens, feed the pig, turn out the cow to graze, sweep the floor,
and make the porridge ready for dinner."

"Don't you bother about all that," said Siôn, "you see to the turnips."

The wife went to the field, Siôn to the house. The baby awoke. For a
long time, Siôn rocked the cradle and tried to sing to the child, which
seemed to make the poor thing worse. Siôn then remembered the pig, which
was squealing very loudly. He went to get some buttermilk to make food
for it but spilt it on the kitchen floor. The pig heard the sound of the bucket
and made so much noise that Siôn could not stand it.

"You wait a bit, you rascal!" he said to himself, but he meant the

*From *Welsh Folklore and Folk-Custom* by Thomas Gwynn Jones (London: Methuen &
Co., 1930), pp. 229–31 (revised by A.ap Gwynn). Reprinted by kind permission, A.ap Gwynn.

pig, "you shall go out to find food for yourself!"

So he opened the door to turn out the pig. Out went the pig like a shot, right between Siôn's legs, throwing him into the dunghill. By the time he got up and tried to scrape a little of the dirt off his clothes, the pig was out of sight. Siôn went into the house. There the pig had gone to lap up the buttermilk from the floor, and had, besides, overthrown another pot of buttermilk and was busy with that,

"You rascal!" shouted Siôn, and catching hold of an axe he struck the pig a blow on the head. The poor pig wobbled like a drunken man, then fell by the door and departed this life.

By this time it was getting late, and Siôn thought of the porridge, but the cow had to be turned out to graze, and he had quite forgotten the hens, poor souls. The field where the cow had to gather its daily bread, as it were, was some distance from the yard, and if Siôn went to take it there, the porridge would never be ready in time. At that moment Siôn happened to remember that there was some fine grass growing on the roof of the house. There was a rise at the back of the house, and the roof reached almost to the ground. Siôn thought the grass on the roof would be a good meal for a cow, and in order to be able to make the porridge as well he took a rope, tied one end round the cow's neck, ran up the roof, and dropped the other end of the rope down the chimney. Then he went to the porridge. So that he might have his two hands free, he tied the end of the rope round his ankle. In grazing on the roof the cow, without thinking, as it were, came to the top and slipped over suddenly. Siôn felt himself being pulled up by the leg, and into the chimney he went, feet first. Somehow, his legs went one on each side of the iron bar from which the kettle was hung over the fire, and there he stuck.

Just at that moment, the wife came back from the turnip field, and was horrified to see the cow dangling in the air. She ran to the door and fell across the dead pig, and without seeing anything else picked up the axe and ran to cut the rope and save the poor cow. Then she ran into the house and the first thing she saw there was Siôn, standing on his head in the porridge.

Notes and Comments

The tales in this section take the listener away from the world of magic and enchantment back to the one that lies outside his own door. The tone, however, remains generally lighthearted, with laughter being heard more often than sharp criticism.

"The Cow on the Roof" is a Welsh tale of foolish imitation also known in ballad form:

> The old 'ummon her tüked the whip in her hand,
>   And went to dräve the plough,
> The old man he tüked the milking pail,
>   And went to milk the cow.
>
> But Cherry, her kicked, and Cherry her flinged,
>   And Cherry her widden be quiet,
> Her gied the old man a kick in the leg,
>   Which made he kick up a riot.
>
> He went to watch the speckitty hen,
>   For fear that her shüde stray,
> But he forgot to wind the yarn
>   His wife spinned yesterday.
>
> Then he swared by the zin, the müne and the stars,
>   And all that wuz in Heaven,
> That his wife cüde do more work in a day,
>   Than he cüde do in zebben.
>
> (Briggs, *Dictionary,* A (2), pp. 209–10)

The tale is found in two basic forms—that in which the husband fails in all his tasks, and a longer version in which the husband spends much of his time complaining about the ease of his wife's work and the difficulties of his own. The cow on the roof motif (J1904.1) is a familiar one and appears in other tales, most noticeably in Type 1450 *Clever Elsie* and Type 1384 *The Husband Hunts Three Persons as Stupid as his Wife.*

Linda Degh collected a variant of this tale in Hungary, and her informant was most precise about the manner in which it should be told.

> She explained that it was a trick, just with anecdotes of this kind, to tell it quickly and to recite it in a quickly flowing language, for otherwise the nagging of the woman and the uncouthness of the man "do not come to light so well."
>
> (*Folktales and Society,* p. 321)

There is more to this tale of marital disharmony than the humor. It exemplifies something essential about the human condition. Few beliefs are more prevalent than the idea that others are having an easier time of things than we. Envy of the rich, the widespread belief in welfare chiselers, justifications for cheating on income tax, all are symptoms of the belief that the grass is greener in someone else's pasture. Of course, it seldom is.

Linda Degh's informant told the story with something of a revolutionary fervor. "It is astonishing to see how much the women like this tale which in the end raises its voice against the position of women in the old patriarchal family structure" (*Ibid.*, p. 321).

It seems extraordinary that so popular a tale as this should have been so sparsely collected. It is found in considerable numbers in Scandinavia (Finland records one hundred variants, Sweden forty-six, and Ireland forty-five), but the tale is undoubtedly far more widespread. Wanda Gag's version of this tale in her picture book *Gone is Gone* has made the marital problems of Fritzl and his wife familiar to the readers of children's literature. The incident of taking the cow on the roof to graze is often told as a complete tale itself, and to understand this motif we should not forget that some early houses were often constructed in such a way as to make it possible for an animal to reach the roof. Early pioneer houses in America were sometimes simply hollowed out of a bank of earth with a sod roof supported by a few cross beams. In Laura Ingalls Wilder's *On the Banks of Plum Creek* the ox, Pete, puts his foot through the roof and precipitates its collapse (Ch. 7).

Tale Type 1408   The Man Who Does His Wife's Work

Principal Motifs:

J2431   A man undertakes to do his wife's work; all goes wrong
J1904.1   Cow taken on roof to graze
J2176   Fool lets wine [milk] run in the cellar [kitchen]
J2132.2   Numskull ties the rope to his leg as the cow grazes on the roof

Parallel Stories in:

Asbjørnsen, #39
Briggs, *Dictionary,* A(2) (4 variants: 2 summaries, 2 ballads)

PICTURE BOOK:

Gone is Gone. Retold and illustrated by Wanda Gag. New York: Coward-McCann, 1935.

9

Crab*

There was once a king who had lost a valuable ring. He looked for it everywhere, but could not find it. So he issued a proclamation that if any astrologer could tell him where it was he would be richly rewarded. A poor peasant by the name of Crab heard of the proclamation. He could neither read nor write, but took it into his head that he wanted to be the astrologer to find the king's ring. So he went and presented himself to the king, to whom he said: "Your Majesty must know that I am an astrologer, although you see me so poorly dressed. I know that you have lost a ring and I will try by study to find out where it is." "Very well," said the king, "and when you have found it, what reward must I give you?" "That is at your discretion, your Majesty." "Go, then, study, and we shall see what kind of an astrologer you turn out to be."

He was conducted to a room, in which he was to be shut up to study. It contained only a bed and a table on which were a large book and writing materials. Crab seated himself at the table and did nothing but turn over the leaves of the book and scribble the paper so that the servants who brought him his food thought him a great man. They were the

*From *Italian Popular Tales* by Thomas Frederick Crane (Boston: Houghton, Mifflin and Company, 1885), pp.314–16.

ones who had stolen the ring, and from the severe glances that the peasant cast at them whenever they entered, they began to fear that they would be found out. They made him endless bows and never opened their mouths without calling him "Mr. Astrologer." Crab, who, although illiterate, was, as a peasant, cunning, all at once imagined that the servants must know about the ring, and this is the way his suspicions were confirmed. He had been shut up in his room turning over his big book and scribbling his paper for a month, when his wife came to visit him. He said to her: "Hide yourself under the bed, and when a servant enters, say: 'That is one;' when another comes, say: 'That is two;' and so on." The woman hid herself. The servants came with the dinner, and hardly had the first one entered when a voice from under the bed said: "That is one." The second one entered; the voice said: "That is two;" and so on. The servants were frightened at hearing that voice, for they did not know where it came from, and held a consultation. One of them said: "We are discovered; if the astrologer denounces us to the king as thieves, we are lost." "Do you know what we must do?" said another. "Let us hear." "We must go to the astrologer and tell him frankly that we stole the ring, and ask him not to betray us, and present him with a purse of money. Are you willing?" "Perfectly."

So they went in harmony to the astrologer, and making him a lower bow than usual, one of them began: "Mr. Astrologer, you have discovered that we stole the ring. We are poor people and if you reveal it to the king, we are undone. So we beg you not to betray us, and accept this purse of money." Crab took the purse and then added: "I will not betray you, but you must do what I tell you, if you wish to save your lives. Take the ring and make that turkey in the court-yard swallow it, and leave the rest to me." The servants were satisfied to do so and departed with a low bow. The next day Crab went to the king and said to him: "Your Majesty must know that after having toiled over a month I have succeeded in discovering where the ring has gone to." "Where is it, then?" asked the king. "A turkey has swallowed it." "A turkey? very well, let us see."

They went for the turkey, opened it, and found the ring inside. The king, amazed, presented the astrologer with a large purse of money and invited him to a banquet. Among the other dishes, there was brought on the table a plate of crabs. Crabs must then have been very rare, because only the king and a few others knew their name. Turning to the peasant the king said: "You, who are an astrologer, must be able to tell me the name of these things which are in this dish." The poor astrologer was very much puzzled, and, as if speaking to himself, but in such a way that the others heard him, he muttered: "Ah! Crab, Crab, what a plight you are in!" All who did not know that his name was Crab rose and proclaimed him the greatest astrologer in the world.

Notes and Comments

This very popular Type 1641 *Doctor Know-All* is diffused in Africa, Asia, and Europe. Over four hundred variants are known. The story is one of those in the category of "lucky accidents" since the central character saves his reputation (and his neck) by some accidental discovery which he passes off as genuine deduction.

The entire story of *Doctor Know-All* is found in the literary tale collections of India. It was certainly known by the end of the first century A.D. Joseph Jacobs includes a variant called "Harisarman" in his *Indian Fairy Tales.* At the climax of that tale, the sham scholar can only recall his pet name and lament his hard fate as he says, "Froggie you will soon become the swift destroyer of your helpless self." Naturally there is a frog hidden in the dish. Other versions have been found in many of the Renaissance jest books. These works, among the first printed books in Europe, are collections of short pointed stories, usually noodle tales, mocking a disliked class such as doctors or scholars.

The structure of the full tale has four parts:

I. The Sham Doctor. A peasant named Crab (Cricket or Rat) poses as Doctor Know-All.

II. Betrayal of the Theft. He is employed to catch thieves but is feasted first. As servants enter, he counts them—"That's one; that's two"—or frowns on them. They confess.

III. The Covered Dish. As a test of his powers he must guess what is in a covered dish. He says in despair, "Poor Crab (Rat, Cricket)." This dish contains the animals that share his name.

IV. The Stolen Horse. He "finds a horse he has just hidden."

American retellings have been almost exclusively black American, though Vance Randolph found a white version in Arkansas. Like almost all black versions, the Arkansas variant contains only the covered dish part of the story and hinges on the colloquial meaning of the word "coon." For example, "You've caught this old coon (i.e., himself) at last." In the dish is a raccoon. In a Chinese variant the cry of despair at the end is "Oh!

Goldhair." Fortunately for the sham doctor, there is a large yellow cat hidden in the sack.

The notion that fortune tellers, astrologers and seers are suspect is an ancient one. Whether or not there are those who possess unusual powers, there have been more than enough fakes and charlatans to make this type of story widely popular.

Tale Type 1641 Doctor Know-All

Principal Motifs:

K1956.2 Sham wise man hides something and is rewarded for finding it
N611 Criminal accidentally detected: "That is the first"—sham wise man
N688 What is in the dish: "Poor Crab"

Parallel Stories in:
Brewer, *Juneteenth* (1932), pp. 24–25
Briggs, *Dictionary*, A (2) (4 variants)
Degh, *Society*, pp. 324 (note)
Dorson, *Michigan*, pp. 51–53
———, *Buying*, pp. 253–56.
Eberhard, *China*, #11
Fansler, *Filipino*, #1 (references)
Grimm, #98
Hurston, *Mules and Men*, pp. 111–12 (reprinted in Botkin, *American*, pp. 445–46)
Jacobs, *Indian*, #11
Kent, *Turkey*, pp. 56–60
Megas, *Greece*, #68
Musick, *Green Hills*, #54
O'Suilleabhain, *Handbook*, p. 584 (summary)
Paredes, *Mexico*, #57
Parsons, *Antilles* 3: 282–84
Randolph, *Devil's*, pp. 133–35
Ranke, *Germany*, #54
Saucier, *Louisiana*, #24
Speers, *Notes*, pp. 284–85

10

Gudbrand on the Hill-side*

O nce on a time there was a man whose name was Gudbrand; he
had a farm which lay far, far away, upon a hillside, and so they
called him Gudbrand on the Hill-side.

Now, you must know this man and his goodwife lived so happily
together, and understood one another so well, that all the husband did the
wife thought so well done, there was nothing like it in the world, and she
was always glad whatever he turned his hand to. The farm was their own
land, and they had a hundred dollars lying at the bottom of their chest, and
two cows tethered up in a stall in their farmyard.

So one day his wife said to Gudbrand,—

"Do you know, dear, I think we ought to take one of our cows into
town and sell it; that's what I think; for then we shall have some money
in hand, and such well to-do people as we ought to have ready money like
the rest of the world. As for the hundred dollars at the bottom of the chest
yonder, we can't make a hole in them, and I'm sure I don't know what we
want with more than one cow. Besides, we shall gain a little in another way,
for then I shall get off with only looking after one cow, instead of having,
as now, to feed and litter and water two."

---

*From *Popular Tales from The Norse* collected by P. C. Asbjørnsen, translated by George
Dasent (Edinburgh: Edmonston and Douglas, 1859), pp. 172–77.

Well, Gudbrand thought his wife talked right good sense, so he set off at once with the cow on his way to town to sell her; but when he got to the town, there was no one who would buy his cow.

"Well, well! never mind," said Gudbrand, "at the worst, I can only go back home again with my cow. I've both stable and tether for her, I should think, and the road is no farther out than in," and with that he began to toddle home with his cow.

But when he had gone a bit of the way, a man met him who had a horse to sell, so Gudbrand thought 't was better to have a horse than a cow, so he swapped with the man. A little farther on he met a man walking along and driving a fat pig before him, and he thought it better to have a fat pig than a horse, so he swapped with the man. After that he went a little farther, and a man met him with a goat; so he thought it better to have a goat than a pig, and he swapped with the man that owned the goat. Then he went on a good bit till he met a man who had a sheep, and he swapped with him too, for he thought it always better to have a sheep than a goat. After a while he met a man with a goose, and he swapped away the sheep for the goose; and when he had walked a long, long time, he met a man with a cock, and he swapped with him, for he thought in this wise, " 'Tis surely better to have a cock than a goose." Then he went on till the day was far spent, and he began to get very hungry, so he sold the cock for a shilling, and bought food with the money, for, thought Gudbrand on the Hill-side, " 'Tis always better to save one's life than to have a cock."

After that he went on home till he reached his nearest neighbor's house, where he turned in.

"Well," said the owner of the house, "how did things go with you in town?"

"Rather so so," said Gudbrand. "I can't praise my luck, nor do I blame it either," and with that he told the whole story from first to last.

"Ah!" said his friend, "you'll get nicely called over the coals, that one can see, when you get home to your wife. Heaven help you, I wouldn't stand in your shoes for something."

"Well," said Gudbrand on the Hill-side, "I think things might have gone much worse with me; but now, whether I have done wrong or not, I have so kind a goodwife, she never has a word to say against anything that I do."

"Oh!" answered his neighbor, "I hear what you say, but I don't believe it for all that."

"Shall we lay a bet upon it?" asked Gudbrand on the Hill-side. "I have a hundred dollars at the bottom of my chest at home; will you lay as many against them?"

Yes, the friend was ready to bet; so Gudbrand stayed there till evening, when it began to get dark, and then they went together to his house, and the neighbor was to stand outside the door and listen, while the man went in to see his wife.

"Good evening!" said Gudbrand on the Hill-side.

"Good evening!" said the goodwife. "Oh, is that you? now God be praised."

Yes! it was he. So the wife asked how things had gone with him in town.

"Oh! only so so," answered Gudbrand; "not much to brag of. When I got to the town there was no one who would buy the cow, so you must know I swapped it away for a horse."

"For a horse," said his wife; "well, that is good of you; thanks with all my heart. We are so well to do that we may drive to church, just as well as other people; and if we choose to keep a horse we have a right to get one, I should think. So run out, child, and put up the horse."

"Ah!" said Gudbrand, "but you see I've not got the horse after all; for when I got a bit farther on the road I swapped it away for a pig."

"Think of that, now!" said the wife; "you did just as I should have done myself; a thousand thanks! Now I can have a bit of bacon in the house to set before people when they come to see me, that I can. What do we want with a horse? People would only say we had got so proud that we couldn't walk to church. Go out, child, and put up the pig in the stye."

"But I've not got the pig either," said Gudbrand; "for when I got a little farther on I swapped it away for a milch goat."

"Bless us!" cried his wife, "how well you manage everything! Now I think it over, what should I do with a pig? People would only point at us and say, 'Yonder they eat up all they have got.' No! now I have got a goat, and I shall have milk and cheese, and keep the goat too. Run out, child, and put up the goat."

"Nay, but I haven't got the goat either," said Gudbrand, "for a little farther on I swapped it away, and got a fine sheep instead."

"You don't say so!" cried his wife; "why, you do everything to please me, just as if I had been with you; what do we want with a goat! If I had it I should lose half my time in climbing up the hills to get it down. No! if I have a sheep, I shall have both wool and clothing, and fresh meat in the house. Run out, child, and put up the sheep."

"But I haven't got the sheep any more than the rest," said Gudbrand; "for when I had gone a bit farther I swapped it away for a goose."

"Thank you! thank you! with all my heart," cried his wife; "what should I do with a sheep? I have no spinning-wheel, nor carding-comb, nor should I care to worry myself with cutting, and shaping, and sewing clothes.

We can buy clothes now, as we have always done; and now I shall have roast goose, which I have longed for so often; and, besides, down to stuff my little pillow with. Run out, child, and put up the goose."

"Ah!" said Gudbrand, "but I haven't the goose either; for when I had gone a bit farther I swapped it away for a cock."

"Dear me!" cried his wife, "how you think of everything! just as I should have done myself. A cock! think of that! why it's as good as an eight-day clock, for every morning the cock crows at four o'clock, and we shall be able to stir our stumps in good time. What should we do with a goose? I don't know how to cook it; and as for my pillow, I can stuff it with cotton-grass. Run out, child, and put up the cock."

"But after all I haven't got the cock," said Gudbrand; "for when I had gone a bit farther, I got as hungry as a hunter, so I was forced to sell the cock for a shilling, for fear I should starve."

"Now, God be praised that you did so!" cried his wife; "whatever you do, you do it always just after my own heart. What should we do with the cock? We are our own masters, I should think, and can lie a-bed in the morning as long as we like. Heaven be thanked that I have got you safe back again; you who do everything so well that I want neither cock nor goose; neither pigs nor kine."

Then Gudbrand opened the door and said,—

"Well, what do you say now? Have I won the hundred dollars?" and his neighbor was forced to allow that he had.

Notes and Comments

In the *Tale-Type Index,* "Gudbrand on the Hill-Side" is classified as Type 1415: *Lucky Hans.* Like Gudbrand, Hans was lucky not in his swappings (which were progressively worse), but in his winning a bet that his wife would not be angry with him (Motif N11).

There are, needless to say, variants of this type in which the wife is cast as a shrew rather than an angel of mercy. The familiar "Mr. Vinegar" is an English tale of a foolish fellow who, having found some money dropped by thieves, proceeds to trade it down from a cow, to bagpipes, to gloves, and finally to a stick. Eventually he loses even that. Being a noodle, Mr. Vinegar naturally tells his wife the whole story and receives such a "cudgeling that she broke every bone in his skin."

Almost without exception the tales of this kind involve family relationships of husband and wife or noodle and mother. The swapping motif is the key to the tale, each exchange being for something of less value. The foolish man is always content with his new possessions and never realizes that he has been taken advantage of. What makes "Gudbrand" so refreshing is that the hero's ignorance of worldly matters is more than outweighed by the patient love of his long-suffering wife.

Other tales employ 1415 as a beginning for Type 1384 *The Husband Hunts Three Persons as Stupid as His Wife*. On a recording Richard Chase tells a Jack tale, "Jack and the Three Sillies," in which Jack ends up with a nice round rock to prop his door open. His actions cause his wife to despair, leave home, search for three people more foolish than her husband, and get back the fifty dollars Jack had lost in the bargain. (Her reaction is less likely to strain the credulity of female readers than that of Gudbrand's wife.)

The "swapping series" is a popular feature in folktales and folk songs. Two other tales in this book—#42 and #63—also employ exchanges, though in different ways and with different results. Type 1415 *Lucky Hans* is well known in Europe and eastward as far as India. It is popular in Scandinavia and has been retold by Hans Christian Andersen as "What the Good Man Does Is Always Right." Additionally, John Langstaff's picture book *The Swapping Boy* prints verses and a tune from his own family tradition. Alongside illustrations of Joe and Beth Krush, some of the verses he lists are:

I swapped my mare and got me a cow,
But then to milk her, I don't know how.

I swapped my cow and got me a calf
And in that trade I lost just half.

I swapped my calf and got me a mule
And then I rode like a doggone fool.

Many verses later he ends up swapping a cat for a mole,

And the darned old thing went straight to its hole!

Tale Type 1415 Lucky Hans

Principal Motifs:

J2081.1 Foolish bargain; horse for cow, cow for hog, etc. Finally nothing left
N11 Wager on wife's complacency

Parallel Stories in:

Afanas'ev, pp. 371–75
Boggs, *North Carolina,* p. 307, and references
Briggs, *Dictionary,* A (1), pp. 310–12; and A (2), pp. 135–36, 548 (summaries)
Fauset, *Nova Scotia,* #170 (variant)
Gardner, *Schoharie,* pp. 172–75
Grimm, #83
Halliwell, *Nursery,* pp. 28–30
Jacobs, *English,* #6
Randolph, *Devil's,* pp. 20–22
Thompson, *One,* #87 (from Asbjørnsen)

RECORDINGS:

Richard Chase, "Jack and the Three Sillies"
Gudrun Thorne-Thompson, "Gudbrand on the Hill-side"

PICTURE BOOKS:

What the Good Man Does is Always Right. Hans Christian Andersen. Illustrated by
Rick Schreiter. New York: Dial Press, 1968.
Happy Go Lucky. Retold and illustrated by William Wiesner. New York: Seabury
Press, 1970. (Set in Poland)
Swapping Boy. John Langstoff. Illustrated by Beth and Joe Krush. New York:
Harcourt, Brace and World, 1960.

11

The Story of Kunz and His Shepherd*

T he proverb runs: "You will be left behind as Kunz was left behind to look after the sheep." And if you ask how Kunz came to be left behind to look after the sheep, I will tell you.

Once upon a time there was a mighty king, who had a counselor called Kunz. Whenever the king needed advice, and the counselors in conference came to a decision, the clever Kunz would go to the king and say: "This is our decision." This fine gentleman always took the credit to himself, pretending that he was responsible for the advice and that the other counselors had to agree with him, for they had neither sense nor understanding. And the good king believed what Kunz told him and considered him as much wiser than the other counselors.

Now the other counselors noticed that the king loved Kunz more than he loved them and they resented it very much, for he was the least important among them. One day they took counsel together how to get the better of Kunz and humiliate him. So they went to the king and said: "Lord king, we beg of you to forgive us, for we wish to ask you how it is that you think

*From the *Ma'Aseh Book of Jewish Tales and Legends* edited by Moses Gaster. (Philadelphia: Jewish Publication Society of America, 1934), II, 571–76. Copyrighted by and used through the courtesy of the Jewish Publication Society of America.

more of Kunz and hold him in higher esteem than the rest of us, although we know that he is the least important among us?" The king replied: "I will tell you how it happens. Whenever you come to a decision on any matter, he reports it to me and says that the idea is his and that you have to acknowledge every time that he is wiser than you and that you have no sense at all. But I do not hold you in disrespect, for you are all good to me." When the counselors heard this, they were very glad and thought: "We will soon bring about his downfall." Then they said to the king: "Be assured that all which Kunz said is a lie, for he has no sense at all. Try every one of us separately and you will see that he cannot give you any advice by himself." The king said: "I will find out very soon," and sent for his beloved counselor Kunz and said to him: "My dear servant, I know that you are loyal and exceedingly wise. Now I have something in my mind that I do not wish to reveal to anyone. Therefore, I want to ask you whether you can find out the truth for me, and if you do, I will reward you liberally." The clever Kunz replied: "My beloved king, ask me and I hope I can give you an answer. Tell me the secret." The king said: "I will ask you three questions. The first is: Where does the sun rise? The second is: How far is the sky from the earth? The third, my dear Kunz, is: What am I thinking?" When Kunz heard these three questions, he said: "Lord king, these are difficult matters, which cannot be answered offhand. They require time. I beg of you, therefore, to give me three days' time, and then I hope to give you the proper answer." The king replied: "My dear Kunz, your request is granted, I will give you three days' time." Kunz went away and thought to himself: "I cannot concentrate my mind very well in the city. I will go for a walk into the country. There I am alone and can reflect better than in the city."

He went out into the country and came upon the shepherd who was tending his flock. Walking along, he talked as it were to himself, saying: "Who can tell me how far the heavens are from the earth? Who can tell me where the sun rises? Who can tell me what the king is thinking?" The shepherd, seeing his master walking about wrapt in thought, said to him: "Sir, pardon me. I see that you are greatly troubled in your mind. If you ask me, I might be able to help you. As the proverb says: 'One can often advise another, though one cannot advise oneself.' " When Kunz heard these words from the shepherd, he thought: "I will tell him. Perhaps after all he may be able to advise me." And he said: "I will tell you why I am so troubled. The king asked me three questions, which I must answer or lose my neck. I have been thinking about them and cannot find the answer." Then the shepherd said: "What are the three questions? Perhaps I may be able to help you in your great trouble." So Kunz thought: "I will tell him, maybe he is a scholar." And he said: "My dear shepherd, these are the three questions which the king asked me. I must tell him where the sun rises, how far the heavens are from the earth, and what the king is thinking." The shepherd thought it was well to know the answers and said to Kunz: "My dear master, give me your fine clothes, and you put on my poor garments and look after the sheep. I will go to the king and he will think that I am you and give me the three questions. Then I shall give him the proper answers and you will be saved from your trouble. Then I shall return here and you will not be in disgrace with your king." Kunz allowed himself to be persuaded, gave the shepherd his good clothes and fine cloak, while he put on the shepherd's rough garments and sat down to look after the sheep, as though he had done it all his life.

When the three days had passed, the shepherd went to the king and said: "Lord king, I have been thinking over the three questions that you asked me." The king said: "Now tell me, where does the sun rise?" The shepherd replied: "The sun rises in the east and sets in the west." The king asked again: "How far are the heavens from the earth?" The shepherd replied: "As far as the earth is from the heavens." Then the king said: "What am I thinking?" The shepherd replied: "My lord king, you are thinking that I am your counselor Kunz, but I am not. I am the shepherd who looks after his flock. My master Kunz was walking in the field one day and saying to himself: 'Who can tell where the sun rises? Who can tell me how far the heavens are from the earth? Who can tell me what the king has in his mind?' He was walking about all the time and talking in such fashion. So I told him he should give me his good clothes and I would give him my rough clothes; he should look after the sheep and I would, with the help of God, guess the answers to these three questions and save him. He allowed himself to be persuaded, and so he is now out in the field, dressed in my rough clothes and tending the sheep, while I am dressed in his beautiful cloak and his best clothes." When the king heard this, he said to the shepherd: "As you succeeded in persuading Kunz, you shall remain my counselor and Kunz can look after the sheep." Hence the proverb: "You will be left behind as Kunz was left behind to look after the sheep." This is what happened to him. May it go better with us.

Notes and Comments

The riddling tradition is an ancient and serious one, with the fate of many a kingdom, the length of a life, or the virtue of a maiden hanging in the balance. Some scholars suggest that the riddle is the most ancient and widespread type of formulated thought; certainly riddles are older than the Hebrew and Greek cultures which contain many famous examples. In the Biblical book of Judges, for example, there is a riddling contest between Samson and the Philistines. Samson asks:

> Out of the eater came something to eat;
> Out of the strong came something sweet.

Even the answer to this riddle, finally given by Samson to his bride-to-be, Delilah, came in the form of a riddle:

> What is sweeter than honey?
> What is stronger than the lion?

The answer to the riddle was a lion's carcass filled with a honeycomb.

The wager on Samson's riddle was only thirty shirts and thirty changes of garments, but the Greek hero Oedipus saves a whole city by his answer to the riddle of the marauding Sphinx:

> What goes on four legs in the morning, on two in the afternoon, and on three in the evening?

The answer was man, for he crawls as a baby, walks upright in the middle of his lifetime, and supports himself with a cane in the evening of his life.

In "The Story of Kunz and His Shepherd" the reputation of Kunz is at stake as well as his neck, and his story serves as a moral exemplum for all those with intellectual pretensions. In this story Kunz not only loses his powerful position at the right hand of the throne, but his experiences are encapsulated in a proverb that persists in Jewish tradition: "You will be left behind as Kunz was left behind to look after the sheep."

The plot of Tale Type 922 is straightforward and simple. For various reasons the authority figure, be he king, cardinal, or landlord, has occasion to pose a riddle to one of his servants. He always asks three riddles, the last one seemingly impossible to answer. It is this third and final riddle that is the crux of the tale; the answer to it almost always involves some kind of disguise or substitution on the part of the servant under fire. The questions are either "What am I thinking?" or even "What is God doing?" The answers are similar, being either "You think I am the abbot and I am only a poor shepherd" or "God is surprised that a shepherd would dare answer in place of the abbot."

This particular tale type has an equally strong tradition as a ballad known as "King John and the Bishop" (Child Ballad #45) where it keeps company with such other famous riddling ballads as Child Ballad #1, "Riddles Wisely Expounded," and Child Ballad #46, "Captain Wedderburn's Courtship."

Tale Type 922   The Shepherd Substituting for the Priest Answers the King's Questions

Principal Motifs:

H540.3   King propounds riddles
J1115.6   Clever peasant
H682.1   Riddle: how far is it from earth to heaven?

Parallel Stories:

Aiken, *Mexico,* pp. 78–82
Briggs, *England,* #63 (from Wilson, *Humorous,* #1)
Campbell, *West Highlands* 2: #50
Child Ballad, #45 (see notes)
Fauset, *Negro,* pp. 259–60
———, *Nova Scotia,* #37
Grimm, #152
Jacobs, *More English,* #72 (from a ballad in Percy, *Reliques* 2: 303–12)
Noy, *Israel,* #38, #61
Paredes, *Mexico,* #44
Parsons, *Cape Verde,* I: #31, #32
Randolph, *Turtle,* pp. 25–27
Thompson, *One,* #82

12

The Most Obedient Wife*

L ong ago there was a rich farmer who had three daughters, all grown up and marriageable, and all three very pretty. The eldest of them was the prettiest, and she was also the cleverest, but she was so quarrelsome and obstinate, that there was never any peace in the house. She constantly contradicted her father, who was a kind, peace-loving man, and she quarreled with her sisters, although they were very good-natured girls.

Many wooers came to the farm, and one of them wished to marry the eldest daughter. The farmer said that he had no objection to him as a son-in-law, but at the same time he thought it his duty to tell the suitor the truth. Accordingly he warned him that his eldest daughter was so violent and strong-minded that no one could live in peace with her. As some compensation for these faults, she would receive three hundred pounds more in her dowry than would her two sisters. That was, of course, very attractive, but the young man thought over the matter and, after he had been visiting the house for some time, he altered his mind and asked for the hand of the second daughter. The daughter accepted him, and, as her father was willing, the two became man and wife and lived very happily together.

*From *Danish Fairy Tales* by Svend Grundtvig (London: George C. Harrap and Co., 1914), pp. 175–83. Reprinted by permission of George C. Harrap & Company Ltd.

Then came another wooer, from another part of the country, and he also wanted to marry the eldest daughter. The father warned him, as he had cautioned the first wooer; telling him that she would receive three hundred pounds more than her youngest sister, but that he must be careful, for she was so stubborn and quarrelsome that nobody could live in peace with her. So the second wooer changed his mind and asked for the hand of the youngest daughter. They married shortly after and lived happily and peacefully together.

The eldest sister was now alone with her father, but she did not treat him any better than before, and grew even more ill-humored because her two sisters had found favor in the eyes of the first two wooers. She was obstinate and quarrelsome, violent and bad-tempered, and she grew more so from day to day.

At last another wooer came, and he was neither from their own district nor even from their country, but from a distant land. He went to the farmer and asked for the hand of his eldest daughter. "I do not want her to marry at all," said the father. "It would be a shame to allow her to do so; she is so ill-tempered and violent that no human being could live in peace with her and I do not want to be the cause of such unhappiness." But the wooer remained firm; he wanted her, he said, whatever her faults might be. At length the father yielded, provided that his daughter were willing to marry the young man, for, after all, he would be glad to get rid of her, and as he had told the suitor the whole truth about her, his conscience was clear. Accordingly, the young man wooed the girl, and she did not hesitate long, but accepted the offer, for she was tired of sitting at home a despised and spurned spinster.

The wooer said that he had no time to remain with them just then, as he must return home at once, and, as soon as the wedding day was fixed, he rode away. He also told them not to wait for him at the farm on the day of the wedding, he would appear in good time at the church. When the day came the farmer drove with his daughter to the church, where a great company of wedding guests had assembled; the bride's sisters and brothers-in-law were there, and all the village people arrived in their Sunday clothes. The bridegroom was there also, but in ordinary traveling garments; and so the couple walked up to the altar and were married.

As soon as the ceremony was over, the bridegroom took his young wife by the hand and led her out of the church. He sent a message to his father-in-law asking him to excuse their absence from the marriage feast, as they had no time to waste. He had not driven in a coach, as is the custom at weddings, but traveled on horseback, on a fine big gray horse, with an ordinary saddle, and a couple of pistols in the saddlebags. He had brought no friends or relations with him, only a big dog, that lay beside the horse during the ceremony. The bridegroom lifted his bride on to the pommel, as if she had been a feather, jumped into the saddle, put the spurs to his horse and rode off with the dog trotting behind. The marriage party standing at the church door looked after them, and shook their heads in amazement. Then they got into their carriages, drove back to the house, and partook of the marriage feast without bride or bridegroom.

The bride did not like this at all, but as she did not want to quarrel with her bridegroom so soon, she held her tongue for a time; but as he did not speak either, she at last broke the ice and said that it was a very fine horse they were riding. "Yes," he replied; "I have seven other horses at home in my stables, but this is my favorite; it is the most valuable of all, and I like it best." Then she remarked that she liked the beautiful dog also. "It is indeed a jewel of a dog," he said, "and has cost me a lot of money."

After a while they came to a forest, where the bridegroom sprang from his horse and cut a thin switch from a willow tree. This he wound three times round his finger, then tied it with a thread and gave it to his bride, saying: "This is my wedding gift to you. Take good care of it, and carry it about with you always! You will not repent it." She thought it a strange wedding gift, but put it in her pocket, and they rode on again. Presently the bride dropped her glove, and the bridegroom said to the dog: "Pick it up, Fido!" But the dog took no notice, and left the glove on the ground. Then his master drew his pistol from the holster, shot the dog, and rode on, leaving it lying dead. "How could you be so cruel?" said his bride. "I never say a thing twice," was the reply, and they journeyed on in silence.

After some time they came to a running stream that they had to cross. There being only a ford, and no bridge, the man said to his horse: "Take good care! Not a drop must soil my bride's dress!" When they had crossed, however, the dress was badly soiled, and the husband lifted his bride from the horse, drew out the other pistol and shot the horse, so that it fell dead to the ground. "Oh, the poor horse!" cried the bride. "Yes, but I never say a thing twice," answered her husband. Then he took saddle, bridle, and cover from the horse; bridle and cover he carried himself, but the saddle he gave to his young wife, and said: "You can carry that; we shall soon be home." He walked on in silence, and the bride quickly put the saddle on her back and followed him; she had no desire to make him say it twice.

Soon they arrived at his dwelling place, a very fine farm. The menservants and maidservants rushed to the door and received them, and the husband said to them: "See, this is my wife and your mistress. Whatever she tells you, you are to do, just as if I had ordered it." Then he led her indoors and showed her everything—livingrooms and bedrooms, kitchen and cellar, brewhouse and dairy—and said to her: "You will look after everything indoors, I attend to everything out-of-doors," and then they sat down to supper, and soon after went to bed.

Days, weeks and months passed; the young wife attended to all household matters while her husband looked after the farm, and not a single angry word passed between them. The servants had been accustomed to obey their master implicitly, and now they obeyed their mistress likewise, and so six months passed without there having arisen any necessity for the husband to say the same thing twice to his wife. He was always kind and polite to her, and she was always gentle and obedient.

One day he said to her: "Would you not like to visit your relations?" "Yes, dear husband, I should like to do so very much, if it is convenient," she replied. "It is quite convenient," he said, "but you have never mentioned it. It shall be done at once; get ready, while I have the horses put to the carriage." He went to the stable and saw to everything, while his wife ran upstairs to dress as quickly as possible for the journey. The husband drove up, cracked his whip and asked: "Are you ready?" "Yes, dear," came the reply, and she came running out and entered the carriage. She had not quite finished dressing and carried some of her things in her hand, and these she put on in the carriage.

Then they started. When they had driven nearly half the distance, they saw a great flock of ravens flying across the road. "What beautiful white birds!" said the husband. "No, they are black, dear!" said his wife. "I think it is going to rain," he said, turned the horses, and drove home again. She understood perfectly why he had done so; it was the first time that she had contradicted him, but she showed no resentment, and the two conversed in quite a friendly fashion all the way home. The horses were put into the stable—and it did not rain.

When a month had passed, the husband said one morning: "I believe it is going to be fine to-day. Would you not like to visit your relations?" She wished to do so very much indeed, and she hastened a little more than the last time, so that when her husband drove up and cracked his whip, she was quite ready and mounted the carriage beside him. They had driven considerably more than half the distance, when they met a large flock of sheep and lambs. "What a fine pack of wolves!" said the husband. "You mean sheep, dear!" said the wife. "I think it will rain before evening," said the husband, looking up at the sky. "It will be better for us to drive home again." With these words he turned the horses and drove back home. They conversed in a friendly manner until they reached home; but it did not rain.

When another month had passed, the husband said one morning to his wife: "We really must see whether we cannot manage to visit your relations.

What do you say to our driving across today? It looks as though the day would be fine." His wife thought so too; she was ready very soon and they set out. They had not traveled far when they saw a great flock of swans flying along over their heads. "That was a fine flock of storks," said the husband. "Yes, so it was, dear," said his wife, and they drove on; there was no change in the weather that day, so that they reached her father's farm in due course. He received them joyfully and sent at once for his two other daughters and their husbands, and a very merry family meeting it was.

The three married sisters went into the kitchen together, because they could talk more freely there, and they had a great deal to tell each other; the two younger ones in particular had many questions to ask their elder sister, because they had not seen her for a very long time. Then they helped to prepare the dinner; it goes without saying that nothing was too good for this festive occasion.

The three brothers-in-law sat meanwhile with their father-in-law in the sitting room and they, too, had much to tell and ask each other. Then said the old farmer: "This is the first time that you have all three been gathered together under my roof, and I should like to ask you frankly how you are pleased with your wives." The husbands who had married the two younger, good-tempered sisters said at once that they were perfectly satisfied and lived very happily. "But how do you get on with yours?" the father-in-law asked the husband of the eldest sister. "Nobody ever married a better wife than I did," was the reply. "Well, I should like to see which of you has the most obedient wife," said the father-in-law, and then he fetched a heavy silver jug and filled it to the top with gold and silver coins. This he placed in the middle of the table before the three men, and said that he would give it to him who had the most obedient wife.

They put the matter to the test at once. The husband who had married the youngest sister went to the kitchen door and called: "Will you come here a moment, Gerda, please; as quickly as possible!" "All right, I am coming," she answered, but it was some time before she came, because as she explained, she had first to talk about something with one of her sisters. "What do you want with me?" she asked. The husband made some excuse, and she went out again.

Now it was the turn of the man who had married the middle sister. "Please come here a moment, Margaret!" he called. She also answered: "Yes, I am coming at once," but it was a good while before she came; she had had something in her hands and was compelled to put it down first. The husband invented some excuse, and she went out again.

Then the third husband went to the kitchen door, opened it slightly and just said: "Christine!"—"Yes!" she answered, as she stood there with a large dish of food in her hands. "Take this from me!" she said quickly to her sisters, but they looked at her in amazement and did not take the dish. Bang! she dropped it right on the middle of the kitchen floor, rushed into the room and asked: "What do you wish, dear?"—"Oh, I only wanted to see you," he said, "but since you are here, you may as well take that jug standing on the table; it is yours, with all that is in it.—You might also show us what you got from me as a marriage gift on your wedding day."—"Yes, dear, here it is," she said, and drew the willow ring from her bosom, where she had kept it ever since. The husband handed it to his father-in-law and asked: "Can you put that ring straight?"—No, that was impossible without breaking it. "Well, you see now," said the husband, "if I had not bent the twig when it was green, I could not have made it into this shape."

After that they sat down to a merry meal, then the husband of the oldest sister returned home with her, and they lived for many years very happily together.

Notes and Comments

This humorous tale (Type 901 *Taming of the Shrew*) is found throughout the world in at least three hundred variants. The central motif is T251.2.3 "Wife becomes obedient on seeing husband slay a recalcitrant horse" (or other animal).

Thompson says the original tale goes back to the exempla of the Middle Ages, where it appears in Juan Manuel's *El Conde Lucanor.* Books of this genre sought to provide models of "right" behavior. The tale was retold later by Straparola in the sixteenth century as a *novella,* a short tale with realistic settings, characters from everyday life, and familiar folktale motifs. Clearly "The Most Obedient Wife" is an example of a literary tale that has become part of the oral tradition of Europe and America.

The Northern European versions of the tale have been elaborated by additions such as the bridegroom's uncouth behavior at the wedding; a series of absurd statements, usually three, with which the wife must agree; and finally a wager in which the shrew is proved to be the most obedient wife. The oral form may well have partly influenced Shakespeare in writing *The Taming of the Shrew* (ca. 1594). Equally important, however, were such literary sources as Straparola's *Notte Piaceveli* (1550) and the Elizabethan poem "A Merry Geste of a Shrewd and Curst Wife" (ca. 1550). Of course shrews are familiar figures in literature; anyone who has seen the medieval play *Noah* will be only too well aware of this. Of the fifty or so

American variants collected by Jan Harold Brunvand in his study of the tale, the majority are brief and condensed. The most extensive New World versions are French-Canadian and Spanish-American (although the former were ultimately of Scots-Irish origin). These bear a striking resemblance to the versions current in Shakespeare's day.

The taming of the shrew motif is not meant to be treated as a serious solution to a psychological problem. There are, it is true, more nagging wives than husbands in traditional tales, but then the vast majority of fools and noodles in folktales are men. The shrew is simply a conventional figure. The willow ring motif is a subtle touch—signifying as it does the value of training and education at the proper time.

Tale Type 901   Taming of the Shrew

Principal Motifs:

H386   Bride test: obedience
T251.2.3   Wife becomes obedient on seeing husband slay a recalcitrant horse

Parallel Stories in:

Afanas'ev, pp. 161–62
Brunvand, *Bond,* pp. 70–71
————, *Study,* pp. 304–16 (major study)
Campbell, *Cloud Walking,* pp. 220–21
Chase, *American Folk,* pp. 226–27
Harris, *Ranch,* p. 175
McIntosh, *Saddle,* pp. 17–19 (reprinted in Dorson, *Buying,* pp. 351–54)
Randolph, *Knapsack,* pp. 71–73
Rezwin, *Sick Jokes,* p. 14

LITERARY TREATMENTS

"A Merry Geste of a Shrewd and Curst Wife"
Shakespeare, *The Taming of the Shrew*

13

Clever Manka*

There was once a rich farmer who was as grasping and unscrupulous as he was rich. He was always driving a hard bargain and always getting the better of his poor neighbors. One of these neighbors was a humble shepherd who in return for service was to receive from the farmer a heifer. When the time of payment came the farmer refused to give the shepherd the heifer and the shepherd was forced to lay the matter before the burgomaster.

The burgomaster, who was a young man and as yet not very experienced, listened to both sides and when he had deliberated he said:

"Instead of deciding this case, I will put a riddle to you both and the man who makes the best answer shall have the heifer. Are you agreed?"

The farmer and the shepherd accepted this proposal and the burgomaster said:

"Well then, here is my riddle: What is the swiftest thing in the world? What is the sweetest thing? What is the richest? Think out your answers and bring them to me at this same hour tomorrow."

*From *The Shepherd's Nosegay: Stories from Finland and Czechoslovakia* by Parker Fillmore (New York: Harcourt, Brace & World, Inc., 1920). Copyright 1920 by Parker Fillmore; renewed 1948 by Louise Fillmore, edited by Katherine Love. Reprinted by permission of Harcourt Brace Jovanovich, Inc.

The farmer went home in a temper.

"What kind of a burgomaster is this young fellow!" he growled. "If he had let me keep the heifer I'd have sent him a bushel of pears. But now I'm in a fair way of losing the heifer for I can't think of any answer to his foolish riddle."

"What is the matter, husband?" his wife asked.

"It's that new burgomaster. The old one would have given me the heifer without any argument, but this young man thinks to decide the case by asking us riddles."

When he told his wife what the riddle was, she cheered him greatly by telling him that she knew the answers at once.

"Why, husband," said she, "our gray mare must be the swiftest thing in the world. You know yourself nothing ever passes us on the road. As for the sweetest, did you ever taste honey any sweeter than ours? And I'm sure there's nothing richer than our chest of golden ducats that we've been laying by these forty years."

The farmer was delighted.

"You're right, wife, you're right! That heifer remains ours!"

The shepherd when he got home was downcast and sad. He had a daughter, a clever girl named Manka, who met him at the door of his cottage and asked:

"What is it, father? What did the burgomaster say?"

The shepherd sighed.

"I'm afraid I've lost the heifer. The burgomaster set us a riddle and I know I shall never guess it."

"Perhaps I can help you," Manka said. "What is it?"

So the shepherd gave her the riddle and the next day as he was setting out for the burgomaster's, Manka told him what answers to make.

When he reached the burgomaster's house, the farmer was already there rubbing his hands and beaming with self-importance.

The burgomaster again propounded the riddle and then asked the farmer his answers.

The farmer cleared his throat and with a pompous air began:

"The swiftest thing in the world? Why, my dear sir, that's my gray mare, of course, for no other horse ever passes us on the road. The sweetest? Honey from my beehives, to be sure. The richest? What can be richer than my chest of golden ducats!"

And the farmer squared his shoulders and smiled triumphantly.

"H'm," said the young burgomaster, dryly. Then he asked:

"What answers does the shepherd make?"

The shepherd bowed politely and said:

"The swiftest thing in the world is thought for thought can run any distance in the twinkling of an eye. The sweetest thing of all is sleep for when a man is tired and sad what can be sweeter? The richest thing is the earth for out of the earth come all the riches of the world."

"Good!" the burgomaster cried. "Good! The heifer goes to the shepherd!"

Later the burgomaster said to the shepherd:

"Tell me, now, who gave you those answers? I'm sure they never came out of your own head."

At first the shepherd tried not to tell, but when the burgomaster pressed him he confessed that they came from his daughter, Manka. The burgomaster, who thought that he would like to make another test of Manka's cleverness, sent for ten eggs. He gave them to the shepherd and said:

"Take these eggs to Manka and tell her to have them hatched out by tomorrow and to bring me the chicks."

When the shepherd reached home and gave Manka the burgomaster's message, Manka laughed and said: "Take a handful of millet and go right back to the burgomaster. Say to him: 'My daughter sends you this millet. She says that if you plant, grow it, and have it harvested by tomorrow, she'll bring you the ten chicks and you can feed them the ripe grain.' "

When the burgomaster heard this, he laughed heartily.

"That's a clever girl of yours," he told the shepherd. "If she's as comely as she is clever, I think I'd like to marry her. Tell her to come to see me, but she must come neither by day nor by night, neither riding nor walking, neither dressed nor undressed."

When Manka received this message she waited until the next dawn when night was gone and day not yet arrived. Then she wrapped herself in a fishnet and, throwing one leg over a goat's back and keeping one foot on the ground, she went to the burgomaster's house.

Now I ask you: did she go dressed? No. she wasn't dressed. A fishnet isn't clothing. Did she go undressed? Of course not, for wasn't she covered with a fishnet? Did she walk to the burgomaster's? No, she didn't walk for she went with one leg thrown over a goat. Then did she ride? Of course she didn't ride for wasn't she walking on one foot?

When she reached the burgomaster's house she called out:

"Here I am, Mr. Burgomaster, and I've come neither by day nor by night, neither riding nor walking, neither dressed nor undressed."

The young burgomaster was so delighted with Manka's cleverness and so pleased with her comely looks that he proposed to her at once and in a short time married her.

"But understand, my dear Manka," he said, "you are not to use that cleverness of yours at my expense. I won't have you interfering in any of my cases. In fact if ever you give advice to any one who comes to me for judgment, I'll turn you out of my house at once and send you home to your father."

All went well for a time. Manka busied herself in her house-keeping and was careful not to interfere in any of the burgomaster's cases.

Then one day two farmers came to the burgomaster to have a dispute settled. One of the farmers owned a mare which had foaled in the market-place. The colt had run under the wagon of the other farmer and thereupon the owner of the wagon claimed the colt as his property.

The burgomaster, who was thinking of something else while the case was being presented, said carelessly:

"The man who found the colt under his wagon is, of course, the owner of the colt."

As the owner of the mare was leaving the burgomaster's house, he met Manka and stopped to tell her about the case. Manka was ashamed of her husband for making so foolish a decision and she said to the farmer:

"Come back this afternoon with a fishing net and stretch it across the dusty road. When the burgomaster sees you he will come out and ask you what you are doing. Say to him that you're catching fish. When he asks you how you can expect to catch fish in a dusty road, tell him it's just as easy for you to catch fish in a dusty road as it is for a wagon to foal. Then he'll see the injustice of his decision and have the colt returned to you. But remember one thing: you mustn't let him find out that it was I who told you to do this."

That afternoon when the burgomaster chanced to look out the window he saw a man stretching a fishnet across the dusty road. He went out to him and asked: "What are you doing?"

"Fishing."

"Fishing in a dusty road? Are you daft?"

"Well," the man said, "it's just as easy for me to catch fish in a dusty road as it is for a wagon to foal."

Then the burgomaster recognized the man as the owner of the mare and he had to confess that what he said was true.

"Of course the colt belongs to your mare and must be returned to you. But tell me," he said, "who put you up to this? You didn't think of it yourself."

The farmer tried not to tell but the burgomaster questioned him until he found out that Manka was at the bottom of it. This made him very angry. He went into the house and called his wife.

"Manka," he said, "do you forget what I told you would happen if you went interfering in any of my cases? Home you go this very day. I don't care to hear any excuses. The matter is settled. You may take with you the one thing you like best in my house for I won't have people saying that I treated you shabbily."

Manka made no outcry.

"Very well, my dear husband, I shall do as you say: I shall go to my father's cottage and take with me the one thing I like best in your house. But don't make me go until after supper. We have been very happy together and I should like to eat one last meal with you. Let us have no more words but be kind to each other as we've always been and then part as friends."

The burgomaster agreed to this and Manka prepared a fine supper of all the dishes of which her husband was particularly fond. The burgomaster opened his choicest wine and pledged Manka's health. Then he set to, and the supper was so good that he ate and ate and ate. And the more he ate, the more he drank until at last he grew drowsy and fell sound asleep in his chair. Then without awakening him Manka had him carried out to the wagon that was waiting to take her home to her father.

The next morning when the burgomaster opened his eyes, he found himself lying in the shepherd's cottage.

"What does this mean?" he roared out.

"Nothing, dear husband, nothing!" Manka said. "You know you told me I might take with me the one thing I liked best in your house, so of course I took you! That's all."

For a moment the burgomaster rubbed his eyes in amazement. Then he laughed loud and heartily to think how Manka had outwitted him.

"Manka," he said, "you're too clever for me. Come on, my dear, let's go home."

So they climbed back into the wagon and drove home.

The burgomaster never again scolded his wife but thereafter whenever a very difficult case came up he always said:

"I think we had better consult my wife. You know she's a very clever woman."

Notes and Comments

This story is the second tale in the book from that small group of widely known folktales that hinge on riddle solving. As in "The Story of Kunz and His Shepherd" (#11) the original questions are not solved by those they are put to but by others, and in both cases complications arise. Kunz loses his position as advisor; Manka's husband is violently displeased when she interferes with his affairs of state.

The story of the clever girl, according to the German scholar Theodor Benfey, can be traced back to India. The original situation consists of testing the wisdom of a minister who has fallen out of favor. The minister successfully advises his royal master in a riddle contest with a neighboring king. Later in the development of the tale, the sagacity tests are transferred to a wife who helps her father or husband out of his difficulties.

Other scholars believe that the last part of the tale—the marriage of the heroine, her disgrace, and her triumph by kidnapping her husband— was native to Europe. Whatever the ultimate source of the tale type, it includes motifs and themes from a variety of cultures. We have already discussed riddles (see notes to #11) whose origins stretch back long before the Hebrew, Greek, and Vedic cultures, all of which contain many riddles. Ranke notes that the task of appearing "neither naked nor clothed" before the king, which is imposed upon Aslaug the daughter of Brunhild and Sigurd, is found even earlier in an Icelandic saga. The riddles of superlatives: "which is the quickest, the sweetest, the fattest" were traditional among the ancient Greeks and were introduced by them into philosophy. The motif of being allowed to take away that which is most beloved was a favorite of Jewish authors of the Talmud.

Tale Type 875 *The Clever Peasant Girl* is found in two main subdivisions. There are those tales like "Clever Manka" where the riddles are solved, and there are those in which the riddle is acquitted by demanding that the riddler first perform another task of no less difficulty. The "countertask" may involve something that is essential for the execution of the first order (as in the German ballads) or it may have no relation to the original riddle request (as in the English ballads).

The "countertask response" is employed, for example, in a Filipino variant "Sagacious Marcela." When asked to catch the waves of the sea, Marcela demands a rope of sand; when asked to make twelve dishes of food from one small bird, she demands that the king give her twelve spoons made from a pin.

Marie Campbell collected a "Clever Manka" tale in eastern Kentucky which is similar to the British tale printed here. The king looks out of his window and sees the girl approaching:

> He could tell that having the fish net wrapped around her was not wearing clothes nor going bare-naked. Traveling a-straddle of the nanny goat was half walking and half riding but neither one nor t'other. He thought to himself,

"What about the present that won't be a present? I've got her outsmarted on that."

The girl came in the castle and said, "Here's your present that won't be a present." She handed him the pigeon, but it flew out of the window and wouldn't be a present. So she had done according to all three of the king's riddling instructions.

(Cloud Walking, p. 199)

While there may be all too few stories in folk literature about the cleverness and resourcefulness of women, much less their bravery and courage, Molly Whuppie and Clever Manka are admirable representatives of their sex.

Tale Type 875　The Clever Peasant Girl

Principal Motifs:

H632.1　What is the swiftest? Thought
H633.1　What is the sweetest? Sleep
H1023.1.2　Task: hatching eggs immediately; countertask: sowing seeds and bringing in crop next morning
H1053.3　Task: coming neither on horse nor on foot (comes with one leg on animal's back, one on ground)
H1057　Task: coming neither by day nor by night (comes at twilight)
H1054.1　Task: coming neither naked nor clad (comes clothed in net or the like)
J1191.1　*Reductio ad absurdum:* the decision about the colt
J1545.4　The exiled wife's dearest possession

Parallel Stories in:

Ausubel, *Jewish,* pp. 95–97
Campbell, *Cloud Walking,* pp. 198–200
Courlander, *Olode,* pp. 77–81
Crane, *Italian,* #108 (reprinted in Thompson, *One,* #78)
Dawkins, *Forty-Five,* #20, #21
———, *Modern Greek,* #65
Fansler, *Filipino,* #7
Foster, *Wit,* pp. 56–59
Grimm, #94
Jacobs, *Europa's,* pp. 188–93
———, *More English,* #54
Kennedy, *Fireside,* pp. 91–94

Megas, *Greece,* #50
Musick, *Green Hills,* #68
Noy, *Israel,* #61
Pino-Saavedra, *Chile,* #36
Ranke, *Germany,* #47
Walker, *Turkey* 2: 135–39

C

Fairies, Pixies, and Other Wee Folk:
FAIRY TALES

Any encounter with Aiken Drum or Robin Goodfellow should dispel the popular misconception that fairies are gauzy-winged poppets waving magic wands. A clear definition of a "fairy story" as a traditional story with fairies as the main characters will go far in sorting out the confusion of many editors who use the term "fairy tale" to describe all kinds and types of folktales.

14. *RUMPELSTILTSKIN*   103
    TT 500—*The Name of the Helper*
    Also known as *Tom Tit Tot, Duffy and the Devil,*
    Perifool, Titeliture, Ramstampeldam

15. *THE FAIRY DWELLING ON SELENA MOOR*   109
    ML 4077—*Caught in Fairyland*
    Also known as *A Fairy History*

16. *THE FIELD OF BOLIAUNS*   115
    F244.2—*Fairy Shows His Treasure*
    Also known as *The Leprechauns and Their Tricks*

17. *THE BROWNIE OF BLEDNOCK* 121
ML 7015—*The New Suit*
Also known as *Aiken-Drum, Cauld Lad of Hilton,
Laying a Brownie*

18. *THE ADVENTURE OF CHERRY OF ZENNOR* 129
ML 4075—*Visit to Fairyland*
ML 5071—*The Fairy Master*
Also known as *The Fairy's Magic Ointment*

19. *THE SEAL'S SKIN* 136
ML 4080—*The Seal Woman*
Also known as *The Silkie of Skule Skerry, The Seal
Wife and Her Skin*

20. *TE KANAWA AND THE FAIRIES* 140
Also known as *The Maori Fairy Host, A Hero Meets
a Troop of Fairies*

14

*Rumpelstiltskin**

O nce there was a miller who was poor, but who had a beautiful daughter. Now it happened that he had to go and speak to the King, and in order to make himself appear important he said to him: "I have a daughter who can spin straw into gold." The King said to the miller: "That is an art which pleases me well; if your daughter is as clever as you say, bring her to-morrow to my palace, and I will put her to the test."

And when the girl was brought to him he took her into a room which was quite full of straw, gave her a spinning-wheel and a reel, and said: "Now set to work, and if by to-morrow morning early you have not spun this straw into gold during the night, you must die." Thereupon he himself locked up the room, and left her in it alone. So there sat the poor miller's daughter, and for the life of her could not tell what to do; she had no idea how straw could be spun into gold, and she grew more and more frightened, until at last she began to weep.

But all at once the door opened, and in came a little man, and said: "Good evening, Mistress Miller; why are you crying so?" "Alas!" answered the girl, "I have to spin straw into gold, and I do not know how to do it."

*From *Grimms' Fairy Tales* by Jakob and Wilhelm Grimm (London: Routledge and Kegan Paul, 1948), #55.

"What will you give me," said the manikin, "if I do it for you?" "My necklace," said the girl. The little man took the necklace, seated himself in front of the wheel, and whirr, whirr, whirr, three turns, and the reel was full; then he put another on, and whirr, whirr, whirr, three times round, and the second was full too. And so it went on until the morning, when all the straw was spun, and all the reels were full of gold. By daybreak the King was already there, and when he saw the gold he was astonished and delighted, but his heart became only more greedy. He had the miller's daughter taken into another room full of straw, which was much larger, and commanded her to spin that also in one night if she valued her life. The girl knew not how to help herself, and was crying, when the door opened again, and the little man appeared, and said: "What will you give me if I spin that straw into gold for you?" "The ring on my finger," answered the girl. The little man took the ring, again began to turn the wheel, and by morning had spun all the straw into glittering gold.

The King rejoiced beyond measure at the sight, but still he had not gold enough; and he had the miller's daughter taken into a still larger room full of straw, and said: "You must spin this, too, in the course of this night; but if you succeed, you shall be my wife." "Even if she be a miller's daughter," thought he, "I could not find a richer wife in the whole world."

When the girl was alone the manikin came again for the third time, and said: "What will you give me if I spin the straw for you this time also?" "I have nothing left that I could give," answered the girl. "Then promise me, if you should become Queen, to give me your first child." "Who knows whether that will ever happen?" thought the miller's daughter; and, not knowing how else to help herself in this strait, she promised the manikin what he wanted, and for that he once more spun the straw into gold.

And when the King came in the morning, and found all as he had wished, he took her in marriage, and the pretty miller's daughter became a Queen.

A year after, she brought a beautiful child into the world, and she never gave a thought to the manikin. But suddenly he came into her room, and said: "Now give me what you promised." The Queen was horror-struck, and offered the manikin all the riches of the kingdom if he would leave her the child. But the manikin said: "No, something alive is dearer to me than all the treasures in the world." Then the Queen began to lament and cry, so that the manikin pitied her. "I will give you three days' time," said he; "if by that time you find out my name, then shall you keep your child."

So the Queen thought the whole night of all the names that she had ever heard, and she sent a messenger over the country to inquire, far and wide, for any other names that there might be. When the manikin came the next day, she began with Caspar, Melchior, Balthazar, and said all the names she knew, one after another; but to every one the little man said: "That is not my name." On the second day she had inquiries made in the neighborhood as to the names of the people there, and she repeated to the manikin the most uncommon and curious. "Perhaps your name is Short-ribs, or Sheepshanks, or Laceleg?" but he always answered: "That is not my name."

On the third day the messenger came back again, and said: "I have not been able to find a single new name, but as I came to a high mountain at the end of the forest, where the fox and the hare bid each other good night, there I saw a little house, and before the house a fire was burning, and round about the fire quite a ridiculous little man was jumping: he hopped upon one leg, and shouted:

"To-day I bake, to-morrow brew,
   The next I'll have the young Queen's child.
Ha! glad am I that no one knew
   That Rumpelstiltskin I am styled."

You may imagine how glad the Queen was when she heard the name! And when soon afterwards the little man came in, and asked: "Now, Mistress Queen, what is my name?" at first she said, "Is your name Conrad?" "No." "Is your name Harry?" "No."

"Perhaps your name is Rumpelstiltskin?"

"The devil has told you that! the devil has told you that!" cried the little man, and in his anger he plunged his right foot so deep into the earth that his whole leg went in; and then in rage he pulled at his left leg so hard with both hands that he tore himself in two.

Notes and Comments

One of the best-known fairies in folklore is a strange little thing, termed a "solitary impet" by Katharine Briggs and categorized by comparative scholars as "a supernatural helper with a secret name." Such famous characters as Rumpelstiltskin in Germany, Tom Tit Tot, Tittle-te-tot, Perifool, and Terrytop in England, Skaane in Norway, Whuppity Stoorie and Titty Tod in Scotland, Gilitrutt in Iceland, Rompetailtailskin in Louisiana, and Tambutoe in black America are just a few of those impets who roam the countryside, bargaining their powers in exchange for children, marriage, or wealth. These strange creatures appear in the form of little old men, fairies, dwarfs, trolls, and grotesque little devils. In almost all cases the supernatural helper lends his services to complete an impossible task for some poor unfortunate who has usually boasted too much. The crux of the story, however, is that the little one is a gambler, and his favorite ploy is that he will perform miraculous tasks without penalty if his intended victim can only guess his name within a certain period of time. The best-known motif in this tale is H1092, "Task: Spinning impossible amount in one night," but the impet sometimes undertakes other tasks such as putting a spire on a church or curing a dying sow. For carrying out the seemingly impossible task, the impet demands payments ranging from a newborn child to take his place in hell to the person of the intended victim herself. In an unusual Norwegian variant involving St. Olaf and the troll who placed the spire on the cathedral of Trondheim, the saint rashly promises the sun, the moon, and his own head if he cannot guess the troll's name.

From the list above it is clear that the names of the helper are not to be found in a usual list of children's names, no matter how exhaustive the list. But perseverance and luck enter in, and the helper's name is overheard in the country as he chants a verse or rhyme in anticipation of his victory on the third day. In glee he dances around a fire and sings:

> Duffy, my lady, you'll never know—what?
> That my name is Terrytop, Terrytop—top!

or

> Today I burn, tomorrow I shall bloom.
> What luck! the queen's child will come take my place.
> No one knows what my name is.
> My name is Rompetailtailskin.

or

> Nimmy nimmy not,
> My name's Tom Tit Tot.

Reactions to the revelation of his name at the last moment are usually violent, as the impet stamps his foot, thrashes about in anger, but ultimately is forced to withdraw, die, or vanish.

The story of the supernatural helper is well known in Europe, especially Germany and Scandinavia, but it has been widely collected in the

British Isles and appears occasionally in America. C. W. von Sydow, the Swedish folklorist, studied this tale extensively in connection with another tale of miraculous spinners, *The Three Old Women Helpers,* Type 501. Edward Clodd examined the primitive name–tabus in an essay "The Philosophy of Rumpelstiltskin" (*Folk-Lore Journal,* 1889) and later in a book, *Tom Tit Tot, an Essay on Savage Philosophy in Folk-Tale* (1898).

The power of the name is strong in many cultures. To know a man's name is to have power over the owner of the name, even power over his soul. The early Egyptian belief of the identification of the name with the soul resulted in their inscribing names on statues so that the statue might become the residence of the soul. In later cultures the road to heaven is made more sure if one dies with the name of his god or personal saint on his lips.

Sometimes merely the mention of the name is sufficient to summon the help of the spirits, especially in those cultures with a strong belief in the ability of family ancestors to help the living as long as the preservation of the family name remains intact. Conversely, in some cultures the cursing of a man is possible only if his name is known. To think that this belief is an ancient one is to forget the context of a playground scene where one child calls another a derogatory made-up name or rhymes a real name with a derogatory substance. Additionally, to misspell a name in print, in a newspaper, or in the bibliography of this book, is to call down the anger of the person involved who could justly claim that his identity has been violated. Serious business, this magic of the name.

The little people are said to be very touchy about their names. They disapprove of the word "fairy." A little rhyme printed by Chambers (*Popular Rhymes,* 1826, p. 264) contains the couplet:

> Gin ye ca' me fairy
> I'll work ye muckle tarrie [much harm]

but call him a "seelie wicht" (helpful spirit) and he will be "your freend baith day and nicht."

When the reluctant hero of *The Hobbit* encounters the dragon Smaug, he is not so unskilled in dragon lore as to let Smaug know his name. Bilbo knows that dragons have to be talked to in riddling talk: Bilbo is "clue finder," "web-cutter," "barrel rider," and "Ringwinner." After all, that "is the way to talk to dragons, if you don't want to reveal your proper name (which is wise), and don't want to infuriate them by a flat refusal (which is also very wise)" (Ch. 12).

Tale Type 500 The Name of the Helper

Principal Motifs:

H521	Guessing unknown propounder's name
H1021.8	Task: spinning gold
H1092	Task: spinning impossible amount in one night
D2183	Magic spinning usually performed by supernatural helper
S211	Child sold (promised) to devil (ogre)
H512	Guessing with life as wager
N475	Secret name overheard by eavesdropper
C432.1	Guessing name of supernatural creature gives power over him

Parallel Stories in:

Briggs, *Dictionary,* A (1), 6 variants. ("Gypsy Woman," pp. 539–41, is a sequel to "Tom Tit Tot." Strictly speaking it would be Type 501.)
———, *England,* #3
Christiansen, *Norway,* #2a, #2b, #69 (variant)
Clodd, *Philosophy* (major study)
Degh, *Society,* pp. 303–4
Groome, *Notes* (elaborated in Clodd, *Philosophy,* pp. 138–43 and in Hartland, *English Fairy,* pp. 28–34)
Hunt, *Popular Romances,* pp. 239–47
Jacobs, *English,* #1 (reprinted from Clodd above with Suffolk dialect reduced)
   Reprinted in Thompson, *One,* #36
Lang, *Ship,* pp. 331–34
Massignon, *France,* #63
R.L., *Titty Tod,* 18
Saucier, *Louisiana,* #11
Simpson, *Icelandic,* pp. 73–75

15

The Fairy Dwelling
on Selena Moor*

The tale is about a Mr. Noy, a well-liked farmer, who lived near Selena Moor and who went out to the neighboring inn one night to order drink for the Harvest Home next day. He left the inn, but never arrived home. They searched for him for three days, and at last, passing within half a mile of his home, they heard dogs howling, and a horse neighing. They went over the treacherous bogland of the moor, and found a great thicket, where Mr. Noy's horse was tethered, with the dogs beside it. The horse had fed well on the rich grass, but the dogs were very thin. The horse led them to a ruined bowjey (or barn) and there they found Mr. Noy fast asleep. He was surprised to see that it was morning already, and was very dazed and bewildered, but at last they got his story from him. He had made a short-cut through the moor, but had lost his way and had wandered, he thought, many miles over country unknown to him, until he saw lights in the distance and heard music. He hurried towards it, thinking that he had come at last to a farmhouse, where they were perhaps holding a Harvest Home supper. His horse and dogs shrank back and would not

*From *The Fairies in Tradition and Literature* by Katharine Briggs (London: Routledge and Kegan Paul, 1967), pp. 16–19. Reprinted by permission of Routledge & Kegan Paul Ltd., and by Chicago University Press. Text from W. Bottrell, *Traditions and Half-Sized Stories of West Cornwall* (Penzance, 1870–80).

come with him, so he tied his horse to a thorn, and went on through a most
beautiful orchard towards a house, outside which he saw hundreds of people
either dancing or sitting drinking at tables. They were all richly dressed, but
they looked to him very small, and their benches and tables and cups were
small too. Quite close to him stood a girl in white, taller than the rest, and
playing a kind of tambourine. The tunes were lively, and the dancers were
the nimblest he had ever seen. Soon the girl gave the tambourine to an old
fellow near, and went into the house to fetch out a black-jack of ale for the
company. Mr. Noy, who loved dancing and would have been glad of a
drink, drew near to the corner of the house, but the girl met his eyes, and
signed to him to keep back. She spoke a few words to the old fellow with
the tambourine, and then came towards him.

"Follow me into the orchard," she said.

She went before him to a sheltered place, and there in the quiet star-
light, away from the dazzle of the candles, he recognized her as Grace
Hutchens, who had been his sweetheart for a long time, but had died, or
was thought to have died, three or four years before.

"Thank the stars, dear William," she said, "that I was on the look-out
to stop ye, or ye would this minute be changed into the small people's state,
like I am, woe is me!"

He would have kissed her, but she warned him anxiously against
touching her, and against eating a fruit or plucking a flower if he wished
ever to reach his home again.

"For eating a tempting plum in this enchanted orchard was my undoing," she said. "You may think it strange, but it was all through my
love for you that I am come to this. People believed, and so it seemed,
that I was found on the moor dead; what was buried for me, however,
was only a changeling or a sham body, never mine, I should think, for it
seems to me that I feel much the same still as when I lived to be your
sweetheart."

As she said this several little voices squeaked, "Grace, Grace, bring us
more beer and cider, be quick, be quick!"

"Follow me into the garden, and remain there behind the house; be
sure you keep out of sight, and don't for your life touch fruit or flower."

Mr. Noy begged her to bring him a drink of cider too, but she said she
would not on his life; and she soon returned, and led him into a bowery
walk, where all kinds of flowers were blooming, and told him how she came
there. One evening about dusk she was out on Selena Moor looking for a
stray sheep, when she heard Mr. Noy hallooing to his dogs, so she took a
short-cut towards him, and got lost in a place where the ferns were above
her head, and so wandered on for hours until she came to an orchard where

music was sounding, but though the music was sometimes quite near she could not get out of the orchard, but wandered round as if she was pixy-led. At length, worn out with hunger and thirst, she plucked a beautiful golden plum from one of the trees, and began to eat it. It dissolved into bitter water in her mouth, and she fell to the ground in a faint. When she revived she found herself surrounded by a crowd of little people, who laughed and rejoiced at getting a neat girl to bake and brew for them and to look after their mortal babies, who were not so strong, they said, as they used to be in the old days.

She said their lives seemed unnatural and a sham. "They have little sense or feeling; what serves them in a way as such, is merely the remembrance of whatever pleased them when they lived as mortals—maybe thousands of years ago. What appear like ruddy apples and other delicious fruit are only sloes, hoggins [haws] and blackberries."

Mr. Noy asked her if any fairy babies were born, and she answered that just occasionally a fairy child was born, and then there was great rejoicing —every little fairy man, however old and wizened, was proud to be thought its father. "For you must remember that they are not of our religion," she said in answer to his surprised look, "but star-worshippers. They don't always live together like Christians and turtle-doves; considering their long existence, such constancy would be tiresome for them; anyhow, the small tribe seem to think so."

She told him also that she was now more content with her condition, since she was able to take the form of a small bird and fly about near him.

When she was called away again Mr. Noy thought he might find a way to rescue them both; so he took his hedging gloves out of his pocket, turned them inside out and threw them among the fairies. Immediately all vanished, Grace and all, and he found himself standing alone in the ruined bowjey. Something seemed to hit him on the head, and he fell to the ground.

Like many other visitors to Fairyland, Mr. Noy pined and lost all interest in life after this adventure.

Notes and Comments

The majority of tales in this section are known as "migratory legends." As such they were believed to be based on fact by the people who told them. For this reason while there is less realism in the tales than in those of the previous section, the listener finds more factual details than he does in magic tales. He is told where the story took place, given names of the principal characters, and supplied with a number of detailed descriptions of setting and locale. Such elements help convince the hearer of the truthfulness of the story.

The word "fairy" is loosely used to denote a supernatural being, usually invisible, living in close proximity to man. Such creatures are found all over the world and have many common characteristics. Fairies are usually diminutive, can become invisible, and often live underground. They are helpful, but love to play pranks. Mortal visitors to fairyland must not drink or eat anything, or they can never leave. Often a river must be crossed (compare with the Chaeron myth of the ancient Greeks) before the fairy kingdom is entered.

In "The Fairy Dwelling on Selena Moor" the events in Mr. Noy's encounter with the fairy folk gives a broad survey of many of the beliefs in traditional fairy lore. Note for instance that the fairies of oral tradition are very different from the pretty, innocuous creatures of the literary tradition. In traditional stories, there is no mention of their having wings, though in the English county of Devon pale moths that flutter around candles are called pisgies. Briggs reports the belief that these moths are the souls of unbaptized children. Such a belief is similar to that which holds that the fairies are the ghosts of the pre-Christian inhabitants of Britain who were too good for hell but not good enough for heaven.

Traditionally fairies can take the shape of animals and birds but, according to stories heard in Cornwall, only if the shape is smaller than the previous one. When they reach ant size, they die. Consequently, the Cornish people are very careful not to hurt ants for fear of offending the pisgies.

Throughout the land, fairy stocks are maintained, but at a dwindling rate, by fresh infusions of stolen children and the souls of those who died of a stroke, or any illness that induces a trancelike state. (Compare the Eastern European traditions on the origins of vampires.) The condition of suspended animation is significant, for time stands still for the fairies as it does for the dead. As a mortal, Mr. Noy could stay for as long as a hundred years in fairyland and think it but one night. Conversely, he could be missing for three days and believe he had been gone a few hours.

Although fairy traditions may vary from district to district, some generalizations about the life and times of the fairies may be made based on the abundant facts available in the stories themselves. The fairy kingdom is ruled over by a king and queen with the latter usually predominant. Their habitation is often underground, in a ruin surrounded by swamps or bogs, or in an old barn or mill which to the mortal eye, deceived by the fairy power of "glamor," becomes a stately house set in a beautiful garden and orchard with many fruit trees.

While fairies apparently do not die, they certainly can be born since stories abound of mortal midwives attending the birth of fairy children. Other humans have been known to serve as nurses to fairy children, and many tales are told of the special prize of human milk coveted by fairies.

Mortal children are especially vulnerable to fairy mischief. Oftentimes a fairy mother will exchange her baby for a mortal baby, ostensibly to strengthen the fairy stock by providing the fairy baby with access to human milk. Usually such children, known as "changelings," ultimately return to fairyland, but they cause a great deal of misery to their mortal families during their stay. Many a mother, gazing down into the screaming, wrinkled, red face of an infant in full cry, has wondered whether such a creature, so different from the Ivory Soap ads, might not in fact be just such a "changeling."

Adult troubles with the fairies are equally dangerous unless one is thoroughly familiar with traditional tabus and spells. It is fortunate for Mr. Noy that he heeded Grace's advice not to eat the food and that he knew that fairies could be frightened away by reversing some object, in this case his glove. Otherwise, he might have met the same fate as Grace Hutchens. As it is, he seems closer to the state of mind that Cherry of Zennor will find herself in, after her visit to fairyland. Indeed, a loss of interest in life is one of the dangers inherent in a visit to fairyland with all its "glamor."

In *Elidor* Alan Garner evokes the mysterious power of glamor to change ordinary objects into something that appears noble and beautiful in another world:

> Roland looked through the windows out over Elidor. He saw the tall figure on the battlements of Gorias, with the golden cloak about him. He saw the life spring in the land from Mondrum to the mountains of the north. He saw the morning. It was not enough.
> "Yes! Take them!"
> He cried his pain, and snatching the cup from Helen, he threw it and the railing at the windows. Nicholas and David threw their Treasures. They stuck together, and the windows blazed outward, and for an instant the glories of stone, sword, spear, and cauldron hung in their true shapes, almost a trick of the splintering glass, the golden light.
> The song faded.
> The children were alone with the broken windows of a slum.
> (Ch. 20)

Tale Type ML 4077 Caught in Fairyland

Principal Motifs:

F200.1	Pixies
F377	Supernatural lapse of time in fairyland
F251.2	Fairies as souls of the departed
C211.1	Tabu: eating in fairyland
F378.7	Tabu: eating while with fairies
F320	Fairies carry people away to fairyland
F376	Mortal as servant in fairyland
F385.1	Fairy spell averted by turning coat [glove]

Parallel Stories in:

Boucher, *Moondaughter,* pp. 134–41
Briggs, *Dictionary,* B (1), pp. 219–20
Campbell, *West Highlands* 2:28 (summaries)

16

*The Field of Boliauns**

T om Fitzpatrick was the eldest son of a comfortable farmer who
lived at Ballincollig. Tom was just turned of nine-and-twenty,
when he met the following adventure, and was as clever, clean, tight,
good-looking a boy as any in the whole county Cork. One fine day in harvest
—it was indeed Lady-day in harvest, that every body knows to be one of
the greatest holidays in the year—Tom was taking a ramble through the
ground, and went sauntering along the sunny side of a hedge, thinking in
himself, where would be the great harm if people, instead of idling and going
about doing nothing at all, were to shake out the hay, and bind and stook
the oats that was lying on the ledge, 'specially as the weather had been
rather broken of late, he all of a sudden heard a clacking sort of noise a little
before him, in the hedge. "Dear me," said Tom, "but isn't it surprising to
hear the stonechatters singing so late in the season?" So Tom stole on, going
on the tops of his toes to try if he could get a sight of what was making the
noise, to see if he was right in his guess. The noise stopped; but as Tom
looked sharply through the bushes, what should he see in a nook of the
hedge but a brown pitcher that might hold about a gallon and a half of
liquor; and by and by a little wee diny dony bit of an old man, with a little

---

*From *Fairy Legends and Traditions of the South of Ireland* by Thomas Croker (London:
John Murray, 1825), pp. 199–205.

motty of a cocked hat stuck upon the top of his head, and a deeshy daushy leather apron hanging before him, pulled out a little wooden stool, and stood up upon it and dipped a little piggin into the pitcher, and took out the full of it, and put it beside the stool, and then sat down under the pitcher, and began to work at putting a heel-piece on a bit of a brogue just fitting for himself. "Well, by the powers!" said Tom to himself, "I often heard tell of the Cluricaune; and, to tell God's truth, I never rightly believed in them —but here's one of them in real earnest. If I go knowingly to work, I'm a made man. They say a body must never take their eyes off them, or they'll escape."

Tom now stole on a little farther, with his eye fixed on the little man just as a cat does with a mouse, or, as we read in books, the rattlesnake does with the birds he wants to enchant. So when he got up quite close to him, "God bless your work, neighbor," said Tom.

The little man raised up his head, and "Thank you kindly," said he.

"I wonder you'd be working on the holiday?" said Tom.

"That's my own business, not yours," was the reply.

"Well, may be you'd be civil enough to tell *us* what you've got in the pitcher there?" said Tom.

"That I will, with pleasure," said he: "it's good beer."

"Beer!" said Tom: "Thunder and fire! where did you get it?"

"Where did I get it, is it? Why, I made it. And what do you think I made it of?"

"Devil a one of me knows," said Tom, "but of malt, I suppose; what else?"

"There you're out. I made it of *heath.*"

"Of heath!" said Tom, bursting out laughing: "sure you don't think me to be such a fool as to believe that?"

"Do as you please," said he, "but what I tell you is the truth. Did you never hear tell of the Danes?"

"And that I did," said Tom: "weren't *them* the fellows we gave such a *licking* when they thought to take Limerick from us?"

"Hem!" said the little man drily—"is that all you know about the matter?"

"Well, but about *them* Danes?" said Tom.

"Why, all the about them there is, is that when they were here they taught us to make beer out of the heath, and the secret's in my family ever since."

"Will you give a body a taste of your beer?" said Tom.

"I'll tell you what it is, young man—it would be fitter for you to be looking after your father's property than to be bothering decent, quiet people with your foolish questions. There now, while you're idling away your time here, there's the cows have broke into the oats, and are knocking the corn all about."

Tom was taken so by surprise with this, that he was just on the very point of turning round when he recollected himself; so, afraid that the like might happen again, he made a grab at the Cluricaune, and caught him up in his hand; but in his hurry he overset the pitcher, and spilt all the beer, so that he could not get a taste of it to tell what sort it was. He then swore what he would not do to him if he did not show him where his money was. Tom looked so wicked and so bloody-minded, that the little man was quite frightened; so, says he, "Come along with me a couple of fields off, and I'll show you a crock of gold."

So they went, and Tom held the Cluricaune fast in his hand, and never took his eyes from off him, though they had to cross hedges, and ditches, and a crooked bit of bog (for the Cluricaune seemed, out of pure mischief, to pick out the hardest and most contrary way), till at last they came to a great field all full of boliaun buies (ragweed), and the Cluricaune pointed to a big boliaun, and, says he, "Dig under that boliaun, and you'll get the great crock all full of guineas."

Tom in his hurry had never minded the bringing a spade with him, so he thought to run home and fetch one; and that he might know the place again, he took off one of his red garters, and tied it round the boliaun.

"I suppose," said the Cluricaune, very civilly, "you've no farther occasion for me?"

"No," says Tom; "you may go away now, if you please, and God speed you, and may good luck attend you wherever you go."

"Well, good bye to you, Tom Fitzpatrick," said the Cluricaune, "and much good may do you, with what you'll get."

So Tom ran, for the dear life, till he came home, and got a spade, and then away with him, as hard as he could go, back to the field of boliauns; but when he got there, lo, and behold! not a boliaun in the field but had a red garter, the very identical model of his own, tied about it; and as to digging up the whole field, that was all nonsense, for there was more than forty good Irish acres in it. So Tom came home again with his spade on his shoulder, a little cooler than he went; and many's the hearty curse he gave the Cluricaune every time he thought of the neat turn he had served him.

Notes and Comments

In the neighborhood of Limerick and Cork the cluracan (or cluri-caune) is often associated with the leprechaun because he is a little old-man fairy who knows the whereabouts of hidden treasure. This particular fairy being was thought of as a tiny shoemaker who dressed in a little leather apron, brewed beer of the first order, and kept pots of gold hidden in the ground. He never kept any of his gold on his person, though, if caught, he would always promise to show the one who captured him where a crock was hidden. Tom Fitzpatrick rightly clutches his prize tightly, for a leprechaun can escape between the blinks of an eye. If escape were not possible, his favorite trick was to distract his captor by saying, "The cows are in the oats." Should the mortal turn his head a fraction, the leprechaun was gone.

Traditionally these tiny creatures were known to be cantankerous and cunning; in most of the stories they are more than a match for the mortals who briefly hold them captive. The cluricaune in this story takes a perverse delight in leading Tom through the most difficult pathways to reach the fabled pot of gold. They come, not by chance, to a field of boliauns, better known as "ragwort" or "ragweed." These plants have long been associated with the fairy folk, for they cannot be used against them, and they often provide a refuge in time of trouble. The fact that ragweed is the most prevalent cause of hay fever is no accident. If the leprechaun can escape in the twinkling of an eye, how much easier can he escape during the paroxysm of a sneeze. The stalks of the ragweed have often been used by fairies as magic horses, and witches ride them with the same ease as they do broomsticks (Motif G242.1.2).

William Butler Yeats has edited a collection of folktales and poems from Ireland. One of them by William Allingham tells of a leprechaun whom he captured a safe distance from the dangerous ragweed. Alas the little fairy was too clever for his captor.

> I caught him at work one day, myself,
>   In the cattle-ditch, where foxglove grows—
> A wrinkled, wizen'd, and bearded Elf,
>   Spectacles stuck on his pointed nose,
>   Silver buckles to his hose.
>   Leather apron—shoe in his lap—
>   "Rip-rap, tip-tap,
>   Tick-tack-too!
>   (A grasshopper on my cap!
>   Away the moth flew!)
>   Buskins for a fairy prince,
>   Brogues for his son,—
>   Pay me well, pay me well,
>   When the job is done!"
> The rogue was mine, beyond a doubt.

I stared at him; he stared at me;
"Servant, Sir!" "Humph!" says he,
    And pull'd a snuff-box out.
He took a long pinch, look'd better pleased,
    The queer little Leprachaun;
Offer'd the box with a whimsical grace—
Pouf! he flung the dust in my face,
    And, while I sneezed,
        Was gone!

The cluricaune has no need of the special properties of the boliaun, for Tom Fitzpatrick is no match for this cunning fellow. The trick of marking all the other plants in an identical manner is a favorite one of tricksters. It is a well-known variant of the motif by which a culprit marks others like himself and thus escapes detection. Perhaps the cluricaune knew the trick of the clever slave girl, Marjaneh in "Ali Baba and the Forty Thieves," for when the robber marked the door of Kasim's house with the piece of chalk, she marked several doors on either side and thwarted his plans. This same technique was employed on a far more noble occasion by the people of an occupied country during the Second World War. When the Nazi high command issued orders that all Jews were to wear the Star of David as an identifying symbol, many of the people of the occupied country, even though they were not Jewish, briefly wore the distinctive yellow arm band.

Such a trick may have passed into international tradition, but the personal characteristics of the fairy cobbler, be he leprechaun or cluricaune, are entirely his own. The country people around Cork believe that the cluricaune shares with the Danes the power to make the finest beer out of heath or heather. This talent, similar to that of spinning flax or straw into gold, and the little one's love of a "wee dram," provides the theme of many a rousing story for adults. Often as a whiskey jug and punch bowl become empty too quickly, the little creatures are given both the credit and the blame, and thus prompt another story.

Perhaps there is even some connection between the tradition of being able to see these creatures only between the blinking of an eye and never by staring or looking for them carefully, and the tradition of their being found most often in the vicinity of a punch bowl or a bottle of spirits. Certainly Mary Norton in *The Borrowers* echoes this tradition when she has Pod in his tiny size appear to Great Aunt Sophy as coming out of a decanter of Fine Old Pale Madeira.

Principal Motifs:

F451.0.1   Luchrupáin (leprechauns) (as fairies)
D1045   Magic beer
F244.2   Fairy shows hiding place of treasure in return for freedom
N538   Treasure pointed out by supernatural creature (fairy, etc.)

Parallel Stories in:

Foster, *Wit,* pp. 191–93
Jacobs, *Celtic,* #3 (from Croker's Fairy Legends)
Keightley, *Fairy Mythology,* pp. 373–75
Kennedy, *Legendary,* pp. 130–31
Protter, *Celtic,* #3
Randolph, *Devil's* pp. 117–18

17

The Brownie of Blednock*

D id you ever hear how a Brownie came to our village of Bled-nock, and was frightened away again by a silly young wife, who thought she was cleverer than anyone else, but who did us the worst turn that she ever did anybody in her life, when she made the queer, funny, useful little man disappear?

Well, it was one November evening, in the gloaming, just when the milking was done, and before the bairns were put to bed, and everyone was standing on their doorsteps, having a crack about the bad harvest, and the turnips, and what chances there were of good prices for the bullocks at the Martinmas Fair, when the queerest humming noise started down by the river.

It came nearer and nearer, and everyone stopped their gossip and began to look down the road. And, deed, it was no wonder that they stared, for there, coming up the middle of the highway, was the strangest, most frightsome-looking creature that human eyes had ever seen.

He looked like a little wee, wee man, and yet he looked like a beast, for he was covered with hair from head to foot, and he wore no clothing

---

*From *Children's Tales from Scottish Ballads* by Elizabeth Grierson (London: A. and C. Black Ltd., 1906), pp. 234–43.

except a little kilt of green rushes which hung round his waist. His hair was matted, and his head hung forward on his breast, and he had a long blue beard, which almost touched the ground.

His legs were twisted, and knocked together as he walked, and his arms were so long that his hands trailed in the mud.

He seemed to be humming something over and over again, and, as he came near us we could just make out the words, "Hae ye wark for Aiken-Drum?"

Eh, but I can tell you the folk were scared. If it had been the Evil One himself who had come to our quiet little village, I doubt if he would have caused more stir. The bairns screamed, and hid their faces in their mothers' gown-tails, while the lassies, idle huzzies that they were, threw down the pails of milk, which should have been in the milkhouse long ago, if they had not been so busy gossiping; and the very dogs crept in behind their masters, whining, and hiding their tails between their legs. The grown men, who should have known better, and who were not frightened to look the wee man in the face, laughed and hooted at him.

"Did ye ever see such eyes?" cried one.

"His mouth is so big, he could swallow the moon," said another.

"Hech, sirs, but did ye ever see such a creature?" cried the third.

And still the poor little man went slowly up the street, crying wistfully, "Hae ye wark for Aiken-Drum? Any wark for Aiken-Drum?"

Some of us tried to speak to him, but our tongues seemed to be tied, and the words died away on our lips, and we could only stand and watch him with frightened glances, as if we were bewitched.

Old Grannie Duncan, the oldest, and the kindest woman in the village, was the first to come to her senses. "He may be a ghost, or a bogle, or a wraith," she said; "or he may only be a harmless Brownie. It is beyond me to say; but this I know that if he be an evil spirit, he will not dare to look on the Holy Book." And with that she ran into her cottage, and brought out the great leather-bound Bible which aye lay on her little table by the window.

She stood on the road, and held it out, right in front of the creature, but he took no more heed of it than if it had been an old song-book, and went slowly on, with his weary cry for work.

"He's just a Brownie," cried Grannie Duncan in triumph, "a simple, kindly Brownie. I've heard tell of such folk before, and many a long day's work will they do for the people who treat them well."

Gathering courage from her words, we all crowded round the wee man, and now that we were close to him, we saw that his hairy face was kind and gentle and his tiny eyes had a merry twinkle in them.

"Save us, and help us, creature!" said an old man reprovingly, "but can ye no speak, and tell us what ye want, and where ye come from?"

For answer the Brownie looked all round him, and gave such a groan, that we scattered and ran in all directions, and it was full five minutes before we could pluck up our courage and go close to him again.

But Grannie Duncan stood her ground, like a brave old woman that she was, and it was to her that the creature spoke.

"I cannot tell thee from whence I come," he said.

" 'Tis a nameless land, and 'tis very different from this land of thine. For there we all learn to serve, while here everyone wishes to be served. And when there is no work for us to do at home, then we sometimes set out to visit thy land, to see if there is any work which we may do there. I must seem strange to human eyes, that I know; but if thou wilt, I will stay in this place awhile. I need not that any should wait on me, for I seek neither wages, nor clothes, nor bedding. All I ask for is the corner of a barn to sleep in, and a cogful of brose set down on the floor at bedtime; and if no one meddles with me, I will be ready to help anyone who needs me. I'll gather your sheep betimes on the hill; I'll take in your harvest by moonlight. I'll sing the bairns to sleep in their cradles, and, though I doubt you'll not believe it, you'll find that the babes will love me. I'll kirn your kirns for you, goodwives, and I'll bake your bread on a busy day; while, as for the men folk, they may find me useful when there is corn to thrash, or untamed colts in the stable, or when the waters are out in flood."

No one quite knew what to say to answer to the creature's strange request. It was an unheard-of-thing for anyone to come and offer their services for nothing, and the men began to whisper among themselves, and to say that it was not canny, and 'twere better to have nothing to do with him.

But up spoke Old Grannie Duncan again. " 'Tis but a Brownie, I tell you," she repeated, "a poor, harmless Brownie, and many a story have I heard in my young days about the work that a Brownie can do, if he be well treated and let alone. Have we not been complaining all summer about bad times, and scant wages, and a lack of workmen to work the work? And now, when a workman comes ready to your hand, ye will have none of him, just because he is not bonnie to look on."

Still the men hesitated, and the silly young wenches screwed their faces, and pulled their mouths. "But, Grannie," cried they, "that is all very well, but if we keep such a creature in our village, no one will come near it, and then what shall we do for sweethearts?"

"Shame on ye," cried Grannie impatiently, "and on all you men for encouraging the silly things in their whimsies. It's time that ye were thinking o' other things than bonnie faces and sweethearts. 'Handsome is that handsome does,' is a good old saying; and what about the corn that stands rotting in the fields, an' it past Hallowe'en already? I've heard that a Brownie can stack a whole ten-acre field in a single night."

That settled the matter. The miller offered the creature the corner of his barn to sleep in, and Grannie promised to boil the cogful of brose, and send her grandchild, wee Jeannie, down with it every evening, and then we all said good-night, and went into our houses, looking over our shoulders as we did so, for fear that the strange little man was following us.

But if we were afraid of him that night, we had a very different song to sing before a week was over. Whatever he was, or whatever he came from, he was the most wonderful worker that men had ever known. And the strange thing was that he did most of it at night. He had the corn safe into the stackyards and the stacks thatched, in the clap of a hand, as the old folk say.

The village became the talk of the countryside, and folk came from all parts to see if they could catch a glimpse of our queer, hairy little visitor; but they were always unsuccessful, for he was never to be seen when one looked for him. One might go into the miller's barn twenty times a day, and twenty times a day find nothing but a heap of straw; and although the cog of brose was aye empty in the morning, no one knew when he came home, or when he supped it.

But wherever there was work to be done, whether it was a sickly bairn to be sung to, or a house to be tidied up; a kirn that would not kirn, or a batch of bread that would not rise; a flock of sheep to be gathered together on a stormy night, or a bundle to be carried home by some weary labourer; Aiken-Drum, as we learned to call him, always got to know of it, and appeared in the nick of time. It looked as if we had all got wishing-caps, for we had just to wish, and the work was done.

Many a time, some poor mother, who had been up with a crying babe all night, would sit down with it in her lap, in front of the fire, in the morning, and fall fast asleep, and when she awoke, she would find that Aiken-Drum had paid her a visit, for the floor would be washed, and the dishes too, and the fire made up, and the kettle put on to boil; but the little man would have slipped away, as if he were frightened of being thanked.

The bairns were the only ones who ever saw him idle, and oh, how they loved him! In the gloaming, or when the school was out, one could see them away down in some corner by the burn-side, crowding round the little dark brown figure, with its kilt of rushes, and one would hear the sound of wondrous low sweet singing, for he knew all the songs that the little ones loved.

So by and by the name of Aiken-Drum came to be a household word amongst us, and although we so seldom saw him near at hand, we loved him like one of our ain folk.

And he might have been here still, had it not been for a silly, senseless young wife who thought she knew better than everyone else, and who took some idle notion into her empty head that it was not right to make the little man work, and give him no wage.

She dined this into our heads, morning, noon, and night, and she would not believe us when we told her that Aiken-Drum worked for love, and love only.

Poor thing, she could not understand anyone doing that, so she made up her mind that she, at least, would do what was right, and set us all an example.

"She did not mean any harm," she said afterwards, when the miller took her to task for it; but although she might not mean to do any harm, she did plenty, as senseless folk are apt to do when they cannot bear to take other people's advice, for she took a pair of her husband's old, mouldy, worn-out breeches, and laid them down one night beside the cogful of brose.

By my faith, if the village folk had not remembered so well what Aiken-Drum had said about wanting no wages, they would have found something better to give him than a pair of worn-out breeks.

Be that as it may, the long and the short of it was, that the dear wee man's feelings were hurt because we would not take his services for nothing, and he vanished in the night, as Brownies are apt to do, so Grannie Duncan says, if anyone tries to pay them, and we have never seen him from that day to this, although the bairns declare that they sometimes hear him singing down by the mill, as they pass it in the gloaming, on their way home from school.

Notes and Comments

Anyone who is still of the opinion, after reading this far in the present section, that gauzy wings and twinkling scepters are the norm for fairies and other wee folk, is probably no more prepared for the appearance of the brown-haired, long blue-bearded, twisty-legged Aiken-Drum than were the people in the village of Blednock. Yet, Old Grannie Duncan at least knew that the wee folk cannot cast spells in the presence of an open Holy Bible, and after Aiken-Drum passes that awesome test, he is pronounced a Brownie and a welcome creature to the village.

The list of duties performed by the Brownie—gathering sheep, harvesting crops, singing babies to sleep, baking bread, churning butter, thrashing corn, taming colts, and a hundred other useful tasks—should encourage even the faintest of heart earnestly to desire one for himself. Anyone so fortunate as to be visited by a helpful Brownie, however, should remember that he must be allowed to do his work without human meddling—in the form of offering clothes, wages, and other gifts.

Unfortunately, many mortals find it difficult to believe that the services of the Brownie are all free, and their meddling usually means the end of the visit. On the other hand, criticism of a Brownie always leads to trouble. The enraged creature will break dishes, spill milk, turn the cows astray, spoil the crops, and do other mischievous deeds. He can, however, always be made to leave if clothes are left out for him. Both troublesome and helpful Brownies will respond, singing:

> Gie brownie coat, gie brownie sark;
> Ye'se get nae mair o' brownie's wark.

Several reasons are given for the Brownie's departure. It may be that his clothes make him too proud to labor. Some suggest he goes to the fairy kingdom now that he is dressed so finely. Others suggest that since he has labored and been rewarded, the Brownie is freed of a curse. Nevertheless, whatever the reason, once the Brownie has been rewarded he will work "nae mair."

The Brownie is similar to his other fairy counterparts in that he can only be seen at his pleasure, never when someone is looking for him; that he can do magical quantities of work almost as miraculous as spinning straw into gold; and that he likes his daily "cog of brose" or drink of local brew. Children are his favorite companions, and Aiken-Drum spends all his idle hours with those still too young to be skeptical of miraculous beings and certainly too sensible to meddle with the workings of the wee folk.

The inevitable "meddling" in the form of a gift of clothes which causes the Brownie to leave is perhaps best known in the Grimm version of "The Elves and the Shoemaker." Although neither the townspeople of Blednock nor the German shoemaker and his wife suffer any harm as a result of their gift of clothes, they do lose the services of the Brownie forever. Only the children of Blednock occasionally hear him singing near the mill and then only at the magical hour of twilight or "the gloaming."

Such a song heard at twilight might indeed be similar to one popular with children today:

There was a man lived in the moon, lived in the
  moon, lived in the moon,
There was a man lived in the moon,
And his name was Aiken-Drum.

CHORUS: And he played upon a ladle, a ladle, a ladle,
And he played upon a ladle, and his name was Aiken-Drum.

And his hat was made of good cream cheese, etc.
And his name was Aiken-Drum. CHORUS

And his coat was made of good roast beef, etc.
And his name was Aiken-Drum. CHORUS

And his buttons made of penny loaves, etc.
And his name was Aiken-Drum. CHORUS

And his breeches made of haggis bags, etc.
And his name was Aiken-Drum. CHORUS

A real ladle to bang in accompaniment makes this Scottish song irresistible
to the very youngest children.

Tale Type ML 7015   The New Suit

Principal Motifs:

F482   Brownie
F233.8   Fairies as brown and hairy
F482.5.4 Helpful deeds of Brownie or other household spirit
F482.5.4c Brownie does farm work for owner
F381.3   Fairy leaves when he is given clothes
F382.4   Opening Holy Bible in presence of fairies nullifies their spells

Parallel Stories in:

Briggs, *Dictionary,* B (1) 11 variants
Chambers, *Popular Rhymes* (1826), pp. 266–77
Christiansen, *Norway,* #62
Grimm, #39
Hunt, *Popular Romances,* pp. 96, 129–30
Jacobs, *English,* #38
Keightley, *Fairy Mythology,* pp. 287 (summary), 357–60
Marwick, *Orkney,* pp. 148–50

Shakespeare, *Midsummer Night's Dream* 2: I, 33–37 (literary)
Simpson, *Sussex,* pp. 57–58

PICTURE BOOKS:

Elves and the Shoemaker. Illustrated by Katrin Brandt. New York: Follett, 1967. (Set in Germany)

Shoemaker and the Elves. Illustrated by Adrienne Adams. New York: Scribners, 1960. (Set in Germany)

Elves and the Shoemaker. Retold by Frances Pavel and illustrated by Joyce H. Hewitt. New York: Holt, Rinehart and Winston, 1961. (Set in Germany)

18

The Adventure of Cherry of Zennor*

O ne fine morning Cherry tied up a few things in a bundle and prepared to start. She promised her father that she would get service as near home as she could, and come home at the earliest opportunity. The old man said she was bewitched, charged her to take care she wasn't carried away by either the sailors or pirates, and allowed her to depart. Cherry took the road leading to Ludgvan and Gulval. When she lost sight of the chimneys of Trereen, she go out of heart, and had a great mind to go home again. But she went on.

At length she came to the four cross roads on the Lady Downs, sat herself down on a stone by the roadside, and cried to think of her home, which she might never see again.

Her crying at last came to an end, and she resolved to go home and make the best of it.

When she dried her eyes and held up her head she was surprised to see a gentleman coming towards her;—for she couldn't think where he came from; no one was to be seen on the Downs a few minutes before.

The gentleman wished her "Good morning," inquired the road to

*From *Popular Romances of the West of England* collected and edited by Robert Hunt (London: John Hotten, 1871), #47 (slightly shortened).

Towednack, and asked Cherry where she was going.

Cherry told the gentleman that she had left home that morning to look for service, but that her heart had failed her, and she was going back over the hills to Zennor again.

"I never expected to meet with such luck as this," said the gentleman. "I left home this morning to seek for a nice clean girl to keep house for me, and here you are."

He then told Cherry that he had been recently left a widower, and that he had one dear little boy, of whom Cherry might have charge. Cherry was the very girl that would suit him. She was handsome and cleanly. He could see that her clothes were so mended that the first piece could not be discovered; yet she was as sweet as a rose, and all the water in the sea could not make her cleaner. Poor Cherry said "Yes, sir," to everything, yet she did not understand one quarter part of what the gentleman said. Her mother had instructed her to say "Yes, sir," to the parson, or any gentleman, when, like herself, she did not understand them. The gentleman told her he lived but a short way off, down in the low countries; that she would have very little to do but milk the cow and look after the baby; so Cherry consented to go with him.

Away they went, he talking so kindly that Cherry had no notion how time was moving, and she quite forgot the distance she had walked.

At length they were in lanes so shaded with trees that a checker of sunshine scarcely gleamed on the road. As far as she could see, all was trees and flowers. Sweetbriars and honeysuckles perfumed the air, and the reddest of ripe apples hung from the trees over the lane.

Then they came to a stream of water as clear as crystal, which ran across the lane. It was, however, very dark, and Cherry paused to see how she should cross the river. The gentleman put his arm around her waist and carried her over, so that she did not wet her feet.

The lane was getting darker and darker, and narrower and narrower, and they seemed to be going rapidly down-hill. Cherry took firm hold of the gentleman's arm, and thought, as he had been so kind to her, she could go with him to the world's end.

After walking a little farther, the gentleman opened a gate which led into a beautiful garden, and said, "Cherry, my dear, this is the place we live in."

Cherry could scarcely believe her eyes. She had never seen anything approaching this place for beauty. Flowers of every dye were around her; fruits of all kinds hung above her; and the birds, sweeter of song than any she had ever heard, burst out into a chorus of rejoicing. She had heard granny tell of enchanted places. Could this be one of them? No. The gentleman was as big as the parson; and now a little boy came running down the garden-walk shouting, "Papa, papa."

The child appeared, from his size, to be about two or three years of age; but there was a singular look of age about him. His eyes were brilliant and piercing, and he had a crafty expression. As Cherry said, "He could look anybody down."

Before Cherry could speak to the child, a very old, dry-boned, ugly-looking woman made her appearance, and seizing the child by the arm, dragged him into the house, mumbling and scolding. Before, however, she was lost sight of, the old hag cast one look at Cherry, which shot through her heart "like a gimblet."

Seeing Cherry somewhat disconcerted, the master explained that the old woman was his late wife's grandmother; that she would remain with them until Cherry knew her work, and no longer, for she was old and ill-tempered, and must go. At length, having feasted her eyes on the garden, Cherry was taken into the house, and this was yet more beautiful. Flowers of every kind grew everywhere, and the sun seemed to shine everywhere, and yet she did not see the sun.

Aunt Prudence—so was the old woman named—spread a table in a moment with a great variety of nice things, and Cherry made a hearty supper. She was now directed to go to bed, in a chamber at the top of the house, in which the child was to sleep also. Prudence directed Cherry to keep her eyes closed, whether she could sleep or not, as she might, per-chance, see things which she would not like. She was not to speak to the child all night. She was to rise at break of day; then take the boy to a spring in the garden, wash him, and anoint his eyes with an ointment, which she would find in a crystal box in a cleft of the rock, but she was not, on any account, to touch her own eyes with it. Then Cherry was to call the cow; and having taken a bucket full of milk, to draw a bowl of the last milk for the boy's breakfast. Cherry was dying with curiosity. She several times began to question the child, but he always stopped her with, "I'll tell Aunt Prudence." According to her orders, Cherry was up in the morning early. The little boy conducted the girl to the spring, which flowed in crystal purity from a granite rock, which was covered with ivy and beautiful mosses. The child was duly washed, and his eyes duly anointed. Cherry saw no cow, but her little charge said she must call the cow.

"Pruit! pruit! pruit!" called Cherry, just as she would call the cows at home; when, lor! a beautiful great cow came from amongst the trees, and stood on the bank beside Cherry.

Cherry had no sooner placed her hands on the cow's teats than four streams of milk flowed down and soon filled the bucket. The boy's bowl was then filled, and he drank it. This being done, the cow quietly walked away, and Cherry returned to the house to be instructed in her daily work.

The old woman, Prudence, gave Cherry a capital breakfast, and then informed her that she must keep to the kitchen, and attend to her work there —to scald the milk, make the butter, and clean all the platters and bowls with water and gard (gravel sand). Cherry was charged to avoid curiosity. She was not to go into any other part of the house; she was not to try and open any locked doors.

After her ordinary work was done on the second day, her master required Cherry to help him in the garden, to pick the apples and pears, and to weed the leeks and onions.

Glad was Cherry to get out of the old woman's sight. Aunt Prudence always sat with one eye on her knitting, and the other boring through poor Cherry. Now and then she'd grumble, "I knew Robin would bring down some fool from Zennor—better for both that she had tarried away."

Cherry and her master got on famously, and whenever Cherry had finished weeding a bed, her master would give her a kiss to show her how pleased he was.

After a few days, old Aunt Prudence took Cherry into those parts of the house which she had never seen. They passed through a long dark passage. Cherry was then made to take off her shoes; and they entered a room, the floor of which was like glass, and all round, perched on the shelves, and on the floor, were people, big and small, turned to stone. Of some, there were only the head and shoulders, the arms being cut off; others were perfect. Cherry told the old woman she "wouldn't cum any furder for the wurld." She thought from the first she was got into a land of Small People underground, only master was like other men; but now she know'd she was with the conjurors, who had turned all these people to stone. She had heard talk on 'em up in Zennor, and she knew they might at any moment wake up and eat her.

Old Prudence laughed at Cherry, and drove her on, insisted upon her rubbing up a box, "like a coffin on six legs," until she could see her face in it. Well, Cherry did not want for courage, so she began to rub with a will; the old woman standing by, knitting all the time, calling out every now and then, "Rub! rub! rub! harder and faster!" At length Cherry got desperate, and giving a violent rub at one of the corners, she nearly upset the box. When, O Lor! it gave out such a doleful, unearthly sound, that Cherry thought all the stone-people were coming to life, and with her fright she fell down in a fit. The master heard all this noise, and came in to inquire into the cause of the hubbub. He was in great wrath, kicked old Prudence out of the house for taking Cherry into that shut-up room, carried Cherry into the kitchen, and soon, with some cordial, recovered her senses. Cherry could not remember what had happened; but she knew there was something fearful in the other part of the house. But Cherry was mistress now—old Aunt Prudence was gone. Her master was so kind and loving that a year passed by like a summer day. Occasionally her master left home for a season; then he would return and spend much time in the enchanted apartments, and Cherry was certain she had heard him talking to the stone-people. Cherry had everything the human heart could desire, but she was not happy; she would know more of the place and the people. Cherry had discovered that the ointment made the little boy's eyes bright and strange, and she thought often that he saw more than she did; she would try; yes, she would!

Well, next morning the child was washed, his eyes anointed, and the cow milked; she sent the boy to gather her some flowers in the garden, and taking a "crum" of ointment, she put it into her eye. Oh, her eye would be burned out of her head! Cherry ran to the pool beneath the rock to wash her burning eye; when Lo! she saw at the bottom of the water, hundreds of little people, mostly ladies, playing,—and there was her master, as small as the others, playing with them. Everything now looked different about the place. Small people were everywhere, hiding in the flowers sparkling with diamonds, swinging in the trees, and running and leaping under and over the blades of grass. The master never showed himself above the water all day; but at night he rode up to the house like the handsome gentleman she had seen before. He went to the enchanted chamber and Cherry soon heard the most beautiful music.

In the morning, her master was off, dressed as if to follow the hounds. He returned at night, left Cherry to herself, and proceeded at once to his private apartments. Thus it was day after day, until Cherry could stand it no longer. So she peeped through the keyhole, and saw her master with lots of ladies, singing; while one dressed like a queen was playing on the coffin. Oh, how madly jealous Cherry became when she saw her master kiss this lovely lady! However, the next day, the master remained at home to gather fruit. Cherry was to help him, and when, as usual, he looked to kiss her, she slapped his face, and told him to kiss the Small People, like himself, with whom he played under the water. So he found out that Cherry had used the ointment. With much sorrow he told her she must go home,—that he would have no spy on his actions, and that Aunt Prudence must come back. Long before day, Cherry was called by her master. He gave her lots of clothes and other things;—took her bundle in one hand, and a lantern in the other, and bade her follow him. They went on for miles on miles, all the time going up hill, through lanes, and narrow passages. When they came at last on level ground, it was near daybreak. He kissed Cherry, told her she was punished for her idle curiosity; but that he would, if she behaved well, come sometimes on the Lady Downs to see her. Saying this, he disappeared. The sun rose, and there was Cherry seated on a granite stone, without a soul within miles of her,—a desolate moor having taken the place of a smiling garden. Long, long did Cherry sit in sorrow, but at last she thought she would go home.

Her parents had supposed her dead, and when they saw her, they believed her to be her own ghost. Cherry told her story, which every one doubted, but Cherry never varied her tale, and at last every one believed it. They say Cherry was never afterwards right in her head, and on moonlight nights, until she died, she would wander on to the Lady Downs to look for her master.

Notes and Comments

The story of Cherry of Zennor's sojourn in fairyland demonstrates the conflict inherent in any encounter with the little folk. On the one hand, Cherry's trip to her new home, her generally pleasant stay there, and her apparently happy romance with Robin Goodfellow illustrate all the allure and fascination of traditional fairy "glamor"—making what seems to be quite different from what is. To all outward appearance this fairy world is the answer to the desire of any young girl's heart. But appearances are deceiving, and tradition tells us that any encounter with the supernatural is fraught with danger.

Note that the fairy master appears when Cherry is in despair, having faltered in her determination to find work and escape the poverty and anonymity of her huge family. She does not enter the enchanted land by choice, however, but is enticed and led. Apparently rescued from her unremarkable life, Cherry is a happy and willing worker until she breaks the tabu by applying the magic ointment to her own eyes, thereby discovering the reality of the fairy world about her. At that point in the story, no matter how hard she might wish to reverse the plot, her knowledge of the true state of the fairy world existing unseen beside the real world prevents her from returning to her blissful ignorance. Once she has seen through the "glamor," the illusion is lost, and she must return home again, to wander the moors for the rest of her life pining for her lost master.

Individual details of fairyland tradition are important in this story as is the story of Cherry's experiences. The listener is given a rare glimpse of the life and world of the little people as he follows Cherry and her mysterious companion. Beginning with the fairy dwelling, down dark, narrow, winding lanes, in wooded subterranean passes, across streams that mortals may not touch, the reader is soon lost in the same kind of fairy time that Cherry experiences when she is "so happy that the year flashed by like a week." Such details as the magic ointment that gives second sight is in the true fairy tradition, and Katharine Briggs says that Cherry was lucky not to have lost an eye for this violation of tabu.

Robin, as Aunt Prudence (grandmother of the fairies) calls the kindly master in this story, is one of the Elizabethan names for Puck, perhaps the best known of all literary fairies because of his Shakespearean fame in *A Midsummer Night's Dream.* In some books Robin Goodfellow is reported to be the child of a marriage between a mortal and a fairy. Perhaps this fact would explain the ease with which Robin inhabits both worlds in "Cherry of Zennor." The little boy in the story, being half-mortal, half-fairy as well, needs the magic ointment to participate fully in the fairy world, while Cherry as an ordinary mortal and an outsider, is not entitled to any such "second" sight and will inevitably offend the fairies by using fairy ointment.

Tale Types: ML 4075   Visits to Fairyland
             ML 5071   The Fairy Master

Principal Motifs:

F376   Mortal as servant in fairyland
F235.4.1 Fairies made visible through use of ointment
F378.6   Tabu: using fairy bathwater, soap or ointment on oneself while bathing
          fairy child
F372   Fairies take human nurse to attend fairy child
F378.2   Tabu: bathing or touching water in lake in fairyland
F378.0.1 Mortal expelled from fairyland for breaking tabu
F377   Supernatural lapse of time in fairyland

Parallel Stories in:

Briggs, *Dictionary,* B (1), pp. 219–20 and 8 variants
Campbell, *West Highlands* 2: 66–67
Christiansen, *Norway,* #26
Jacobs, *English,* #40
O'Sullivan, *Folklore,* #17
———, *Ireland,* #26
Protter, *Celtic,* #6

19

The Seal's Skin*

There was once some man from Myrdal in Eastern Iceland who went walking among the rocks by the sea one morning before anyone else was up. He came to the mouth of a cave, and inside the cave he could hear merriment and dancing, but outside it he saw a great many sealskins. He took one skin away with him, carried it home, and locked it away in a chest. Later in the day he went back to the mouth of the cave; there was a young and lovely woman sitting there, and she was stark naked, and weeping bitterly. This was the seal whose skin it was that the man had taken. He gave the girl some clothes, comforted her, and took her home with him. She grew very fond of him, but did not get on so well with other people. Often she would sit alone and stare out to sea.

After some while the man married her, and they got on well together, and had several children. As for the skin, the man always kept it locked up in the chest, and kept the key on him wherever he went. But after many years, he went fishing one day and forgot it under his pillow at home. Other people say that he went to church one Christmas with the rest of his

*From *Icelandic Folktales and Legends* by Jacqueline Simpson (Berkeley, California: University of California Press, 1972), pp. 100–102. Copyright 1972 by Jacqueline Simpson; reprinted by permission of the University of California Press; and by B. T. Batsford Limited.

household, but that his wife was ill and stayed at home; he had forgotten to take the key out of the pocket of his everyday clothes when he changed. Be that as it may, when he came home again the chest was open, and both wife and skin were gone. She had taken the key and examined the chest, and there she had found the skin; she had been unable to resist the temptation, but had said farewell to her children, put the skin on, and flung herself into the sea.

Before the woman flung herself into the sea, it is said that she spoke these words:

Woe is me! Ah, woe is me!
I have seven bairns on land,
And seven in the sea.

It is said that the man was broken-hearted about this. Whenever he rowed out fishing afterwards, a seal would often swim round and round his boat, and it looked as if tears were running from its eyes. From that time on, he had excellent luck in his fishing, and various valuable things were washed ashore on his beach. People often noticed, too, that when the children he had had by this woman went walking along the seashore, a seal would show itself near the edge of the water and keep level with them as they walked along the shore, and would toss them jellyfish and pretty shells. But never did their mother come back to land again.

Notes and Comments

People who live near the sea say that the eyes of a baby seal bear an uncanny resemblance to those of a human being. Even the sound of a seal in pain can scarcely be distinguished from the cries of a human being. Because seals can come onto land and because their heads, when seen in the water, look somewhat human, it is also said that seals are human beings under a spell. This totemic tabu accounts for the fact that many families in the Scottish islands who trace their ancestry to sealmen will not eat seal meat.

It is easy to understand why the people so closely bound to the sea would tell so many tales about this graceful creature. Most of the stories are based upon the motif B651.8, "Marriage to seal in human form" (seal maidens are among the commonest of fairy brides), and deal with the tragedy inherent in such a union. Almost always the marriage is held together by coercion, usually by the hiding of the seal skin. Generally the marriage is a happy one for a time with only a few moments of strange, sad dreaming on the part of the seal lover. But there is always an ending; the seal skin, without which the maiden would drown, is rediscovered and put on; and the unnatural marriage that was never meant to be is no more.

In many stories the seal lover returns frequently to bring the husband good luck on the sea, or to bring offerings of fish for her children so that they will never go hungry. In others, such as Child Ballad #113, the "Silkie of Skule Skerry," tragedy follows the return of the lover to the sea, as the mortal husband is destined to kill both the seal lover and his supernatural son.

One theory about the popularity of this kind of traditional story is described by Norman Kennedy, Scottish weaver and singer. According to him, many people believe that at one time someone from an island far to the north, Greenland, for example, became caught in the strong Gulf Stream current and was washed, kayak and all, onto the shores of Scotland, Iceland, or the Orkney Islands—all places where such stories of seal lovers abound. This creature from the far north would indeed be clothed in many skins for warmth and would perhaps shed them in the relatively warmer climates of the southern islands, as if taking off its own skin. Another less pragmatic belief is that seals or sea people are descended from the pharaoh's soldiers drowned in the Red Sea. These men presumably shed their skins and resume human form once a year on Midsummer Eve or on the twelfth day of Christmas.

Whatever the origin of these rather sad seal alliances, similar marriages of mortals to fairy figures are a common motif in tales. For example, a popular story in Europe is Type 400 *The Man on a Quest for his Lost Wife* (The Swan Maiden), in which wings and feathers are shed in a manner similar to the way the seal maiden's skin is shed.

Tale Type ML 4080   The Seal Woman

Principal Motifs:

D327.2   Transformation: seal to person
C31.10   Tabu: giving garment back to supernatural wife
B651.8   Marriage to seal in human form

Parallel Stories in:

Briggs, *Dictionary,* A(1), 5 variants B (1), 4 variants
Child Ballad, #113
Marwick, *Orkney,* pp. 27–28
O'Sullivan, *Folklore,* #21
Protter, *Celtic,* #19
Thomson, *People* (major study)

20

Te Kanawa and the Fairies*
told by Te Wherowhero
Waikato 1853

I t was Te Kanawa who saw the fairies; he saw them on Mount
Pukemore in the Waikato. He had gone there to hunt kiwis with
his dogs, and when evening came he and his companions lit a fire to give
them light where they were camped. By this time it was night. They were
lying under a great tree that stood there on its own; they were very glad
to have such a good spot, with the roots of the tree to lie between and the
fire in front of them.

No sooner had evening come than they heard what sounded like peoples' voices: the voices of women and men and children, just as though there
were a great party of travellers. Now they knew that these were fairies and
they were very much afraid, for where could they run to, there on the
mountain in the darkness?

After a time the fairies came closer, then closer still, right up to the
edge of the fire; Te Kanawa and his companions were completely overcome
with fear. The fairies crowded round to gaze at Te Kanawa, who was a
magnificent figure of a man; staring at him, they craned forward over the
roots of the tree where the men were lying; they stood there gazing at him,

*From *Maori Folktales* introduced and translated by Margaret Orbell (New York: Humanities Press, Inc., 1968), pp. 31–33. Reprinted with permission of Margaret Orbell and Humanities Press, Inc.

140

while his companions were nearly frightened to death. Whenever the fire blazed up they would move a short distance away, and whenever its glow died down they would come back very close; they were singing this song.

Here you are climbing up Tirangi,
To the multitude of Ati Puhi—
Turn round and go back!

Then Te Kanawa thought of the pendant with the greenstone toggle which he wore around his neck, and he unfastened it. He was desperately afraid—half dead with fear. The fairies did not rush to attack the men, but just kept coming close to look at them. Te Kanawa took the pendant with the toggle from around his neck, and also his shark's-tooth earrings, and spreading them out, he presented them to the multitude that crowded around him; he fastened a stick in the ground and on it he hung the pendant and the earrings.

Soon, when they had finished their song, the fairies took the forms of the earrings and passed them around from hand to hand. Then they suddenly disappeared, and nothing more was seen of them.

The shapes and forms of the treasures were taken by the fairies, but the pendant and earrings themselves were left behind, and Te Kanawa took them away with him again. With these treasures he had satisfied the hearts of the fairy people, showing them that he was well disposed towards them. As soon as morning came, Te Kanawa went down the mountain again; he did not hunt there.

The fairies were a most numerous people—as numerous as cicadas. They were similar in appearance to human beings, and looked much like Pakehas. Their skins were white, and their hair was fair in colour. They were not at all like the Maori people; they were quite different.

Te Kanawa died before the Pakehas came to this country.

Notes and Comments

This Maori tale of an encounter with a supernatural fairy host, because it is obviously outside the more familiar European tradition, carries a flavor of the tropical islands rather than of the mist-laden coasts and moors of Britain. Yet many similar motifs exist despite the exotic setting of Te Kanawa. Even on this faraway island, fairies travel in troops, frequent isolated places, appear to live under a hollow knoll or large tree, seem to be unacquainted with fire, and accept gifts and bribes as tokens of friendship. Even in these islands the power of fairy "glamor" is very strong, and the Maori fairies can take the shapes and forms of the treasures that Te Kanawa offers them and still leave the pendant and earrings themselves. By this ability to take the substance of a gift and leave its form, they demonstrate a traditional power of their European counterparts. Such power has been illustrated in "Selena Moor," where the fairies take the soul of Grace Hutchens and leave her body a "changeling or sham body."

The Maori have always had an implicit belief in the existence of *patupaiarehe* (white-skinned fairies often dangerous to mortals). They resembled human beings and could be either spirits of the dead or the living. The *patupaiarehe* were of medium height, lived in forests, and ventured forth on wet misty days. Some played plaintive tunes on flutes to attract young women to their fairy homes and young men to their deaths. Only two defenses were possible: cooked food or kokowai, a red ocher which was a sacred color to the Maori. Like spirits everywhere, they shared a healthy respect for fire. (Reed, *Maori,* pp. 205–07.)

Finally, no matter what the culture, fairies and other supernatural beings are often conceived of as being quite different from whoever encounters them. Thus the small size, hairy body, and seal skin coverings set apart the leprechaun, the Brownie, and the seal lover from the mortals they visit or deal with. Here too, in a land of dark-skinned Polynesians, the white-skinned, fair-haired fairies are seen as quite different from the Maori people. Their presence also seems to fit into some racial schema of subsequent visitors to the island, since the fairies are thought to be the forerunners of the Pakehas who came to the island after the death of Te Kanawa. In a similar schema, albeit reversed, the fairies of Great Britain are thought by some to be the ghosts of the old Druids, prehistoric remnants of ancient days.

Principal Motifs:

F167.8   Otherworld creatures unacquainted with fire
F239.4.3   Fairies are tiny
F233.6   Fairies fair (fine, white)
F211   Fairyland under a hollow knoll

Parallel Story in:

Reed, *Maori,* 209–10

D

Fur and Feather:
ANIMAL TALES

The constant battle of wits in the animal kingdom produces tales that ridicule the stupid, victimize the unimaginative, and glorify the clever in ways that would never be acceptable if the characters were human. Happily, these animal characters who talk and act in hauntingly human ways delight us with their antics without arousing our moral indignation.

21. *BUH FOX'S NUMBER NINE SHOES*   145
    TT 1—*The Theft of Fish*
    Also known as *Some Animals Never Learn, A Good Trick Today Is Bad Luck Tomorrow*

22. *THE THREE BILLY-GOATS GRUFF*   150
    TT 122E—*Wait for the Fat Goat*
    Also known as *The Fat Goat and the Troll, The Troll Under the Bridge*

23. *THE CAT THAT WENT A-TRAVELING*   154
    TT 130—*The Animals in Night Quarters*
    Also known as *The Bremen Town Musicians, The Ram and the Pig Who Went into the Woods*

24. *THE THREE HARES*   159
TT 124—*Blowing the House In*
Also known as *The Three Little Pigs, By the Hair of
My Chinny-Chin Chin*

25. *THE HARE AND THE HEDGEHOG*   164
TT275A—*Hare and Tortoise Race: Sleeping Hare*
TT 1074—*Race Won by Deception: Relative Helpers*
Also known as *The Look-Alike Relatives, Race
between Hedgehog and Hare*

21

Buh Fox's Number Nine Shoes*

Y ou children ever study about how come Buh Rabbit generally get the best of things, particularly with Buh Fox? You'd think Buh Fox goin' to learn a few tricks, the way Rabbit always outsmartin' him. Buh Fox sort of figure it that way too, and that's why he never give up tryin' to out-trick Buh Rabbit. Just about everything Buh Rabbit do in his dealin's with Buh Fox is a little different. He never do the same trick twice, and that's the secret of it. Every time Fox get the worst of it from Rabbit, he say, "Man, I'm goin' to remember that trick. Rabbit ain't *never* goin' to catch me with it again." Well then, next time it's a different trick Rabbit does. Fox is smart enough in his way. He never make the same mistake twice. But just the same, every one of his mistakes has a big resemblance to all the others.

That's the way it was the time Fox had Buh Rabbit holed up in a hollow log. Log had a hole at both ends, but Fox wouldn't go in either way 'cause he's afraid Buh Rabbit go out the other way. So he just set there waitin'. He say, "Buh Rabbit, come on out. Ain't no use hidin' in there, 'cause if you do I'll just starve you to death."

Buh Rabbit say, "I don't know about that, Mr. Fox. Reckon I can wait just as long as you."

*From *Terrapin's Pot of Sense* by Harold Courlander (New York: Henry Holt and Company, 1957), pp. 37–40. Reprinted by permission of Harold Courlander.

So Buh Fox just wait, settin' there in the hot sun with his tongue hangin' out. Rabbit don't mind it where he's at, it's nice and cool in there. Buh Fox commence to get hungry.

After a while Rabbit say, "Mr. Fox, you must get mighty tired eatin' nothin' but rabbit and chicken. How'd you like to try a big mess of fish for a change?"

"Well," Fox say, "what you got on your mind?"

"The way it is," Buh Rabbit say, "Buh Bear went fishin' this mornin', and pretty soon he's comin' home with a cartful. Man, it sure makes my mouth water."

"Mine too," Fox say, "but you made a big fool of me before, Buh Rabbit, and I ain't takin' no chances. Besides, ain't nobody can get them fish away from Buh Bear."

" 'Cept me," Rabbit say, "But if you don't want to go partners on this trick, don't make no difference to me. I got a big pile of greens in here and I'm fixed to stay a couple of weeks."

"I'll tell you what," Buh Fox say. "You come on out and we'll get the fish."

Buh Rabbit say, "How I know you ain't foolin' me, Buh Fox? I think I'm goin' to hole up here for a while."

"Come on, Rabbit," Fox say. "You got my mouth waterin' for fish."

So Buh Rabbit come out of the log. He say, "You stay here in the bushes and keep quiet. I'll go down the road a ways and wait for Buh Bear."

Fox he suspicious what Rabbit goin' to do, but he set in the bushes while Rabbit went down the road. When Rabbit see Buh Bear comin' along with his load of fish, he took off one of his shoes and set it right in the middle of the road, and then he hid himself in the grass. Pretty soon Buh Bear get there hollerin' giddap to his mule. When he see that one lonesome shoe there in the road he stop. "That shoe might just fit me," Bear say, "but what good is one shoe?" After that he left the shoe where it was and went on his way with his cartload of fish.

Well, Buh Rabbit take that shoe, the very same one, and run way 'round the field till he get ahead of Buh Bear again, and he put the shoe back in the road. When Buh Bear get there he say, "What you know, there's the other one!" And he left the cart right where it was and went back to get the first shoe.

Soon as he's gone, Buh Rabbit put his shoe on and take all the fish out of Buh Bear's cart. He gave some to Buh Fox and headed home with all the rest.

Now Buh Fox see everything that Buh Rabbit do. "That's a mighty smart trick," he say, "I think I can do it myself." So next day he wait for

Buh Bear to come along with a load of fish, and he put one of his own shoes, number nine, out in the road where Buh Bear will see it. Buh Bear he been fooled once, but he been doin' some thinkin' since he lost all his fish the day before. So when he see Buh Fox's shoe, he pick it up and throw it in the cart. Don't wait to find the other one.

Buh Fox he run way ahead of the cart, and of course he's only got one shoe left now, so he puts that one in the road and wait for Mr. Bear to come along. Naturally there wasn't no purpose in it any more, but Buh Fox didn't get the point of it. When Buh Bear come along, he stop just long enough to pick up the other shoe.

"Well, now, I got a mighty fine pair of number nines," Bear say. "Giddap, mule."

Fox find out he's got no shoes at all, and no fish either. So he run after Bear, sayin', "Mornin', Buh Bear. You happen to find a nice pair of shoes this mornin'?"

"Maybe I did," Buh Bear say. "What size you wear?"

"Number nine," Fox say.

"I learned a lot about shoes since yesterday," Bear say, "Come on here and tell me are these shoes yours."

"Yeah, they sure look like my shoes, Buh Bear," Fox say.

"Look close," Bear say.

Buh Fox put his nose right up there. "They're mine all right," he say.

Bear grab Fox by the scruff of the neck. "You got my fish yesterday, Buh Fox," he say, "and I got you today!"

Well, the whuppin' Bear gave Buh Fox was a sight to see. Fox yelpin' and hollerin', Buh Bear cuffin' him first on one side then the other, and red fur flyin' every-which-way. When Fox got out of there he was a sad sight. Had to go home and grow a new coat of fur, and ain't *nobody* see him for four weeks and seven days.

Like I said before, the moral is—it don't do you no good to learn the right trick at the wrong time. Trouble with Buh Fox, if he'd done that trick on *Wednesday* 'stead of *Thursday* he'd made good on it. *Time* is one element you can't fool around with.

Notes and Comments

One of the most interesting literary products of the Middle Ages was a collection of animal tales that eventually formed an epic that we know as *Reynard the Fox.* Kaarle Krohn, the Finnish folklorist, believes that the whole cycle developed in the folk tradition of nothern Europe. Krohn estimates that the tales had existed for over a thousand years. He finds that the fox's antagonist changes according to locale.

Literally hundreds of tales of this cycle have been collected, especially around the Baltic, and during the last four hundred years the tales were probably exported to the New World.

Kaarl Krohn analyzed the tales and discovered that one particular series of episodes was ordinarily handled as a unit. These were tales like "Buh Fox's Number Nine Shoes" where a stupid animal is placed in opposition to a sly fox (i.e., Reynard). Ironically, by way of many tellings and retellings, as well as journeys across the Atlantic, the clever Reynard of European fame has been transformed into the slow-witted Buh Fox in this particular southern tale, and he appears here as the dupe who always seems to let Buh Rabbit get the best of him. But the heart of the animal tale remains the same: in the concluding words of the narrator, it approaches an eternal truth that the same trick never works twice, or the right trick at the wrong time "don't do you no good."

The battle of wits between animals in stories is a continuing one repeated endlessly, and gamesmanship prevails in the animal world where every hour someone is king of some mountain, or at least "one up" on some other fellow creature. When the Fox and the Rabbit can call a "King's X" (time out) from their stalemate of the hollow log, they shift easily from the roles of hunter-hunted, and the ensuing partnership to dupe the recent fisherman, Buh Bear, is a profitable one. Yet though the two animals work freely side by side in their plan to steal the fish, the reader or hearer is never allowed to forget for a moment who is the more clever of the two. In case there is the slightest doubt, the narrator points out that while Buh Rabbit never plays the same trick twice and Buh Fox never makes the same mistake twice, every one of the latter's mistakes "has a big resemblance to all the others."

A favorite method of tale tellers is to combine several types to produce a long story. Resultant plots are generally episodic and even repetitive, but this does not spoil the listeners' pleasure. They know also that Brer Rabbit is always going to escape and that probably Brer Fox *could* catch him if he *really* tried.

A rather interesting question of the diffusion of Tale Type 1 is raised by Keigo Seki in *Folktales of Japan.* Although the tale has an important position in Japanese oral tradition (sixty-eight versions recorded), it has not been extensively reported in India and has not been found in China. Just how the adventures of a European fox reached Japan and established themselves so firmly remains a mystery.

These scholarly questions, however, need not concern those readers beginning to discover the international cycle of animal tales. Happily these stories can ridicule the stupid, victimize the steady and dull, and glorify the clever in ways that would never be acceptable if the characters were human. In the same way that seeing someone slip on a banana peel is funny only if the person is anonymous and not your grandmother, these animal characters who talk and act in hauntingly human ways delight us with their tricks and antics without calling down our parental judgment.

Perhaps it is this sense of vicarious mischief that has entertained generations of storytellers and listeners. A parallel series in children's books by H. E. Rey creates much the same atmosphere to the delight of many children who would never ever think of being as bad as Curious George, even if they sometimes, ever so secretly, wanted to do some of those very same mischievous tricks.

Tale Type 1　The Theft of Fish

Principal Motifs:

K341.6　Shoes dropped to distract owner's attention
K371.1　Trickster throws fish out of wagon
K401　　Blame for theft fastened on dupe
K1026　Dupe imitates trickster's theft and is caught

Parallel Stories in:

Dorson, *American Negro,* #12
————, *"Negro Tales,"* pp. 83–84
————, *World,* pp. 445–48
Edmonds, *Trickster Tales,* pp. 99–102
Massignon, *France,* #54
O'Sullivan, *Ireland,* #3
Parsons, *Bahamas,* #8, #9
————, *Sea Islands,* #25, #26
Seki, *Japan,* #1

22

The Three Billy-Goats Gruff*

Once on a time there were three Billy-goats, who were to go up to the hill-side to make themselves fat, and the name of all three was "Gruff."

On the way up was a bridge over a burn they had to cross; and under the bridge lived a great ugly Troll, with eyes as big as saucers, and a nose as long as a poker.

So first of all came the youngest billy-goat Gruff to cross the bridge.

"Trip, trap; trip, trap!" went the bridge.

"WHO'S THAT tripping over my bridge?" roared the Troll.

"Oh! it is only I, the tiniest billy-goat Gruff; and I'm going up to the hill-side to make myself fat," said the billy-goat, with such a small voice.

"Now, I'm coming to gobble you up," said the Troll.

"Oh, no! pray don't take me. I'm too little, that I am," said the billy-goat; "wait a bit till the second billy-goat Gruff comes, he's much bigger."

"Well! be off with you," said the Troll.

A little while after came the second billy-goat Gruff to cross the bridge.

*From *Popular Tales From the Norse* collected by P. C. Asbjørnsen, translated by George Dasent (Edinburgh: Edmonston and Douglas, 1859), pp. 303–5.

"TRIP, TRAP! TRIP, TRAP! TRIP, TRAP!" went the bridge.

"WHO'S THAT tripping over my bridge?" roared the Troll.

"Oh! it's the second billy-goat Gruff, and I'm going up to the hill-side to make myself fat," said the billy-goat, who hadn't such a small voice.

"Now, I'm coming to gobble you up," said the Troll.

"Oh, no! don't take me, wait a little till the big billy-goat Gruff comes, he's much bigger."

"Very well! be off with you," said the Troll.

But just then up came the big billy-goat Gruff.

"TRIP, TRAP! TRIP, TRAP! TRIP, TRAP!" went the bridge, for the billy-goat was so heavy that the bridge creaked and groaned under him.

"WHO'S THAT tramping over my bridge?" roared the Troll.

"IT'S I! THE BIG BILLY-GOAT GRUFF," said the billy-goat, who had an ugly hoarse voice of his own.

"Now, I'm coming to gobble you up," roared the Troll.

Well, come along! I've got two spears,
And I'll poke your eyeballs out at your ears;
I've got besides two curling-stones.
And I'll crush you to bits, body and bones.

That was what the big billy-goat said; and so he flew at the Troll and poked his eyes out with his horns, and crushed him to bits, body and bones, and tossed him out into the burn, and after that he went up to the hill-side. There the billy-goats got so fat they were scarce able to walk home again; and if the fat hasn't fallen off them, why they're still fat; and so,—

Snip, snap, snout,
This tale's told out.

Notes and Comments

A large number of tales are classified as Type 122 *The Wolf Loses His Prey*. All such tales deal with an animal that persuades its captor to delay eating it for some reason. Appeals can be made to vanity (122B *The Rat Persuades the Cat to Wash her Face Before Eating;* 122C *The Sheep Persuades the Wolf to Sing*), but the basic appeal is to greed. Thus in *Type 122E Wait for the Fat Goat* ("Three Billy-Goats Gruff"), the troll is convinced that a better meal is in the offing.

Type 122E is one of the best-known tales, but it has been collected in only four countries outside Norway. The only substantial variation in its content occurs in those versions that pit a wolf against the three goats. The familiar story is remarkably unchanged, though the reply of the billy goat in a Hungarian variant is amusing enough.

> The billy goat came walking up.
> "Where are you bound for, billy goat?"
> "To the thicket."
> "Aren't you afraid that I'll eat you?"
> "Why should I be afraid; I carry a pair of pistols over my head, and I've got a pouch between my legs."
> Gee willikers! That wolf got scared and took to his heels.
> And that's the end of it.

This brief action-packed story is a great favorite with younger children and animated storytellers alike, telling as it does of a relatively rare encounter between animals and ancient otherworld beings. In folktales the troll is one of the more grotesque characters encountered, but here, in spite of his "eyes as big as saucers and his nose as long as a poker," he seems to be more frightful looking than dangerous, especially to the strong and the brave.

Historically trolls have always been extraordinarily ugly, and tradition has characterized them as meat eaters, even sometimes giving them the reputation of preferring human flesh. The troll hiding under the dark damp bridge in this story (he would burst if the sun shone on his face) seems willing to settle for billy goat, and probably would have succeeded in procuring his supper had he not been so greedy and had he not insisted on eating the largest and fattest of the three.

The significant distinction of trolls from their other supernatural counterparts is their connection with the long and distant past of legend. They are closely related to the Jotuns of Norse mythology who fought so constantly against the gods, most especially with Thor. Their general homeland in mythology, a dark ice-covered expanse called Trolleborn, is almost always to the far north in a cold and forbidding frozen world. When they appear in folktales such as the one we have here, they often leave their more awesome natures behind and seem more stupid and ugly than frightful and dangerous.

Because the plot of the Billy Goat Gruff tale is simple and straightforward, as is true with many animal stories, much of the excitement of retelling comes from the voice characterizations possible with the three different sizes of goats, the obviously deep-throated responses of the ill-tempered troll, the taunting verse chant of the big Billy Goat threat, and the formula ending of the narrator:

Snip snout
My tale's told out.

Evaline Ness has done a classic woodcut illustration of this tale that embodies the simplicity and directness of the tale itself and reflects the feeling of the ancient so appropriate for any sketch of a creature with the long history and legendary tradition of the troll.

Tale Type 122E   Wait for the Fat Goat

Principal Motif:

K553.2   Wait for the fat goat

Parallel Stories in:

Degh, *Hungary,* #28
Jones, *Scandinavian,* pp. 102–4

PICTURE BOOKS:

Three Billy Goats Gruff. Retold and illustrated by Marcia Brown. New York: Harcourt, Brace, and World, 1957.

23

The Cat that Went
a-Traveling *

B ad luck to kill a cat. Best just tote it off from home and turn it
loose and leave it. A cat's a shifty creature, and it'll manage
somehow to get a new place to live. Seems to me like I know where that
stray cat on your porch came from, though I'm not naming no names. And,
speaking of stray cats, from times when I was a boy I always knowed a tale
about a cat that went a-traveling and got itself a new home.

This here olden tale says a cat heard an old woman say she was going
to kill it, for no good reason but she hated cats. The old cat gathered up
her kittens and set out a-traveling.

Down the road a piece she met up with a dog. She told the dog how
come she was a-traveling. The dog said, "Think I'll just go along with you.
Folks don't treat me too good where I been living. Won't let me lay by the
fire in the wintertime."

The cat said, "Come along and welcome."

A little piece on down the road, they met up with a cow. They
told the cow how come they were a-traveling. The cow said, "Think I'll
just go along with you. Folks don't treat me too good where I been liv-

*From *Tales from the Cloud Walking Country* by Marie Campbell (Bloomington, Indiana:
Indiana University Press, 1958), pp. 226–28. Copyright © 1958 by Indiana University Press.
Reprinted by permission of the publisher.

ing. Don't feed me nothing but little, old nubbins."

They said, "Come along and welcome."

Next they met up with a guinea hen. They told the guinea hen how come they were a-traveling. The guinea hen said, "Think I'll just go along with you. Folks don't treat me too good where I been living. They hunt my nest in the high weeds and take out my eggs with a big spoon."

They said, "Come along and welcome."

After that they met a gander. They told the gander how come they were a-traveling. The gander said, "Think I'll just go along with you. Folks don't treat me too good where I been living. Pick all my feathers off of my back and sides to make them a featherbed."

They said, "Come along and welcome."

Then they met a rooster. They told the rooster how come they were a-traveling. The rooster said, "Think I'll just go along with you. Folks where I live don't treat me too good. Been talking about killing me to make a big pot of chicken and dumplings."

They said, "Come along and welcome."

They kept on a-traveling till nigh-dark. Then they found a little house. Seemed like nobody was living there. So they took up for the night. The dog lay by the fire. The rooster and the guinea hen flew up to the rafters. The cow stood behind the door. The gander squatted in a corner. And the cat and her kittens took the bed for their share.

In the night, all the animal creatures woke up with the voice of some men talking in the little house. They listened, and it was robbers counting the money they stole. The animal creatures were scared so bad they made their own noises as loud as they could. The cat and her kittens mewed, the dog barked, the cow mooed, the guinea hen pot-racked, the rooster crowed, and the gander screamed and hissed.

All the animal creatures named in this here tale are mighty noisy creatures, and all put together they scared the robbers so bad they ran off and left their money.

The cat said, "They'll be back. They won't give up the money they stole without trying." So the animal creatures planned out how they would scare the robbers so bad they would stay gone after that.

The next night the robbers came sneaking back to get their money. All at the same time and in the dark, the animals made their noises, and acted out what they planned. The cat and her kittens mewed and scratched. The dog barked and bit. The cow mooed and kicked. The guinea hen pot-racked and pecked at the robbers' eyes. The rooster done the same thing and crowed. The gander screamed and hissed and beat the robbers with his wings.

Hearing all the different noises mixed together at the same time, the robbers had no idea what all it might be. And being come at in the dark with all them things trying to hurt them made the robbers scared of their lives. They ran off in the dark and left their money again and never did come back.

The cat took the little house for her home and let all the animal creatures live with her and her kittens. They used the money the robbers left to live on, for they had no idea who it belonged to and couldn't give it back. The robbers ought not had it, for they never came by it honest.

Notes and Comments

Type 130 *The Animals in Night Quarters* has four basic forms, depending on the nature of the flight and denouement of the story. Type 130C *Animals in Company of a Man* has been reported in America where the animals travel with Jack to seek their fortunes. Types 130A *Animals Build Themselves a House* and 130B *Animals in Flight after Threatened Death* are less widespread though they have been located in sizeable numbers in Scandinavia and eastern Europe.

A related type, 210, *Cock, Hen, Duck, Pin, and Needle on a Journey,* is widely diffused in the East but is less well known in Europe. The objects travel together, have a fight in darkness—each one defending and attacking in his own characteristic fashion—and ultimately frighten away the robbers, the landlord, or the owner of the house they choose to live in.

In the basic Type 130 *The Animals in Night Quarters,* the animals are forced to leave home for a variety of reasons. Often they are to be killed —a sheep or bull always making good eating; a goose being a traditional Christmas dinner; and a cock sufficing when no hen is available. Though it is of little comfort to the animals just mentioned, they do at least die for a rational purpose; the fate of dogs and cats is less predictable. While they might expect to live out their old age in relative comfort, these domestic animals have been regarded by some as suitable sacrifices. Campbell reports that in Scotland cats were roasted alive on a spit to summon the devil and as a means of finding a treasure, and dogs were once sacrificed to Hecate, goddess of the night, on the thirtieth of each month.

Surprisingly, in view of the popularity of the tale, very few versions have been found in America or England. Those that have been located seem to be retellings of Grimm #27, "The Bremen Town Musicians," probably because the tale has been anthologized so often. The Kentucky version printed here, while it seems to share the ancient distrust of cats, is nevertheless, as one would expect, markedly different in tone from the older European variants. The Norwegian formulaic ending of the preceding tale—

Snip snout
My tale's told out

compared with the abrupt, homespun beginning of "Bad luck to kill a cat. Best just tote it off from home," emphasizes sufficiently the significant role cultural variation can play in the narrative style of any story.

Scrambled guinea hen eggs, gander-grown featherbeds, and big pots of chicken and dumplings—all serve to emphasize just how different are the clothes and cultural trappings one single story may put on and still remain true to the emotional or structural core formed centuries ago. Certainly "The Cat That Went A-Traveling" is the same story as "The Bremen Town Musicians" or "The Ram and Pig Who Went into the Woods," but when placed side by side, they illustrate the rich and indispensable contribution of each culture and every individual storyteller.

So well known is this tale type that the city of Bremen still sells small donkeys, cats, and roosters of terra cotta, wood, brass, and pewter—which according to Bertha Dobie, are used throughout Germany as paperweight emblems of the ancient folktale.

Not to be missed in any examination of this particular story is the exciting version recorded by Richard Chase in his rendition of the *Jack Tales,* complete with dialect, abundant animal noises and characterizations, and the background laughter of the children who so love this story.

Tale Type 130   The Animals in Night Quarters

Principal Motifs:

B296	Animals go a-journeying
K1161	Animals hidden in various parts of house attack owner with their characteristic powers
K335.1.4.1	Animals cry out; frighten robbers

Parallel Stories in:

Asbjørnsen, *Fjeld,* pp. 283–88
Boggs, *North Carolina,* p. 294
Briggs, *Dictionary,* A (1), pp. 313, 174 (short); A (2), pp. 543–46

Campbell, *West Highlands* 1: 11
Carrière, *Missouri,* #1 (summary in English)
Chase, *Jack,* p. 191 (references) #4
Crane, *Italian,* #88
Dobie, *Texas Household,* pp. 33–38 (references)
Dorson, *American Negro,* #215
————, *Michigan,* p. 189
Eberhard, *China,* #63 (variant)
Fauset, *Negro,* p. 258
Grimm, #27
Jacobs, *English,* #54
Kennedy, *Legendary,* pp. 5–12 (reprinted in Jacobs, *Celtic,* #14)
Massignon, *France,* #52
Parsons, *Bahamas,* #83
Ranke, *Germany,* #4
Reaver, *Four Lithuanian,* pp. 262–64
Roberts, *Sang Branch,* #112
————, *South,* #1
Seki, *Japan,* #6 (variant)

24

The Three Hares*

O nce upon a time, or so they say, there lived three baby hares, who dwelt with their father and mother in a deep and narrow hole. When they were just a month old their father called them all before him.

"My little ones," he said, "pay attention to what I am going to say to you."

The three little hares pricked up their ears, and began to listen very carefully.

"You are now," said their father, "quite well grown. This very day your first month of life is at an end, and your second month is beginning. To-night or to-morrow your brothers will be born, and this hole of ours is narrow: we cannot all take refuge in it. Each one of you, therefore, must go out, and dig his own run, and make his own nest. It is the custom of hares. Your mother and I, when we were a month old, also left our father's home. But settle somewhere very near to us: let us keep close to each other."

Father Hare, when he had finished his talk, went away, and left his children alone. For a little while they talked about what they should do, and

*From *Fairy Tales From Turkey* translated by Margery Kent (London: George Routledge and Sons, 1946), pp. 61–64. Reprinted by permission of Routledge & Kegan Paul Ltd.

then they said good-bye to their mother and father, came up from the hole, and left it.

The first little hare said to himself, he said:

"I am not going to stay in this place, or dig any such hole. That dark, drain-like den of Father's simply made me sick. I have had enough of it. The weather's lovely, too. I shall build a beautiful little cottage in the nicest place I can find, somewhere near the woods and the meadows; and there I shall live. Whenever I like I shall go out and eat my fill, and I shall sit and look out of my windows and enjoy myself."

So this little hare did just as he said. He collected leaves, moss, sticks, brushwood and tufts of bushes and whatever else he could find, and piled them up and arranged them into a lovely little house. Then he went inside and settled down. Presently he felt hungry, so he went out to look for food. And while he was sitting in a meadow a fox came up to him and said:

"Hare, hare, little downy hare, stop, let us talk to each other. Don't run away from me, I wouldn't hurt you."

But the little hare answered:

"Fox, fox, cunning-eyed fox, you would like to catch and eat me, but you shall not!"

And with these words away he went, leaping and bounding, into his house, and hid himself. But in a few minutes the fox was there and had pulled down the house and had eaten the poor little hare, scrunch, munch. Such was the price this heedless one paid for his folly.

The second young hare, likewise, said to himself:

"I know what I shall do. How tired I had grown of a life in dark lairs and dens! Now let me make a nest for myself, in the roots of a tree."

And he, too, did just as he said he would do. He carried twigs and straw and moss, and scraps of everything that he could find, to the roots of a tree, crept inside, and sat. When he began to feel hungry out he came to find some food, and while he was grazing in a meadow along came the fox.

"Hare, hare," called the cunning fox, "little downy hare, don't run away from me. I mean no harm to you! Stay, let us talk to each other."

This put the little hare into a fright.

"Fox, fox, cunning-eyed fox," he cried, "I know well enough what you are after. You would like to eat me if you could, but you'll never catch me!"

And off he ran, leaping and bounding, into his nest. But when the fox saw the nest he began to laugh.

"Hare, hare, silly little hare," he cried, "now you shall see! I am going to eat you up and swallow you down in a single gulp!"

In a few minutes he had torn down the nest of sticks and straws, and had eaten the poor little hare, scrunch, munch. And so this one, too, was lost by his own foolish act. Alas! he had not stopped to think that homes made like birds' nests are of no use to hares.

The third little hare said to himself:

"I shall dig a hole somewhere near my father's den, but I shall make it deeper and longer than his. Then I shall get inside it and make myself at home."

So he set to work at a great pace, and day and night he dug. In a few days he had made a winding run, which was deep and long and safe, and when it was finished he went inside and hid himself. As soon as he felt in need of food he came out again, and went to a field, and there, sure enough, he met the fox. To this hare, too, the crafty fox called out:

"Hare, hare, little downy hare, do come and talk to me. I wouldn't hurt you."

But this little hare was wiser than his brothers.

"Fox, fox, cunning-eyed, sharp-nosed fox, I know your tricks!" said he. "Do you think I didn't hear that only yesterday you gobbled up one of my brothers? But you won't catch me!"

And straightway off he ran, leaping and bounding, and so into his narrow twisty lair, and sat. Along came fox, but try as he might he could not get into the hole. He waited awhile, but at last he had to take himself off, and that was the end of him. And this is how the third little hare proved himself cleverer than his brothers. From all foxes, dogs, and hunters, may he live safely for ever!

Notes and Comments

Tale Type 124 *Blowing the House In* is rather thinly scattered over western Europe, the British Isles, and the New World. Its extraordinary popularity is due, in large measure, to the favor it receives among young listeners. Rather than reproduce a familiar text, we have selected a Turkish variant, "The Three Hares."

This tale type, with its simple plot structure, has encouraged a great deal of cultural modification. An Italian variant, for instance, has a wolf who, having successfully devoured two goslings, is scalded to death by a third. Using a technique familiar to readers of the folktale (see also "The Cat and the Parrot," Section F, Tale 35), the third gosling cuts open the wolf, and all three goslings sit down to a meal of macaroni and cheese, the latter thoughtfully provided by the wolf.

While English readers are generally brought up to believe the wolf meets his nemesis from a pig, it is worth noting that the refrain, "No, no, by the hair of my chiny, chin, chin" is confusing in its reference to pigs. A variant, located by Richard Chase in North Carolina, transfers the beard to the fox. Outside in the cold the fox shouts (in rhyme!):

> By the beard of my chin
> I'll blow your house in.

It seems logical to suppose that this tale is closely related to Tale Type 123 *The Wolf and the Kids,* in which goats are eaten by the wolf only to be let out later when the wolf is cut open.

Katharine Briggs found a strange version of the tale in Devon, England. Since pixies are generally called "pigsies" in that part of the world, a tale evolved in which the fox gobbles up two pixies before the third can cast a spell on him and force him into a box where he soon perishes.

The fate of the wolf (or fox) is generally an unpleasant one. A New York State variant collected by Emelyn Gardner has the wolf threatening, "I'll get up on your ruff-tree. I'll huff and I'll paw till I get your ruff off," and climbing down the "chimbly." There he is caught on the trammel hook and burned to a crisp. In a Missouri version told to Vance Randolph (*Church House?*, pp. 84–86), the wolf, who had just been singing gayly—

> Bakebilly boo! Bakebilly boo!
> Pig and peas for supper!
> Pig and peas!

is "scalded plumb to death." The fate of the third pig in this tale is left deliberately ambiguous. We are told that he "lived happy in his rock house till the butcher cut him down." This is a sorry fate for an animal that was once held sacred among the Gauls and fed on acorns in the sacred oak groves of the Druids.

Children are, of course, very familiar with the little rhymes: "Little Pig, Little Pig, Let me come in!" and "Not by the hair of my chinny-chin-chin." They enjoy the story of a small animal who is smart enough to outwit a fox or a wolf by building a house with solid walls and a firm foundation. Such a resourceful animal somehow deserves to make it in a rough and tough world. Even Biblical echoes of the wise man who built his house upon the rock and the foolish man who built his on the sand are to be found in similar animal stories about pigs or ducks or hares. In all the folktales the hero is a small, weak animal; the adversary is a cunning, strong animal; and the winner of the encounter between the two is the one who keeps his wits about him.

In this Turkish story about two foolish and one wise hare, the listener encounters the traditional cycle of nature as well as the very important aspects of custom and parental advice. Father Rabbit points out that he and his mate left their nest after a month; that they went into the world alone and dug their own run and made their own nest; and that such a pattern is "the custom of hares."

But some hares, some pigs, some geese, and even some children do not appreciate the importance of tradition and custom in everyday life, and as the young always have and always will, they look for the new and exotic. Perhaps the moralizing is a bit too strong for some tastes, but the story is a good one, the rhythmic effect of the repetition is fun, and the encounter of a new version of a familiar tale will perhaps appeal to those students who will always prefer the exotic to the traditional.

Tale Type 124   Blowing the House In

Principal Motif:

Z81   Blowing the house in

Parallel Stories in:

Boggs, *North Carolina,* pp. 293–94
Briggs, *Dictionary,* A (2), pp. 568–74 (3 versions)
Bryant, *Edgerfield County,* p. 198
Campbell, *West Highlands* 1: introduction p. lxxxvi (summary)
Chase, *Grandfather,* #8
Crane, *Italian,* #86
Fauset, *Negro,* p. 240
Gardner, *Schoharie,* pp. 100–103 (references)
Grimm, #5
Harris, *Nights,* "The Story of the Pigs"
Jacobs, *English,* #14
Lang, *Green,* pp. 100–105 (in Briggs, *Dictionary,* A (2), pp. 569–72)
Owen, *Coyote,* pp. 64–65
Parsons, *Aiken,* #19
Randolph, *Church House?,* pp. 84–86, 205 (extensive references)

25

The Hare and the Hedgehog*

E arly one Sunday morning, when the cowslips or paigles were showing their first honey-sweet buds in the meadows and the broom was
in bloom, a hedgehog came to his little door to look out at the weather. He
stood with arms a-kimbo, whistling a tune to himself—a tune no better and
no worse than the tunes hedgehogs usually whistle to themselves on fine
Sunday mornings. And as he whistled, the notion came into his head that,
before turning in and while his wife was washing the children, he might take
a little walk into the fields and see how his young nettles were getting on.
For there was a tasty beetle lived among the nettles; and no nettles—no
beetles.

Off he went, taking his own little private path into the field. And as
he came stepping along around a bush of blackthorn, its blossoming now
over and its leaves showing green, he met a hare; and the hare had come
out to look at his spring cabbages.

The hedgehog smiled and bade him a polite "Good-morning." But the
hare, who felt himself a particularly fine sleek gentleman in this Sunday
sunshine, merely sneered at his greeting.

*From *Tales Told Again* by Walter de la Mare (New York: Alfred A. Knopf Inc., 1927),
pp. 9–14. Reprinted by permission of the Literary Trustees of Walter de la Mare and the
Society of Authors as their representative.

"And how is it," he said, "*you* happen to be out so early?"

"I am taking a walk, sir," said the hedgehog.

"A walk!" sniffed the hare. "I should have thought you might use those bandy little legs of yours to far better purpose."

This angered the hedgehog, for as his legs were crooked by nature, he couldn't bear to have bad made worse by any talk about them.

"You seem to suppose, sir," he said, bristling all over, "that you can do more with your legs than I can with mine."

"Well, perhaps," said the hare, airily.

"See here, then," said the hedgehog, his beady eyes fixed on the hare, "I say you *can't.* Start fair, and I'd beat you nowt to ninepence. Ay, every time."

"A race, my dear Master Hedgehog!" said the hare, laying back his whiskers. "You must be beside yourself. It's *childish.* But still, what will you wager?"

"I'll lay a Golden Guinea to a Bottle of Brandy," said the hedgehog.

"Done!" said the hare. "Shake hands on it, and we'll start at once."

"Ay, but not quite so fast," said the hedgehog. "I have had no breakfast yet. But if you will be here in half an hour's time, so will I."

The hare agreed, and at once took a little frisky practice along the dewy green border of the field, while the hedgehog went shuffling home.

"He thinks a mighty deal of himself," thought the hedgehog on his way. "But we shall see what we *shall* see." When he reached home he bustled in and looking solemnly at his wife said:

"My dear, I have need of you. In all haste. Leave everything and follow me at once into the fields."

"Why, what's going on?" says she.

"Why," said her husband, "I have bet the hare a guinea to a Bottle of Brandy that I'll beat him in a race, and you must come and see it."

"Heavens! husband," Mrs. Hedgehog cried, "are you daft? Are you gone crazy? You! Run a race with a hare!"

"Hold your tongue, woman," said the hedgehog. "There are things simple brains cannot understand. Leave all this fussing and titivating. The children can dry themselves; and you come along at once with me." So they went together.

"Now," said the hedgehog, when they reached the ploughed field beyond the field which was sprouting with young green wheat, "listen to me, my dear. This is where the race is going to be. The hare is over there at the other end of the field. I am going to arrange that he shall start in that deep furrow, and I shall start in this. But as soon as I have scrambled along a few inches and he can't see me, I shall turn back. And what *you*, my dear, must do is this: When he comes out of his furrow *there*, you must be sitting puffing like a porpoise *here.* And when you see him, you will say, 'Ahah! so you've come at last?' Do you follow me, my dear?" At first Mrs. Hedgehog was a little nervous, but she smiled at her husband's cunning, and gladly agreed to do what he said.

The hedgehog then went back to where he had promised to meet the hare, and he said, "Here I am, you see; and very much the better, sir, for a good breakfast."

"How shall we run," simpered the hare scornfully, "down or over; sideways, longways; three legs or altogether? It's all one to me."

"Well, to be honest with you," said the hedgehog, "let me say this: I have now and then watched you taking a gambol and disporting yourself with your friends in the evening, and a pretty runner you are. But you never keep straight. You all go round and round, and round and round, scampering now this way, now that and chasing one another's scuts as if you were crazy. And as often as not you run uphill! But you can't run *races* like that. You must keep straight; you must begin in one place, go steadily on, and end in another."

"I could have told you that," said the hare angrily.

"Very well then," said the hedgehog. "You shall keep to that furrow, and I'll keep to this."

And the hare, being a good deal quicker on his feet than he was in his wits, agreed.

"One, Two! Three!—and AWAY!" he shouted, and off he went like a little whirlwind up the field. But the hedgehog, after scuttling along a few paces, turned back and stayed quietly where he was.

When the hare came out of his furrow at the upper end of the field, the hedgehog's wife sat panting there as if she would never be able to recover her breath, and at sight of him she sighed out, "Ahah! sir, so you've come at last?"

The hare was utterly shocked. His ears trembled. His eyes bulged in his head. "You've run it! You've run it!" he cried in astonishment. For she being so exactly like her husband, he never for a moment doubted that her husband she actually was.

"Ay," said she, "but I was afraid you had gone lame."

"Lame!" said the hare, "lame! But there, what's one furrow? 'Every time' was what you said. We'll try again."

Away once more he went, and he had never run faster. Yet when he came out of his furrow at the bottom of the field, there was the hedgehog! And the hedgehog laughed, and said: "Ahah! So here you are again! At last!" At this the hare could hardly speak for rage.

"Not enough! not enough!" he said. "Three for luck! Again, again!"

"As often as you please, my dear friend," said the hedgehog. "It's the long run that really counts."

Again, and again, and yet again the hare raced up and down the long furrow of the field, and every time he reached the top, and every time he reached the bottom, there was the hedgehog, as he thought, with his mocking, "Ahah! So here you are again! At last!"

But at length the hare could run no more. He lay panting and speechless; he was dead beat. Stretched out there, limp on the grass, his fur bedraggled, his eyes dim, his legs quaking, it looked as if he might fetch his last breath at any moment.

So Mrs. Hedgehog went off to the hare's house to fetch the Bottle of Brandy; and, if it had not been the best brandy, the hare might never have run again.

News of the contest spread far and wide. From that day to this, never has there been a race to compare with it. And lucky it was for the hedgehog he had the good sense to marry a wife like himself, and not a weasel, or a wombat, or a whale!

Notes and Comments

Stories about races between slow and fast animals are among the oldest tales in the world. The earliest analyses of these tales divided them into three principal forms:

1. By perseverance the slow animal beats the faster one who is too contemptuous of his rival to take the race seriously. Often the swift animal falls asleep.

2. The cunning animal is slow, but he hangs onto the tail of the fast animal and claims to have been waiting for his rival at the finish line.

3. Finally, the slow animal defeats the fast one with a trick by placing relatives along the route. The last relative claims to be the original animal. It is a version of a tale from this group that is reprinted here as "The Hare and the Hedgehog."

There are many versions of this general tale type found in Africa and in areas populated by those of African descent. A variant collected by Richard Dorson in Michigan tells of a race between rabbit and hogshead. The latter is described by the informant as being "a big old worm with one horn in the top of his head, and he will sting you. He stays mostly in cotton." With the help of his wife, hogshead wins the race against the proud rabbit. The narrator concludes: "So the Hogshead beat the Rabbit at his game, outslicked him that time—took 'em both to do it though." (*Michigan,* p. 38).

In this selection Walter de la Mare has retold a traditional tale in a style distinctly his own. Scholars of folklore generally frown upon this practice and seek, wherever possible, to transcribe what they collect faithfully, making an exact copy of what they were told by their informants. The foundation of folklore scholarship depends upon such faithful renditions in any area of current study. The student of the folktale, however, will encounter many older collections and even some recent ones where the author and the collector have intruded upon the tale. Three main types of author intrusion exist, and the student should be aware of them.

1. The "tidying-up" of a tale by its collector—smoothing out the language and details. Joseph Jacobs, for instance, changes the American version of "The Bremen Town Musicians" which he found in the *Journal of American Folklore,* Vol. I, by eliminating "a malodorous and un-English skunk." Other authors have intruded more boldly and in fact have "censored" their tales so that, in their opinion, they became more suitable for children.

2. The transcription of a tale generally as it was told but with moralistic insertions here and there of the "Dear Reader" type. The tale of "The Three Hares" in Section D is perhaps an example of such heavy-handed tampering, but such practice is generally recognizable for what it is and is certainly passé.

3. Stories that are colored and dressed in the elaborate trappings of the consumate literary artist who uses the folktale as a vehicle for his own finely-wrought prose. Though "The Hare and the Hedgehog" exists in tradition as a version of Tale Type 275A *Hare and Tortoise Race: Sleeping Hare,* as well as Tale Type 1074 *Race Won by Deception: Relative Helpers,* the version we have printed here is the creation of a master literary artist who uses the essential plot of the tale type as a framework for a retelling.

Walter de la Mare was born near London in 1873. He wrote poems and short stories for magazines while working as a clerk. His first book was *Songs of Childhood* (1902), a collection of poems. Eight years later he published *The Three Mulla Mulgars,* a poetical fantasy, but it was the publication in 1913 of *Peacock Pie,* a collection of rhymes and verses for and about children, which established his reputation as a first-rank author for children. Over the next forty years he wrote many stories and poems for children. His classic poetry anthology, *Come Hither,* was published in 1923. *Told Again,* from which "The Hare and the Hedgehog" was taken followed in 1927.

De la Mare was made a companion of honor in 1948 and received the Order of Merit in 1953. He died in 1956.

Tale Types: 275A   Hare and Tortoise Race: Sleeping Hare
           1074   Race Won by Deception: Relative Helpers

Principal Motif:

K11.1   Race won by deception: relative helpers

Parallel Stories in:

Aesop, "The Hare and the Tortoise"
Afanas'ev, p. 310
Briggs, *Dictionary,* A (1), pp. 113–15, 116–17; B (1), p. 66
Burton, *Magic Drum,* pp. 95–98
Courlander, *Terrapin's,* pp. 28–30
Cushing, *Zuni,* pp. 277–84
Dorson, *American Negro,* #9
———, *Michigan,* pp. 37–38
———, *Richardson,* #1
Grimm, #187
Harris, *Remus,* "Mr. Rabbit Finds His Match at Last"
Parsons, *Cape Verde* 1: #100
———, *Guilford County,* #5, #6
Reaver, *Lithuanian,* pp. 162–63
Seki, *Japan,* #10

E

Broomsticks and Night Ride:
STORIES OF WITCHES AND DEVILS

Ghosts, devils, vampires, werewolves, even the horrible Baba Yaga—all the dark psychological fears rattle and scream in these tales of superstition and ignorance. Yet, withal, beware . . . lest ye read them in the light of the full moon without the comfort of a proper talisman.

26. *THE WITCHES' RIDE*   173
    ML 3045—*Following the Witch*
    Also known as *The Ride to the Witches' Sabbath,*
    Magic Incantations

27. *THE BABA YAGA*   179
    TT 313H—*The Flight from the Witch,* subtype of
    313 *The Girl as Helper in the Hero's Flight*

28. *THE TOAD WITCH*   185
    ML 3055—*The Witch that Was Hurt*
    Also known as *The Cat Witch's Paw; Goody, My*
    Neighbor

29. THE TINKER AND THE GHOST 188
TT 326A—*Soul Released from Torment*
Also known as *Dead Man as Helper, Staying in the Haunted House*

30. *THE GOLDEN ARM* 194
TT 366—*The Man from the Gallows*
Also known as *Teeny Tiny, The Silver Toe, Chunk o'Meat, The Big Black Toe*

31. *THE COFFIN-LID* 197
TT 363—*The Vampire*
Also known as *The Corpse and the Shroud, The Peasant and the Corpse*

32. *THE WOLF-CHILD* 202
ML 4005—*The Werewolf Husband*
Also known as *The Crescent and the Wolf Child, The Wolf-Changeling*

33. *THE KING O' THE CATS* 210
TT 113A—*King of the Cats Is Dead*
ML 6070B—*The King of the Cats*
Also known as *Tom Tildrum's Dead, Suzy Truth Is Dead, Tell Puss Thy Catten*

34. *THE SHROVE TUESDAY VISITOR* 214
TT 817—*Devil Leaves at Mention of God's Name*
Also known as *Dancing Past Midnight, The Devil and the Fiddler*

26

The Witches' Ride*

O nce, in the days of long ago, there lived in Costa Rica a widow who had an only son. Now this son was considered a *bobo,* or simpleton, because he was lazy and, more than that, because in one way or another he muddled everything he set out to do.

One day the bobo's mother was preparing to cook the *chayote* hash and rice which were to be their supper. She went to the shed for wood to burn in the stove, but the shed was empty. So she told the bobo to go to the forest yonder and bring her some sticks for the fire.

Since it was already late afternoon and a chill wind was blowing, the bobo wrapped himself up in a coarse old blanket, wearing it like a cape. Then he set off. He soon entered the forest, but there were no broken branches at hand and since he had no machete, or long, sharp knife, with him to cut branches from the trees, he went on farther and farther, from one thicket to another. Before long he was deep in the forest.

Soon it grew dark and he lost the path. As he groped his way through the dense underbrush and hanging vines, not knowing which way to turn,

*From *The Witches' Ride and Other Tales from Costa Rica,* Told and Illustrated by Lupe de Osma (New York: William Morrow and Co., Inc., 1957), pp. 13–21. Copyright © 1957 by Lupe de Osma. By permission of William Morrow & Company, Inc.

he suddenly came upon a hut. He was glad to find a shelter and knocked a good round knock. No one answered. So he opened the door and went in. Finding the hut deserted, he proceeded to make himself at home. In a corner behind a pile of straw he found an old mat woven of reeds, and there he snuggled down. Soon, in good comfort, he was fast asleep.

He slept and slept till at the hour of midnight he was awakened with a start by the sound of merry voices. He raised his head a wee bit and looked around with one eye.

Through the open window of the hut the moonlight shone on the clay floor, turning it white. There the bobo saw twelve black shadows—the shadows of twelve old witches. They were jesting and laughing and having altogether a merry time as each witch took a sip from a big drinking gourd, then smacked her lips and passed it on.

Meantime, the bobo lay quiet and still behind the pile of straw, scarcely daring to draw his breath lest the witches find him and change him into some bird or beast.

And the riot and revelry went on until the gourd ran dry. Then without any warning at all, a witch cried out in a croaking voice, "Time to be off!" At the same moment she picked up a broom from a pile on the floor, placed herself nimbly upon it, and said these magic words:

Fly me faster than a fairy,
Without God—without Saint Mary!

Away out of the window she flew and soared gracefully up into the air. The others followed quickly—each pouncing upon a broomstick from the pile, then repeating the magic words.

High in the night sky they flew, one behind the other, like a long black waving ribbon. They circled once and again around the big yellow moon and then vanished swiftly from sight beyond the tall mountain peaks.

"A week of Sundays!" cried the bobo in surprise. "Wasn't that neatly done! I wouldn't mind doing it myself! And why not?"

Well, as soon as the last witch had disappeared, up sprang the bobo from the reed mat and straightway went to the corner where the pile of brooms had been. He hoped that the witches might have left one behind. And they had! He snatched it up, and fastening the blanket around his shoulders good and tight, he placed himself upon the stick. Then he shouted with all his might:

Fly me faster than a fairy,
Without God—without Saint Mary!

These words were scarcely out of his mouth when up he shot into the air like a whizzing arrow, and out of the window he flew. Faster and faster he soared, low over the treetops and high toward the moon, like a bird. And he flew and flew and flew, and the higher he went, the more he liked it— so much that every once in a while he would say the magic words again to the broom.

But, alas, he was not called a bobo for nothing. In his great glee he muddled the words, and said to the broomstick:

Fly me faster than a fairy,
Fly with God and good Saint Mary!

No sooner were these words out of his mouth than the broom began to fall. Fast—and faster than fast—it dropped. The poor bobo had no time to think of the right magic words as he tumbled and somersaulted through the air.

Now then, it so happened that some robbers were hiding at the edge of the forest that night. Their booty was spread out on a large cloth, and they were seated around it, counting out each one's share of the treasure by the weak light of their lantern.

"Ho! The Devil himself must have been with us today," cried one of the robbers in delight. "Hope he doesn't take a fancy to drop in for his share!"

And at this very moment the bobo, who was coming down full tilt, saw the group and shouted, "Out of the way! Look out there, all of you! Make way for this poor devil!"

The robbers looked up, each and all of them afraid of the strange sight the bobo made. For his blanket flapped and danced behind him like two big black wings as he plunged down upon them. They sprang up in great fear, thinking they had the Devil on their backs.

"The Devil! The Devil is loose! Here he comes!" they cried in terror. "Run! Let us fly! Away . . . away!" They took to their heels as if they were running a race. And they left their booty behind.

The bobo came down in one enormous swoop upon the pile of riches —*plump!* There he sat, gazing rapturously at the heap of gold and silver coins. "Bless my soul! Bless my little soul!" he cried.

Straightway he jumped up and piled the coins together again in the center of the large cloth. Then he made a bundle out of it, slung it over his shoulder, and hobbled home very happy, humming a merry tune.

And as for the robbers, they were never seen again.

Notes and Comments

Practitioners of the black mass claim to be descendents of the superstitious people of medieval times who chose to give homage to the Prince of
Darkness (Satan) rather than the high and authoritarian church. The black
mass was held on the witches' sabat, although the day on which the orgy
was celebrated is not exactly known.

The chief concern of these early church fathers centered around the
fact that the black mass and all its rituals mocked the most sacred rituals
of Christianity and the solemnity of the church service. The witches burned
a foul-smelling incense, turned the crucifix upside down, recited the scriptures (especially the Lord's Prayer) backwards, drank symbolic blood from
the skull of a criminal, and cavorted nude with great hilarity and merriment. Such witches had allegedly signed a pact with the devil to worship
him in return for the gratification of their desires, and the evil one himself
usually made an appearance at the sabbat celebration, often in the form of
a black goat. The twelve old witches in "Witches' Ride" are preparing to
go to such a congregational meeting to pay homage and respect to his
satanic majesty.

Prior to gathering in a secret place, witches usually drink and feast
until satiated. Then the actual flight through the air is preceded by the
repetition of an inverted Christian word formula. Two famous literary
variants of this formula are as follows:

> The Hag is astride,
> This night for to ride:
> The Devil and she together;
> Through thick, and through thin,
> Now out, and then in,
> Though ne'er so foule be the weather.

> Robert Herrick, "The Hag," *Hesperides*

> Over hill, over dale,
> Through bush, through brier,
> Over park, over pale,
> Through flood, through fire,
> I do wander everywhere.

> Shakespeare, *A Midsummer Night's Dream,* II, i (2–6)

Obviously, as we see from the Costa Rican bobo's disastrous mistake, this formula must be spoken exactly in order for the flight to succeed. The method of flight, however, can be varied according to local custom and belief. Some witches are said to smear themselves with magic ointment made from the fat and marrow of unbaptized infants. Thus anointed, the witches fly through the air with ease. Other witches use broomsticks or straws, flying either up the chimney or out the window after repeating the magic formula. Still others possess magic bridles which turn ordinary calves into winged steeds who soar away into the moonlight and carry the witch to the orgy of the witches' sabbat.

The magic bridle is also sometimes used to turn humans into beasts suitable for riding. Indeed, the greatest fear of the bobo is not being caught by the witches but being changed into some bird or beast. Stories about the transformation of men into beasts, especially by use of a magic bridle, often end by turning the tables so that the victim is able to steal the bridle and ride the old witch.

The conclusion of this Costa Rican story employs yet another motif in the witches' ride tales—the mysterious fall through the air, a fall that frightens the robbers below into believing that the devil himself must have had a hand in their successful robbery. The chance remark of the poor falling bobo who cries "Make way for this poor devil!" only reinforces that belief.

Tale Type ML 3045   Following the Witch

Principal Motifs:

G224.1	Witch's charm opposite of Christian
G243	Witch's Sabbath
G248	Witches feast on rich food and drink
G242.1	Witch flies through air on broomstick
G242.7	Person flying with witches makes mistake and falls
D1681	Charm incorrectly uttered will not work
J1786.1	Man costumed as demon thought to be devil; thieves flee

Parallel Stories in:

Campbell, *West Highlands* 2: 69–71
Christiansen, *Norway,* #17a
Cox, *Witch Bridle,* pp. 203–9

Dorson, *American Negro*, #122
Folk-Lore Scrapbook, pp. 240–41
Gardner, *Schoharie*, pp. 62–65
Hyde, *Beside the Fire*, 104–28
Jacobs, *Celtic*, #2 (from Hyde, *Beside the Fire*)
Leather, *Herefordshire*, p. 176
Protter, *Celtic*, #1
Randolph, *Devil's*, pp. 47–49 (extensive references)
————, *Missouri*, pp. 79–80

27

The Baba Yaga*

O nce upon a time there was an old couple. The husband lost his wife and married again. But he had a daughter by the first marriage, a young girl, and she found no favor in the eyes of her evil stepmother, who used to beat her, and consider how she could get her killed outright. One day the father went away somewhere or other, so the stepmother said to the girl, "Go to your aunt, my sister, and ask her for a needle and thread to make you a shift."

Now that aunt was a Baba Yaga. Well, the girl was no fool, so she went to a real aunt of hers first, and says she:

"Good morning, auntie!"

"Good morning, my dear! what have you come for?"

"Mother has sent me to her sister, to ask for a needle and thread to make me a shift."

Then her aunt instructed her what to do. "There is a birch tree there, niece, which would hit you in the eye—you must tie a ribbon round it; there are doors which would creak and bang—you must pour oil on their hinges; there are dogs which would tear you in pieces—you must throw them these

*From *Russian Folk-Tales* by W. R. Ralston (London: Smith, Elder and Co., 1873), pp. 139–142.

rolls; there is a cat which would scratch your eyes out—you must give it a piece of bacon."

So the girl went away, and walked and walked, till she came to the place. There stood a hut, and in it sat weaving the Baba Yaga, the Bony-Shanks.

"Good morning, auntie," says the girl.

"Good morning, my dear," replies the Baba Yaga.

"Mother has sent me to ask you for a needle and thread to make me a shift."

"Very well; sit down and weave a little in the meantime."

So the girl sat down behind the loom, and the Baba Yaga went outside, and said to her servant-maid:

"Go and heat the bath, and get my niece washed; and mind you look sharp after her. I want to breakfast off her."

Well, the girl sat there in such a fright that she was as much dead as alive. Presently she spoke imploringly to the servant-maid, saying:

"Kinswoman dear, do please wet the firewood instead of making it burn; and fetch the water for the bath in a sieve." And she made her a present of a handkerchief.

The Baba Yaga waited awhile; then she came to the window and asked:

"Are you weaving, niece? are you weaving, my dear?"

"Oh yes, dear aunt, I'm weaving." So the Baba Yaga went away again, and the girl gave the Cat a piece of bacon, and asked:

"Is there no way of escaping from here?"

"Here's a comb for you and a towel," said the Cat; "take them, and be off. The Baba Yaga will pursue you, but you must lay your ear on the ground, and when you hear that she is close at hand, first of all throw down the towel. It will become a wide, wide river. And if the Baba Yaga gets across the river, and tries to catch you, then you must lay your ear on the ground again, and when you hear that she is close at hand, throw down the comb. It will become a dense, dense forest; through that she won't be able to force her way anyhow."

The girl took the towel and the comb and fled. The dogs would have rent her, but she threw them the rolls, and they let her go by; the doors would have begun to bang, but she poured oil on their hinges, and they let her pass through; the birch tree would have poked her eyes out, but she tied the ribbon around it, and it let her pass on. And the Cat sat down to the loom, and worked away; muddled everything about, if it didn't do much weaving. Up came the Baba Yaga to the window, and asked:

"Are you weaving, niece? are you weaving, my dear?"

"I'm weaving, dear aunt, I'm weaving," gruffly replied the Cat.

The Baba Yaga rushed into the hut, saw that the girl was gone, and took to beating the Cat, and abusing it for not having scratched the girl's eyes out. "Long as I've served you," said the Cat, "you've never given me so much as a bone; but she gave me bacon." Then the Baba Yaga pounced upon the dogs, on the doors, on the birch tree, and on the servant-maid, and set to work to abuse them all, and to knock them about. Then the dogs said to her, "Long as we've served you, you've never so much as pitched us a burnt crust; but she gave us rolls to eat." And the doors said, "Long as we've served you, you've never poured even a drop of water on our hinges; but she poured oil on us." The birch tree said, "Long as I've served you, you've never tied a single thread round me; but she fastened a ribbon around me." And the servant-maid said, "Long as I've served you, you've never given me so much as a rag; but she gave me a handkerchief."

The Baba Yaga, bony of limb, quickly jumped into her mortar, sent it flying along with the pestle, sweeping away the while all traces of its flight with a broom, and set off in pursuit of the girl. Then the girl put her ear to the ground, and when she heard that the Baba Yaga was chasing her, and was now close at hand, she flung down the towel. And it became a wide, such a wide river! Up came the Baba Yaga to the river, and gnashed her teeth with spite; then she went home for her oxen, and drove them to the river. The oxen drank up every drop of the river, and then the Baba Yaga began the pursuit anew. But the girl put her ear to the ground again, and when she heard that the Baba Yaga was near, she flung down the comb, and instantly a forest sprang up, such an awfully thick one! The Baba Yaga began gnawing away at it, but however hard she worked, she couldn't gnaw her way through it, so she had to go back again.

But by this time the girl's father had returned home, and he asked: "Where's my daughter?"

"She's gone to her aunt's," replied her stepmother.

Soon afterwards the girl herself came running home.

"Where have you been?" asked her father.

"Ah, father!" she said, "mother sent me to aunt's to ask for a needle and thread to make me a shift. But aunt's a Baba Yaga, and she wanted to eat me!"

"And how did you get away, daughter?"

"Why like this," said the girl, and explained the whole matter. As soon as her father had heard all about it, he became wroth with his wife, and shot her. But he and his daughter lived on and flourished, and everything went well with them.

Notes and Comments

This Russian Baba Yaga tale is a variant of Type 313H *Flight From the Witch.* It is a very widely distributed tale, and the motif of the obstacle flight was known in ancient Greece as evidenced by the story of Jason and Medea.

We have chosen this tale because it has a rather complete description of one of the more fascinating witch characters in all folk literature—the Baba Yaga, a personification of evil. She is one of the hateful tribe of malevolent enchantresses found all over the world. Baba Yaga possesses supernatural powers, but her wits are dull, and she is often defeated by her intended victims.

Baba Yaga in all her terrible ferocity is kin to other marvelous beings peculiar to their own countries, such as the "glaestigs" of the Scottish Highlands, the "jinns" of the Near East, and the "rakshasas" of India. Each of these supernatural creatures dominates tales in his or her own region, although the tales themselves are almost always international. Thus it is that Baba Yaga is the central character in this widespread and well-known tale of the obstacle flight, but her very bony presence there declares the story to be uniquely Russian.

Baba Yaga is said by many to be the grandmother of the devil, and she resembles other ogresses and witches by her preference for the flesh of young children. She lives in a hut surrounded by a fence of human bones. The fence stakes are skeletons that glare at visitors through empty sockets. Instead of doorways and a gate, there are scrawny chicken feet, and instead of bolts there are hands. In place of the lock there is a mouth of sharp teeth. When the right words are addressed to it, the hut revolves so as to present its back instead of its front to the forest.

Baba Yaga is pictured as a devourer. She is associated with dark places like the forest and has an aura of menace. Her iron teeth are used to rend her victim's flesh. Inside her hut, the Baba Yaga customarily perches with her head to the door, a foot in either corner, and her nose touching the ceiling. Any child being pursued by such a creature is never certain whether sight or sound is more frightening, for the Baba Yaga chases her victims in a giant iron kettle that bumps along with frightful racket, or else she flies through the air in a mortar which she propels by a pestle as she sweeps her traces from the air with a broom.

The great variations in Type 313H lie with "localizing" the obstacles. In an Ozark variant Ruthie-ma-Toothy and Alf Knight run off from the devil, throwing behind them bramble briars, little gravels, and a bottle of water that causes barns and "haystacks with chickens a-riding on 'em" to float downstream. The devil is persistent, but Ruthie throws down her Bible and the countryside is filled with holy writ. The devil goes home in disgust. The basic elements of Type 313H are the flight of the young couple and pursuit by the witch or ogre (often related to the heroine). The basic Type 313 is very long and complicated, and American variants tend to place emphasis on the flight and the magic objects. These objects vary a great deal, from an umbrella in a Chinese variant to the above-mentioned Bible. The presence of Baba Yaga is in fact incidental to the story; any witch or ogre could be the villain—except, of course, in a Russian tale.

Tale Type 313H   Flight from the Witch

Principal Motifs:

G204   Girl in service of witch
D671   Transformation flight
D672   Obstacle flight
L55   Stepdaughter heroine
G273.4   Witch powerless to cross stream

Type 313 Parallel Stories in:

Briggs, *Dictionary*, A(1) (12 variants)
Chase, *Jack*, #15, p. 198 (references given)
Christiansen, *Norway*, #78
Claudel, *Louisiana*, pp. 192–95
Clouston, *Popular*, 1, 441–43 (2 variants)
Dawkins, *Modern Greek*, #49 (summary)
Degh, *Hungary*, #65
Eberhard, *China*, #27
MacCurdy, *Spanish*, #11 (in Spanish)
Massignon, *France*, #6
Megas, *Greece*, #22
Paredes, *Mexico*, #30
Parsons, *Antilles* 3: #172 (abstracts and references)
Randolph, *Devil's*, pp. 3–6 (references; see also *Missouri*, pp. 77–79)

BABA YAGA TALES (A SELECTION):

Afanas'ev gives 14 Baba Yaga tales.
Hoke, "Baba Yaga and the Little Girl with the Kind Heart," in *Witches*, pp. 19–30.
Magnus, "Baba Yaga and Zamoryshek" and "Vasilisa the Fair" in *Russian*, pp. 48–51, 109–18.

Ralston, "Vasilissa the Fair," in *Russian,* pp. 150–58.
Ransome, "Baba Yaga," in *Old Peter's,* pp. 88–105.

PICTURE BOOKS:

Baba Yaga. Retold by Ernest Small and illustrated by Blair Lent. Boston: Houghton Mifflin, 1966 (48 pp).

Vasilisa the Beautiful. Retold by Thomas Whitney and illustrated by Nonny Hogrogian. New York: Macmillan, 1970. (Has Baba Yaga character)

28

The Toad Witch*

This story takes place in my grandmother's village in Poland. Some people of the village were having trouble with their milk cows. Some cows were drying up and some were giving too much milk. One day a beggar came to my grandmother's farm and asked for some food. She agreed but told him she could not give him any milk because her cows were drying up. She explained that some cows were giving too much and others none. He said he would travel into town and see if he could find out a reason. On his return from town, the begger told my grandmother to watch whatever was the last thing to follow the cows into the barn and to cut off one of its hands. She watched the cows go into the barn and saw a toad following the herd. She cut off its hand, and the next morning the cows were giving milk again. That same morning a neighbor woman was seen with her hand all bandaged up. It was the same side as the hand cut from the toad.

*Collected by K. Laliberte from a Polish-American informant in 1971. Eastern Michigan University Folklore Archive. Used with permission of K. Laliberte.

Notes and Comments

References to milk-stealing witchcraft are found in Europe as early as the twelfth century. But witches could also take away the milk of a nursing mother, or suck human breasts till blood flowed. The connection between nursing mothers' milk and witchcraft is scarcely coincidental. The life-giving potential of mother's milk (at least in preformula days), the suscepti-bility of children to evil forces, and the miracle of human milk production itself undoubtedly account for the fact that the dairy became a focus of superstition.

Methods used by the witches to steal milk vary, but three categories predominate. In the first, the witch uses her craft to draw milk from a wooden ax or spigot stuck in a post or from some other inanimate object. Her belief in a covenant with the devil accounts for the magic, for it is the devil himself who milks the cow and brings the invisible milk underground to the wooden object. The second method involves the construction by the witch of a leather bag or other container that she empowers to slink through the dairy and fill itself. In the third method, found in this story, the witch transforms herself into an animal and steals the milk directly from the cow. The more popular English animals for this type of transformation, accord-ing to Professor George Lyman Kittredge, are hares, hedgehogs, snakes, or even English goblins called hobthursts. In his notes, he adds that in Poland witches often become toads when raiding the dairy. He cites at least one method of thwarting them—burning a live toad in a closed pot (*Witchcraft,* p. 484). Interestingly enough, the story reprinted here, collected from a Polish informant living in Michigan, has retained the traditional form of witch transformation from the old country.

Protecting milk from the witch and identifying just which neighbors were guilty of meddling in the dairy are problems faced by anyone whose dairy seems bewitched. Besides the fact that witches can assume almost any shape at will and work all kinds of mischief with their power, they can scarcely be detected even by the most suspicious and superstitious eye. The common folk belief, however, holds that a wound received by the trans-formed witch will remain with the creature when she resumes her normal body. Richard Dorson in *Michigan* (p. 146) cites a historical parallel in which a servant, suspicious of a mischievous cat, cut off one of its paws which instantly became a woman's hand with a gold ring on one finger. Ultimately the mistress of the house was found to have a severed hand. The informant declares that this event happened in North Carolina where her grandmother worked as a house slave.

Tale Type ML 3055   The Witch that Was Hurt

Principal Motifs:

D2083.1   Cows magically made dry
G252   Witch in form of cat (toad) has hand cut off; recognized next morning
           by missing hand

Parallel Stories in:

Addy, *Household*, #44
Boggs, *North Carolina*, p. 296
Brewer, *American Negro*, pp. 308–9
Briggs, *Dictionary*, B (2) (17 variants)
Chase, *Jack*, #8, p. 192 (references)
Cox, *Witch Bridle*, pp. 203–9 (references)
Dorson, *American Negro*, #124
——, *Bloodstoppers*, pp. 77–78
——, *Michigan*, pp. 146–47
Emmons, *Cats*, pp. 95–96
——, *Nacogdoches*, pp. 132–34 (references)
Fauset, *Nova Scotia*, #125
Gardner, *Schoharie*, p. 74 (references)
Halpert, *Indiana Storyteller*, #17
Harland, *Lancashire*, pp. 5–7
Im, *Korean*, pp. 42–43
Kittredge, *Witchcraft*, p. 563 (references)
Paredes, *Mexico*, #8 (witch mother-in-law)
Parsons, *Guilford County*, #54
——, *Sea Islands*, #12
Randolph, *Knapsack*, pp. 103–4
Roberts, *South*, #36b
Thompson, *Boots*, pp. 112–13

29

The Tinker and the Ghost*

O n the wide plain not far from the city of Toledo there once stood a great gray Castle. For many years before this story begins no one had dwelt there, because the Castle was haunted. There was no living soul within its walls, and yet on almost every night in the year a thin, sad voice moaned and wept and wailed through the huge, empty rooms. And on All Hallows' Eve a ghostly light appeared in the chimney, a light that flared and died and flared again against the dark sky.

Learned doctors and brave adventurers had tried to exorcise the ghost. And the next morning they had been found in the great hall of the Castle, sitting lifeless before the empty fireplace.

Now one day in late October there came to the little village that nestled around the Castle walls a brave and jolly tinker whose name was Esteban. And while he sat in the market place mending the pots and pans the good wives told him about the haunted Castle. It was All Hallows' Eve, they said, and if he would wait until nightfall he could see the strange, ghostly light flare up from the chimney. He might, if he dared go

*From *Three Golden Oranges and Other Spanish Folk Tales* by Ralph Steele Boggs and Mary Gould Davis (London: Longmans, Green, 1936), pp. 99–108. Copyright © 1936 by Ralph Boggs and Mary Davis. Reprinted by permission of the David McKay Company, Inc.

near enough, hear the thin, sad voice echo through the silent rooms.

"If I dare!" Esteban repeated scornfully. "You must know, good wives, that I—Esteban—fear nothing, neither ghost nor human. I will gladly sleep in the Castle tonight, and keep this dismal spirit company."

The good wives looked at him in amazement. Did Esteban know that if he succeeded in banishing the ghost the owner of the Castle would give him a thousand gold *reales?*

Esteban chuckled. If that was how matters stood, he would go to the Castle at nightfall and do his best to get rid of the thing that haunted it. But he was a man who liked plenty to eat and drink and a fire to keep him company. They must bring to him a load of faggots, a side of bacon, a flask of wine, a dozen fresh eggs and a frying pan. This the good wives gladly did. And as the dusk fell, Esteban loaded these things on the donkey's back and set out for the Castle. And you may be very sure that not one of the village people went very far along the way with him!

It was a dark night with a chill wind blowing and a hint of rain in the air. Esteban unsaddled his donkey and set him to graze on the short grass of the deserted courtyard. Then he carried his food and his faggots into the great hall. It was dark as pitch there. Bats beat their soft wings in his face and the air felt cold and musty. He lost no time in piling some of his faggots in one corner of the huge stone fireplace and in lighting them. As the red and golden flames leaped up the chimney Esteban rubbed his hands. Then he settled himself comfortably on the hearth.

"*That* is the thing to keep off both cold and fear," he said.

Carefully slicing some bacon he laid it in the pan and set it over the flames. How good it smelled! And how cheerful the sound of its crisp sizzling!

He had just lifted his flask to take a deep drink of the good wine when down the chimney there came a voice—a thin, sad voice—and *"Oh me!"* it wailed, *"Oh me! Oh me!"*

Esteban swallowed the wine and set the flask carefully down beside him.

"Not a very cheerful greeting, my friend," he said, as he moved the bacon on the pan so that it should be equally brown in all its parts. "But bearable to a man who is used to the braying of his donkey."

And *"Oh me!"* sobbed the voice, *"Oh me! Oh me!"*

Esteban lifted the bacon carefully from the hot fat and laid it on a bit of brown paper to drain. Then he broke an egg into the frying pan. As he gently shook the pan so that the edges of his egg should be crisp and brown and the yolk soft, the voice came again. Only this time it was shrill and frightened.

"Look out below," it called. *"I'm falling."*

"All right," answered Esteban, "only don't fall into the frying pan." With that there was a thump, and there on the hearth lay a man's leg! It was a good leg enough and it was clothed in the half of a pair of brown corduroy trousers.

Esteban ate his egg, a piece of bacon and drank again from the flask of wine. The wind howled around the Castle and the rain beat against the windows.

Then, *"Look out below,"* called the voice sharply. *"I'm falling!"* There was a thump, and on the hearth there lay a second leg, just like the first!

Esteban moved it away from the fire and piled on more faggots. Then he warmed the fat in the frying pan and broke into it a second egg.

And, *"Look out below!"* roared the voice. And now it was no longer thin, but strong and lusty. *"Look out below! I'm falling!"*

"Fall away," Esteban answered cheerfully. "Only don't spill my egg." There was a thump, heavier than the first two, and on the hearth there lay a trunk. It was clothed in a blue shirt and a brown corduroy coat.

Esteban was eating his third egg and the last of the cooked bacon when the voice called again, and down fell first one arm and then the other.

"Now," thought Esteban, as he put the frying pan on the fire and began to cook more bacon. "Now there is only the head. I confess that I am rather curious to see the head."

And: "LOOK OUT BELOW!" thundered the voice. "I'M FALLING —FALLING!"

And down the chimney there came tumbling a head!

It was a good head enough, with thick black hair, a long black beard and dark eyes that looked a little strained and anxious. Esteban's bacon was only half cooked. Nevertheless, he removed the pan from the fire and laid it on the hearth. And it is a good thing that he did, because before his eyes the parts of the body joined together, and a living man—or his ghost—stood before him! And *that* was a sight that might have startled Esteban into burning his fingers with the bacon fat.

"Good evening," said Esteban. "Will you have an egg and a bit of bacon?"

"No, I want no food," the ghost answered. "But I will tell you this, right here and now. You are the only man, out of all those who have come to the Castle, to stay here until I could get my body together again. The others died of sheer fright before I was half finished."

"That is because they did not have sense enough to bring food and fire with them," Esteban replied coolly. And he turned back to his frying pan.

"Wait a minute!" pleaded the ghost. "If you will help me a bit more, you will save my soul and get me into the Kingdom of Heaven. Out in the courtyard, under a cypress tree, there are buried three bags—one of copper coins, one of silver coins, and one of gold coins. I stole them from some thieves and brought them here to the Castle to hide. But no sooner did I have them buried than the thieves overtook me, murdered me and cut my body into pieces. But they did not find the coins. Now you come with me and dig them up. Give the copper coins to the Church, the silver coins to the poor, and keep the gold coins for yourself. Then I will have expiated my sins and can go to the Kingdom of Heaven."

This suited Esteban. So he went out into the courtyard with the ghost. And you should have heard how the donkey brayed when he saw them!

When they reached the cypress tree in a corner of the courtyard: "Dig," said the ghost.

"Dig yourself," answered Esteban.

So the ghost dug, and after a time the three bags of money appeared.

"Now will you promise to do just what I asked you to do?" asked the ghost.

"Yes, I promise," Esteban answered.

"Then," said the Ghost, "strip my garments from me."

This Esteban did, and instantly the ghost disappeared, leaving his clothes lying there on the short grass of the courtyard. It went straight up to Heaven and knocked on the Gate. St. Peter opened it, and when the spirit explained that he had expiated his sins, gave him a cordial welcome.

Esteban carried the coins into the great hall of the castle, fried and ate another egg and then went peacefully to sleep before the fire.

The next morning when the village people came to carry away Esteban's body, they found him making an omelette out of the last of the fresh eggs.

"Are you alive?" they gasped.

"I am," Esteban answered. "And the food and the faggots lasted through very nicely. Now I will go to the owner of the Castle and collect my thousand gold *reales*. The ghost has gone for good and all. You will find his clothes lying out in the courtyard."

And before their astonished eyes he loaded the bags of coins on the donkey's back and departed.

First he collected the thousand gold *reales* from the grateful lord of the Castle. Then he returned to Toledo, gave the copper coins to the *cura* of his church, and faithfully distributed the silver ones among the poor. And on the thousand *reales* and the golden coins he lived in idleness and a great contentment for many years.

Notes and Comments

Ghost stories often reflect great extremes in human experience. Such stories are either related as true happenings that illustrate just how frightened the narrator was, or are told with an air of understatement that emphasizes the courage of a narrator in fearsome circumstances. It is the air of seeming nonchalance and the interaction of supernatural and commonplace that makes "The Tinker and the Ghost" an effective story. Despite the warnings of terrified villagers and a symphony of terrifying sounds, the tinker, Esteban, calmly builds up the huge fire, busies himself with cracking eggs and slicing bacon, and directs his senses to the warmth of the hearth, the sound of the cooking, and the smell of the delicious food. Warmth and sustenance are all this unlikely hero needs "to keep off both cold and fear."

Nevertheless, for the audience, all the narrative trappings of a good ghost story abound: a thin, sad voice moaning and wailing through huge empty rooms, a dark night with the chill wind on All Hallows' Eve, a strange ghostly light from the chimney, insistent warnings to "look out below," and finally the grotesque thumps and scrapings of falling body parts which assemble themselves into a complete corpse. Small wonder Estaban's predecessors died of fright, but then they "did not have sense enough to bring food and fire with them" as did this practical and brave tinker who quickly gets the better of his ghostly visitor.

The tradition of the restless ghost who needs to expiate his sins, who returns to finish a forgotten chore, who is compelled to redress a wrong or make right an undiscovered wrong, to punish or protect, to impart information, or even to reenact his death is a longstanding tradition. These restless dead, called revenants, have reportedly appeared in various forms: sometimes they cannot be detected until they vanish; frequently they are characterized by a wraithlike quality.

Related motifs dealing with ghosts who direct the living to buried treasure are particularly prominent. In these cases the revenant's motive might be to see that the money is used for some good purpose—to help the poor, to reward someone. In many American tales the ghost gives away the money because he "cain't get no rest until somebody finds the stuff and spends it for something useful" (Randolph, *Ozark*, p. 220). The dismembered revenant in "The Golden Arm" will provide another example of the frightening phenomenon of the restless dead. (See Tale #30.)

Tale Type 326A   Soul Released from Torment

Principal Motifs:

H1411.1	Fear test: staying in haunted house where corpse drops piecemeal down the chimney
E371.4	Ghost of man returns to point out buried treasure
E352	Dead returns to restore stolen goods
E373.1	Money received from ghost as reward for bravery
E451.5.1	Money must be distributed to beggars so that ghost may be laid
E31	Limbs of dead voluntarily reassemble and revive
E459.3	Ghost laid when wishes are acceded to

Parallel Stories in:

Addy, *Household,* #4
Boggs, *North Carolina,* pp. 296–97 (2 variants)
Boucher, *Moondaughter,* pp. 34-39
Briggs, *Dictionary,* A (1) (9 variants, references to 5 more)
Dorson, *American Negro,* #195
Gardner, *Schoharie,* pp. 191–94 (references given, 2 variants)
Grimm, #4
Halpert, *Indiana Folktales,* pp. 9–11 (references given)
Hampden, *Gypsy,* pp. 51–56
Jacobs, *More English,* #46
Jansen, *Steel Town,* #1
Kennedy, *Legendary,* pp. 154–56 (reprinted in *Schoharie,* pp. 193–94)
Parsons, *Sea Islands,* #62, #169
Porter, *East Anglia,* pp. 108–9, 170–73
Protter, *Celtic,* #11
Randolph, *Turtle,* pp. 22–24, 186–87 (references)
Roberts, *South,* #9 (4 variants)

30

The Golden Arm*

There was once a man who travelled the land all over in search of a wife. He saw young and old, rich and poor, pretty and plain, and could not meet with one to his mind. At last he found a woman, young, fair, and rich, who possessed a right arm of solid gold. He married her at once, and thought no man so fortunate as he was. They lived happily together, but, though he wished people to think otherwise, he was fonder of the golden arm than of all his wife's gifts besides.

At last she died. The husband put on the blackest black, and pulled the longest face at the funeral; but for all that he got up in the middle of the night, dug up the body, and cut off the golden arm. He hurried home to hide his treasure, and thought no one would know.

The following night he put the golden arm under his pillow, and was just falling asleep, when the ghost of his dead wife glided into the room. Stalking up to the bedside it drew the curtain, and looked at him reproachfully. Pretending not to be afraid, he spoke to the ghost, and said: "What hast thou done with thy cheeks so red?"

"All withered and wasted away," replied the ghost in a hollow tone. "What hast thou done with thy red rosy lips?"

*From *English Fairy Tales* collected by Joseph Jacobs (London: David Nutt, 1898), pp. 143–44.

"All withered and wasted away."
"What hast thou done with thy golden hair?"
"All withered and wasted away."
"What hast thou done with thy *Golden Arm?*"
"THOU HAST IT!"

Notes and Comments

Of all ghost stories told for the purpose of frightening the audience, this "startle" tale is perhaps the most popular. The method of frightening the audience is by a loud and explosive shout—"THOU HAST IT!" "YOU'VE GOT IT!" or "TAKE IT!" at the end of the tale. Even when prepared for the explosive refrain, there are those who feel the hair rising on the back of their necks. In a closely related form, the English "Teeny Tiny," a teeny-tiny woman takes a teeny-tiny bone from the churchyard to make some teeny-tiny soup. The story is generally told in a "teeny-tiny" voice, until the final episode where the owner demands the return of the bone, and the storyteller shouts "TAKE IT!"

Thompson says that Tale Type 366 *The Man from the Gallows* is well known both in Europe and America with its greatest popularity being in Denmark, although it is also found in the Malay Peninsula and among the Hausa in Africa (*Folktale,* p. 42). Roberts cites this type as being the most widespread short tale collected in Kentucky (*South,* p. 223).

The restless revenant in all these variants is a familiar character akin to the dismembered ghost in the Spanish tale "The Tinker and the Ghost." Its reason for returning to earth is usually fairly simple: a piece of clothing, some false teeth, or a part of the body is disturbed in death, either taken from the gallows before burial, removed from the coffin in secret, or accidentally dug up in a field or in a cemetery. In the more grisly versions, the body part is put in a soup and eaten by mistake.

In all cases the ghost returns, retrieves the missing part, and leaves (if the story has been well told) amidst the screams of the audience. Jacobs's version here is perhaps most successful when the narrator presents the repetitive ghostly dialogue of "All withered and wasted away" in a faint singsong, lulling the audience's senses just prior to the shout at the end.

Other chants equally effective are "Give-me-my-silver-toe"; "Where's my false teeth—I'm going to eat you up with 'em!"; and "Bzzz-zzz-zzz—W-h-o—g-o-t—m-y—g-o-l-d-e-n—a-r-m?" This latter example comes from Mark Twain's essay "How to Tell a Story and Other Essays." In this example Twain suggests that the storyteller "set your teeth together and imitate the wailing and wheezing singsong of the wind" in the first part of the chant. Later on in the story, the teller "must begin to shiver violently" when the midnight thief realizes that he has disturbed a corpse. But in order to achieve the proper frightful effect, Twain is very specific in his instructions for the conclusion:

> You must wail it out very plaintively and accusingly; then you stare steadily and impressively into the face of the farthest-gone auditor—a girl, preferably—and let that awe-inspiring pause begin to build itself right into the deep hush. When it has reached exactly the right length, jump suddenly at that girl and yell, "You've got it!"

For the beginning storyteller, Twain admits getting the conclusion just right is "the most troublesome and aggravating and uncertain thing you ever undertook."

Tale Type 366   The Man from the Gallows

Principal Motif:

E235.4.1   Return from dead to punish theft of golden arm from grave

Parallel Stories in:

Boggs, *North Carolina,* p. 296 (big toe)
Botkin, *American,* pp. 502–3 (reprinted from Samuel L. Clemens, *How to Tell a Story and Other Essays,* pp. 7–15
Briggs, *Dictionary,* A (2) (9 variants)
Campbell, *Cloud Walking,* pp. 175–76
Chase, *Grandfather,* #25 (big toe eaten)
Cox, *Negro Tales,* pp. 341–42 (1934)
Dobie, *Texas Household,* pp. 41–42 (1927)
Gilchrist, *Bone,* pp. 378–79 (1939)
Goldstone, *From Uncle Remus,* p. 242 (note)
Grimm #109 (variant)
Hunt, *Popular Romances,* pp. 452–53 (teeth)
Jacobs, *English,* #12
Lowrimore, *Six California,* #5 (toe)
Randolph, *Turtle,* pp. 22–24, 186–87 (references)
Roberts, *South,* #12
Simpson, *Icelandic,* pp. 111–13 (2 variants)

31

The Coffin-Lid*

Amoujik was driving along one night with a load of pots. His horse grew tired, and all of a sudden it came to a stand-still alongside of a graveyard. The moujik unharnessed his horse and set it free to graze; meanwhile he laid himself down on one of the graves. But somehow he didn't go to sleep.

He remained lying there some time. Suddenly the grave began to open beneath him: he felt the movement and sprang to his feet. The grave opened, and out of it came a corpse—wrapped in a white shroud, and holding a coffin-lid—came out and ran to the church, laid the coffin-lid at the door, and then set off for the village.

The moujik was a daring fellow. He picked up the coffin-lid and remained standing beside his cart, waiting to see what would happen. After a short delay the dead man came back, and was going to snatch up his coffin-lid—but it was not to be seen. Then the corpse began to track it out, traced it up to the moujik, and said:

"Give me my lid: if you don't, I'll tear you to bits!"

"And my hatchet, how about that?" answers the moujik. "Why, it's I who'll be chopping you into small pieces!"

*From *Russian Folk-Tales* by William Ralston (London: Smith, Elder and Co., 1873), pp. 309–11.

"Do give it back to me, good man!" begs the corpse.

"I'll give it when you tell me where you've been and what you've done."

"Well, I've been in the village, and there I've killed a couple of youngsters."

"Well then, now tell me how they can be brought back to life."

The corpse reluctantly made answer:

"Cut off the left skirt of my shroud, and take it with you. When you come into the house where the youngsters were killed, pour some live coals into a pot and put the piece of the shroud in with them, and then lock the door. The lads will be revived by the smoke immediately."

The moujik cut off the left skirt of the shroud, and gave up the coffin-lid. The corpse went to its grave—the grave opened. But just as the dead man was descending into it, all of a sudden the cocks began to crow, and he hadn't time to get properly covered over. One end of the coffin-lid remained sticking out of the ground.

The moujik saw all this and made a note of it. The day began to dawn; he harnessed his horse and drove into the village. In one of the houses he heard cries and wailing. In he went—there lay two dead lads.

"Don't cry," says he, "I can bring them to life!"

"Do bring them to life, kinsman," say their relatives. "We'll give you half of all we possess."

The moujik did everything as the corpse had instructed him, and the lads came back to life. Their relatives were delighted, but they immediately seized the moujik and bound him with cords, saying:

"No, no, trickster! We'll hand you over to the authorities. Since you knew how to bring them back to life, maybe it was you who killed them!"

"What are you thinking about, true believers! Have the fear of God before your eyes!" cried the moujik.

Then he told them everything that had happened to him during the night. Well, they spread the news through the village; the whole population assembled and swarmed into the graveyard. They found out the grave from which the dead man had come out, they tore it open, and they drove an aspen stake right into the heart of the corpse, so that it might no more rise up and slay. But they rewarded the moujik richly, and sent him away home with great honour.

Notes and Comments

The dozens of films based upon the vampire legend attest to the continuing popularity of this grisly character in tradition—in many ways the most dangerous species of the undead. Belief in vampires is worldwide, but it is predominantly a Slavic concept. The traditional vampire is a revenant who spends the night searching for victims but who at dawn must return to his coffin. Such creatures are themselves traditionally victims who were bitten by vampires. Other candidates are suicides, witches, those under a curse, the seventh son of a seventh son, and any corpse whom cats have jumped over. At burial, should a corpse's mouth be open, it must be stuffed with clay before the coffin is closed or the body will become a vampire.

The detection and identification of vampires can be a rather scientific matter, according to Anthony Masters, author of *The Natural History of the Vampire,* but only if one proceeds according to the following checklist immediately upon disinterment of a suspected vampire:

1. Are there a number of holes about the breadth of a man's finger in the soil above the grave?
2. Does the revealed corpse have any of the following:
   a. Wide open eyes?
   b. A ruddy complexion?
   c. No signs of corruption?
3. Have the nails and hair grown as in life?
4. Are there two small livid marks on the neck?
5. Is the shroud partially devoured?
6. Is there blood in the veins of the corpse?
7. Is the coffin full of blood?
8. Does the body look well fed?
9. Are the limbs fully flexible?

Mr. Masters then suggests: "If the answer to these questions is yes, refer to your neighborhood *Dhampir,* priest, or witch to provide exorcism recipe."

In order to account for such a well-defined belief in the behavior of the restless dead, Mr. Masters also offers a natural explanation for the phenomena of the disturbed corpse which, albeit theory, is sufficiently plausible to be interesting. He suggests that

> owing to the rudimentary methods of defining death, many people were buried alive, and upon being exhumed were found in an entirely different position from that in which they were buried. The victim would be face down in the coffin so as to inhale the maximum amount of air. During the process of

suffocating, the victim would bite his lips and fingers, draining blood and often filling the coffin with gore.

He concludes this theory by suggesting that when coffins were opened in order to determine whether the corpse had "ascended or descended," the unfortunate victim of a premature burial was immediately assumed to be a "bloodsucking vampire."

Whatever the origin of the belief in vampires, traditional methods of protection were widely known and practiced. Besides the well-known method of exorcism by driving a wooden stake through the heart, success in eliminating vampires has also been reported with other methods such as chopping off the head, burning the corpse, shooting with a silver bullet, tearing out the heart, and throwing boiling water or oil into the grave. One writer suggests that, depending on the age of the vampire at the time of exorcism, one could expect him first "to commence visibly to decay, and if he were old enough . . . literally to disintegrate into bones of dust." One is assured that although the vampire will writhe in agony, his soul will rest later.

For the individual wishing to protect his person rather than rid the countryside of vampires, he might try spreading garlic in front of his doors and windows, wearing a crucifix or rosary at all times, or as a last resort, sprinkling a circle of holy water and standing inside it, since all vampires are powerless to cross such a protective circle. All these talismans and rituals are well documented in the folklore of Europe.

The peasant in this tale is unusually fearless. By retaining possession of the coffin lid, he places the vampire in grave danger of detection since he must lie in that coffin during the daylight hours. Using this power of persuasion, the peasant is able to extract life-giving remedies to save the vampire's most recent victims. Later, the vampire's coffin is easily spotted, for there is not time to secure the lid before it is spotted by the villagers. The same villagers, steeped in the traditions of their region, put an end to the vampire with a stake of aspen—the same kind of wood that was traditionally used for the Holy Cross.

Tale Type 363   The Vampire

Principal Motifs:

E251   Vampire. Corpse which comes from grave at night and sucks blood
E251.1   Vampire's power overcome

E251.3   Deeds of vampire
E442   Ghost laid by piercing grave (corpse) with stake
E592.2   Ghost carries coffin on back

Parallel Stories in:

Afanas'ev, pp. 593–98
Briggs, *Dictionary,* A (1), p. 553
Magnus, *Russian,* pp. 6–12 (3 tales)
Massignon, *France,* #28 (variant; TT 307)
Ralston, *Russian,* pp. 314–18
Ranke, *Germany,* #23

32

*The Wolf-Child**

I n the North of Portugal there are many sequestered spots where the
enchanted Moors and the wizards meet when it is full moon. These
places are generally situated among high rocks on the precipitous sides of
the hills overlooking rivers; and when the wind is very boisterous their
terrible screams and incantations can be distinctly heard by the peasantry
inhabiting the neighboring villages.

On such occasions the father of the family sets fire to a wisp of straw,
and with it makes the sign of the cross around his house, which prevents
these evil spirits from approaching. The other members of the family place
a few extra lights before the image of the Virgin; and the horse-shoe nailed
to the door completes the safety of the house.

But it will so happen that sometimes an enchanted Moor, with more
cunning than honesty, will get through one of the windows on the birth of
a child, and will brand the infant with the crescent on his shoulder or arm,
in which case it is well known that the child, on certain nights, will be
changed into a wolf.

The enchanted Moors have their castles and palaces under the ground

---

*From *Tales From the Lands of Nuts and Grapes* by Charles Sellers (London: Field and
Tuer, The Leadenhall Press, 1888), pp. 17–25.

or beneath the rivers, and they wander about the earth, seeing but not seen; for they died unbaptized, and have, therefore, no rest in the grave.

They seem to have given preference to the North of Portugal, where they are held in great fear by the ignorant peasantry; and it has been observed that all such of the natives as have left their homes to study at the universities, on their return have never been visited by the enchanted Moors, as it is well known that they have a great respect for learning. In fact, one of the kings has said that until all his subjects were educated they would never get rid of the enchanted Moors and wizards.

In a village called Darque, on the banks of the Lima, there lived a farmer whose goodness and ignorance were only equalled by those of his wife. They were both young and robust, and were sufficiently well off to afford the luxury of beef once or twice a month. Their clothes were home-spun, and their hearts were homely. Beyond their landlord's grounds they had never stepped; but as he owned nearly the whole village, it is very evident that they knew something of this world of ours. They were both born and married on the estate, as their parents had been before them, and they were contented because they had never mixed with the world.

One day, when the farmer came home to have his midday meal of broth and maize-bread, he found his wife in bed with a newborn baby boy by her side, and he was so pleased that he spent his hour of rest looking at the child, so that his meal remained untasted on the table.

Kissing his wife and infant, and bidding her beware of evil eyes, he hurried out of the house back to his work; and so great was his joy at being a father that he did not feel hungry.

He was digging potatoes, and in his excitement had sent his hoe through some of them, which, however, he did not notice until he happened to strike one that was so hard that the steel of his hoe flashed.

Thinking it was a pebble, he stooped to pick it up, but was surprised to see that it was no longer there.

However, he went on working, when he struck another hard potato, and his hoe again flashed.

"Ah," said he, "the evil one has been sowing this field with stones, as he did in the days of good Saint Euphemia, our patroness." Saying which, he drew out the small crucifix from under his shirt, and the flinty potato disappeared; but he noticed that one of its eyes moved.

He thought no more of this untoward event, and went on hoeing until sunset, when, with the other laborers, he shouldered his hoe and prepared to go home.

Never had the distance seemed so great; but at last he found himself by his wife's bedside. She told him that while he was absent an old woman had called, asking for something to eat, and that as she seemed to have met with some accident, because there was blood running down her face, she invited her in, and told her she might eat what her husband had left untasted.

Sitting down at the table, the old woman commenced eating without asking a blessing on the food; and when she had finished she approached the bed, and, looking at the infant, she muttered some words and left the house hurriedly.

The husband and wife were very much afraid that the old woman was a witch; but as the child went on growing and seemed well they gradually forgot their visitor.

The infant was baptized, and was named John; and when he was old enough he was sent out to work to help his parents. All the laborers noticed that John could get through more work than any man, he was so strong and active; but he was very silent.

The remarkable strength of the boy got to be so spoken about in the village that at last the wise woman, who was always consulted, said that there was no doubt but that John was a wolf-child; and this having come to the ears of his parents, his body was carefully examined, and the mark of the crescent was found under his arm.

Nothing now remained to be done but to take John to the great wise woman of Arifana, and have him disenchanted.

The day had arrived for the parents to take John with them to Arifana, but when they looked for him he could nowhere be found. They searched everywhere—down the well, in the river, in the forest—and made inquiries at all the villages, but in vain; John had disappeared.

Weeks went by without any sign of him; and the winter having set in, the wolves, through hunger, had become more undaunted in their attacks on the flocks and herds. The farmer, afraid of firing at them, lest he might shoot his son, had laid a trap; and one morning, to his delight, he saw that a very large wolf had been caught, which one of his fellow-laborers was cudgelling. Fearing it might be the lost wolf-child, he hastened to the spot, and prevented the wolf receiving more blows; but it was too late, apparently, to save the creature's life, for it lay motionless on the ground as if dead. Hurrying off for the wise woman of the village, she returned with him; and, close to the head of the wolf, she gathered some branches of the common pine-tree, and lighting them, as some were green and others dry, a volume of smoke arose like a tower, reaching to the top of a hill where lived some notorious enchanted Moors and wizards; so that between the wolf and the said Moors the distance was covered by a tunnel of smoke and fire. Then the wise woman intoned the following words, closing her eyes, and bidding the rest do so until she should tell them they might open them:—

Spirit of the mighty wind
    That across the desert howls,
Help us here to unbind
    All the spells of dreaded ghouls;
Through the path of smoke and fire
    Rising to the wizards' mound,
Bid the cursèd mark retire
    From this creature on the ground;
Bid him take his shape again,
    Free him from the Crescent's power,
May the holy Cross remain
    On his temple from this hour.

She now made the sign of the Cross over the head of the wolf, and continued:—

River, winding to the west,
    Stay thy rippling current, stay,
Jordan's stream thy tide has blest,
    Help us wash this stain away;
Bear it to the ocean wide,
    Back to Saracenic shore.
Those who washed in thee have died
    But to live for evermore.

Then she sprinkled a few drops over the fire, which caused a larger amount of smoke, and exclaimed—

Hie thee, spirit, up through smoke,
    Quenched by water and by fire;
Hie thee far from Christian folk,
    To the wizard's home retire.
Open wide your eyelids now,
    All the smoke has curled away;
'Neath the peaceful olive bough
    Let us go, and let us pray.

Then they all rose, and the wolf was no longer there. The fire had burned itself out, and the stream was again running. In slow procession they went to the olive grotto, headed by the wise woman; and, after praying, they returned to the house, where they found, to their delight, John fast asleep in his bed; but his arms showed signs of bruises which had been caused by the cudgelling he had received when he was caught in the trap.

There were great rejoicings that day in the village of Darque; and no one was better pleased than John at having regained his proper shape.

He was never known to join in the inhuman sport of hunting wolves for pleasure, because, as he said, although they may not be wolf-children, they do but obey an instinct which was given them; and to be kind-hearted is to obey a precept which was given us. And, owing to the introduction into Portugal of the Book in which this commandment is to be found, wolf-children have become scarcer, and the people wiser.

Notes and Comments

Closely akin to a fear of the vampire is a similar universal fear of the werewolf. Even in cultures where no wolf exists, beliefs are remarkably similar, except that the prevailing fiercest animal takes the place of the wolf. For example, in India and western Asia, stories appear of the weretiger; in North America, the bear or wolf; in South America, the jaguar; in Greece and Turkey, the boar. In Africa, stories of shape shifting from man to animal involve the hyena, leopard, lion, and even crocodile. The similarity of the vampire and wolf traditions is such that in Greece a man who is a werewolf in life becomes a vampire after burial. One writer on the werewolf, Montague Summers, suggests that "the desire of blood and the desire of flesh are found to be never far apart." But perhaps there is an even closer connection with the fear of these supernatural creatures in general—werewolf, vampire, ghosts, perhaps even pixies. Perhaps they are merely variant manifestations of our darkest psychological imagingings.

On the one hand, Hartland tells us that "no positive distinction can be drawn between ghosts and witches." For his proof he cites certain facts in common:

> evilly disposed ghosts, like black witches, require for their deadliest work, the cover of darkness; souls as well as witches ride on the wind, and hence are associated with drafts and chilling blasts of air; ghosts, like witches, possess knowledge of the location of buried treasure, and have the power to arrest the movement of animals and persons; ghosts are rendered as helpless as witches by the sanctity of the Bible, and name of the Lord, a cross or its sign, a circle, a bit of mountain ash, or a horseshoe. Both ghosts and witches are subject to injury by a silver bullet or by the purifying influence of fire.

An even closer link can be seen in the theory of the origin of fairies as seen in "The Fairy Dwelling on Selena Moor" where fairies are said to be the souls of unbaptized children as well as those who died of a stroke, catalepsy, or any trancelike illness. Similar details were noted in the annotation to "The Peasant and the Corpse" and the vampire legend. In Ireland, the ghosts and fairies are said to dance together on Halloween.

In the Portuguese tale, "The Wolf-Child," the mysterious Moors are closely allied to the fairies of British folklore. They live underground in beautiful castles and palaces; they wander about the earth "seeing but not seen," just as their counterparts in fairyland; and they have died unbaptized and have "therefore, no rest in the grave," just as fairies and vampires and ghosts.

The idea that Moors are unbaptized underscores the universal fear of potential harm that can come to children not yet christened. Folk belief has it that children especially need protection even before they are born, and most mothers-to-be are warned to avoid the "evil eye," to seek and be given all unusual fancies in the way of food, and to be provided with a host of protective charms and amulets to ward off evil dangers. Safely born, the baby has to be christened as soon as possible in order to safeguard it not only against witches and the fairy people—groups always eager to exchange their own unattractive offspring for an unchristened human child—but also against the devil himself. If the newborn lives in Portugal, he must be protected even against the wizards and enchanted Moors who may slip in unawares, brand the child with the mark of the Crescent, and turn him later into a Wolf-Child.

In many areas, baptism is a good safeguard. But not even holy water is always sufficiently effective where witchcraft or the darker supernatural is concerned. Numerous other charms and protectives have long been thought necessary to ward off evil from the newborn child. Herrick's *Hesperides* lists surrounding the child's cradle with rowan leaves; placing a knife or other iron object beneath the foot of the bed—especially since witches are known to fear the power of iron—and even placing a piece of Communion bread or a crust blessed by a priest.

> Bring the holy crust of bread,
> Lay it underneath the head;
> 'Tis a certain charm to keep
> Hags away while children sleep.

>   (Charmes, p. 336)

In our story of "The Wolf-Child" many of the same charms and rituals are employed to keep away the evil spirits in general. When the howling of wizards and enchanted Moors are heard during the full moon, the peasant father sets fire to a wisp of straw, makes the sign of the cross with it all around the house, places a few extra lights before the image of the Virgin, and checks the security of the horseshoe nailed to the door, a universal protection against witches, the devil, and certainly enchanted Moors.

The narrator makes an interesting comment on superstition, however tongue-in-cheek, by citing education and learning as an even greater talisman against such evil spirits on the theory that "it is well known that they [the enchanted Moors] have a great respect for learning." He goes on to add that the king of the land believes that "until all his subjects were educated, they would never get rid of the enchanted Moors and wizards."

But our peasant couple are as ignorant as they are happy, and for whatever reasons the evil forces do invade their house in the form of an old woman with unusual characteristics: 1) blood on her face (vampires and other revenants are often found with traces of blood on their faces); 2) no blessing before eating her food (evil spirits universally fear the name of the Holy One and reverse Christian ritual if they employ it at all); and 3) muttering above the cradle of the infant (witches, devils and other spirits use language spells, charms and incantations to work their evil). The result is that the child becomes a werewolf.

Traditionally two forms of werewolf are said to exist—those transformed into wolves by enchantment and those having the power to assume wolf shape at will. Of these two types, the latter is perhaps the most to be feared, for he can apparently take off his wolf skin during the day and hide it, becoming to all appearances a normal human being during the daylight hours, although his extraordinary strength may give him away. The wolf-child in this story is obviously the latter kind, even if his untimely transformation and disappearance is strongly motivated by the impending disenchantment. Nevertheless, both kinds of werewolves share a love for human flesh. Like witches, they carry any wounds given them in their animal form on their human form the next day.

Historically, the Moors as worshippers of Islam were deadly enemies of the Portuguese Christians, and their influence had to be replaced by Christian symbols and rituals. Thus it is that the charm uttered by the "wise woman" to disenchant the boy is notable not only for its poetry and precision, but also its invocation of Christianity. The crescent is replaced by the mark of the Cross; a rebaptism from Jordan's stream is accomplished by sprinkling drops into the fire; and the evil spirit, now quenched by water and by fire, is banished to the wizard's home in the mountains.

Tale Type ML 4005   The Werewolf Husband (similar)

Principal Motifs:

G272.12	Straws as protection against witch
G273.1	Witch powerless when one makes sign of the cross
G272.4	Fires burnt in street to ward off witches
G272.11	Horsehoe hung up as protection against witches
G303.3.4.6	Devil in shape of a stone
D113.1.1	Werewolf
D789.6.1	Disenchantment by speaking proper words
D793	Disenchantment made permanent

Parallel Stories in:

Barbeau, *Anecdotes,* #33 (in French)
Christiansen, *Norway,* #23a, #23b
Dorson, *Bloodstoppers,* pp. 76–77
Randolph, *Tales from Missouri,* pp. 38–39
Thompson, *Boots,* pp. 116–17
Ure, *Romanian,* pp. 65–68
Wallace, *Larocque,* pp. 42–46

STUDIES:

Fodor, *Lycanthropy*
Smith, *Werwolf*
Steward, *Werewolf Superstitions*
Summers, *Werewolf*

33

The King o' the Cats*

One winter's evening the sexton's wife was sitting by the fireside with her big black cat, Old Tom, on the other side, both half-asleep and waiting for the master to come home. They waited and they waited, but still he didn't come, till at last he came rushing in, calling out, "Who's Tommy Tildrum?" in such a wild way that both his wife and his cat stared at him to know what was the matter.

"Why, what's the matter?" said his wife, "and why do you want to know who Tommy Tildrum is?"

"Oh, I've had such an adventure. I was digging away at old Mr. Fordyce's grave when I suppose I must have dropped asleep, and only woke up by hearing a cat's *Miaou.*"

"*Miaou!*" said Old Tom in answer.

"Yes, just like that! So I looked over the edge of the grave, and what do you think I saw?"

"Now, how can I tell?" said the sexton's wife.

"Why, nine black cats all like our friend Tom here, all with a white spot on their chestesses. And what do you think they were carrying? Why,

*From *More English Fairy Tales* collected and edited by Joseph Jacobs (London: David Nutt, 1894), pp. 156–58.

a small coffin covered with a black velvet pall, and on the pall was a small coronet all of gold, and at every third step they took they cried all together, *Miaou—*"

"*Miaou!*" said Old Tom again.

"Yes, just like that!" said the sexton; "and as they came nearer and nearer to me I could see them more distinctly, because their eyes shone out with a sort of green light. Well, they all came towards me, eight of them carrying the coffin, and the biggest cat of all walking in front for all the world like—but look at our Tom, how he's looking at me. You'd think he knew all I was saying."

"Go on, go on," said his wife; "never mind Old Tom."

"Well, as I was a-saying, they came towards me slowly and solemnly, and at every third step crying all together, *Miaou—*"

"*Miaou!*" said Old Tom again.

"Yes, just like that, till they came and stood right opposite Mr. Fordyce's grave, where I was, when they all stood still and looked straight at me. I did feel queer, that I did! But look at Old Tom; he's looking at me just like they did."

"Go on, go on," said his wife; "never mind Old Tom."

"Where was I? Oh, they all stood still looking at me, when the one that wasn't carrying the coffin came forward and, staring straight at me, said to me—yes, I tell 'ee, *said* to me—with a squeaky voice, 'Tell Tom Tildrum that Tim Toldrum's dead,' and that's why I asked you if you knew who Tom Tildrum was, for how can I tell Tom Tildrum Tim Toldrum's dead if I don't know who Tom Tildrum is?"

"Look at Old Tom, look at Old Tom!" screamed his wife.

And well he might look, for Tom was swelling and Tom was staring, and at last Tom shrieked out, "What—old Tim dead! then I'm the King o' the Cats!" and rushed up the chimney and was never more seen.

Notes and Comments

The narrator of "The Cat that Went A-Traveling" voiced a warning about cats in general when he said: "Bad luck to kill a cat. Best just tote it off from home and turn it loose and leave it. A cat's a shifty creature . . ." (see Story 23). Aloof and inscrutable, the cat has walked alone through the ages, according to Rudyard Kipling in "The Cat Who Walked by Himself," and is perhaps best known for his amazing complement of nine lives as well as for his unusual position as favored familiar of witches. Kittredge tells us that "the cat appears as a familiar in the first of the really notable Elizabe-than witch trials, at Chelmsford in 1566" (*Witchcraft,* p. 178).

But more than familiars, the cat is also reported to be witches' favorite choice for shape shifting, for they are thought to be able to assume cat form at will. Vance Randolph tells one such story that comes from gossip about women who disguise as house cats to visit lovers. His personal experience is as follows:

> A big yellow cat once walked into a cabin where I was sitting with an aged tie hacker and his wife. The woman began to shout "Witch! Witch!" at the top of her voice. The old man sprang up, crossed the fingers of both hands, and chanted something that sounded like "Pulley-bone holy-ghost double-yoke! Pulley-bone holy-ghost double-yoke!' The cat walked in a wide circle past the hearth, stared fixedly at the old gentleman for a moment, and then strolled out across the threshold. We followed a moment later, but the animal was nowhere in sight.
>
> (*Ozark Magic and Folklore,* p. 269)

Folklore has traditionally associated cats and corpses. Beliefs are quite diverse: cats mutilate corpses, change them to vampires, even steal the souls of the dead. Kittredge quotes a widespread tradition as follows: "Never take a cat near a dead person, lest the cat take the soul of the dead" (*Witchcraft,* p. 178). Confirmation of this tradition is amplified by the explanation that the soul often issues from the mouth of a sleeping man in the shape of a mouse *(Ibid.).*

With such an array of folk belief concerning the unusual nature of cats, it is easy to understand the sexton's concern at the procession of cats bearing a coffin, crying *"Miaou"* in unison, and bemoaning the death of their leader. Variations in this enigmatic story are threefold. In one a cat speaks directly to a man who then hurries home to recount the message to his wife; in another, a cat comes down the chimney with the message. In the third one reprinted here, a man accidentally glimpses a solemn cat funeral and over-hears the cats talking. In any case, the otherwise placid housecat immedi-ately reacts with the "King of the Cats" refrain and is seen no more.

Part of the attraction of this tale lies in the variety of names of the cat-king: in England Mally Dixon is dead; in the Ozarks, Old Kitty Rollins. Some versions change Tom Tildrum or Tim Toldrum to Dildrum and Doldrum. Equally attractive is the variation in rhythmic intensity of the fearful message. Some announcements are relatively straightforward: "Good man, tell Lucy Truth that Suzy Truth is dead"; others are almost Shakespearean in their rhythm:

Commend me to Titten Tatten and to pus thy catten, and tell her that Grimalkin is dead.

An interesting variant from Scandinavia has a cat who was formerly a troll. His metamorphosis is a punishment for becoming too familiar with a troll-wife. While he is biding his time in the form of a "noble tortoise-shell tomcat" in the house of one Mr. Plat, he hears the joyful news of his rival's death:

Harkye Plat,
Tell your cat,
That Knurremurre is dead.

The troll-cat immediately runs out of the window to console the widow.

Tale Types: 113A   King of the Cats is Dead
ML 6070B   The King of the Cats

Principal Motifs:

B241.2.3	King of cats
B342	Cat leaves house when report is made of death of one of his companions
F982.2	Four cats carry coffin

Parallel Stories in:

Briggs, *Dictionary,* B (1) (4 variants)
Burne, *Two* (reprinted in Hartland, *English Fairy,* pp. 126–27)
C., D., *Dildrum*
Emmons, *Cats,* pp. 99–100 (1933) (reprinted in Botkin, *Southern,* pp. 540–41)
Halliwell, *Nursery,* pp. 48–49
Harland, *Lancashire,* pp. 12–13
Hudson, *Versions,* pp. 225–31 (references to 31 variants in British Isles)
Jansen, *Steel Town* #2
Keightley, *Fairy Mythology,* pp. 120–21
Leather, *Herefordshire,* 167–68
O'Suilleabhain, *Handbook,* #52, #53, p. 622 (summaries)
Randolph, *Church House?,* pp. 40, 191–92
———, *Ozark* pp. 236–37
Thompson, *Boots,* p. 109

34

The Shrove Tuesday Visitor*

I n olden times in Canada, Shrove Tuesday, the day before the beginning of Lent, was more strictly observed than it is to-day. The night
was always one of great merriment and feasting. Boys and girls of the
villages and country places gathered there for the last time before the long
period of quiet. They danced until midnight, but the youth or maiden who
dared to dance after the hour of twelve was henceforth followed with little
luck. This rule was not often broken, for when it was broken the Spirits of
Evil always walked the earth and brought disaster to the youthful dancers.

In a remote village on the banks of a great river there dwelt in the
seventeenth century a French peasant, a kind and devout old man. He had
but one child, a daughter. She was a handsome girl, and naturally enough
she had many suitors among the young men of the place. One of these she
prized above all the others, and she had promised to become his wife. On
the evening of the Shrove Tuesday before the date set for the wedding, as
was the custom the young people of the village gathered at her home. It was
a simple but joyous gathering, the last which the girl could attend before
her marriage. Right merrily the dance went on, and all the guests were in

*From *Canadian Wonder Tales* by Cyrus Macmillan (London: John Lane, The Bodley
Head, 1920), pp. 162–67. Reprinted by permission of The Bodley Head.

high spirits. Soon after eleven o'clock a sleigh drawn by a great coal-black horse stopped at the door. It contained but one man. Without knocking at the door, the newcomer entered. The rooms were crowded, but the rumor soon spread whisperingly around that a new presence had appeared, and the simple villagers strove to get a look at the tall figure in fine clothes. The old man of the house received the stranger kindly and offered him the best he had in his home, for such was the custom in the old days. One thing the gathering particularly noted—the stranger kept his fur cap on his head, and he did not remove his gloves; but as the night was cold this caused but little wonder.

After the silence caused by the stranger's entrance the music swelled, and again the dance went on. The newcomer chose the old man's daughter as his partner. He came to her and said, "My pretty lass, I hope you will dance with me to-night, and more than once, too." "Certainly," replied the girl, well pleased with the honor, and knowing that her friends would envy her. During the remainder of the evening the stranger never left her side, and dance after dance they had together. From a corner of the room the girl's lover watched the pair in silence and anger.

In a small room opening from that in which the dancers were gathered was an old and pious woman seated on a chest at the foot of a bed, praying fervently. She was the girl's aunt. In one hand she held her beads, with the other she beckoned to her niece to come to her.

"It is very wrong of you," she said, "to forsake your lover for this stranger; his manner is not pleasing to me. Each time I utter the name of the Saviour or the Virgin Mary as he passes the door, he turns from me with a look of anger." But the girl paid no heed to her aunt's advice.

At last it was midnight, and Lent had come. The old man gave the signal for the dance to cease. "Let us have one more dance," said the stranger. "Just one more," pleaded the girl; "my last dance before my marriage." And the old man wishing to please his only child,—for he loved her well,—consented, and although it was already Ash Wednesday the dance went on. The stranger again danced with the girl. "You have been mine all the evening," he whispered; "why should you not be mine for ever?" But the girl laughed at his question. "I am a strange fellow," said the stranger, "and when I will to do a thing it must be done. Only say yes, and nothing can ever separate us." The girl cast a glance towards her dejected lover in the corner of the room. "I understand," said the stranger. "I am too late; you love him."

"Yes," answered the girl, "I love him, or rather I did love him once," for the girl's head had been turned by the attentions of the stranger.

"That is well," said the stranger; "I will arrange all, and overcome all difficulties. Give me your hand to seal our plight."

She placed her hand in his, but at once she withdrew it with a low cry of pain. She had felt in her flesh the point of some sharp instrument as if the stranger held a knife in his hand. In great terror she fainted and was carried to a couch. At once the dance was stopped and the dancers gathered around her, wondering at the sudden happenings. At the same time two villagers came in and called the old man to the door to see a strange sight without. The deep snow for many yards around the stranger's horse and sleigh had melted in the hour since his arrival, and a large patch of bare ground was now showing. Terror soon spread among the guests; they spoke in whispers of fear, and shrank from the centre of the room to the walls as if eager to escape; but the old man begged them not to leave him. The stranger looked with a cold smile upon the dread of the company. He kept close to the couch where the girl was slowly coming back to life. He took from his pocket a beautiful necklace, and said to her, "Take off the glass beads you wear, and for my sake take this beautiful necklace." But to her glass beads was attached a little cross which she did not want to part with, and she refused to take his gift.

Meanwhile, in the home of the priest, some distance away, there was a strange happening. While he prayed for his flock the old priest had fallen asleep. He saw in his slumber a vision of the old man's home and what was happening there. He started quickly from his sleep and called his servant and told him to harness his horse at once, for not far away a soul was in danger of eternal death. He hurried to the old man's home. When he reached there, the stranger had already unfastened the beads from the girl's neck and was about to place his own necklace upon her and to seize her in his arms. But the old priest was too quick for him. He passed his sacred stole around the girl's neck and drew her towards him, and turning to the stranger he said, "What art thou, Evil One, doing among Christians?" At this remark terror was renewed among the guests; some fell to their knees in prayer; all were weeping, for they knew now that the stranger with the stately presence and the velvet clothes was the Spirit of Evil and Death. And the stranger answered, "I do not know as Christians those who forget their faith by dancing on holy days. This fair girl has chosen to be mine. With the blood that flowed from her hand she sealed the compact which binds her to me for ever."

In answer, the old curé struck the stranger hard across the face with his stole, and repeated some Latin words which none of the guests understood. There was a great crash, as if it thundered, and in a moment amid the noise the stranger disappeared; with his horse and sleigh he had vanished as mysteriously and quickly as he had come.

The guests were long in recovering from their fear, and all night they prayed with the curé that their evil deeds might be forgiven. That she might be cleansed from her sins and that her promise to the stranger might be rightly broken, the girl entered a convent to pass the remainder of her life. A few years later she died. And since that day in her little village on the banks of the great river, the Shrove Tuesday dancers have always stopped their dance at midnight; for youths and maidens still keep in mind the strange dancer in the fine clothes who wooed the peasant's only daughter and almost carried her off.

Notes and Comments

Tabus exist in every culture, and they are enforced by tales and legends that illustrate the unhappy fate that befalls anyone foolhardy enough to violate them. "The Shrove Tuesday Visitor" is just such a cautionary tale. It illustrates the dangers that follow anyone who dares to dance during the holy days of Lent. Its lesson is apparently effective, for in the conventionally structured ending we are told: "Since that day in her little village on the banks of the great river, the Shrove Tuesday dancers have always stopped their dance at midnight," remembering the close call one maiden had with the devil himself.

The concept of the devil in folktales is a confusing one. Sometimes the narrator means an oriental demon, an Arabian djinn, a German ogre, or Satan himself. In many stories the terms "stupid ogre," "stupid giant," and "stupid devil" are used interchangeably, but almost all these figures appear to be dangerous, almost unconquerable in verbal or physical combat, and supernaturally powerful.

Physical characteristics of the devil vary also, as well as the methods of detecting his presence. Thanks to medieval artists and writers, a general picture of the devil now includes such items as his cloven hooves, a tail, either pointed ears or horns, and a well-trimmed and pointed beard. Sometimes he is a well-dressed gentleman, as in the "Shrove Tuesday Visitor," but other times he appears inconspicuously dressed, looking no different from the ordinary folk of whatever neighborhood he chooses to frequent. One fellow in the Ozarks described him as wearing "blue overalls, slouch hat, skinny face, long hair, shotgun on shoulder, and so on." When questioned, however, as to why he was so sure he had in fact encountered the devil, he whispered most fearfully: "He didn't throw no shadder! He didn't leave no tracks!" (Randolph, *Ozark Superstitions,* p. 276).

The well-dressed gentleman who appears at the dance on Shrove Tuesday—a significant day because it precedes Ash Wednesday, the first day of Lent—gives many clues to his true identity, especially to one as suspicious and pious as the heroine's old aunt. It is the latter who notices that the stranger grows angry at the mention of the Savior or the Virgin Mary. Later everyone is amazed to find the sleigh has given off enough heat to melt the snow for yards around. Other guests might have suspected that the fur cap he failed to remove was covering either his horns or his pointed ears, or that the gloves he failed to remove covered his devilish claws. But even after he pierces the maiden's hands with these same claws, the guests are more concerned with her swoon, the mysterious happenings of the evening, and their own terror to take any of the traditional protections to ward off the influences of evil.

Fortunately, the priest who has been forewarned in his dream knows that he must accost the devil with his own name, protect the girl with his sacred stole, and drive the fiend away by calling on God. The villagers do not understand Latin, but the devil does, and at the mention of God's name he leaves in a fury. As long as this tale of "The Shrove Tuesday Visitor" is remembered, no one in the village will forget the tabu against dancing on Ash Wednesday.

Tale Type 817   Devil Leaves at Mention of God's Name

Principal Motifs:

G303.4.1.6	Devil has horns
G303.4.4	Devil has claws
G303.3.1.2	Devil as a well-dressed gentleman
G303.9.4.7	Devil tempts girl
G303.10.4.5	Devil dances with maid and puts his claws through her hands
G303.16.3	Devil's power avoided by the cross
G303.16.2.2	Person saved from devil by prayer to Virgin
G303.16.14.1	Priest chases devil away
G303.16.8	Devil leaves at mention of God's name
G303.17.2.5	Devil retreats into Hell amid thunder and lightning
Q386.1	Devil punishes girl who loves to dance
C631	Tabu: breaking the Sabbath
Q223.6.4(B)	Punishment for dancing on Sunday
C631.6	Tabu: Playing music on the Sabbath
G303.16.11.2	Devil prevented from revenge by pious priest
G303.17.2.9	Devil disappears in carriage drawn by four [one] black horses

Parallel Stories in:

Briggs, *Dictionary*, B (1), pp. 95–96
Jones, *Devil*, pp. 16–19 (2 variants)
Laskowski, *Polish*, pp. 169–70
Paredes, *Mexico*, #7
Randolph, *Knapsack*, pp. 12–14
Rose, *Quebec*, pp. 251–52
Wallrich, *Spanish-American*, pp. 52–54 (6 variants)

F

Pattern and Rhythm:
FORMULA TALES

Clickety-clack and pitty-ti-pat: these tales scarcely wind up to a formulaic spiral before SPRONGG . . . they all tumble down again in a riotous rhythmic conclusion. Although these tales vary widely in content and origin, all are categorized by a definite structure that inexorably controls the movement of the plot to its last breathless moment, regardless of the number and nature of characters present.

35. *THE CAT AND THE PARROT*　　　　　　　　223
　　　TT 2027—*The Fat Cat*
　　　TT 2028—*The Troll (Wolf) who was Cut Open*
　　　Also known as *A Swallowing Story*

36. *TALK*　　　　　　　　　　　　　　　　　229
　　　TT 1705—*Talking Horse and Dog*
　　　Also known as *"Imagine That, A Talking Yam!"*

37. *PLOP!*　　　　　　　　　　　　　　　　233
　　　TT 2033—*A Nut Hits the Cock's Head*
　　　Also known as *Henny Penny, Chicken Licken,*
　　　Chickie Birdie

38. *THE CAT AND THE MOUSE* 237
TT 2034—*The Mouse Regains its Tail*
Also known as *The Old Woman and Her Pig, One Fine Day*

39. *THE GINGERBREAD BOY* 242
TT 2025—*The Fleeing Pancake*
Also known as *The Wee Bannock, The Journey-Cake Ho! The Doughnut*

40. *ENDLESS TALES*
    a. *An Endless Story* 247
    TT 2300—*Endless Tales*
    Also known as *And This Sheep Jumped over the Fence*

    b. *A Dark and Stormy Night* 249
    TT 2320—*Rounds*
    Also known as *The Bear Went Over the Mountain; My Eyes Are Dim, I Cannot See*

41. *THE TRAVELS OF A FOX* 251
TT 1655—*The Profitable Exchange*
TT 170—*The Fox Eats his Fellow Lodger*
Also known as *The Bumblebee in the Bag; Going to Squintum's*

35

The Cat and the Parrot*

O nce there was a cat, and a parrot. And they had agreed to ask
each other to dinner, turn and turn about: first the cat should
ask the parrot, then the parrot should invite the cat, and so on. It was the
cat's turn first.

Now the cat was very mean. He provided nothing at all for dinner
except a pint of milk, a little slice of fish, and a biscuit. The parrot was too
polite to complain, but he did not have a very good time.

When it was his turn to invite the cat, he cooked a fine dinner. He
had a roast of meat, a pot of tea, a basket of fruit, and, best of all, he
baked a whole clothesbasketful of little cakes!—little, brown, crispy,
spicy cakes! Oh, I should say as many as five hundred. And he put four
hundred and ninety-eight of the cakes before the cat, keeping only two
for himself.

Well, the cat ate the roast, and drank the tea, and sucked the fruit, and
then he began on the pile of cakes. He ate all the four hundred and ninety-
eight cakes, and then he looked round and said:—

"I'm hungry; haven't you anything to eat?"

*From *How to Tell Stories to Children* by Sara Cone Bryant (Boston: Houghton Mifflin,
1905), pp. 159–63.

"Why," said the parrot, "here are my two cakes, if you want them?" The cat ate up the two cakes, and then he licked his chops and said, "I am beginning to get an appetite; have you anything to eat?"

"Well, really," said the parrot, who was now rather angry, "I don't see anything more, unless you wish to eat me!" He thought the cat would be ashamed when he heard that—but the cat just looked at him and licked his chops again,—and slip! slop! gobble! down his throat went the parrot!

Then the cat started down the street. An old woman was standing by, and she had seen the whole thing, and she was shocked that the cat should eat his friend. "Why, cat!" she said, "how dreadful of you to eat your friend the parrot!"

"Parrot, indeed!" said the cat. "What's a parrot to me?—I've a great mind to eat you, too." And—before you could say "Jack Robinson"—slip! slop! gobble! down went the old woman!

Then the cat started down the road again, walking like this, because he felt so fine. Pretty soon he met a man driving a donkey. The man was beating the donkey, to hurry him up, and when he saw the cat he said, "Get out of my way, cat; I'm in a hurry and my donkey might tread on you."

"Donkey, indeed!" said the cat, "much I care for a donkey! I have eaten five hundred cakes, I've eaten my friend the parrot, I've eaten an old woman,—what's to hinder my eating a miserable man and a donkey?"

And slip! slop! gobble! down went the old man and the donkey.

Then the cat walked on down the road, jauntily, like this. After a little, he met a procession, coming that way. The king was at the head, walking proudly with his newly married bride, and behind him were his soldiers, marching, and behind them were ever and ever so many elephants, walking two by two. The king felt very kind to everybody, because he had just been married, and he said to the cat, "Get out of my way, pussy, get out of my way,—my elephants might hurt you."

"Hurt me!" said the cat, shaking his fat sides. "Ho, ho! I've eaten five hundred cakes, I've eaten my friend the parrot, I've eaten an old woman, I've eaten a man and a donkey; what's to hinder my eating a beggarly king?"

And slip! slop! gobble! down went the king; down went the queen; down went the soldiers,—and down went all the elephants!

Then the cat went on, more slowly; he had really had enough to eat, now. But a little farther on he met two land-crabs, scuttling along in the dust. "Get out of our way, pussy," they squeaked.

"Ho, ho ho!" cried the cat in a terrible voice. "I've eaten five hundred cakes, I've eaten my friend the parrot, I've eaten an old woman, a man with a donkey, a king, a queen, his men-at-arms, and all his elephants; and now I'll eat you too."

And slip! slop! gobble! down went the two land-crabs.

When the land-crabs got down inside, they began to look around. It was very dark, but they could see the poor king sitting in a corner with his bride on his arm; she had fainted. Near them were the men-at-arms, treading on one another's toes, and the elephants, still trying to form in twos, —but they couldn't, because there was not room. In the opposite corner sat the old woman, and near her stood the man and his donkey. But in the other corner was a great pile of cakes, and by them perched the parrot, his feathers all drooping.

"Let's get to work!" said the land-crabs. And, snip, snap, they began to make a little hole in the side, with their sharp claws. Snip, snap, snip, snap,—till it was big enough to get through. Then out they scuttled.

Then out walked the king, carrying his bride; out marched the men-at-arms; out tramped the elephants, two by two; out came the old man, beating his donkey; out walked the old woman, scolding the cat; and last of all, out hopped the parrot, holding a cake in each claw. (You remember, two cakes was all he wanted?)

But the poor cat had to spend the whole day sewing up the hole in his coat!

Notes and Comments

This cumulative tale is one of several that involve the motif of extraordinary swallowing, either by eating great quantities or by swallowing an impossible chain of objects. In almost all swallowing tales, those creatures unfortunate enough to have been eaten manage to escape with little damage either to themselves or, in some instances, to the swallower himself. Thompson has assigned numbers F911–F929 to motifs of the extraordinary swallowings. Some of the more famous examples are found as early as Greek mythology or the Bible.

In one myth Cronus, the ancient Greek Titan, fears a prophecy that his sons will rise up and kill him; therefore, he swallows them all as soon as they are born. His wife, Rhea, in angry despair, at last presents her husband Cronus with a stone wrapped in a blanket instead of the baby Zeus. Zeus later grows to manhood, slays his father, and fulfills the prophecy, whereupon all the previously swallowed children emerge from his stomach unharmed, along with, of course, a single large stone wrapped in a blanket.

The folktale of "The Wolf and Seven Little Kids" (Tale Type 123) is similar to this Greek myth in that the wolf eats all the baby goats and goes to the riverbank to sleep. Later, the mother goat finds him, cuts open his stomach, and replaces the kids with large stones. The goat awakens, goes for a drink, and is dragged into the lake by all those heavy stones in his stomach. Tom Thumb (Tale Type 700) is swallowed by a cow, a fish, and a giant; Puss in Boots (Tale Type 545B) swallows the ogre in the form of a mouse; and Little Red Riding Hood (Tale Type 333) assists in rescuing her grandmother who has been swallowed by the wolf.

The biblical story of Jonah and the whale is still another ancestor of swallowing stories. Jonah's adventures, however, parallel a second type of story, the pourquoi tale such as "The Prisoner" from the South Seas. In that story the maiden is swallowed by a large fish too, but she escapes by slashing the sides of the fish with some *tapa* shells she has in her sarong. This act, the islanders claim, is why all fish have gills today.

The version of "The Cat and the Parrot" printed here is a third type of swallowing story—swallowing an impossible chain of objects. While our cat merely swallows five hundred cakes, his friend the parrot, an old woman, a man and a donkey, a king, a queen, and an entire wedding procession including elephants and soldiers, and two lowly land crabs, other swallowers have been similarly expansive. One animal has an entire card game going on inside his stomach (F911.3.3); one voracious monster has entire towns of people and buildings inside (F911.6); and one small louse in an Indian tale eats a crow, a loaf of bread, a she goat, a cow buffalo, five sepoys, a wedding procession with one lac (an indefinitely large number) of people, an elephant, and a tank of water.

"Drakestail" in Andrew Lang's famous story, needs all the help he can get in order to get his money back from the king. On his journey to the palace, he swallows friend Fox, lady-friend Ladder, friend River, and comrade Wasp's nest. All these helpers turn out to be most necessary at the time of the great battle when Drakestail confronts the king singing:

Quack, quack, quack,
When shall I get my money back.

For effective narration, such a repetitive refrain often accompanies the repetitive swallowings. In "The Cat and the Parrot" the cat consumes his chain of objects with a "slip! slop! gobble!" Another swallower in Kentucky sings:

Take a bite of honey
Take a bite of hay—
Gobble you up!

A Negro informant in Michigan sings:

I eat a barrel of pickle,
I drink a barrel of wine,
I'll eat you if I catch you,

prior to swallowing a little girl, a little boy, an old lady, an old farmer, and almost a rabbit. But while chasing the rabbit, he trips over barbed wire and bursts open.

This method of the victim's escape is essentially what distinguishes Tale Type 2027 *The Fat Cat* from Tale Type 2028 *The Troll (Wolf) who was Cut Open.* In the former, the swallower bursts from excessive eating or from falling. In the latter, the swallower is indiscriminate in the objects he swallows, and either fails to check whether the person swallowed has a sharp object in his pocket or whether the usually inconspicuous animals once swallowed have sharp claws.

The hero of Robert McCloskey's *Burt Dow, Deep Water Man* chooses a third method of escape. Bert, a house painter who happens to have a few cans of leftover paint on hand when he is swallowed by a whale, creates brilliant Pollock-like pictures on the walls of the whale's stomach with the paint, until an enormous belch of rumbling wind finally expels him, boat, paint, and all, onto the sea again where still further adventures await him.

Tale Type 2027 The Fat Cat
2028 The Troll (Wolf) who was Cut Open

Principal Motif:

Z33.2 The fat cat

Parallel Stories in:

Briggs, *Dictionary,* A (2), p. 347
Chase, *Grandfather,* #7
Dorson, *Michigan,* p. 199
———, *Cante Fable,* pp. 84–85
Roberts, *South,* #77b, #77c

PICTURE BOOKS:

The Wolf and the Seven Kids. Felix Hoffmann. New York: Harcourt, Brace and World, 1959. (Set in Germany)

The Fat Cat. Jack Kent. New York: Parent's Magazine Press, 1971. (Set in Germany)

Burt Dow, Deep Water Man. Robert McCloskey. New York: Viking Press, 1963. (Set in Maine)

36

*Talk**

An Ashanti Tale

O nce, not far from the city of Accra on the Gulf of Guinea, a country man went out to his garden to dig up some yams to take to market. While he was digging, one of the yams said to him, "Well, at last you're here. You never weeded me, but now you come around with your digging stick. Go away and leave me alone!"

The farmer turned around and looked at his cow in amazement. The cow was chewing her cud and looking at him.

"Did you say something?" he asked.

The cow kept on chewing and said nothing, but the man's dog spoke up. "It wasn't the cow who spoke to you," the dog said. "It was the yam. The yam says leave him alone."

The man became angry, because his dog had never talked before, and he didn't like his tone besides. So he took his knife and cut a branch from a palm tree to whip his dog. Just then the palm tree said, "Put that branch down!"

The man was getting very upset about the way things were going, and

*From *The Cow-Tail Switch and Other West African Stories* by Harold Courlander and George Herzog (New York: Henry Holt & Co., 1947), pp. 25–29. Copyright 1947, © 1975 by Holt, Rinehart and Winston. Reprinted by permission of Holt, Rinehart and Winston, Publishers.

he started to throw the palm branch away, but the palm branch said, "Man, put me down softly!"

He put the branch down gently on a stone, and the stone said, "Hey, take that thing off me!"

This was enough, and the frightened farmer started to run for his village. On the way he met a fisherman going the other way with a fish trap on his head.

"What's the hurry?" the fisherman asked.

"My yam said, 'Leave me alone!' Then the dog said, 'Listen to what the yam says!' When I went to whip the dog with a palm branch the tree said, 'Put that branch down!' Then the palm branch said, 'Do it softly!' Then the stone said, 'Take that thing off me!' "

"Is that all?" the man with the fish trap asked. "Is that so frightening?"

"Well," the man's fish trap said, "did he take it off the stone?"

"Wah!" the fisherman shouted. He threw the fish trap on the ground and began to run with the farmer, and on the trail they met a weaver with a bundle of cloth on his head.

"Where are you going in such a rush?" he asked them.

"My yam said, 'Leave me alone!' " the farmer said. "The dog said, 'Listen to what the yam says!' The tree said, 'Put that branch down!' The branch said, 'Do it softly!' And the stone said, 'Take that thing off me!' "

"And then," the fisherman continued, "the fish trap said, 'Did he take it off?' "

"That's nothing to get excited about," the weaver said. "No reason at all."

"Oh, yes it is," his bundle of cloth said. "If it happened to you you'd run too!"

"Wah!" the weaver shouted. He threw his bundle on the trail and started running with the other men.

They came panting to the ford in the river and found a man bathing. "Are you chasing a gazelle?" he asked them.

The first man said breathlessly, "My yam talked at me, and it said, 'Leave me alone!' And my dog said, 'Listen to your yam!' And when I cut myself a branch the tree said, 'Put that branch down!' And the branch said, 'Do it softly!' And the stone said, 'Take that thing off me!' "

The fisherman panted, "And my trap said, 'Did he?' "

The weaver wheezed, "And my bundle of cloth said, 'You'd run too!' "

"Is that why you're running?" the man in the river asked.

"Well, wouldn't you run if you were in their position?" the river said.

The man jumped out of the water and began to run with the others. They ran down the main street of the village to the house of the chief. The chief's servant brought his stool out, and he came and sat on it to listen to their complaints. The men began to recite their troubles.

"I went out to my garden to dig yams," the farmer said, waving his arms. "Then everything began to talk! My yam said, 'Leave me alone!' My dog said, 'Pay attention to your yam!' The tree said, 'Put that branch down!' The branch said, 'Do it softly!' And the stone said, 'Take it off me!' "

"And my fish trap said, 'Well, did he take it off?' " the fisherman said.

"And my cloth said, 'You'd run too!' " the weaver said.

"And the river said the same," the bather said hoarsely, his eyes bulging.

The chief listened to them patiently, but he couldn't refrain from scowling. "Now this is really a wild story," he said at last. "You'd better all go back to your work before I punish you for disturbing the peace."

So the men went away, and the chief shook his head and mumbled to himself, "Nonsense like that upsets the community."

"Fantastic, isn't it?" his stool said. "Imagine, a talking yam!"

Notes and Comments

The Ashanti tale "Talk" is a cumulative chain tale with the final chain being presented to the wisdom and judgment of the chief for his verdict. The surprise ending is characteristic of a whole genre of tales known collectively as "Shaggy Dog Stories." Jan Brunvand in *The Study of American Folklore* (p. 114) offers a definition of a shaggy dog story as follows: "A nonsensical joke that employs in the punchline a psychological non sequitur, a punning variation of a familiar saying, or a hoax, to trick the listener who expects conventional wit or humor." As the reader listens along with the Ashanti chief to the story of the magical talking yam, he certainly doesn't expect the stool of the chief to talk.

A similar tale type centered around Motif B210.2, "Talking animal or object refuses to talk on demand," depicts just the opposite predicament. Vance Randolph uses one version of this type as the lead story in *The Talking Turtle and Other Ozark Folk Tales.* There a man noted throughout the town not only for always telling the truth but also for talking too much is warned by the turtle that he talks too much. When the man realizes excitedly that he has just heard a turtle talking, he runs to get all the people from the tavern to listen to the turtle. Of course the turtle doesn't say a word, and the townspeople in anger kick the poor man into the ditch, whereupon the turtle laughs and says "Didn't I tell you? . . . You talk too damn much." Randolph then notes that in the original form of this story told in the Gold Coast, the man is put to death when the turtle refuses to talk.

Tale Type 1705   Talking Horse and Dog

Principal Motifs:

B211.1.7 Speaking dog
F990   Inanimate objects act as if living
D1610   Magic Speaking Object

Variant motif:

B210.2   Talking animal or object refuses to talk on demand

Parallel Stories in:

Briggs, *England,* #84
Halpert, *City Jests,* p. 19
Hurston, *Mules and Men,* pp. 217–18 (reprinted in Botkin, *American,* pp. 440–41)
Parsons, *Aiken,* #13
Thomas, *Tall Stories,* pp. 7–8

Variants of Motif B210.2 in:

Barker, *West African,* pp. 119–21
Botkin, *Southern,* p. 510
Brewer, *Juneteenth,* pp. 48–50
Frobenius, *African Genesis,* pp. 161–62
Hurston, *Mules and Men,* pp. 219–20
Parsons, *Guilford County,* #11
Randolph, *Turtle,* pp. 3–5, 179–80

37

Plop!*

M any, many years ago there were six rabbits who lived on the shore of a lake, in a forest. One fine day, a big ripe fruit on one of the biggest trees fell down into the lake, making a loud "plop!" when it hit the water. The rabbits were terrified, not knowing what the noise could be, and at once made off as fast as their four legs could carry them.

A fox saw them fleeing and called out, "Why are you flying?" The rabbits said, "Plop is coming!" When the fox heard this, he immediately started to flee with them. Next they ran into a monkey, who queried, "Why are you in such a hurry?" "Plop is coming!" replied the fox. So the monkey also joined in their flight.

Thus the news spread from mouth to mouth until a deer, a pig, a buffalo, a rhinoceros, an elephant, a black bear, a brown bear, a leopard, a tiger, and a lion were all running away, helter-skelter.

They had no thought at all, except to fly. The faster they ran, the more frightened they became.

At the foot of the hill there lived a lion with a great long mane. When he caught sight of the other lion running, he roared to him, "Brother, you

*From *I Saw A Rocket Walk a Mile* edited by Carl Withers (New York: Holt, Rinehart and Winston, 1965), pp. 123–25. Copyright © 1965 by Carl Withers. Reprinted by permission of Holt, Rinehart and Winston, Publishers.

have claws and teeth and you are the strongest of all animals. Why are you running like mad?"

"Plop is coming!" the running lion panted.

"Who's Plop? What is he?" the lion with the long mane demanded.

"Well, I really don't know," he faltered.

"Why make such a fuss then?" the long-maned lion went on. "Let's find out what it is first. Who told you about it?"

"The tiger told me."

The inquisitive lion with the long mane asked the tiger, who said that the leopard had told him, so the lion turned to the leopard, and the leopard answered that he had heard it from the brown bear. The question was passed on to the brown bear, who said he had heard it from the black bear. In this way, the black bear, the elephant, the rhinoceros, the buffalo, the pig and the deer were all asked, one by one, and each of them said he was told by someone else. Finally it came down to the fox's testimony, and he said, "The rabbits told me." Then the lion went up to the rabbits, who squeaked in chorus:

"All six of us heard this terrible Plop with our own ears. Come with us, we'll show you where we heard him."

They led him to the forest, and pointing at it, they said, "The terrible Plop is there."

Just at this moment another big fruit fell from the tree and dropped into the water with a deep "plop!"

The lion sneered. "Now, look, all of you!" he said. "You've all seen what that plop is. It's only the sound of a fruit dropping into the water. What is so terrifying about that? You almost ran your legs off!"

They breathed a sigh of relief. The panic was all for naught.

Notes and Comments

American readers of this Tibetan tale, long familiar with the repetitive "Henny-Penny," "Turkey-Lurkey," "Duckey-Daddles," and "Chicken-Licken" may be surprised to learn that this tale type has an ancient literary ancestry reaching back as far as *The Jataka Tales,* a collection of over five hundred stories written in India during the second and third centuries B.C. These ancient stories are primarily about the many rebirths of the Buddha and concern his adventures when he walked on earth in animal form. Several stories, omitting reference to the Buddha, have reappeared as popular folk tales, for example, the story of "The Tar Baby." (See notes to tale 42.)

The central character in one Jataka tale is a little nervous hare who, like her sillier human sister in "Bastianelo" (see Noodles section), worries about those things that might come to pass. In "Bastianelo," the new bride worries about the demise of her yet unconceived son; the little hare's greatest concern is "Suppose the Earth were to fall in, what would happen to me?" Preoccupied with such fears, she runs frantically when she hears a heavy fruit fall on a rustling leaf. Later the kind and gentle Buddha, now in the form of a wise lion, takes the little hare back to the scene of the fearful crash, carrying her on his back and supporting her fears with his strength.

Readers of C. S. Lewis's *Narnia* books will recall a similar triumphant ride on the back of the great lion Aslan in *The Lion, The Witch and The Wardrobe,* with Lucy and Susan holding on tightly to his mane. Lewis describes such a ride as the ultimate fantasy of every child:

> Have you ever had a gallop on a horse? Think of that; and then take away the heavy noise of the hoofs and the jingle of the harness and imagine instead the almost noiseless padding of the great paws. Then imagine instead of the black or grey or chestnut back of the horse the soft roughness of golden fur, and the mane flying back in the wind. And then imagine you are going about twice as fast as the fastest racehorse. But this is a mount that doesn't need to be guided and never grows tired. He rushes on and on, never missing his footing, never hesitating, threading his way with perfect skill between tree-trunks, jumping over bush and briar and the smaller streams, wading the larger, swimming the largest of all. (Ch. 15)

Like the kind and gentle Aslan, the great Buddha-lion of the Jataka tale offers no reproof to the little hare after she discovers her mistake about the earth falling in—only a compassionate suggestion to her: "Shall we go back and tell the other animals?"

Such compassion is typical of the Buddhistic attitude and the tales of the Jataka, but it is not always evident in the tales that bypass the original cultural and religious elements. In "Plop!" the lion with the great long mane is still the one who has the wisdom to sort out the situation and to prevent a generalized panic, but his arrogant and sneering remarks are quite different from the gentleness of the Jataka lion.

Different too, is the reason for the panic in the two stories. In the Jataka tale, the inner nervousness of the little hare, her constant worrying about things that might be and disasters that might befall, causes her to jump at the first sign that her worst fears have been realized. In "Plop!" there is not even any safety in numbers, for six timid hares abandon their reasons and magnify the sound of a ripe fruit falling until it becomes a monster in their imaginations. Fear overcomes common sense; panic spreads; and all the animals except the lion with the great long mane can think of nothing else but to flee, shouting and pointing to the surface of the water, "The terrible Plop is there."

Neither compassion nor arrogance is present in the Henny-Penny type tales popular with children today. Hilarity is the rule, and cumulative rhyming words of animal names is the method in such tales as "Chickie Birdie," "Chicken Licken," or "The Hen and Her Fellow Travelers." The fate of all these silly animals is little different from that of another swift-running character, the Pancake, and they all are usually eaten by a fox in the end. Henny-Penny tales indeed illustrate the changes that can take place when a tale is passed on through time and retold by those who know nothing of its original cultural content.

Tale Type 2033   A Nut Hits the Cock's Head

Principal Motif:

J1810   Physical phenomena misunderstood

Parallel Stories in:

Briggs, *Dictionary*, A (2) (4 versions)
Burlingame, *Elephant*, #15
Feldman, *Storytelling*, p. 156
Halliwell, *Nursery*, pp. 31–32
Jacobs, *English*, #20
Kennedy, *End* (reprinted in Kennedy, *Fireside*, p. 25)
Morrison, *Manx*, pp. 78–82
Shedlock, *Eastern Stories*, pp. 3–6

38

The Cat and the Mouse*

The Cat and the Mouse
Played in the malt-house.
The Cat bit the Mouse's tail off.

Pray, puss," said the Mouse, "give me my long tail again."
"No," said the Cat, "I'll not give you your tail again till you go to the cow and fetch me some milk."

First she leaped, and then she ran,
Till she came to the cow, and thus began:

"Pray, cow, give me some milk that I may give to the Cat, so she may give me my long tail again."
"No," said the cow, "I will give you no milk till you go to the farmer and get me some hay."

---

*From *Tales of Laughter* by Kate Wiggin (New York: Doubleday, Page, and Co., 1927), pp. 222–23. Copyright 1908, 1926 by Doubleday & Company, Inc. Used by permission of Doubleday & Company, Inc.

First she leaped, and then she ran,
Till she came to the farmer, and thus began:

"Pray, farmer, give me some hay that I may give to the cow, so she may give me some milk that I may give to the Cat, so she may give me my long tail again."

"No," says the farmer, "I'll give you no hay till you go to the butcher and fetch me some meat."

First she leaped, and then she ran,
Till she came to the butcher, and thus began:

"Pray butcher, give me some meat that I may give to the farmer, so he may give me some hay that I may give to the cow, so she may give me some milk that I may give to the Cat, so she may give me my long tail again."

"No," said the butcher, "I'll give you no meat till you go to the baker and fetch me some bread."

First she leaped, and then she ran,
Till she came to the baker, and thus began:

"Pray, baker, give me some bread that I may give to the butcher, so he may give me some meat that I may give to the farmer, so he may give me some hay that I may give to the cow, so she may give me some milk that I may give to the Cat, so she may give me my long tail again."

"Yes," said the baker, "I'll give you some bread,
But if you eat my meal, I'll cut off your head."

The baker gave the Mouse bread, which she brought to the butcher; the butcher gave the Mouse meat, which she brought to the farmer; the farmer gave the Mouse hay, which she brought to the cow; the cow gave the Mouse milk, which she brought to the Cat; and the Cat gave to the Mouse her long tail again.

Notes and Comments

Cumulative tales depend for their effect on repetition of actions and reactions. The scholarly term for such an effect in traditional ballads is "incremental repetition," in which each repetition builds on the last action in a "same song—second verse" pattern. The effect is of a slowly building spiral with each event adding to the preceding one until the climax of the tale is reached, at which point all details turn around and slide rapidly back down the same spiral.

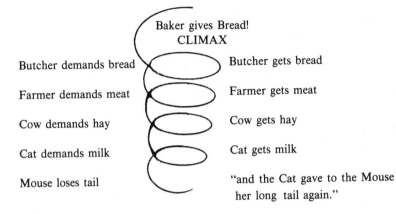

Baker gives Bread!
CLIMAX

Butcher demands bread   Butcher gets bread

Farmer demands meat   Farmer gets meat

Cow demands hay   Cow gets hay

Cat demands milk   Cat gets milk

Mouse loses tail   "and the Cat gave to the Mouse her long tail again."

One informant in the Ozarks referred to these stories as "buildup stories"; another informant speaking of a similar tale remembers: "This foolish tale I loved when I was little. What the old woman says to different things belongs to be said kinda quick and devilish." Many writers commenting on the effect of the downward spiral sense the feel of the story as "unwinding."

Many versions of Type 2034 *The Mouse Regains its Tail* exist, and they differ from Type 2030 *The Old Woman and her Pig* only in the nature of the problem. The mouse needs to get its tail put back on; the old woman needs to get her pig over the fence in time for supper. Otherwise, the form of the tales is exactly the same and should be considered an archetype of the cumulative tale.

This particular version of "The Cat and the Mouse" is included because of the interesting rhythm of the refrain as well as the unusual setting in the beginning. The refrain functions much as a refrain in a traditional ballad does by allowing the storyteller to pause a moment on familiar ground in order to sort out the next sequence of events. But even while the teller pauses, the fast rhythm of the refrain keeps the story moving briskly forward. An equally interesting refrain was given by a Texas informant who remembers:

And away he went trittety trot;
The faster he went the sooner he got.

A refrain also appears in the cante-fable form of "The Old Woman and Her Pig" in a Kentucky version collected by Leonard Roberts:

I can't get to my little boy tonight,
It's almost dark but the moon shines.

Roberts reports that the singing "is repeated after each cumulation, singing the first phrase with some speed, but slowing on the second and holding the last word." (*Sang Branch,* p. 217.)

The function of this tale is primarily to entertain, but Campbell reports that in the Scottish Highlands at the turn of the century "it is the infant ladder to learning a chain of cause and effect, and fully as sensible as any of its kind." He notes that it is the best known of all Gaelic tales and adds that "it used to be commonly taught to children of five or six years of age, and repeated by school boys, and . . . is still remembered by grown-up people in all parts of the Highlands." (*West Highlands* I, p. 164).

The continuing popularity of this cumulative tale was evident when it received the Caldecott Medal in 1971 as a picture book by Nonny Hogrogian entitled *One Fine Day,* a version in which a fox loses his extremely fine and bushy tail.

Tale Type 2034   The Mouse Regains its Tail

Principal Motif:

Z41.4   The mouse regains its tail

Variant motif:

Z41   The old woman and her pig

Parallel Stories in:

Afanas'ev, pp. 17–19
Dobie, *Texas Household,* p. 38–41 (references)
Jacobs, *English,* #34
Johnson, *What They Say,* pp. 141–42
Newall, *Passover Song,* p. 34, fn. #3 for bibliography on "The Cat and the Mouse"
Nichols, *Nursery,* p. 229
Roberts, *Sang Branch,* #131
Saucier, *Louisiana,* #29

Variants of 2030 in:

Beckwith, *Jamaica Anansi,* #138
Brewster, *House,* pp. 209–12 (study)
Campbell, John, *West Highlands,* 1:161–65
Campbell, Marie, *Cloud Walking,* pp. 202–05
Emeneau, *India* (major study)
Fauset, *Nova Scotia,* #15 (3 variants)
Halliwell, *Nursery* (1849), pp. 34–35
Jacobs, *English,* #4
Johnson, *What They Say,* 135–39
Kent, *Turkey,* pp. 122–27
Newall, *Passover Song,* pp. 33–48 (major study)
Randolph, *Turtle,* pp. 61–62, 196–97 (references)
Roberts, *Sang Branch,* #105
———, *Cante Fable,* pp. 86–88

PICTURE BOOKS:

TT2030   *The Monkey's Whiskers.* Anne Rockwell. New York: Parents' Magazine Press, 1971.

TT2030   *The Old Woman and Her Pig.* Paul Galdone, New York: McGraw Hill, 1960.

TT2034   *One Fine Day.* Nonny Hogrogian. New York: Macmillan, 1971.

39

The Gingerbread Boy*

Now you shall hear a story that somebody's great-great-grandmother told a little girl ever so many years ago:

There was once a little old man and a little old woman, who lived in a little old house in the edge of a wood. They would have been a very happy old couple but for one thing—they had no little child, and they wished for one very much. One day, when the little old woman was baking gingerbread, she cut a cake in the shape of a little boy, and put it into the oven.

Presently, she went to the oven to see if it was baked. As soon as the oven door was opened, the little gingerbread boy jumped out, and began to run away as fast as he could go.

The little old woman called her husband, and they both ran after him. But they could not catch him. And soon the gingerbread boy came to a barn full of threshers. He called out to them as he went by, saying

I've run away from a little old woman,
  A little old man,
And I can run away from you, I can!

*From St. Nicholas 2 (May 1875): 448–49.

Then the barn full of threshers set out to run after him. But, though they ran fast, they could not catch him. And he ran on till he came to a field full of mowers. He called out to them:

I've run away from a little old woman,
  A little old man,
  A barn full of threshers,
And I can run away from you, I can!

Then the mowers began to run after him, but they couldn't catch him. And he ran on till he came to a cow. He called out to her:

I've run away from a little old woman,
  A little old man,
  A barn full of threshers,
  A field full of mowers,
And I can run away from you, I can!

But, though the cow started at once, she couldn't catch him. And soon he came to a pig. He called out to the pig:

I've run away from a little old woman,
  A little old man,
  A barn full of threshers,
  A field full of mowers,
  A cow
And I can run away from you, I can!

But the pig ran, and couldn't catch him. And he ran till he came across a fox, and to him he called out:

I've run away from a little old woman,
  A little old man,
  A barn full of threshers,
  A field full of mowers,
  A cow and a pig,
And I can run away from you, I can!

Then the fox set out to run. Now foxes can run very fast, and so the fox soon caught the gingerbread boy and began to eat him up.

Presently the gingerbread boy said: "Oh, dear! I'm quarter gone!" And then: "Oh, I'm half gone!" And soon: "I'm three-quarters gone!" And at last: "I'm all gone!" and never spoke again.

Notes and Comments

This cumulative tale is the mirror image of "The Cat and the Parrot," but the main boast of the hero is not that he has eaten so many items but that he himself has not been eaten during a chain of encounters. If the central character is a gingerbread boy, he may taunt his pursuers:

> Run, run as fast as you can,
> You can't catch me, I'm the Gingerbread Man.

If the central character is an American pancake, a Scottish bannock, or a Russian bun, it may roll merrily along with the old man and old woman chasing it and asking those they meet, "Did you see a johnny-cake going by here flippity-flop, flippity-flop?" Or the bannock itself may sing as it rolls by:

> I've beat a wee wife,
> And I've beat a wee man,
> And I've beat a wee sheep,
> And I've beat a wee goat,
> And I'll try and beat ye too if I can.

But the ending is almost always the same; the wily fox waits somewhere just around the corner. The unfortunate bannock's last words are "Oh, ye're nippin's, ye're nippin's," or the gingerbread boy wails, "Oh dear! I'm quarter gone!" or the poor pancake never manages a word as he is carried across the stream on an animal's snout and swallowed in one gulp, and the narrator is left with: "as the poor pancake could go no farther, why—this story can go no farther either."

Almost all cumulative stories are fun to tell, and Fanny D. Bergen recalls (in *JAF* 2) how she heard this story when she was a little girl in northern Ohio:

> The chorus of the tale . . . was repeated to us in a sort of hoarse chant and, I remember, gave the impression of being loudly and tauntingly called back to the listener, by the rapidly vanishing Johnny-cake. The final word, too, of this chorus, was always pronounced very slowly, in a specially loud tone.

Then in a scaring technique similar to the one always employed when telling any version of "The Golden Arm," Mrs. Bergen remembers that at the climax, when the sly fox grabs the unsuspecting Johnny-cake, the narrator would make a spring at the rapt listeners to the tale and scream OH! so as to make the children jump.

While modern readers may be able to recall hearing this story as children, they may not be able to remember just how a johnny-cake was made. One eighty-year-old grandmother in Texas, fearful that such culinary knowledge would be forgotten, wrote down the method of making these pancakes around the middle of the last century:

> People would have an oak or hickory board, much like the middle of a barrel head, about six inches across. On this board they would pat out cornmeal dough about an inch thick, and then spread cream all over it with a knife and make it smooth, and put the board down on the hearth before a bed of coals or a hot fire and bake the edges first. Then, when the dough was baked about the edges, they would set the board up straight with a flat iron behind it to hold it up. When the lower side was brown, they would turn the upper side down so that the johnny-cake might bake an even brown.

The same procedure was then repeated for the other side, and she remembers "there never was a sweeter bread to eat with butter or milk than this" (Dobie, *Texas Household,* p. 31).

The version of "The Gingerbread Boy" printed here was first published in the *St. Nicholas Magazine* in May 1875 and has formed the basis for the versions most commonly found in children's books. The *St. Nicholas Magazine* was the most famous children's magazine ever published and marked a turning point in the concept of the nature of children's literature. Mary Mapes Dodge, the editor, wrote in 1873, "Let there be no sermonizing, no spinning out of facts, no rattling of dry bones. . . . The ideal child's magazine is a pleasure ground." Thus with the advent of *St. Nicholas,* didacticism as the chief element in reading for children began to fade away.

The revolutionary idea that literature for children should be enjoyable and imaginative was popular with many of the most famous authors of the day. Such well-known writers for children as Louisa May Alcott, Robert Louis Stevenson, Rudyard Kipling, Francis Hodgson Burnett, Lucretia Hale, and Laura E. Richards wrote for this magazine which guided children's reading for over half a century. The inclusion of this favorite nursery tale, "The Gingerbread Boy," in a magazine designed to please children was in tune with the times in the nineteenth century.

Tale Type 2025   The Fleeing Pancake

Principal Motif:

Z33.1   The fleeing pancake

Parallel Stories in:

Afanas'ev, pp. 447–49
Asbjørnsen, *Fjeld,* pp. 121–25
Bergen, *Johnny-Cake,* pp. 60–62 (reprinted in Jacobs, *English,* #28)
Briggs, *Dictionary,* A (2), pp. 540–41, 575–76
Dobie, *Texas Household,* pp. 30–33
Harris, *Remus* (Fate of Mr. Jack Sparrow)
Jacobs, *English,* #28
——, *More English,* #57
Kennedy, *Fireside,* pp. 19–20
Kittredge, *English Folk-Tales,* pp. 291–92
Whiting, *English Folk,* pp. 217–18

PICTURE BOOKS:

The Gingerbread Boy. Retold by Nova Nestrick and illustrated by Bonnie and Bill
  Rutherford and Eulalie. New York: Platt and Munk, 1961. (Set in England)
Journey Cake Ho! Retold by Ruth Sawyer and illustrated by Robert McCloskey.
  New York: Viking Press, 1953. (Set in America)

40a

*An Endless Story**

L ong ago all the rats in Nagasaki got together and decided that
since there was nothing left to eat in Nagasaki, they would cross
over to Satsuma. They boarded a ship and set out. It happened that on the
way they met a ship on which all the rats in Satsuma had gone aboard,
intending to go to Nagasaki. They asked one another how things were and
discovered that there was nothing to eat in either Satsuma or Nagasaki.
There was no use in going to Nagasaki nor any use in going to Satsuma,
so they decided to jump into the sea and drown.

The first rat began to cry, *chu chu,* and jumped over with a splash.
Then another rat cried, *chu chu,* and jumped over with a splash. Then
another cried, *chu chu,* and jumped over with a splash . . .

Notes and Comments

Certain European countries, Hungary in particular, are especially fond
of telling endless tales. The tale (if it may be called such) is the repetition

*From *Folktales of Japan* edited by Keigo Seki. Translated by Robert J. Adams (Chicago:
University of Chicago Press, 1963). Reprinted by permission of the publisher. Text from
Japanese Folktales. Tokyo: Iwanami Shoten, 1956–57.

of a particular task that must be repeated an infinite number of times. Either the listener interrupts the tale in total exasperation or he is stupefied into unconsciousness.

The tales show little variation beyond the item that is taken and the animal that removes it. Thus O'Suilleabhain notes an Irish version in which corn is taken, grain by grain, by an ant. In an Ozark variant, locusts come in through a hole in the barn and take the corn out grain by grain.

In Addy's *Household Tales* there is another endless tale of Type 2301A *Making the King Lose Patience*. The frame of the tale is a suitor test— whoever can tell an endless tale will marry the princess. The successful poor man tells the tale of a locust removing corn grain by grain. The king loses patience and the poor man wins the princess.

Vance Randolph says of these "teaser yarns" that they are

> a familiar type of bedtime story, an answer to boys and girls who set up a clamor for entertainment. Such tales are drawled out in a deliberately sedative, hypnotic monotone; no attention is paid to interruptions or comments. If the storyteller sticks to his last, the child soon falls asleep.

> (Randolph, *Devil's*, p. 192)

Tale Type 2300   Endless Tales

Principal Motif:

Z11   Endless tales

Parallel Stories in:

Addy, *Household*, #14
Briggs, *Dictionary* (A2), pp. 519–20
Barbeau, *Contes Populaires*, #25c
Brendle, *Pennsylvania German*, p. 134
Lanctôt, *Contes*, #15[3] (in French, 3 variants)
O'Suilleabhain, *Handbook*, p. 588
Randolph, *Devil's*, p. 75

40b

A Dark and Stormy Night*

I t was a dark and stormy night, and the captain and all his men were around the campfire. One of the men rose and said "Captain, tell us a story." So the captain began.

"It was a dark and stormy night, and the captain and all his men were around the campfire. One of the men rose and said, 'Captain, tell us a story.' So the captain began."

"It was a dark and stormy night, and the captain and all his men were around the campfire. One of the men rose and said, 'Captain, tell us a story.' So the captain began . . ."

Notes and Comments

The round is another kind of endless tale that usually employs as its framework a request for a tale that is included in the telling of the tale. A continuous verbal loop is thus formed, and the narrative has no way of

*Collected by M. Brockie from her grandmother, Mrs. Ethel Royce in 1971. Mrs. Royce heard it from her husband who learned it in the cavalry in 1902. Eastern Michigan University Archive. Reprinted by permission of Marian L. Brockie.

developing. A black South Carolina variant employs a slightly different approach in which a preacher is echoed by his congregation:

"My eyes are dim. I can't see. I left my spec' at home." His members begin to sing, "My eyes are dim, I can't see. I left my spec' at home." He said, "I didn't mean for you to sing. I said my eyes are dim." His members sang again, "I didn't mean for you to sing. I said my eyes are dim."

Vance Randolph collected an Indiana variant in which a hunter sees "an old iron" at the top of a tree. He calls up all his dogs, fourteen of them, individually by name. When he has done so, the old iron jumps to another tree, forcing the hunter to call them all once more. The story is even more pointless since no one knows exactly what an old iron is. The informant said she thought of it as "a great flatiron, with head and feet like a cat" (Randolph, *Church House?*, p. 202).

Katharine Briggs notes that there was a popular round, "The Bear Went Over the Mountain," that was sung to the tune of "For He's a Jolly Good Fellow." It is important to remember that rounds appear more frequently as songs than they do as tales.

Tale Type 2320   Rounds

Principal Motif:

Z17   Rounds

Parallel Stories in:

Alderson, *Circular,* p. 288
Briggs, *Dictionary* (A2), p. 520
Halpert, *University Students,* #5
Hoffman, *Repeating Games,* p. 209 (2 variants)
Lanctôt, *Fables,* #46 (in French)
Randolph, *Devil's,* pp. 25–26
Stimson, *Defiance,* p. 129
Withers, *Rocket,* p. 130

41

The Travels of a Fox*

A fox digging behind a stump found a bumblebee. The fox put the bumblebee in his bag, and traveled.

The first house he came to he went in, and said to the mistress of the house, "Can I leave my bag here while I go to Squintum's?"

"Yes," said the woman.

"Then be careful not to open the bag," said the fox.

But as soon as the fox was out of sight the woman just took a little peep into the bag, and out flew the bumblebee, and the rooster caught him and ate him all up.

After a while the fox came back. He took up his bag, and he saw that his bumblebee was gone, and he said to the woman, "Where is my bumblebee?"

And the woman said, "I just untied the string, and the bumblebee flew out, and the rooster ate him up."

"Very well," said the fox; "I must have the rooster, then."

So he caught the rooster and put him in his bag, and traveled.

And the next house he came to he went in, and said to the mistress of the house, "Can I leave my bag here while I go to Squintum's?"

*From *Outlook* 57, no. 11 (November 13, 1897): pp. 689–90. Collected by Clifton Johnson.

"Yes," said the woman.

"Then be careful not to open the bag," said the fox.

But as soon as the fox was out of sight the woman just took a little peep into the bag, and the rooster flew out, and the pig caught him and ate him all up.

After a while the fox came back. He took up his bag, and he saw that his rooster was gone, and he said to the woman, "Where is my rooster?"

And the woman said, "I just untied the string, and the rooster flew out, and the pig ate him up."

"Very well," said the fox; "I must have the pig, then."

So he caught the pig and put him in his bag, and traveled.

And the next house he came to he went in, and said to the mistress of the house, "Can I leave my bag here while I go to Squintum's?"

"Yes," said the woman.

"Then be careful not to open the bag," said the fox.

But as soon as the fox was out of sight the woman just took a little peep into the bag, and the pig jumped out, and the ox gored him.

After a while the fox came back. He took up his bag, and he saw that his pig was gone, and he said to the woman, "Where is my pig?"

And the woman said, "I just untied the string, and the pig jumped out, and the ox gored him."

"Very well," said the fox; "I must have the ox, then."

So he caught the ox and put him in his bag, and traveled.

And the next house he came to he went in, and said to the mistress of the house, "Can I leave my bag here while I go to Squintum's?"

"Yes," said the woman.

"Then be careful not to open the bag," said the fox.

But as soon as the fox was out of sight the woman just took a little peep, and the ox got out, and the woman's little boy broke off his horns and killed him.

After a while the fox came back. He took up his bag, and he saw that his ox was gone, and he said to the woman, "Where is my ox?"

And the woman said, "I just untied the string, and the ox got out, and my little boy broke off his horns and killed him."

"Very well," said the fox; "I must have the little boy, then."

So he caught the little boy and put him in his bag, and traveled.

And the next house he came to he went in, and said to the mistress of the house, "Can I leave my bag here while I go to Squintum's?"

"Yes," said the woman.

"Then be careful not to open the bag," said the fox.

The woman was making cake, and her children were around her teasing for it.

"Oh, ma, give me a piece!" said one, and "Oh, ma, give me a piece!" said the others.

And the smell of the cake came to the little boy weeping and crying in the bag, and he heard the children beg for the cake, and he said, "Oh, mammy, give me a piece!"

Then the woman opened the bag and took the little boy out, and she put the house-dog in the bag in the little boy's place. And the little boy stopped crying and joined the other children.

After a while the fox came back. He took up his bag, and he saw that it was tied fast, and he put it on his back, and traveled deep into the woods. Then he sat down and untied the bag, and if the little boy had been in the bag things would have gone badly with him.

But the little boy was safe at the woman's house, and when the fox untied the bag the house-dog jumped out and caught the fox and killed him.

Notes and Comments

Although the text of "The Travels of a Fox" reprinted here has apparently a strong literary tradition (there are few versions available that do not follow this text line closely, even to the repetition of the mysterious "Squintum's" as a person or place name), still there are strong ties to classical mythology through the Pandora myth and to universal folktales through the swapping story.

The Pandora myth relies on the tabu motif, which is sure to be broken whenever it appears in mythology or folklore. Thus, when Pandora receives a lovely box as a gift from Zeus with instructions not to open it, the reader is put on a collision course with the inevitable ending, knowing that only time stands between her and the open box. So it is with our wily fox, who may be certain to improve his fortunes by playing both on the goodwill of the various people to whom he entrusts his bag and on their predictably curious nature as they invariably violate the tabu and open the bag.

As the fox improves his lot from household to household, the swapping story motif found in such tales as "Gudbrand on the Hillside" emerges. Sometimes the swapping is done on the initiative of the hero, although, as in Gudbrand's story, the swapping chain does not always spiral upward from an insignificant object to one of great value. In fact, in one famous Jack tale collected by Richard Chase, the hero, Jack, is sent to town with a cow to sell at market, does a lot of trading on the way, and finally ends up with a "nice round rock," a rock that he assures his wife will be just perfect "to prop the door back." (His wife was last seen searching for three persons more stupid than her husband—cf. Tale Type 1384 in the Noodle Section.) Other swapping stories are based on unfortunate accidents, such as the swallowing of a chick pea by a chicken, who is in turn eaten by a pig, who is then killed by a calf, who is then killed and cooked by an innkeeper's wife for her sick daughter, who recovers and is given in marriage to the original owner of the chick pea. This forced swapping is closer to the story of "The Travels of a Fox" and perhaps exists in its most famous form in the "Rat's Wedding," where the rat goes from modest beginnings to a marriage with the king's daughter, only to meet his fate on a footstool especially prepared by the Queen Mother for such upstart rodents.

An interesting Negro variant collected by Parsons is quoted below for its unusual alterations of the story line. The narrator begins his story with the farmer as the hero, but midway he apparently remembers more of the story as he first heard it, and reverts to a cast list of a fox and a bumblebee and a bag:

> There was a farmer who had a bumble-bee in a bag. He went to Puntious Pilot to get some pum'kin to make some pies. So he travel through the woods. Soon he came to a house, and went in and asked the lady of the house to let his bag stay 'til he go Puntious Pilot's to get some pumpkins, and told the lady to be careful not to open the bag. But as soon as the fox was out of sight, the lady untied the bag, and the bumble-bee flew out of the bag. So the lady's little boy ran out to catch the bee, but could not; so the lady put her little boy in the bag.
>
> (*Aiken*, p. 21)

While this story is a good addition to a repertory of formula tales, it is perhaps best studied in light of much larger traditions, such as the great tabu stories—Adam and Eve, Lot's Wife, Orpheus and Eurydice, or the tradition of the swapping stories that are often used as introductions to other kinds of folktales, such as "Jack and His Wife."

Tale Type 1655   The Profitable Exchange
170   The Fox Eats his Fellow Lodger

Principal Motifs:

C322   Tabu: looking into a bag
K251.1   The eaten grain and the cock as damages
K526   Captor's bag filled with animals or objects while Captive escapes

K525.6 Escape, leaving dog as substitute
Z47   Series of trick exchanges

Parallel Stories in:

Beckwith, *Jamaica Anansi,* #63 (references)
Dorson, *World,* pp. 284–86 (variant)
Harris, Nights, "Bro Rabbit Rescues Bro
   Terrypin" (variant)
O'Suilleabhain, *Handbook,* p. 585 (summary)
Pino-Saavedra, *Chile,* #47

G

A Clever Fellow
by Any Other Name:
TRICKSTER TALES

A traditional trickster is not merely a rascal who plays a trick on someone and gets away with it. These tricksters have been such rogues for so long that entire cycles of tales have grown up around them. So it is that while Jack or Brer Rabbit or Anansi may appear as central characters in many different tale types, they are always their own recognizable selves, unrepentant, and unreformed.

42. *ANANSI PLAYS DEAD*   259
     TT 175—*The Tarbaby and the Rabbit*
     Also known as *The Gum Baby, The Demon With
     the Matted Hair* from the *Jataka Tales*

43. *JACK AND THE VARMINTS*   264
     TT 1640—*The Brave Tailor*
     Also known as *Seven at a Whack, Brave Kong* (see
     Noodle section), *Jack the Giant Killer*

44. *SHEER CROPS*   272
     TT 1030—*The Crop Division*
     Also known as *A Brer Rabbit Trick, Tops and*

*Bottoms, Sharing the Crops, Brer Rabbit's Harvest
Time Tricks*

45. *BOOTS AND HIS BROTHERS*   277

   TT 577—*The King's Tasks*
   Also known as *How to Fell the Oak, How to Dig the
   Well, How to Marry the Princess*

46. *COYOTE TRICKS THE WHITE MAN*   283

   TT 1539—*Cleverness and Gullibility*
   TT 1542A—*Return for Tools*
   Also known as *Tools for a Horse Thief, The Wily
   Coyote, Tricking the Gringo*

47. *BABY IN THE CRIB*   286

   TT 1525M—*Mak and the Sheep*
   Also known as *Pig in the Cradle, Hog in the
   Cadillac, John and Marster and the Stolen Meat*

48. *NASR-ED-DIN HODJA IN THE PULPIT*   289

   TT 1826—*The Parson Has No Need to Preach*
   Also known as *No Need for the Parson, Let Them
   What Knows Tell Them What Don't Know*

49. *PEDRO DE URDEMALAS*   293

   TT 1539—*Cleverness and Gullibility*
   TT 1004—*Hogs in the Mud, Sheep in the Air*
   Also known as *The Tale of the Tails*

42

Anansi Plays Dead*

O ne year there was a famine in the land. But Anansi and his wife
Aso and his sons had a farm, and there was food enough for
all of them. Still the thought of famine throughout the country made Anansi
hungry. He began to plot how he could have the best part of the crops for
himself. He devised a clever scheme.

One day he told his wife that he was not feeling well and that he was
going to see a sorcerer. He went away and didn't return until night. Then
he announced that he had received very bad news. The sorcerer had informed him, he said, that he was about to die. Also, Anansi said, the
sorcerer had prescribed that he was to be buried at the far end of the farm,
next to the yam patch. When they heard this news, Aso, Kweku Tsin, and
Intikuma were very sad. But Anansi had more instructions. Aso was to
place in his coffin a pestle and mortar, dishes, spoons, and cooking pots, so
that Anansi could take care of himself in the Other World.

In a few days, Anansi lay on his sleeping mat as though he were sick,
and in a short time he pretended to be dead. So Aso had him buried at the

*From *The Hat-Shaking Dance and Other Ashanti Tales Ghana* by Harold Courlander
(New York: Harcourt, Brace and Company, 1957), pp. 20–24. © 1957 by Harold Courlander.
Reprinted by permission of Harcourt Brace Jovanovich, Inc.

far end of the farm, next to the yam patch, and they put in his coffin all of the cooking pots and other things he had asked for.

But Anansi stayed in the grave only while the sun shone. As soon as it grew dark, he came out of the coffin and dug up some yams and cooked them. He ate until he was stuffed. Then he returned to his place in the coffin. Every night he came out to select the best part of the crops and eat them, and during the day he hid in his grave.

Aso and her sons began to observe that their best yams and corn and cassava were being stolen from the fields. So they went to Anansi's grave and held a special service there. They asked Anansi's soul to protect the farm from thieves.

That night Anansi again came out, and once more he took the best crops and ate them. When Aso and her sons found out that Anansi's soul was not protecting them, they devised a plan to catch the person who was stealing their food. They made a figure out of sticky gum. It looked like a man. They set it up in the yam patch.

That night Anansi crawled out of his coffin to eat. He saw the figure standing there in the moonlight.

"Why are you standing in my fields?" Anansi said.

The gum-man didn't answer.

"If you don't get out of my fields, I will give you a thrashing," Anansi said.

The gum-man was silent.

"If you don't go quickly, I will have to beat you," Anansi said.

There was no reply. The gum-man just stood there. Anansi lost his temper. He gave the gum-man a hard blow with his right hand. It stuck fast to the gum-man. Anansi couldn't take it away.

"Let go of my right hand," Anansi said. "You are making me angry!"

But the gum-man didn't let go.

"Perhaps you don't know my strength," Anansi said fiercely. "There is more power in my left hand than in my right. Do you want to try it?"

As there was no response from the gum-man, Anansi struck him with his left hand. Now both his hands were stuck.

"You miserable creature," Anansi said, "so you don't listen to me! Let go at once and get out of my fields or I will really give you something to remember! Have you ever heard of my right foot?"

There was no sound from the gum-man, so Anansi gave him a kick with his right foot. It, too, stuck.

"Oh, you like it, do you?" Anansi shouted. "Then try this one, too!"

He gave a tremendous kick with his left foot, and now he was stuck by both hands and both feet.

"Oh, are you the stubborn kind?" Anansi cried. "Have you ever heard of my head?"

And he butted the gum-man with his head, and that stuck as well.

"I'm giving you your last chance now," Anansi said sternly. "If you leave quietly, I won't complain to the chief. If you don't, I'll give you a squeeze you will remember!"

The gum-man was still silent. So Anansi took a deep breath and gave a mighty squeeze. Now he was completely stuck. He couldn't move this way or that. He couldn't move at all.

In the morning when Aso, Kweku Tsin, and Intikuma came out to the fields, they found Anansi stuck helplessly to the gum-man. They understood everything. They took him off the gum-man and led him toward the village to be judged by the chief. People came to the edge of the trail and saw Anansi all stuck up with gum. They laughed and jeered and sang songs about him. He was deeply shamed, and covered his face with his headcloth. And when Aso, Kweku Tsin, and Intikuma stopped at a spring to drink, Anansi broke away and fled. He ran into the nearest house, crawled into the rafters, and hid in the darkest corner he could find.

From that day until now, Anansi has not wanted to face people because of their scoffing and jeering, and that is why he is often found hiding in dark corners.

Notes and Comments

Anansi is the spider hero and trickster of a considerable number of West African tales. Under a variety of names, the animal is outrageously cunning and wily. He is known everywhere in the West Indies and other parts of the New World. In many tales Anansi appears sometimes as a spider and sometimes as a man. In Ghana and parts of the Ivory Coast he is known as Kwaku Anansi. In South Carolina and the Sea Islands, he is generally known as Miss Nancy; in the Gullah region of the United States he is specifically Aunt Nancy. In many other areas, however, Anansi remains defiantly Anansi.

Tricksters are interchangeable fellows, and the reader should not be surprised to find Anansi playing the tricks with which the name Brer Rabbit is synonymous in the United States. The "capture by tarbaby" motif (K741) is found in every corner of the world. Tarbabies come in all shapes and sizes: in Mexico "tarbaby" is a doll made of wax to protect an onion patch; in Kentucky "tarbaby" is a tar man protecting a cabbage patch; in Peru a tar doll sits on a water pipe to prevent a mouse from stealing a gentleman's flowers; in Chile "Tarbaby" is a clay doll guarding a fig tree; and in the Philippines he is a crooked little old man of wax planted to trap a monkey who steals corn.

In a Bahamian variant the tarbaby is set up because the foolish Boukee "done dirtiness in the well," and in a closely related version from North Carolina, rabbit muddies the well by washing his face in it. Other African tales cluster around the theme of stealing water from a well. Here the tarbaby is a trap against the thief. In the Bahamas, Tarbaby is referred to as an *obeah* baby, or "witch baby." When this is taken in conjunction with the Islands' practice of "fixin" or "dressing" fields against thieves, it seems clear that the tarbaby has often been thought of as a charm against thieves and trespassers. In Angola, the gum baby is, indeed, "medicine" supplied by the "old one" to catch thieves.

The motif's enormous popularity in the United States owes a great deal to its inclusion in Joel Chandler Harris's "The Wonderful Tar Baby" which was included in *Uncle Remus: His Songs and His Sayings.* This is the familiar story in which Brer Fox, tired of Brer Rabbit's insolence, "fix up a contrapshun wat he call a Tar-Baby." Brer Rabbit coming by greets the tarbaby very civilly, but receiving no answer finally comes to blows and is securely held at five points, hands, feet, and head. Brer Fox who has "lain low" now saunters out and accuses Brer Rabbit of being "sorter stuck up."

Joseph Jacobs makes an ingenious attempt to link the Brer Rabbit story and all others like it to an original Jataka Tale ("The Demon with the Matted Hair," *Indian Fairy Tales,* #25) which he believes was carried from India to South Africa and thence to America. In the original Jataka, the Buddha himself sticks in five places—hands, feet and head. This incident is so ludicrous that it is unlikely it would have been invented by accident.

"Anansi Plays Dead" is significant as being the bare story (with only a few minor additions) of the Anansi–tarbaby combination as told of Hare in Angola, of Jackal among the Hottentots, or Brer Rabbit among Southern blacks, and of Coyote, Pitcher, Skunk, and others among North American Indians. The story is still the same even in a Chilean variant in which there are no animals at all—only two men who disguise themselves as "ghosts."

Aurelio M. Espinosa has made an exhaustive study of the tarbaby tale (based on 267 versions) in *JAFL* 43 (1930): 129–209 and *JAFL* 56 (1943): 31–37.

Tale Type 175   The Tarbaby and the Rabbit

Principal Motifs:

K741   Capture by tarbaby
A2433.5.3   Haunts of spider

Parallel Stories in:

Arnott, *African Myths,* pp. 16–21
Barker, *West African,* pp. 69–72
Boas, *Mexican,* pp. 235–36, 249–59 (notes and references)
Brewer, *American Negro,* pp. 7–9
Burlingame, *Elephant,* #9
Cowell, *Jataka,* #55
Dorson, *Buying,* pp. 248–49
Espinosa, *Classification*
Harris, *Remus,* "The Wonderful Tar-Baby Story" (reprinted in Botkin, *American,*
    pp. 653–54 and in Brewer, *American Negro,* pp. 4–5)
Jacobs, *Indian,* #25
Paredes, *Mexico,* #26
Parsons, *Antilles* 2:325–26
———, *Bahamas,* #10, #11, #12 (references)
———, *Sea Islands,* #13, #14, #15
Pino-Saavedra, *Chile,* #2
Puckett, *Folk Beliefs,* pp. 39–41 (with notes)
Roberts, *Sang Branch,* #139
Saucier, *Louisiana,* #31, #33

PICTURE BOOKS:

Beeswax Catches a Thief. Retold and illustrated by Ann Kirn. New York: W. W.
    Norton, 1968. (Set in the Congo)
The Clever Turtle. Retold and illustrated by A. K. Roche. Englewood Cliffs, N.J.:
    Prentice Hall, 1969. (Set in Angola)
Punia and the King of the Sharks. Retold by Beverly Mohan and illustrated by Don
    Bolognese. Chicago: Follett, 1964. (US variants of African tales)
A Story a Story. Retold and illustrated by Gail E. Haley. New York: Atheneum,
    1970. (Set in Africa)

43

Jack and the Varmints*

Jack was a-goin' about over the country one time, happened he passed by a place where a man had been rivin' boards, saw a little thin piece and picked it up, started in to whittlin' on it. Jack was so lazy he never noticed much what he was doin' till he'd done made him a little paddle. He didn't know what he'd do with it, just carried it along. Directly he came to a muddy place in the road where a lot of little blue butterflies had lit down to drink. So Jack slipped up right close to 'em and came down with that paddle right in the middle of 'em—*splap!* Then he counted to see how many he'd killed.

Went on down the road, came to a blacksmith shop. He got the blacksmith to take some brads and make him a sign in big letters on his belt; buckled that around him and went on.

Pretty soon here came the King on his horse, says, "Hello, Jack."

"Howdy do, King."

"What's all that writin' you got around ye, Jack? Turn around so's I can read it."

The old King read it off:

---

*From *The Jack Tales* edited by Richard Chase (Cambridge, Mass.: Houghton, Mifflin Co., 1943), pp. 58–66. Copyright 1943 and © renewed 1971 by Richard Chase. Reprinted by permission of Houghton Mifflin Company.

STRONG-MAN-JACK—
KILLED-SEVEN-AT-A-WHACK.

"You mean you've done killed seven at one lick, Jack? You must be gettin' to be an awful stout feller. I reckon you could do pretty nigh anything, couldn't ye?"

"Well," says Jack, "I don't know. I've pulled a few tricks."

King says, "Well, now, Jack, if you're up to that adver-tize-ment you got on your belt there, you're the very man I'm a-lookin' for. There's a big wild hog been tearin' around in my settle-ment, killin' lots of sheep. If you help us get shet of that hog, I'll pay ye a thousand dollars. All my men are scared of it."

"Well," says Jack, "I'll try."

So the King took Jack over on the mountain where that wild hog was a-usin'. Time he got up in the holler a ways, he turned his horse around, says, "You go on up in the mountain and find it, Jack. I got im-portant business back home."

And the King gave his horse a lick and made it go back in a hurry.

Jack he knowed that if the King was so scared of that hog, it must be awful dangerous. Decided he'd just not get mixed up with such a varmint. Said he'd wait a little while and then he'd slip out and get away 'fore that old hog smelled him. Well, directly Jack got to plunderin' around in there tryin' to get out, heard that hog a-breakin' bresh up the mountain, and then he saw it comin'. So Jack lit out through the woods—him and the hog . . .

Whippety cut!
Whippety cut!
Whippety cut!

and the wild hog right in behind him.

Jack looked behind and saw it was gettin' closer; they say Jack commenced jumpin' fifteen feet ever' step, but the old hog kept right on a-gainin'. Jack came out in a field, looked down it a ways and saw a old waste-house standin' there with no roof on it. Jack made for that house, ran in the door, and scrambled up the wall. That old hog was so close it grabbed hold on Jack's coat-tail, but Jack was a-goin' so fast it jerked his coat-tail plumb off. Jack got up on top of the wall, looked down at the hog standin' there with his forefeet up on the logs a-lookin' up after him. Then Jack jumped down and ran around outside, pushed the door to and propped it right quick with some timbers. Saw the hog couldn't get out, so then he pulled back to the King's house.

"Hello, Jack. Did ye do any good?"

"Why, no, King. I couldn't find no wild hog up there. Hunted all over that mountain, didn't see nothin'."

"Why Jack, that old hog just *makes* for ever'body goes up there. You must 'a seen it."

"Well, there wasn't nothin' but a little old boar shoat, came bristlin' up to me, kept follerin' me around. I ran it off a time or two, but it kept on taggin' after me. The blame thing got playful after a while, jumped up and jerked a piece out of my coat-tail. That made me a little mad, so I took it by the tail and ear and throwed it in a old waste-house up there, barred it in. I don't reckon that was what you wanted. You can go up and see if ye want to."

When the King rode up there and saw it was that wild hog, he like to beat his horse to death gettin' back. Blowed his horn and fifty or sixty men came runnin' up. They took a lot of Winchester rifles and went on up to that old house; but they were so scared they wouldn't go close enough to get a shoot at it. So fin'ly Jack he went on down there, poked around with a rifle and shot two or three times. That old hog went to tearin' around and when it fell it had tore that house plumb down.

So the King's men skinned it out. Hit made two wagonloads of meat.

The King paid Jack the thousand dollars, and Jack started to pull out for home.

The King called him, says, "I got another job for ye, Jack. They say there's a unicorn usin' back here on another mountain, doin' a sight of damage to people's livestock. Hit's a lot more dangerous than that hog, but a brave feller like you oughtn't to have no trouble killin' it. I'll pay ye another thousand dollars, too."

Well, Jack tried to back out of it, but he saw he couldn't, so the King took him up there where they said the unicorn was, turned his horse around and just burnt the wind.

Jack watched the King out of sight, says, "Thousand dollars'll do me a right long while. I don't want to get mixed up with no unicorn. I'll get out of here and go back another way. I'm not a-goin' to fool around here and get killed."

But Jack hadn't gone very far 'fore he heard that varmint breakin' bresh and a-comin' straight down the mountain. So Jack started runnin' around in amongst the trees as hard as he could tear. Looked around directly and saw that old unicorn so close to him it was just about to make a lunge and stick that horn right through the middle of his back. Jack reached out and grabbed hold on a white oak tree, swung around behind it. The unicorn swerved at him, hit that oak tree and stove its horn plumb through it. Horn came out the other side, and like to stuck Jack. Time he saw that, he snatched some nails out'n his overhall pocket, grabbed him up a rock right quick and wedged the horn in tight. Then he got him a switch and swarped the unicorn a few times to see could it break loose; saw it couldn't, so he pulled on back down to the King's house.

"What luck did ye have this time, Jack?"

"Why, King, I didn't see no unicorn."

"Now, that's a curious thing to me, Jack. Nobody else ever went in there but what that old unicorn came right for 'em. What did ye see, Jack?"

"Nothin' much, just some kind of a little old yearlin' bull, didn't have but one horn. Came down there actin' big, a-bawlin' and pawin' the ground. Got to follerin' me around pretty close and sort of gougin' at me with that horn, till fin'ly hit kind of aggravated me. So I took it by the tail and neck, stove its horn through a tree. I reckon it's still fastened up there where I left it at. We can all go on up and see it if ye want to."

So Jack took the King and his men with all them rifles up where the unicorn was. They wouldn't none of 'em get close enough to get a good aim, so Jack went on up to it, cut him a little branch and switched it two or three times, says, "See, men? There's not a bit of harm in him."

The men fin'ly shot it, and when it fell, they say it tore that oak tree plumb up by the roots.

Then they skinned it and brought back the hide.

The King paid Jack another thousand dollars, says, "Now, Jack, they've just brought in word here that a lion has come over the mountains from somewhere in Tennessee, been makin' raids on a settle-ment over the other end of this county, killin' ever'thing it comes across: cattle, and horses, and they say it's done killed several men tried to go after it. I told 'em about you, Jack, and they made me promise to send ye."

"Well, King, that sounds like the dangerest thing of all."

"I'll pay ye another thousand dollars, Jack."

"I don't know as I favor workin' any more right now, King. They'll be worried about me if I don't get back in home 'fore dark. Besides, my daddy's cuttin' tobacco and he needs me bad."

"Come on now, Jack. I'll pay ye two thousand dollars."

"Well, I don't know. I'll have to study on it awhile."

"Here's a thousand dollars down, right now, Jack, and I'll pay ye the other thousand when ye get it killed. I'd sure like to get shet of that lion."

"I reckon I'll do it then," says Jack—"try to."

So the King took Jack up behind him on his horse and they rode over to where they said the lion was last seen.

The King says, "Now, Jack, that lion's right up in yonder somewhere. I'll not venture any further."

Jack slipped off the horse.

The King turned him around, says, "When hit smells ye, Jack, you'll sure hear from it!" And then the King left there a-gallopin'.

Well, Jack felt of that three thousand dollars he had down in his overhall pocket, said he'd try to get out of there for good and go on back home. But 'fore he'd hardly took a step or two, that old lion smelled him and com-menced roarin' up there in the woods, roared so hard it jarred the mountain. Then Jack saw it comin'—tearin' down trees, breakin' logs in two, bustin' rocks wide open—and Jack didn't waste no time tryin' to run. He made for the tree nearest to him and skinned up it like a squirrel. He didn't stop neither, till he was clean to the top.

The old lion growled around down there, smelled up the tree a time or two, and then it went right in to gnawin' on the tree-trunk. Jack looked, and it was a sight in the world how the bark and the splinters flew. It nearly shook Jack out the tree.

But it seemed like the lion got tired when he had the tree about half gnawed through; he quit, laid up against the foot of the tree and went sound asleep.

Jack waited awhile till his heart quit beatin' so fast, and then he 'lowed he might have a chance to slip down and get away from there 'fore the old lion woke up. So he started slidin' down the tree. He was keepin' such close watch on that lion's eyes to see would he wake up or not, Jack never noticed when he set his foot on a brickly snag. Put all his weight on that rotten limb, and hit broke, and Jack went scootin' down, landed right straddle the old lion's back.

Well, that lion started in roarin' and jumpin' around, but Jack he just held on. Then the old lion got to runnin' and he was so scared he didn't know he was headed right for town. Got on the public highway and kept right on till next thing Jack knowed they were sailin' all around the courthouse. All the people were runnin' in the stores and climbin' trees gettin' out the way, and everybody shoutin' and hollerin', and the King's men came and started in tryin' to shoot the lion without hittin' Jack, till fin'ly one of 'em drawed a bead on the old lion's head and tumbled him up.

Jack picked himself up out the dirt, com-menced breshin' it off. Ever'-body came over directly to see that lion, when they saw it was sure 'nough dead.

The King came along right soon and Jack says to him, says, "Look-a-here, King. I'm mad."

"Why, how come, Jack?"

"These men have done killed your lion."

"My lion? What ye mean, Jack?"

"Why, I'd 'a not had it killed for three thousand dollars, King. After I'd caught it and 'gun to get it gentled up, now, bedads, your men have done shot it. I was just a-ridin' it down here to get it broke in for you a ridey-horse."

So the old King went over to where his men were and raised a rumpus with 'em, says, "Why, I'd 'a felt big ridin' that lion around. Now you men will just have to raise Jack three thousand dollars for killin' our lion."

So Jack went on home after that; had a whole pile of money down in his old ragged overhall pocket.

And the last time I went down there Jack was still rich, and I don't think he's worked any yet.

Notes and Comments

The Jack in this story is none other than an American cousin of his famous English namesake. Most of the American Jack tales seemed to come from Beech Mountain, North Carolina, where they were told by the descendants of Council Harmon (1803–1896), but others have been found in Virginia. The tales are closely associated with Richard Chase who went to Beech Mountain to collect many of them. There he discovered that the tales were particularly employed as a means of "keeping kids on the job." Telling took place while communal tasks were completed: stringing beans for canning or threading them up to make the dried pods called "leather britches." This use of the tales was a common one in that region, and this natural oral process has led the Appalachian giant-killer to acquire an easy-going, unpretentious, essentially unheroic nature which makes him so different from his cocksure, more dashing English relative.

It is interesting to note not only how stories and anecdotes cluster about a central character in almost every culture, but also how there are always people eager to identify the real Robin Hood, King Arthur, or our brave little tailor, Jack. Katharine Briggs quotes two statements about the identification of Jack among the country folk of England. One man suggests that his name was really Jacky or Jack Kent and identifies him with John of Kentchurch, provincial of the Franciscans and an Oxford professor of the fifteenth century. Perhaps corroborating and further adding to the legend are the comments of yet another contributor.

E. M. Leather [writing in the *Folk-Lore of Herefordshire,* p. 163] says "Jack o'Kent is the name given by the folk to a mysterious personage who formerly lived in the neighbourhood of Kentchurch and Grosmont. He has been supposed by some to be Owen Glendower in hiding . . . while others are sure that he was Sir John Oldcastle, who was long a fugitive upon the Welsh Border."

(Briggs, *Dictionary,* B (1), p. 108)

Other names are suggested as well, but most importantly Mr. Leather confirms the one fact upon which the English countryside seems to be in agreement: "There certainly was a real John Kent, Vicar of Kentchurch, in the reign of Henry V." Whether or not the parchments and documents record exactly his feats as well as his genealogy, his personality has been such that it has attracted a score of legendary anecdotes about his cunning and trickery, so much so that he can be cited as the single most important trickster figure in both Great Britain and the United States.

"Jack and the Varmints" lacks the giant episodes that frequently accompany Type 1640 *The Brave Tailor.* Those episodes are found in the first story in *The Jack Tales* by Richard Chase, "Jack in the Giant's New Ground." (For further discussion of Tale Type 1640, refer to the notes in Section J, Tale 61.)

The reader should perhaps be advised that Richard Chase's tales are not field collections in the strictest sense. He retells his stories taking "the best of many retellings" and the "best of all material" to arrive at his final version. The device of an all-night story-telling session is used, for he rightly wants his readers to see folklore alive and functioning in its environment. In attempting these praiseworthy ideals, Chase may give a somewhat distorted view of mountain life, but the speech patterns and rhythms and the native democratic sentiments are those of North Carolina, and these tales are both refreshing and amusing. After all, where else can a tale depart from its traditional ending to give us:

> So Jack went on home after that; had a whole pile of money down in his old ragged overhaul pocket.
> And the last time I went down there Jack was still rich, and I don't think he's worked any yet.

Throughout this story and other Jack tales the "hero" remains the thoroughly human, unassuming representative of the free world where the democratic spirit moves in easy proximity with the feudal world of the märchen, where the king can pass by and say "Howdy" to Jack jes' sittin' on his porch, rocking.

Tale Type 1640   The Brave Tailor

Principal Motifs:

K1700	Deception through bluffing
K1951	Sham warrior

Parallel Stories in:

Briggs, *Dictionary* (A1) (3 variants)
Campbell, *West Highlands* 3:#45
Carrière, *Missouri,* #67 (summary in English)
Carter, *Mountain White,* #6, #8
Dorson, *Michigan,* pp. 54–55
Grimm, #20
Hyde, *Beside the Fire,* pp. 3–15
Jacobs, *English,* #19
———, *More English,* #58, #79 (variant)
Lang, *Blue,* pp. 337–45
Massignon, *France,* #4
Parsons, *Bahamas,* #82
Roberts, *South,* #62b
Thompson, *One,* #94 (Grimm)

PICTURE BOOKS:

Sixty at a Blow. Illustrated by Christine Price. New York: E. P. Dutton and Co., 1968.
The Valiant Tailor. Illustrated by Kurt Werth. New York: Viking Press, 1965.

44

Sheer Crops*

B r'er Bear en Br'er Rabbit dey wuz farmers. Br'er Bear he has acres en acres uf good bottom land, en Br'er Rabbit has des' er small sandy-land farm. Br'er Bear wuz allus er "raisin' Cain" wid his neighbors, but Br'er Rabbit was er most engenerally raisin' chillun.

Arter while Br'er Rabbit's boys 'gun to git grown, en Br'er Rabbit 'lows he's gwine to have to git more land if he makes buckle en tongue meet.

So he goes ober to Br'er Bear's house, he did, en he say, sez he, "Mo'nin', Br'er Bear. I craves ter rent yer bottom field nex' year."

Br'er Bear he hum en he haw, en den he sez, "I don't spec I kin 'commodate yer, Br'er Rabbit, but I moughten consider hit, bein's hit's yer."

"How does you rent yer land, Br'er Bear?"

"I kin onliest rent by der sheers."

"What is yer sheer, Br'er Bear?"

"Well," said Br'er Bear, "I takes der top of de crop fer my sheer, en yer takes de rest fer yer sheer."

*From "Brazos Bottom Philosophy" by A. W. Eddins. PTFLS 9:153–64 (1931). Reprinted from *Southwestern Lore,* edited by J. Frank Dobie. Used with permission of Texas Folklore Society.

Br'er Rabbit thinks erbout it rale hard, en he sez, "All right, Br'er Bear, I took it; we goes ter plowin' ober dare nex' week."

Den Br'er Bear goes back in der house des' er-laughin'. He sho is tickled ez to how he hez done put one by ole Br'er Rabbit dat time.

Well, 'long in May Br'er Rabbit done sont his oldest son to tell Br'er Bear to come down to the field to see erbout dat are sheer crop. Br'er Bear he comes er-pacin' down to de field en Br'er Rabbit wuz er-leanin' on de fence.

"Mo'nin', Br'er Bear. See what er fine crop we hez got. You is to hab de tops fer yer sheer. Whare is you gwine to put 'em? I wants ter git 'em off so I kin dig my 'taters."

Br'er Bear wuz sho hot. But he done made dat trade wid Br'er Rabbit, en he had to stick to hit. So he went off all huffed up, en didn't even tell Br'er Rabbit what to do wid de vines. But Br'er Rabbit perceeded to dig his 'taters.

'Long in de fall Br'er Rabbit 'lows he's gwine to see Br'er Bear ergin en try to rent der bottom field. So he goes down to Br'er Bear's house en after passin' de time of day en other pleasant sociabilities, he sez, sez he, "Br'er Bear, how erbout rentin' der bottom field nex' year? Is yer gwine ter rent hit to me ergin?"

Br'er Bear say, he did, "You cheat me out uf my eyes las' year, Br'er Rabbit. I don't think I kin let yer hab it dis year."

Den Br'er Rabbit scratch his head er long time, en he say, "Oh, now, Br'er Bear, yer know I ain't cheated yer. Yer jes' cheat yerself. Yer made de trade yerself en I done tuck yer at yer word. Yer sed yer wanted de tops fer yer sheer, en I gib um ter yer, didn't I? Now yer jes' think hit all ober ergin and see if yer can't make er new deal fer yerself."

Den Br'er Bear said, "Well, I rents to yer only on dese perditions: dat yer hab all de tops fer yer sheer en I hab all de rest fer my sheer."

Br'er Rabbit he twis' en he turn en he sez, "All right, Br'er Bear, I'se got ter hab more land fer my boys. I'll tuck hit. We go to plowin' in dare right erway."

Den Br'er Bear he amble back into de house. He wuz shore he'd made er good trade dat time.

Way 'long in nex' June Br'er Rabbit done sont his boy down to Br'er Bear's house ergin, to tell him to come down ter de field ter see erbout his rent. When he got dare, Br'er Rabbit say, he did:

"Mo'nin', Br'er Bear. See what er fine crop we hez got? I specks hit will make forty bushels to der acre. I'se gwine ter put my oats on der market. What duz yer want me ter do wid yer straw?"

Br'er Bear sho wuz mad, but hit wa'n't no use. He done saw whar Br'er

Rabbit had 'im. So he lies low en 'lows to hisself how he's gwine to git eben wid Br'er Rabbit yit. So he smile en say, "Oh, der crop is all right, Br'er Rabbit. Jes' stack my straw anywheres eround dare. Dat's all right."

Den Br'er Bear smile en he say, "What erbout nex' year, Br'er Rabbit? Is yer cravin' ter rent dis field ergin?"

"I ain't er-doin nothin' else but wantin' ter rent hit, Br'er Bear," sez Br'er Rabbit.

"All right, all right, yer kin rent her ergin. But dis time I'se gwine ter hab der tops fer my sheer, en I'se gwine ter hab de bottoms fer my sheer too."

Br'er Rabbit wuz stumped. He didn't know whatter do nex'. But he finally managed to ask, "Br'er Bear, ef yer gits der tops en der bottoms fer yer sheer, what will I git fer my sheer?"

Den ole Br'er Bear laff en say, "Well, yer would git de middles."

Br'er Rabbit he worry en he fret, he plead en he argy, but hit do no good.

Br'er Bear sez, "Take hit er leave hit," en jes' stand pat.

Br'er Rabbit took hit.

Way 'long nex' summer ole Br'er Bear 'cided he would go down to der bottom field en see erbout dat dare sheer crop he had wid Br'er Rabbit. While he wuz er-passin' through de woods on hiz way, he sez to himself, he did:

"De fust year I rents to de ole Rabbit, I makes de tops my sheer, en ole Rabbit planted 'taters; so I gits nothin' but vines. Den I rents ergin, en der Rabbit is to hab de tops, en I de bottoms, en ole Rabbit plants oats; so I gits nothin' but de straw. But I sho is got dat ole Rabbit dis time. I gits both de tops en de bottoms, en de ole Rabbit gits only de middles. I'se bound ter git 'im dis time."

Jes' den de old Bear come ter de field. He stopped. He look at hit. He shet up his fist. He cuss en he say, "Dat derned little scoundrel! He done went en planted dat fiel' in corn."

Notes and Comments

A whole group of anecdotes has to do with bargaining—the simpler the bargain sounds, the more complicated the results turn out to be. The deceptive crop division is well known in India, Japan, and throughout eastern Europe and North America. There is only one version from China, and it is an interesting one, for it appears to be a Communist tale whose purpose is to emphasize the exploitative nature of land owners and the cleverness of the peasants.

Undoubtedly black slaves in America had similar objectives in mind when they retold the tale employing either the familiar Brer Rabbit or a human character as trickster. Obviously the tale had a deeper, symbolic meaning, for its hero was no less than the slave himself who could secretly delight in overcoming his master—if only in his imagination. Even when animal characters are used, as in this tale, the imagery evoked is that of a poor black sharecropper and the grasping white landowner.

It is hard to see how a folktale could be better structured. Brer Bear (a symbol of all the truly stupid people who love to think of themselves as smart) makes a deal that he believes will be only to his advantage. His first defeat is a setback, but Brer Bear recovers and drives what he regards as an even shrewder bargain. When that fails, Brer Bear is beside himself, but he exercises his low cunning. Having been tricked when his share was the top of the crop, and also when it was the bottom, he forces a smile and drives the impossible bargain for his third attempt. A crop can only have a top and bottom, he believes, so he demands both for his share. We now see Brer Rabbit stumped, but just when all is lost, and Brer Bear is walking down to the trickster's field, he pulls up short. Brer Rabbit has done it again. The field is in corn—a crop where only the middle is edible.

One of the more interesting aspects of Type 1030 *The Crop Division* is the need to adapt the tale to the crops grown in different regions of the world. In one English variant, the devil and Jack share a crop of wheat (the devil gets the stalks) and a crop of turnips (the devil gets the tops). Next day they agree to mow hay, and Jack sticks harrow tines in the field which blunt the devil's scythe. Finally they go threshing and the devil takes the top of the barn and Jack the bottom—where all the grain collected.

English variants often include a boggart (a squat hairy man, strong as a six-year-old horse and arms as long as tackle poles). In "The Farmer and the Boggart" the boggart first takes tops, so the farmer plants potatoes, leaving the boggart "the haulms and twitch." Next time the farmer plants corn, leaving the boggart stubble. The third time they sow wheat, but the farmer plants thin iron rods that blunt the boggart's scythe.

A French variant from Vienne follows the American version faithfully except that God and the devil are the farmers. It concludes, however, with God building a castle of ice. The devil wishes to swap his castle of iron for the brilliant one of ice. God then makes the sun melt the ice.

Tale Type 1030   The Crop Division

Principal Motif:

K171.1   Deceptive crop division: above the ground, below the ground

Parallel Stories in:

Briggs, *Dictionary*, B(1), pp. 28–29
Carrière, *Missouri*, #22, #62 (summaries in English)
Chase, *Grandfather*, #9
Courlander, *Terrapin's*, pp. 104–7
Dorson, *World*, pp. 347–49
Eberhard, *China*, #70
Grimm, #189
Massignon, *France*, #33
Roberts, *South*, #39

45

Boots and His Brothers*

O nce upon a time there was a man who had three sons, Peter, Paul, and John. John was Boots, of course, because he was the youngest.

I can't say the man had anything more than these three sons, for he hadn't one penny to rub against another. So he told his sons over and over again they must go out into the world and try to earn their bread, for there at home there was nothing to be looked for but starving to death.

Now, a short way from the man's cottage was the King's palace, and you must know, just against the King's windows a great oak had sprung up, which was so stout and big that it took away all the light from the palace. The King had said he would give many, many dollars to the man who could fell the oak, but no one was man enough for that, for as soon as ever one chip of the oak's trunk flew off, two grew in its stead.

A well, too, the King would have dug, which was to hold water for the whole year; for all his neighbors had wells, but he hadn't any, and that he thought a shame. So the King said he would give any one who could dig him a well that would hold water for a whole year round, both money and

*From *Popular Tales from the Norse* collected by Peter C. Asbjørnsen, translated by George Webbe Dasent (Edinburgh: Edmonston and Douglas, 1859), pp. 380–86.

goods. But no one could do it, for the King's palace was high, high up on a hill, and they hadn't dug a few inches before they came upon solid rock.

But as the King had set his heart on having these two things done, he had it given out far and wide, in all parts of his kingdom, that he who could fell the big oak in the king's courtyard and dig a well that would hold water the whole year round should have the Princess and half the kingdom.

Well! As you can easily guess, there was many a man who came to try his luck. But all their hacking and hewing, and all their digging and delving did them no good. The oak got bigger and stouter at every stroke, and the rock didn't get softer either.

One day the three brothers thought they'd set off to try too, and their father hadn't a word against it. Even if they didn't get the Princess and half the kingdom, they might get a place somewhere with a good master; and that was all he wanted. When the brothers said they thought of going to the palace, their father agreed at once. So the three brothers started out.

They hadn't gone far before they came to a fir wood, and up along one side of it rose a steep hillside. As the brothers went along, they heard something hewing and hacking away up on the hill among the trees.

"I wonder now what it is that is hewing away up yonder," said Boots.

"You're always so clever with your wonderings," said his brothers both at once. "What wonder is it, pray, that a woodcutter should stand and hack on a hillside?"

"Still, I'd like to see what it is, after all," said Boots; and up he went.

"Oh, if you're such a child, 'twill do you good to go and take a lesson," bawled out his brothers after him.

But Boots didn't care for what they said. He climbed the steep hillside toward the noise, and when he reached the place, what do you think he saw? Why, an ax that stood there hacking and hewing, all of itself, at the trunk of a fir.

"Good day," said Boots. "So you stand here all alone and hew, do you?"

"Yes; here I've stood and hewed and hacked a long, long time, waiting for you," said the ax.

"Well, here I am at last," said Boots.

He took the ax, pulled it off its handle, and stuffed both head and handle into his wallet.

When he got down again to his brothers, they began to jeer and laugh at him.

"And now, what funny thing was it you saw up yonder on the hillside?" they said.

"Oh, it was only an ax we heard," said Boots.

When they had gone a bit farther, they came under a steep spur of rock; and up above the rock they heard something digging and shoveling.

"I wonder now," said Boots, "what it is digging and shoveling up yonder at the top of the rock."

"Oh, you're always so clever with your wonderings," said his brothers again. "As if you'd never heard a woodpecker hacking and pecking at a hollow tree!"

"Well, well," said Boots, "I think it would be a piece of fun just to see what it really is."

So off he set to climb the rock, while the others laughed and made game of him. But he didn't care a bit for that. Up he climbed, and when he got near the top, what do you think he saw? Why, a spade that stood there digging and delving.

"Good day," said Boots. "So you stand here all alone and dig and delve?"

"Yes, that's what I do," said the spade. "And that's what I've done this many a long day, waiting for you."

"Well, here I am," said Boots.

He took the spade and knocked it off its handle and put them into his wallet. Then he went down again to his brothers.

"Well, what was it, so rare and strange," said Peter and Paul, "that you saw up there at the top of the rock?"

"Oh," said Boots, "nothing more than a spade; that was what we heard."

So they went on again a good bit, till they came to a brook. They were thirsty, all three, after their long walk, and they lay down beside the brook to have a drink. ·

"I wonder now," said Boots, "where all this water comes from."

"I wonder if you're right in your head," said Peter and Paul, in one breath. "If you're not mad already, you'll go mad very soon, with your wonderings. Where the brook comes from, indeed! Have you never heard how water rises from a spring in the earth?"

"Yes, but still I've a great fancy to see where this brook comes from," said Boots.

Up alongside the brook he went. In spite of all that his brothers bawled after him, nothing could stop him.

On he went. As he went up and up, the brook got smaller and smaller; and at last, a little way farther on, what do you think he saw? Why, a great walnut, and out of that the water trickled.

"Good day," said Boots. "So you lie here and trickle and run all alone?"

"Yes, I do," said the walnut. "And here have I trickled and run this many a long day, waiting for you."

"Well, here I am," said Boots.

He took up a lump of moss and plugged up the hole, that the water mightn't run out. Then he put the walnut into his wallet and ran down to his brothers.

"Well, now," said Peter and Paul, "have you found out where the water comes from? A rare sight it must have been!"

"Oh, after all, it was only a hole it ran out of," said Boots. And so the others laughed and made game of him again, but Boots didn't mind that a bit.

"After all, I had the fun of seeing it," said he.

When they had gone a bit farther, they came to the King's palace. Everyone in the kingdom had heard how a man might win the Princess and half the realm, if he could only fell the big oak and dig the King's well. Many had come to try their luck, so many that the oak was now twice as stout and big as it had been at first. Two chips grew for every one they hewed out with their axes.

Peter and Paul did not let themselves be scared by that; they were quite sure they could fell the oak. Peter, as he was the eldest, was to try his hand first. But it went with him as with all the rest who had hewn at the oak; for every chip he cut out, two grew in its place.

Now Paul was to try his luck, but he fared just the same. When he had hewn two or three strokes, they began to see the oak grow and so the King's men seized him and made him stop.

Now Boots was to try.

"You might as well save yourself the bother," said the King, for he was angry with him because of his brothers.

"Well, I'd just like to try," said Boots, and so he got leave. Then he took his ax out of his wallet and fitted it to its handle.

"Hew away!" said he to his ax.

Away it hewed, making the chips fly, so that it wasn't long before down came the oak.

When that was done, Boots pulled out his spade and fitted it to its handle.

"Dig away!" said he to his spade.

The spade began to dig and delve till the earth and rock flew out in splinters, and soon he had the well dug.

When he had got it as big and deep as he chose, Boots took out his walnut and laid it in one corner of the well. He pulled out the plug of moss.

"Trickle and run!" said Boots.

The nut trickled and ran, till the water gushed out of the hole in a stream. In a short time the well was brimful.

Now Boots had felled the oak which shaded the King's palace and dug a well in the palace yard; so he got the Princess and half the kingdom, as the king had said.

Then Peter and Paul had to say, "Well, after all, Boots wasn't so much out of his mind when he took to wondering."

Notes and Comments

A very familiar figure in folktales is the youngest son—call him Jack, Pedro, or Boots. In English versions of Norwegian tales the name Boots has been given to the Askefis or Espen Askefjis of the original. In Norway the term is almost universally applied to the youngest son of the family. He is Cinderella's brother in fact, and just as she is given all the dirty work to do, so Boots meets a similar fate at the hands of his brothers. Almost always he is the youngest brother of three. The names of his older brothers are often Peter and Paul, and they look down on Boots, giving him the meanest jobs to do. Deep down Boots has great strength of character, integrity, and kindness, and as a result he is the one upon whom fortune smiles. After his brothers encounter their inevitable failure, Boots triumphs over trolls, makes princesses laugh or speak, steals silver ducks and golden harps, rides up glass hills, tames wild horses, and so forth.

Boots shares his qualities with the Pinkel of Sweden, the Dummling of Germany, and the Jack of England and Appalachia. When his time comes, he is ready to brave the scorn of others and accomplish tasks with the aid of those he has befriended on the way.

Tale Type 577 *The King's Tasks* is not widespread. Leonard Roberts heard a version somewhat like the Norse one from an old woman in Kentucky whose tales sometimes seem to have come directly from northern Europe. No other examples of Type 577 are noted by Baughman in his *Type and Motif Index.*

Tale Type 577   The King's Tasks

Principal Motifs:

D950.2   Magic oak tree
D1581   Task performed by use of magic object

D1601.14   Self-chopping ax
F715.1.1   River issues from nut
H335   Tasks assigned suitor
L10   Victorious youngest son
T68   Princess offered as prize

Parallel Stories in:

Briggs, *Dictionary,* A (1), pp. 507–9 (variant)
Fauset, *Nova Scotia,* #18
Hand, *Humaniora* (major study by Christiansen on The King's Tasks, entitled "Displaced Folktales," pp. 161–71)
Musick, *Green Hills,* #44
Roberts, *South,* #24

46

Coyote Tricks the White Man*

oyote was walking down a road when he saw somebody riding toward him on horseback. When the rider came up Coyote saw that it was a white man. Coyote kept looking at him, already thinking up some way to cheat him.

The man pointed toward Coyote and said, "I'm looking for the cleverest coyote. Are you the one that tricks all the people; are you that clever one?"

Coyote said, "No, I am not that one."

But the white man insisted, "You are the man that cheats the people." Coyote kept denying that he was the clever one. "Hurry up," said the white man, "cheat me, perform some trick on me."

Coyote said, "Oh, I'm not that kind of man. They just call me that."

The white man said, "I know about you; let's have a match."

Finally Coyote said, "It's true, I'm that one, but my medicine for cheating the people is at home. I left it way back west and it would take me a long time to go get it."

The white man said, "Well, you go get it."

*From "Kiowa Apache Tales" edited by J. Gilbert McAllister, in *PTFLS* 22, 1949. Reprinted by permission of the Texas Folklore Society.

Coyote answered, "I'm pretty tired. I've traveled a long ways. If you want to have a match, you lend me your horse and I'll go get my medicine."

The man got off his horse and said, "All right, you go get your medicine."

Coyote picked up a little stick and went to the opposite side from the white man in order to get on the horse. Coyote then jabbed the horse as he pretended to try to get on him. The horse gave a snort and jumped away from him. "Your horse is afraid of me because I have no hat," Coyote said.

"All right, I'll give you my hat," the man said.

Coyote pretended to get on the horse, jabbing him again. "Your horse is afraid of me because I have no coat," Coyote explained. The white man gave Coyote his coat.

Coyote again caused the horse to snort and jump. "Your horse is afraid of me because I have no boots." The man gave Coyote his boots.

Again Coyote tried to get on the horse, but as usual the horse appeared to be afraid. "Your horse is scared of me because I have no pants." The man took off his pants and gave them to Coyote.

Coyote did the same thing to the horse and said, "I haven't any gun." The man strapped his gun on Coyote. This kept up until the white man did not have a stitch of clothes.

When Coyote got all the white man had, he got on the horse and rode away, leaving the man with nothing on. After riding a short distance he turned and said, "Say, white man, you know it now. I am a clever Coyote; this is how I cheat people." The white man called him to come back, but Coyote did not listen and rode off and left him there. He took everything the man had.

Notes and Comments

One of the most characteristic tales of the North American Indian is the story of the trickster. The name of the trickster varies according to location. Coyote is perhaps best known, but there are many more: Raven, Mink, Sendeh, Nihansan, Inkotomi, Nanabozho, Wisakedjak, to name a few. Stories about a trickster tend to form loosely knit cycles, and many of the same tales are told about different tricksters.

Coyote's adventures are generally set in the prehuman mythical age when animals lived and talked as people. He is often accompanied in the tales by a companion—Wolf, Wildcat, Fox, Rabbit, Lynx, Porcupine, or Badger. In some tales Coyote and his companions are represented as looking like men; in others they appear as animals. The companions may serve as stooges for the boastful Coyote, while on other occasions they are the ones who outwit him and steal his game.

Characteristically, trickster stories have a formulaic opening, "Coyote was going along . . ." followed by an anecdote of violence, deceit, or knavery. Coyote may die at the end of the tale, but he is always revived in time for the next account of his adventures.

The most incongruous feature of the American Indian trickster is his tendency to become a dupe or play the buffoon even though he was the wily, clever trickster in a story told the day before. Coyote can still be Coyote and become greedy, stupid, erotic, licentious, even a bully. A typical case of this darker side of Coyote is the widely distributed tale of "The Bungling Host." Here Coyote manages to tangle himself in his own snare net where he is mercilessly pounded by his intended victim. In order to separate one Coyote personality from another, the Navaho of the Southwest go so far as to call him by two names: "Coyote" for the clever, helpful trickster, and "Trotting Coyote" for the greedy buffoon.

Trickster tales are told chiefly for amusement, though many tribes have definite tabus about the recital of them in the summertime. To the extent that there is a moral to these tales, it is that Coyote's behavior should not be imitated.

Tale Types: 1539   Cleverness and Gullibility
             1542A   Return for Tools

Principal Motifs:

K330.1   Man gulled into giving up his clothes
K341.8.1   Trickster pretends to ride home for tools to perform tricks
X600   Humor concerning races or nations

Parallel Stories:

Type 1539 found in:
Aiken, *Pack Load,* pp. 49–55
Dorson, *World,* pp. 558–63 (from Pino-Saavedra)
Paredes, *Mexico,* #53a, 53b
Pino-Saavedra, *Chile,* #44
Ranke, *Germany,* #53

Type 1542A found in:
Dorson, *Comic Indian,* p. 124
Marriott, *Winter-Telling,* pp. 74–82

47

Baby in the Crib

(E. L. Smith)*

John stole a pig from Old Marsa. He was on his way home with him and his Old Marsa seen him. After John got home he looked out and seen his Old Marsa coming down to the house. So he put this pig in a cradle they used to rock the babies in in them days (some people called them cribs), and he covered him up. When his Old Marster come in John was sitting there rocking him.

Old Marster says, "What's the matter with the baby, John?"

"The baby got the measles."

"I want to see him."

John said, "Well you can't; the doctor said if you uncover him the measles will go back in on him and kill him."

So his Old Marster said, "It doesn't matter; I want to see him, John." He reached down to uncover him.

John said, "If that baby is turned to a pig now, don't blame me."

*Reprinted from *Negro Folktales in Michigan,* collected and edited by Richard M. Dorson. Originally published in 1956 by Harvard University Press; reprinted with the permission of Richard M. Dorson by Greenwood Press, 1974. Pp. 56–57.

Notes and Comments

The major black American trickster cycle concerns a plantation slave named John or George and his endless attempts to get the better of his Old Marster (or Old Boss, after the Civil War). The stories themselves ventilated many strong feelings in a way that occasionally made plantation life a little more tolerable.

On the plantation John was his own kind of folk hero, and narrators describe him with some admiration. One man began his story: "Old Marster had this main fellow on his farm he put his confidence in, John" (Dorson, *Michigan,* p. 59). Another is more explanatory:

> You take in the South, they always have one strong colored guy on all the plantations. He's given a lot of consideration by the boss—usually he be foreman. Can put two or three of the others in his back pocket.
>
> (*Ibid.,* p. 55)

Actually the Old Boss himself takes a certain amount of pride in his number-one field hand, often bragging about him to other plantation owners, even setting up wagers on John's physical prowess or his powers of divination. The resulting relationship suggests a dangerous partnership, since there was no denying the lash that lay just around the corner. But John treads happily on this thin line between intimacy and disaster. He accidentally or cleverly wins the contests and guesses what is hidden under a box. If he is caught in some petty theft, he somehow manages to talk his way around it; and in most stories it is Old Marster who is left with the bump on his head or with a quizzical look on his face.

While the composite characters of John and Old Marster come directly from the soil of antebellum plantation days, some of the stories that cluster around this trickster figure are much older. The central incident of "Baby in the Crib," for example, can be traced to the most famous English mystery play of the fifteenth century, *The Second Shepherd's Play,* which contains a sheep-stealing incident. In this play a rogue named Mak steals a lamb and hides it in a cradle in his cottage. When the shepherds come seeking their lamb, Mak is singing the "child" a lullaby. Even after the lamb has been discovered, Mak and his wife insist that the child must have been bewitched.

Variations in the old prank are limited, but explanations for the unusual baby are often localized. Part of the appeal of this tale is the way the cornered thief pretends surprise or concern about what his supposedly innocent "child" may turn out to be. In one version, John declares "Master it may be a shoat [little pig] now, but it sure was a possum while ago when I put 'im in this sack" (Botkin, *Burden,* p. 4). Another seems totally amazed at the discovery of maternity and cries, "Great Gawd, my wife has done bawned a hawg!" In still another, John the trickster has the good sense to escape before the discovery is made, using an exit line such as "You kin pull de kivver offen 'im if yuh wants ter, but Ah ain't gwine stay hyeah and see 'im die."

The most widely known example of a baby actually becoming a pig is in Lewis Carroll's *Alice's Adventures in Wonderland,* "Pig and Pepper" (Ch. 6). This transformation, however, is more a reflection of an old bachelor's dislike for little children than a borrowing from folk literature.

Tale Type 1525M   Mak and the Sheep

Principal Motifs:

K406   Stolen animal disguised as person so that thief may escape detection
K406.2   Stolen sheep dressed as baby in cradle

Parallel Stories in:

Allsopp, *Arkansas* 2: pp. 174–75
Botkin, *Burden,* pp. 3–4
Brewer, *John Tales,* pp. 81–83
———, *Juneteenth,* pp. 11–12
———, *Juneteenth, PTFLS* 26: pp. 55–56
Parsons, *Aiken,* #23
Randolph, *Devil's,* pp. 19–20
Robe, *Basque,* p. 156
Smyser, *Analogues,* p. 379
Stroup, *Analogues,* p. 380
———, *Mak,* pp. 5–6
Whiting, *Mak,* p. 552

PLAY:

Second Shepherds' Play (Towneley Cycle)

48

Nasr-ed-Din Hodja in the Pulpit*

Nasr-ed-Din Hodja one day addressed his congregation from the pulpit in the following words: "I beseech you to tell me truly. O brethren! O true believers! if what I am going to say to you is already known to you."

And the answer came, as in one voice, from his congregation, that they did not know, and that it was not possible for them to know, what the Hodja was going to say to them. "Then," quoth the preacher, "of what use to you or to me is an unknown subject?" And he descended from the pulpit and left the mosque.

On the following Friday his congregation, instead of having decreased, had greatly increased, and their anxiety to hear what he was going to say was felt in the very atmosphere.

The Hodja ascended the pulpit and said, "O brethren! O true believers! I beseech you to tell me truly if what I am going to say to you is already known to you."

The answer that came to the Hodja was so spontaneous as to suggest prearrangement. They all shouted, "Yes, Hodja, we do know what you are going to say to us."

---

*From *Tales From Turkey* collected and translated by Allan Ramsay and Francis McCullagh (London: Simpkin, Marshall, Hamilton, Kent, and Co., Ltd., 1914), pp. 46–47.

"That being the case," quoth the Hodja, "there is no need either of you wasting your time or of me wasting my time." And, descending from the pulpit, he left the mosque. His congregation, having prayed, also left gradually, one by one and in groups.

On the following Friday Nasr-ed-Din Hodja again mounted the pulpit, and saw that his mosque was so crowded that not a nook or corner in it was empty. He addressed his congregation in exactly the same manner. "O brethren! O true believers!" said he, "I ask you to tell me truly if what I am going to say is already known to you?"

And again the answer of his numerous congregation had evidently been prepared beforehand, for one half of them rose and said, "Yes, Hodja, we do know what you are going to say to us," and the other half rose and said, "O Hodja effendi, how could we poor ignorant people know what you intend to say to us?"

The Hodja answered, "It is well said; and now if the half that knows what I am going to say would explain to the other half what it is, I would be deeply grateful, for, of course, it will be unnecessary for me to say anything."

Whereupon he descended from the pulpit and left the mosque.

Notes and Comments

Tales of the Turkish trickster Nasredden Hodja (spellings vary) are highly popular in Turkey as well as almost all other Near and Middle Eastern countries. Scholars have yet to agree on whether or not such a man actually lived, but the Turkish government in 1960 published an "official" book of his tales, proclaimed his birthplace as the village of Hortu, and declared the tombstone (dated 1284 A.D.) in the cemetery at Akeshehir to be his authentic grave. At the same time, the Turkish government upgraded tourism to the status of a separate ministry.

That such a folk character would achieve national prominence is a remarkable feature of a trickster cycle. The Hodja has been around for so long and played so many roguish tricks that stories of wide international circulation cluster about him. Reading Kohja, the first English translation of the Hodja stories by Barnham in 1924, is like going down the list of anecdotes in the Aarne/Thompson Index. Plots are the same, whether they are told about Boots in Norway or Jack in Appalachia, but the Hodja stories are decidedly Turkish because the hero is a fat little man in an enormous turban waddling along on a donkey, ready to match wits with the great

Tamburlaine, the Mongol emperor, or to draw verbal swords in the market-place with one of his neighbors. The core of the story remains the same wherever it is told, but there's no one at all quite like the Hodja.

In prerepublican Turkey, a hodja was a Moslem priest and teacher, a scholar of the Koran and religious law. He is a character venerated on the one hand for his wisdom and quick repartee, but he also takes on some of the characteristics of the absent-minded professor. The result is another trickster with a dual character similar to Coyote, Anansi, and the rest. He is sometimes just as stupid as he is shrewd; at other times he is both naïve and wise. But always he is Turkish, and always he is Hodja. And he runs up and down the list of international jests and anecdotes with such familiarity that it is easy to forget the tales did not originate with him, that he has no more claim on many of the tales than does the Arabian Kjuha or the Persian Mullah. To survey a collection of Hodja stories as they are still told in the marketplace today is to understand the nature of the traditional anecdote and to appreciate the ease with which the same story takes on and discards the cultural clothes and climate of whichever country the trickster happens to find himself enshrined.

Sampling the variety of international tale types found in one collection · of Hodja stories will give an idea of the role the trickster plays in traditional literature. In the Barnham book, for example, there is 1351 *The Silence Wager,* 1365A *Wife Falls into a Stream,* and Type 1313 *The Man who Thought Himself Dead.* Even the classic noodle tale 1335A *Rescuing the Moon* has the Hodja pulling the moon out of the well, falling on his back after the effort, and sighing, "Ah! Thank God! . . . I had a tough job to do it, but the moon is back in its place."

On the other hand, since much of the Hodja's clever exploits have to do with the turn of a witty phrase, the clever solution to an impossible riddle, or the witty repartee over the price of the smell of food, much of the charm of the stories depend heavily on a skillful translation. Unfortunately because many puns and wordplays are untranslatable, some of the best Turkish wit of the Hodja may be lost forever for the non-native speaker.

The story reprinted here, "Hodja in the Pulpit," can obviously have little variation in the plot, for the verbal manipulation is as rigid and prescribed as any traditional formula. Only the setting can change as the story is told in different cultures. One black preacher in the deep South saves "a powerful lot of time" by using the same device when he concludes " 'Pears to me that if you all know what I'm talkin' about, ain't no use of my sayin' a word" (Courlander, *Terrapin,* p. 103).

The setting need not always be a church and a sermon. An Ozark story takes place in a secret lodge meeting, complete with a meeting hall, a guard at the door, fine badges, but no "secret wisdom." A wise man from Little Rock collects $25, asks if the boys "know the holy words," and concludes that the crowd is not yet ready for the "secret wisdom." Another $25, another evening, and the answer is "yes." Finally, yet another $25 produces the wisdom that lodge brothers are "all brothers in the bond. . . . Them that knows is obliged to tell them that don't know."

Tale Type 1826   The Parson has no Need to Preach

Principal Motif:

X452   The parson has no need to preach

Parallel Stories in:

Barnham, *Khoja,* pp. 208–9
Courlander, *Terrapin's,* pp. 102–3
Crane, *Italian,* #52
Kelsey, *Hodja,* pp. 21–28
Randolph, *Knapsack,* pp. 129–31

MAJOR STUDY:

Wesselski, Albert. *Der Hodscha Nasreddin.* 2 vols. Weimar: A. Duncker, 1911. (In German)

49

Pedro de Urdemalas*

Pedro de Urdemalas lives by his wits. In a way he is a liar but, different from Don Cacahuate, Tío Aurelio, and Compadre Doroteo, he does not lie for the glory of lying. His *mentiras* are a means to an end, and the most desirable end to him is to skin the fellow who is out to get the other man's hide. However, he often tricks the innocently gullible. Also, being a man of chance, he is a plaything of fate; one day he is rich and the next poor.

Once when considerably the worse for his manner of living and while wandering along a highway tired, hungry, and without money, he came to a hog ranch. It was the first of its kind he had ever seen and, despite his low spirits, he was greatly amused by the great array of swine tails.

"There are many tails," said he, "and wherever there is a tail there is a hog. This gives me an idea, and if it works I shall have money to spend."

He took his knife and cut the tails from the hogs and continued on his way until he came to a *resaca,* or swamp. There he busied himself sticking the hog-end of the tail stumps in the mud. Then, after tramping around and digging up the earth about each, he sat beneath a willow and began to weep.

Presently a man rode up horseback.

*From "A Pack Load of Mexican Tales," by Riley Aiken in *Publications of the Texas Folklore Society* 12 (1935): 49–52. Reprinted by permission of the Texas Folklore Society.

"Why are you weeping?" he asked.

Pedro wept louder than ever and said, "Why shouldn't I weep? I have lost a fortune in this bog hole. Those tails you see are all that is left to show for hogs that were."

"Poor fellow," said the stranger, "weep no more. I shall buy your herd and have my servants come and dig them out of this *atascadero*. How much do you want for them?"

"*Señor,*" said Pedro de Urdemalas, "it is not my wish to sell them, for life is wrapped up in my hogs, but you see how hopeless things are. Rather than lose them, I will sell them to you for one thousand dollars."

The trade was made. Pedro went away weeping until he was out of sight and then took to his heels.

The stranger brought his servants, and he wasn't long finding out how well he had been swindled. Frantic, he directed a search for Pedro but all to no avail. He gave up the hunt and did the only thing left for him to do, and that was to swear revenge in case he should ever again meet Pedro de Urdemalas.

Well, sir, true to form, there came a day when again Pedro was broke and hungry. Immediately he began devising a new lie with which to snare some sucker.

"I need twenty cents worth of *frijoles,* a pot, an underground furnace, and a little time," said he to himself.

He bought beans and pot, dug a furnace, and, after having burned some wood to coals, he put the pot over them and hid all traces of the fire. Presently the pot began to boil, and Pedro, with a long thorn, speared those frijoles that boiled to the top and ate them. He was amusing himself in this manner when a traveler approached.

"*Buenas tardes, buen amigo* (good-day, good friend)," he said. "What are you doing?"

"No, nothing," said Pedro de Urdemalas, "just waiting for those who are to arise and observing those who go."

"Pardon," said the traveler, pointing at the pot, "what makes that thing boil?"

"Nothing; it is a magic pot," Pedro informed him. "In the preparation of my meals I never have to bother with fire. So soon as the food is in it and it is placed on the ground it begins to boil."

Now, the stranger was a traveling man and figured that he needed just such a pot.

"How much do you want for it?" he asked.

"I don't care to sell it," said Pedro.

"I will give you a thousand dollars," bartered the traveler.

"See here, *amigo,*" said Pedro de Urdemalas, "I am badly in need of money; otherwise I would not think of disposing of such a rare pot. It is a bargain, but we will have to take care lest it discover the change in masters and refuse to boil. Sit down very quietly and give me the money. Don't speak or move until I am out of hearing."

It was with the utmost caution that the trade was made. The stranger, almost afraid to breathe, sat by the boiling pot and Pedro tiptoed away. After an hour of patient watching the new owner of the magic vessel noticed that the beans and water were not boiling. He picked up the pot and immediately realized that he had been skinned. At first he swore revenge, but after a second thought he was so humiliated by his gullibility that he was glad to forget about it.

It was late in the afternoon when Pedro de Urdemalas decided it would be safe to rest his weary legs. Tired out by the haste with which he left his last victim, he sat beneath a mesquite not far from the road and wondered how he might add another thousand dollars to his ill-gotten gain. Presently, he began by boring holes in the coin he carried, and, when this was done, he hung it to the branches of the tree in such a manner that it appeared to have grown there.

The following morning two wagon masters on their way up the road were amazed by what they saw. They went to the mesquite and were at the point of plucking the rare fruit when Pedro saw them.

"*Eit, eit!*" he shouted. "Leave my tree alone."

They asked the name of the tree.

"This is the only one in existence," said Pedro de Urdemalas. "It bears twice a year and it is time to gather this season's crop."

"How much do you want for this plant?" they asked.

"Don't insult me," said Pedro. "Why should I want to sell a tree like this? It would be foolish."

"We can pay your price," they insisted. "Besides, it isn't our intention to leave here before you agree to sell."

"Oh, well," said Pedro, "give me a thousand dollars and the presnt crop and the bargain is closed."

They agreed. Pedro gathered the coin from the tree, collected the purchase money, and left for parts unknown.

The wagon masters built homes near the mesquite, pruned it, watered it, and did all in their power to aid in a rich crop of coin the following season.

It being only a mesquite, their reward was mesquite beans.

These poor fools, like the others, had been beaten, but were thankful to have come off no worse.

Pedro, in the meantime, was, as an old *corrido* says, "*siempre caminando,*" always traveling.

Notes and Comments

Stories of tricksters, jokers, braggarts, and noodles are frequently told in Spanish about the rogue called Pedro de Urdemalas. Pedro has been called "dissatisfied," "ever wishing for more," "a genius who is not subject to ordinary rules or limitations," and simply "Peter the Mischiefmaker." The epithet is very old; Cervantes wrote a play, *Pedro de Urdemalas,* about a stupid creature rather than an intelligent trickster. Tales of Pedro were certainly current in Cervantes' day, and the episodes now associated with his name may be associated with the *novela picaresca* of the sixteenth century. "Urdir" means to warp and "mal" means evil.

In such a long series of episodes it is to be expected that the order has become confused and some elements have been added. Several incidents of the entire cycle stand out. Pedro is a shiftless *viajero* (peddler) who lives by his wits. When his old mother lies dying, he hastens her end by bathing her in scalding water, strapping her body to a donkey, and driving it to a farmer's field. The irate farmer throws stones at the burro, and Pedro accuses him of killing his mother. For this not so subtle blackmail Pedro receives a sum of money, and his mother gets a better burial than she anticipated.

Another of Pedro's tricks is the familiar one of scattering gold pieces behind his burro which he sells at a vastly inflated price as a gold-producing donkey. The trickster also secures a job as a pig-keeper but sells his patron's animals to a cattleman, keeping only the tails. These he buries in the swamp (Type 1004) and claims they all fell in. After many such incidents, Pedro visits purgatory where he makes a nuisance of himself by doing good, and the devils complain. Finally he asks for a view of heaven (or flies there as a bird) and sneaks in. God turns him to stone, and he becomes the doorstep of heaven.

Much of the popularity of Pedro lies in his symbolizing the little man who pits his wits against the Establishment and the rich and powerful. The scholar Aurelio Espinosa considers Pedro tales as narratives of social protest, pointing out that stereotypes and epithets once applied to the peninsula Spaniards have now been transferred to the new "oppressor," the North American *gringo.* Whether or not Espinosa's theory is correct, it is clear that the ordinary folk feel the need of a hero from their own background and class—they will accept no other. Tales and motifs about other tricksters are taken and adapted to the home product. This process explains why it is that identical stories are told about such a variety of tricksters—Hodja, Boots, Coyote, and John.

The two tale types are combined in the Pedro tale printed here: 1004 *Hogs in the Mud, Sheep in the Air,* and 1539 *Cleverness and Gullibility*— though only one incident is taken from the latter. The first type is a jest in origin and often accompanies Type 1539. The latter tale includes several episodes that often appear as independent stories with Pedro as protagonist.

Tale Types: 1004   Hogs in the Mud; Sheep in the Air
       1539   Cleverness and Gullibility

Principal Motifs:

K404.1   Tails in the ground
K111   Pseudo-magic treasure-producing object sold
K112.1   Alleged self-cooking kettle sold

Parallel Stories:

Type 1004 found in:

Carrière, *Missouri,* #61 (in French with English summary)
Cleare, *Fortune Island,* pp. 228–29 (references)
Mason, *Porto-Rican,* pp. 162, 172, 179 (in Spanish)
Miller, *Los Angeles,* pp. 324–33 (summary in English, extensive references.Tale is about Juan Tonto.)
Parsons, *Sea Islands,* #18
———, *Zapoteca,* #14
Pino-Saavedra, *Chile,* #41
Robe, *Los Altos,* #114 (summary in English)
Smiley, *Virginia,* #21
Thompson, *One,* #85
Toor, *Mexican,* p. 530
Wheeler, *Jalisco,* #148, #149 (summaries in English)

Type 1539 found in:

Mason, *Porto-Rican,* p. 176
Paredes, *Mexico,* #53
Pino-Saavedra, *Chile,* #44
Robe, *Los Altos,* #41

H

Wisdom of the Ages:
MORALITY TALES

The darker side of reality is prominent in the morality tales, which serve both for instruction and entertainment, sugarcoating with narrative dexterity the nugget of wisdom each contains. The pessimism of these morality tales merely reflects that point of view of life seen through a smoked glass mirror, a slice of life, as it were, cut with a serrated edge.

50. *THE HONEY GATHERER'S THREE SONS*   301
    TT 513—*The Extraordinary Companions*
    Also known as *Six Go Through the World,*
    Cooperation Always Wins

51. *THE RIDICULOUS WISHES*   305
    TT 750A—*The Wishes*
    Also known as *Hospitality Rewarded, The Sausage*
    on the Nose, The Saint's Visit

52. *THE MAN WHO KNEW HOW TO CURE A SNAKEBITE*   309
    TT 155—*The Ungrateful Serpent Returned to*
    Captivity

Also known as *Good Is Always Repaid with Evil,
Good Guys Always Finish Last, The Tiger, the
Brahmin and the Jackal*

53. *THE TALE OF IVAN*   314
 TT 910B—*The Servant's Good Counsels*
 Also known as *Advice Is Better than Wages, Wise
 Through Experience*

54. *THE FOOLISH MAN*   319
 TT 460A—*The Journey to God to Receive Reward*
    460B—*The Journey in Search of Fortune*
 Also known as *Happiness is Often Close at Hand*

55. *THE OLD MAN AND HIS GRANDSON*   324
 TT 980B—*Wooden Drinking Cup for Old Man*
 Also known as *The Child Is Father of the Man, The
 Wooden Bowl for the Aged*

50

The Honey Gatherer's Three Sons*

A honey gatherer had three sons, all born at the same time. Their names were Hear-it-however-faint-the-sound, Follow-it-however-great-the-distance and Put-it-together-however-small-the-pieces. These names are sufficient to indicate the skill of these young men, but their friends called them simply Hear, Follow and Piece.

One day the honey gatherer went on a long, long journey into the forest until he came to a tree that was as high as a hill, and the bees that buzzed in and out showed clearly that it must be full of honey. He climbed up, but, treading on a rotten branch, fell to the ground and was broken into ten pieces.

Hear was sitting beside the hut in the village, but he promptly jumped to his feet, saying, "Father has fallen from a tree. Come! Let us go to his help."

His brother Follow set out and led them along the father's tracks until they came upon the body lying in ten pieces. Piece then put all the parts together, fastened them up, and the father walked home while the sons carried his honey.

*From *The Magic Drum: Tales from Central Africa* by William F. P. Burton (New York: Criterion Books, 1962), pp. 39–41. Copyright © 1961 by W. F. P. Burton. Published by Criterion Books. By permission of Thomas Y. Crowell.

Next day the honey gatherer again set out to look for honey, while his sons sat at home, each boasting that he was more important than the others.

"You could not have heard him without me," said Hear.

"Though you had heard him you could not have found him without me," said Follow.

"Even though you had found him, you could not have put him together without me," said Piece.

Meanwhile, the old honey gatherer had gone far into the forest till he came to a tree as high as the clouds, and the bees buzzing in and out showed clearly that it must be full of honey. He climbed up, but, treading on a rotten branch, fell to the ground and was broken into a hundred pieces. His sons were sitting at home boasting about their prowess, when Hear jumped up, saying, "Father has fallen!"

Follow reluctantly set out to follow the footprints, and found the hundred pieces on the ground. Pointing to them he said, "See how indispensable I am. I have found him for you."

Piece then put the hundred pieces together very grudgingly, saying, "I, and I alone, have restored Father."

Their father walked home, while the sons carried the honey.

Next day the old honey gatherer went farther than ever into the forest and he found a tree that reached to the stars. The bees buzzing in and out showed that it must be full of honey. He climbed up, but, treading on a rotten branch, fell to the ground and was broken into a thousand pieces.

Hear heard the fall, but would not tell his brothers. Follow knew that there must have been an accident since his father did not return, while Piece realized that his father needed his assistance, but would not condescend to ask his brothers to find him so that he might piece him together.

So the old honey gatherer died, because the selfish sons each thought more of his own reputation than of his father's. In truth, each needed the others, and none was wiser or better than the rest.

Notes and Comments

Over many hundreds of years, according to Burton, the Congolese have developed an efficient system for preparing the young for adult life in Central Africa. While most of the vocational skills are learned by doing, the education for communal living comes from the wise men of the tribe who constitute the *bamfumu* or chief's council. Many of these elders delight in the art of storytelling and are especially adept at sugarcoating a pill so that the listeners are seldom aware of just how much moral teaching they are absorbing.

The object of all tales such as "The Honey Gatherer's Three Sons" is to teach, and its lesson is clear. The sons have marvelous gifts, but they lack the sense to use them for good. Instead of working constructively as a team, Hear, Follow, and Piece are much more concerned about whose powers are the most indispensable. In the tragic ending of this tale, none of the brothers is able to help the honey gatherer because it would involve cooperation. The father dies a victim because each of the brothers "needed the others, and none was wiser or better than the rest." The fundamental lesson that "no man is an island" is one that no listener can prudently ignore.

There are many tales whose main ingredient is a series of men (or animals) with extraordinary powers. As Stith Thompson points out, the popularity of extraordinary companions has led to widespread use of this motif in both oral and literary narratives (*Folktale,* pp. 54–55). Extraordinary companions accompany Jason in his search for the golden fleece, are found in the Welsh lore that evolved into the King Arthur epic, and occur in Buddhist scriptures. In the magic tale "Six Go Through the World" (Tale Type 513A), the hero generally finds six companions who help him accomplish tasks for which he is extremely well (though reluctantly) paid. In most magic tales, the unusual powers are used in pursuit of a common goal with a happy outcome, but the "Honey Gatherer," like the other tales in this section, shows the darker side.

Tale Type 513   The Extraordinary Companions

Principal Motifs:

F600   Persons with extraordinary powers
F601.5   Extraordinary companions are brothers
F641   Person of remarkable hearing

Parallel Stories in:

Afanas'ev, pp. 410–14
Basile, *Pentamerone* 1: 5 (Lit.)
Campbell, *West Highlands* 1: #16
Campbell, *Cloud Walking,* pp. 143–47
Carrière, *Missouri,* #30 (summary in English)

Delarue, *Borzoi,* #18 (reprinted in Thompson, *One,* #43)
Grimm, #134
Parsons, *Cape Verde* 1: #82 and variant a
Saucier, *Louisiana,* #9
Seki, *Japan,* #18
Yates, *Gypsy,* pp. 18–20

PICTURE BOOKS:

Five Chinese Brothers. Retold by Claire H. Bishop and illustrated by Kurt Wiese. New York: Coward-McCann, 1938. (Set in China)
The Fool of the World and the Flying Ship. Retold by A. Ransome and illustrated by Uri Shulevitz. New York: Farrar, Strauss, Giroux, 1968. (Set in Russia)
Four Clever Brothers. Illustrated by Felix Hoffmann. New York: Harcourt, Brace and World, 1967. (Set in Germany)
Long, Broad and Quickeye. Adapted and illustrated by Evaline Ness (from Andrew Lang). New York: Charles Scribner's Sons, 1969. (Set in Czechoslovakia)
Seven Simeons. Retold and illustrated by Boris Artzybasheff. New York: Viking Press, 1937. (Set in Russia)

51

The Ridiculous Wishes*

O nce there was a poor woodcutter who, growing weary of a life of toil, wished that he could be at rest in the Stygian realm. Never, he declared, since the day he was born, had cruel heaven granted a single one of his desires.

One day when he was in the woods, complaining of his miserable lot, Jupiter appeared to him, thunderbolt in hand. The poor man cowered before him in terror. "I ask for nothing," he cried. "I'll drop my wishes, master, if you drop your thunder. Surely that's a fair bargain."

"There is no need to be afraid," replied Jupiter. "I have heard your complaints and have come to show you how wrongly you judge me. I, the sovereign master of the world, promise to grant the first three wishes you make, whatever they may be. Now think carefully before you make them, for your whole happiness depends on them."

So saying, Jupiter went back to heaven, while the woodcutter gaily shouldered his bundle of wood and made off for home.

"Yes," he said to himself. "I must decide nothing lightly. I must ask my wife what she thinks."

*From *The Fairy Tales of Charles Perrault* translated by Geoffrey Brereton (London: Penguin Books, 1957), pp. 107–10. © Geoffrey Brereton, 1957. Reprinted by permission of Penguin Books Ltd.

"Hey, Fanny," he cried, as he entered his cottage, "let's have a big fire and a good meal. We are rich for life. We have only to make three wishes."

Thereupon he told his wife all that had happened. The good woman began to form vast schemes in her mind, but, remembering the importance of acting prudently, she said:

"Blaise, my dear, we must spoil nothing by impatience. We must talk this over very carefully. We had better sleep on it and leave our first wish for to-morrow."

"That is just what I think," said her husband. "But now, go and draw some of that special wine from the cellar."

When she came back, he drank a deep draught and, leaning back in his chair before the fire, said: "To go with such a fine blaze, we could do very well with a few feet of black pudding."

He had no sooner spoken than, to his wife's amazement, a very long sausage issued from a corner of the fireplace and came snaking towards her.

She gave a cry, then, realizing that this was the answer to the wish which her husband had so stupidly uttered, she began to abuse him violently. "When you could have an empire, with gold, pearls, rubies, diamonds, splendid clothes, all you can wish for is black pudding!"

"Well," he said, "I was wrong. I have done an extremely silly thing. I will do better next time."

"Yes, yes," she cried. "That is what you say. But only a donkey would make such a wish."

Purple with rage, the husband almost wished his wife to the devil, and perhaps he might have done worse.

"Man," he said, "is born to suffering. A plague on this sausage! I wish to heaven that it would stick to your nose!"

The wish was immediately granted, for no sooner had he spoken than four feet of black pudding fastened themselves to the end of his wife's nose. The effect was not pretty, although by hanging over her mouth the sausage prevented Fanny from talking—an advantage which the husband appreciated for a few peaceful moments.

"With the last remaining wish," he said to himself, "I could still become a king at a single throw. But we must consider the queen's appearance and whether she would like to sit on the throne with a nose over a yard long. She must decide whether she will become a princess and keep that horrible nose, or remain a woodcutter's wife and have a face like other people."

Fanny well knew the power of royalty—when one wears a crown, one's nose is always perfect. Yet, since the desire to look pleasant is stronger still, she decided after all to keep her peasant's bonnet.

So the woodcutter was still a woodcutter. He never became a mighty king. His purse was not filled with gold. He was only too glad to use his last wish to restore his wife to her former state.

Notes and Comments

The story of "The Ridiculous Wishes" (Type 750A) which the Grimms called "The Poor Man and the Rich Man" is a tale that demonstrates human greed and the dangers of unlimited power in a humorous, even facetious manner. Ranke notes that stories of three wishes being granted to a foolish couple are to be found in the works of Marie de France in Europe (twelfth century), in the works of the Middle High German poet Stricker (thirteenth century), and in Arabian narrative literature of the thirteenth and fourteenth century.

But the laws of hospitality date back to Greek mythology when Zeus and the other gods were wont to wander the earth. Perhaps the best known of such visits that resulted in wishes being granted occurs in the myth of Baucis and Philemon. A model couple for all time, these two hospitable people used the wish granted them by Zeus both wisely and lovingly, for they wished they might perish in the same hour so that neither would be left to mourn the other.

The circumstance of the visit is similar when the visitors are Christ and St. Peter, but storytellers have perhaps been more interested in the host and hostess who have not made wise use of their wishes. Such foolish couples usually waste their wishes entirely, with the result that they are no better off than they were before they were granted unlimited power through wish fulfillment. The general pattern followed in most of the wishing stories has the first wish transferred from the husband to the wife who wastes it on some trifle. Then, in a fit of anger, the husband wishes that trifle were on some part of his wife's body. Finally, they both must use the final wish to remove or undo the effects of the first two wishes. The details of the wishes vary a great deal, but the basic idea is always the same: either a reward or a punishment according to the treatment given the holy visitors.

"The Ridiculous Wishes" combines three kinds of oral tradition—tales of wonder (filled with magic), the saint's legend, and the droll. The three wishes motif is found in all of Europe with variants as far afield as Indonesia and Korea. In the Americas it is a popular story among blacks and is easily adapted to the burlesque, such as that version collected by Vance Randolph in *Who Blowed Up the Church House?* The Grimm version is very widely diffused in Europe where over eighty versions have been recorded. The Perrault version printed here is typical of those French versions that have had so much influence on children's editions since the seventeenth century.

Charles Perrault (1628–1703) is a landmark figure in children's literature for many reasons, one of which is his publication of eight folktales in 1697, a century before the work of the Brothers Grimm. "The Ridiculous Wishes" was published two years earlier, originally as a verse tale. Geoffrey Brereton suggests that Perrault "probably took it from one of the 16th century collections of tales which, in turn, had drawn on the medieval fableaux of humorous anecdotes in verse." (p. x1). ⸺

Tale Type 750A   The Wishes

Principal Motifs:

D1761.0.2   Limited number of wishes granted
J2071   Three foolish wishes
J2075   The transferred wish
J2075.2   Two transferred wishes used unwisely

Parallel Stories in:

Djurklo, *Swedish,* pp. 27–32
Dorson, *American Negro,* #206
⸺, *Buying,* p. 83
⸺, *Michigan,* pp. 191–92
Grimm, #87
Grundtvig, *Danish,* 193–98
Harland, *Lancashire,* pp. 15–16
Hartland, *English Fairy,* pp. 251–52
Jacobs, *More English,* #65
Kennedy, *Legendary,* pp. 287–88
Musick, *Green Hills,* #37
O'Suilleabhain, *Handbook,* p. 573 (summary)
Perrault, "Les Souhaits Ridicules"
Randolph, *Church House?,* pp. 139–40
Ranke, *Germany,* #56 (reprinted in Thompson, *One,* #73)

PICTURE BOOK:

The Three Wishes. Joseph Jacobs. Illustrated by Paul Galdone. New York: McGraw Hill, 1961.

52

The Man Who Knew
How to Cure a Snakebite*

Once upon a time, long ago in the Kingdom of Cambodia, there lived a man called Sokh—kind Sokh he was known as.

One day, Sokh set off into the forest to cut firewood. As he was going along he suddenly came to a clearing where he saw a tiger, lying dead at the foot of a rise by the side of the path. Sokh stopped and walked all round the tiger to see what had happened. He decided that the tiger had been bitten by a snake because, just under the tiger's body, he saw a snake's hole.

Now Sokh had a very kind heart towards the dead tiger, and so he opened up the bundle of things he was carrying and took out some snake-bite ointment which he rubbed in over the tiger's body. In a moment the tiger recovered and got to his feet. He saw that his body was covered all over with something dark and sticky. Of course, it was only Sokh's oint-ment, but the tiger was furious and growled at Sokh, "How dare you go and make me all dirty like this?" "Brother Tiger," replied kind Sokh, "I was walking along in the forest when I suddenly saw you lying dead from a snake bite. All I did was to rub and smear some snake-bite ointment on your

*From *Mr Basket Knife and Other Khmer Folktales* translated by A. R. Milne (London: George Allen & Unwin Ltd., 1972), pp. 23–25. Reprinted by permission of the publisher.

body, to bring you back to life." "Stuff and nonsense," said the tiger. "When was I ever dead? When was I ever bitten by a snake? I was just taking a little nap there. Now I shall certainly kill you and eat you up for my dinner."

Poor Sokh trembled with fear at the tiger's words. "Have pity on me, Brother Tiger," said kind Sokh. "Don't kill me now, just wait until I can fetch someone to judge this issue between us. If he says I am in the wrong, then you can certainly eat me up. But if he says I am in the right, you must let me go free." The tiger agreed and so Sokh set off to find a judge. Soon he met a horse and a buffalo standing near his path. "Brothers," Sokh said to them, "have pity on me and come and help to save my life. There is a tiger who was bitten dead by snake, but I brought him back to life again, by smearing him with my snake-bite ointment. But now he wants to eat me all up because he says I woke him up from a sleep and made him all dirty." The horse and the buffalo discussed the matter between themselves. "For sure," they said, "we ought to decide the case in favor of the man and against the tiger, but if we do that, the tiger will be very angry with us and come and eat us up." So they turned to Sokh and said: "Oh no, you are quite in the wrong. We feel that you should offer yourself to the tiger to be eaten up." Poor Sokh grew more and more frightened, so he politely said goodbye to the horse and the buffalo and quickly set off on his way again.

Before long, Sokh met old Judge Rabbit. So Sokh explained the whole matter to him and laid a complaint against the tiger. Judge Rabbit considered the whole story very carefully and then said to Sokh: "I want you to go back and discuss the matter with the tiger again. I will meet you there."

Well, sure enough, just as Sokh was arguing with the tiger again, Judge Rabbit appeared. "What are you two arguing about?" asked Judge Rabbit innocently. The tiger and kind Sokh each explained his case. Judge Rabbit listened carefully and then gave his judgment. "We will just rehearse all the facts once more," he said. "You, Brother Tiger, must go and sleep in the exact spot where you were sleeping before. If, when it is time for you to wake up, you have not died, then you may kill and eat this man."

So the tiger went to sleep as he was told, lying in exactly the same spot as before. The snake came out of his hole again and bit the tiger dead. When Judge Rabbit saw that the tiger was properly dead, he turned to the man and said: "Brother Sokh, that concludes the first part of the case, but this time, do not rub your ointment on!" Then Judge Rabbit took his leave of kind Sokh and went off to his home.

MORAL: Doing good does not always pay.

Notes and Comments

The literary origins of this tale of the ungrateful animal date back to the *Fables of Aesop,* the *Panchatantra* of India, and the *Arabian Thousand and One Nights.* The theme of the story that "Good is repaid with evil" is as old as pessimism itself and corresponds to a modern concept that "Nice guys finish last." Such an attitude reflects the point of view of life seen through a smoked glass mirror, to the extent that he who examines the human experience only sees the darker version.

This "half-empty glass" pessimism corresponds to the thorough-going optimism of the tales of magic, where the young hero is noble, kind, courageous, loyal, brave, and true, marries the king's daughter and lives happily ever after, with his glass always half full. With such an abundance of optimism for the average peasant, it is little wonder that a handful of moralists would choose to reflect the darker side of life. Their assumptions were based on the theory that if things can get any worse, they will. That their stories would serve both for instruction and entertainment is as natural as that proverbs, which attempt to encapsulate the human experience even more tersely, should coexist happily in total contradiction of each other. For example: "Absence makes the heart grow fonder" is balanced by "out of sight—out of mind." For all those who would advocate "look before you leap," there are others standing in the wings shouting, "he who hesitates is lost." No wonder then that there should be a few voices crying in the wilderness of the average man's existence that "good is repaid with evil," and for many a peasant or poor sharecropper, a thousand times over.

The story of "The Man Who Knew How to Cure a Snakebite" is a typical story of the ungrateful animal that has been set free and threatens to injure its rescuer. In the Aesop version below, the man's period of instruction is brief and fatal:

> One winter a Farmer found a Viper frozen and numb with cold, and out of pity picked it up and placed it in his bosom. The Viper was no sooner revived by the warmth than it turned upon its benefactor and inflicted a fatal bite upon him; and as the poor man lay dying, he cried, "I have only got what I deserved, for taking compassion on so villainous a creature."

That such an experience transmits a convincing moral is illustrated by the Negro informant in Michigan who, after relating the fable above in a folktale form, added the following comment about human nature:

Now you know there's people will confidence you just like that snake ... [Gives example of a man he knows]. Yeah, he was crooked as a barrel of scales. He'd steal his own hat off his hoe, just to keep in practice. And as fine-looking a young man as you ever seen. He just loved to steal, and he'd sell for nothing. . . . Anybody'd fall for him. He was a snake. You put him in your bosom and he'd bite you.

(Dorson, *Negro Folktales in Michigan,* p. 197)

Such comments may indicate that man can and does learn from such experiences, as another and more ruthless version of this ungrateful animal story illustrates. In a story close to the text of "The Man Who Knew How to Cure a Snakebite," but with an additional twist of the knife at the end, one man illustrates that sometimes a proverb can be doubly valid. In this form of the story, a man rescues a serpent from a burning tree or from underneath a fallen rock, only to have the serpent threaten his life. After two other animals agree with the serpent that man is no good and doesn't deserve to live, a fox agrees to help the man in return for a reward. The original situation is reconstructed; this time the man leaves the serpent to his fate and goes off to fetch the reward for the helpful fox. At this point, however, the man illustrates just how well he has learned his lesson. Rather than reward the fox with plump chickens as he has promised, the man brings her a bag containing a vicious dog. When the exhausted fox stops on a mountainside during the chase that ensues, she can only wonder in amazement, "And how was this your business . . . to set yourself up as judge?" At least one fox has double reason to believe that "good is always repaid with evil."

Tale Type 155   The Ungrateful Serpent Returned to Captivity

Principal Motifs:

W154.2.1   Rescued animal threatens rescuer
J1172.3   Ungrateful animal returned to captivity

Parallel Stories in:

Afanas'ev, pp. 273–75
Aiken, *Pack Load,* pp. 4–7
Boas, *Mexican,* pp. 209–10, 247
Dawkins, *More Greek,* #3

Eberhard, *China,* #67
Grundtvig, *Danish,* p. 184–86
Megas, *Greece,* #10
Miller, *Los Angeles,* #64 (references)
Paredes, *Mexico,* #25
Taylor, *Varifron,* pp. 93–94 (4 variants summarized)

53

The Tale of Ivan*

There were formerly a man and a woman living in the parish of Llanlavan, in the place which is called Hwrdh. And work became scarce, so the man said to his wife, "I will go search for work, and you may live here." So he took fair leave, and travelled far toward the East, and at last came to the house of a farmer and asked for work.

"What work can ye do?" said the farmer.

"I can do all kinds of work," said Ivan.

Then they agreed upon three pounds for the year's wages.

When the end of the year came his master showed him the three pounds. "See, Ivan," said he, "here's your wage; but if you will give it me back I'll give you a piece of advice instead."

"Give me my wage," said Ivan.

"No, I'll not," said the master; "I'll explain my advice."

"Tell it me, then," said Ivan.

Then said the master, "Never leave the old road for the sake of a new one."

After that they agreed for another year at the old wages, and at the end of it Ivan took instead a piece of advice, and this was it: "Never lodge

*From *Celtic Fairy Tales* edited by Joseph Jacobs. (London: David Nutt, 1892), pp. 195–99.

where an old man is married to a young woman."

The same thing happened at the end of the third year, when the piece of advice was: "Honesty is the best policy."

But Ivan would not stay longer, but wanted to go back to his wife.

"Don't go to-day," said his master; "my wife bakes to-morrow, and she shall make thee a cake to take home to thy good woman."

And when Ivan was going to leave, "Here," said his master, "here is a cake for thee to take home to thy wife, and, when ye are most joyous together, then break the cake, and not sooner."

So he took fair leave of them and travelled towards home, and at last he came to Wayn Her, and there he met three merchants from Tre Rhyn, of his own parish, coming home from Exeter Fair. "Oho! Ivan," said they, "come with us; glad are we to see you. Where have you been so long?"

"I have been in service," said Ivan, "and now I'm going home to my wife."

"Oh, come with us! you'll be right welcome."

But when they took the new road Ivan kept to the old one. And robbers fell upon them before they had gone far from Ivan as they were going by the fields of the houses in the meadow. They began to cry out, "Thieves!" and Ivan shouted out "Thieves!" too. And when the robbers heard Ivan's shout they ran away, and the merchants went by the new road and Ivan by the old one till they met again at Market-Jew.

"Oh, Ivan," said the merchants, "we are beholding to you; but for you we would have been lost men. Come lodge with us at our cost, and welcome."

When they came to the place where they used to lodge, Ivan said, "I must see the host."

"The host," they cried; "what do you want with the host? Here is the hostess, and she's young and pretty. If you want to see the host you'll find him in the kitchen."

So he went into the kitchen to see the host; he found him a weak old man turning the spit.

"Oh! oh!" quoth Ivan, "I'll not lodge here, but will go next door."

"Not yet," said the merchants, "sup with us, and welcome."

Now it happened that the hostess had plotted with a certain monk in Market-Jew to murder the old man in his bed that night while the rest were asleep, and they agreed to lay it on the lodgers.

So while Ivan was in bed next door, there was a hole in the pine-end of the house, and he saw a light through it. So he got up and looked, and heard the monk speaking. "I had better cover this hole," said he, "or people in the next house may see our deeds." So he stood with his back against it while the hostess killed the old man.

But meanwhile Ivan out with his knife, and putting it through the hole, cut a round piece off the monk's robe.

The very next morning the hostess raised the cry that her husband was murdered, and as there was neither man nor child in the house but the merchants, she declared they ought to be hanged for it.

So they were taken and carried to prison, till at last Ivan came to them. "Alas! alas! Ivan," cried they, "bad luck sticks to us; our host was killed last night, and we shall be hanged for it."

"Ah, tell the justices," said Ivan, "to summon the real murderers."

"Who knows," they replied, "who committed the crime?"

"Who committed the crime!" said Ivan. "If I cannot prove who committed the crime, hang me in your stead."

So he told all he knew, and brought out the piece of cloth from the monk's robe, and with that the merchants were set at liberty, and the hostess and the monk were seized and hanged.

Then they came all together out of Market-Jew, and they said to him: "Come as far as Coed Carrn y Wylfa, the Wood of the Heap of Stones of Watching, in the parish of Burman." Then their two roads separated, and though the merchants wished Ivan to go with them, he would not go with them, but went straight home to his wife.

And when his wife saw him she said: "Home in the nick of time. Here's a purse of gold that I've found; it has no name, but sure it belongs to the great lord yonder. I was just thinking what to do when you came."

Then Ivan thought of the third counsel, and he said: "Let us go and give it to the great lord."

So they went up to the castle, but the great lord was not in it, so they left the purse with the servant that minded the gate, and then they went home again and lived in quiet for a time.

But one day the great lord stopped at their house for a drink of water, and Ivan's wife said to him: "I hope your lordship found your lordship's purse quite safe with all its money in it."

"What purse is that you are talking about?" said the lord.

"Sure, it's your lordship's purse that I left at the castle," said Ivan.

"Come with me and we will see into the matter," said the lord.

So Ivan and his wife went up to the castle, and there they pointed out the man to whom they had given the purse, and he had to give it up and was sent away from the castle. And the lord was so pleased with Ivan that he made him his servant in the stead of the thief.

"Honesty's the best policy!" quoth Ivan, as he skipped about in his new quarters. "How joyful I am!"

Then he thought of his old master's cake that he was to eat when he was most joyful, and when he broke it, lo and behold, inside it was his wages for the three years he had been with him.

Notes and Comments

Many scholars have attempted to define and categorize the proverb as well as to determine its nature and function in society. The consensus is that a proverb is a popular saying in a relatively fixed form that is, or has been, in oral circulation (Jan Brunvand's definition). Its functions in society are to synthesize the group experience, to reaffirm the accepted precedents of society, and to validate the wisdom of the past as a pattern for the future.

To use a series of proverbs or good counsels as the basis for a realistic tale is an obvious device for some storytellers. That the proverbs would not always be the same ones, however, and that the subsequent methods of validating each proverb in the story would be different is also to be expected. Thus it is that Tale Type 910B *The Servant's Good Counsels* is found in different forms all over Europe as a folktale or in medieval and Renaissance books of *exempla* and jests. While the *Gesta Romanorum* may be the chief literary influence, Thompson finds these tales in the older literary collections from India as well as in Arabian and Persian reworkings.

In the folktale versions, advice is offered in two basic situations. In some stories the young man receives the advice from the deathbed of his father. In other stories the pieces of advice are purchased at great price, either from a stranger at the request of a new bride, or from an overseer after an apprenticeship has been completed. At any rate, the recipient usually has reason soon enough to try out the advice, and in all cases he learns the importance of benefiting from experience.

These proverbs, often dearly bought, are not so unusual as their purchasers might have thought. Thompson in the *Motif Index* lists seventy-nine different counsels under J21 "Counsels proved wise by experience." In this list he includes such gems as:

"Do not act when angry."

"Sleep before committing suicide."

"Do not walk half a mile with a man without asking his name."

"Do not send your wife for a long visit to her parents."

The hero soon has occasion to test the counsel he has been given. In all cases he counts himself fortunate to have escaped the forewarned dangers and concludes that the advice was well worth the price.

Usually the hero heeds each counsel as the opportunity to do so occurs. In one story from the Irish Celts, however, the hero, a young prince, hears the advice but decides to test it in another way. He is told "never to bring home a beast from a fair after having been offered a fair price for it." He takes a mare to the fair; refuses a good offer; and loses the mare on the way home as she stumbles in a riverbed and is killed. He is also told "never to call in ragged clothes on a friend when he wanted a favor from him." In this instance he borrowed the clothes of a beggar, called on the house of his sister, and was refused entry because she had guests. Finally, he was told "not to marry a wife with whose family he was not well acquainted." Again, he does not heed the advice, arranges a marriage, and discovers rather unsatisfactory information about his bride-to-be just in time. All in all, the ultimate result is the same as that experienced by the hardworking Ivan in the Welsh tale, but the doubting prince chooses to learn his lessons the hard way.

Tale Type 910B The Servant's Good Counsels

Principal Motifs:

J163.4	Good counsels bought (worked for)
J21.5	Do not leave the highway
J21.3	Do not go where an old man has a young wife
J21.2	Do not act when angry
J21	Counsels proved wise by experience

Parallel Stories in:

Afanas'ev, pp. 289–91
Aiken, *Pack Load,* pp. 7–10
Beckwith, *Jamaica Anansi,* #122
Crane, *Italian,* #41
Dawkins, *Modern Greek,* #75a (reprinted in Thompson, *One,* #81)
Hunt, *Popular Romances,* pp. 344–46
Kennedy, *Legendary,* pp. 73–77
Kent, *Turkey,* pp. 48–50, 119–21
Musick, *Green Hills,* #64
Protter, *Celtic,* #21
Roberts, *South,* #32a

54

The Foolish Man*

Once there was and was not in ancient Armenia a poor man who worked and toiled hard from morn till night, but nevertheless remained poor.

Finally one day he became so discouraged that he decided to go in search of God in order to ask Him how long he must endure such poverty —and to beg of Him a favor.

On his way, the man met a wolf.

"Good day, brother man," asked the wolf. "Where are you bound in such a hurry?"

"I go in search of God," replied the man. "I have a complaint to lodge with Him."

"Well," said the wolf, "would you do me a kindness? When you find God, will you complain to Him for me, too? Tell Him you met a half-starved wolf who searches the woods and fields for food from morning till night—and though he works hard and long, still finds nothing to eat. Ask God why He does not provide for wolves since He created them?"

*From *Once There Was and Was Not* by Virginia Tashjian (New York: Little, Brown and Co., 1966), pp. 3–10. Copyright © 1966 by Virginia A. Tashjian. Reprinted by permission of Little, Brown and Co.

"I will tell Him of your complaint," agreed the poor man, and continued on his way.

As he hurried over the hills and through the valleys, he chanced to meet a beautiful maid.

"Where do you go in such a hurry, my brother?" asked the maid.

"I go in search of God," replied the man.

"Oh, kind friend, when you find God, would you ask Him something for me? Tell Him you met a maid on your way. Tell Him she is young and fair and very rich—but very unhappy. Ask God why she cannot know happiness. What will become of her? Ask God why He will not help her to be happy."

"I will tell Him of your trouble," promised the poor man, and continued on his way.

Soon he met a tree which seemed all dried up and dying even though it grew by the side of a river.

"Where do you go in such a hurry, O traveler?" called the dry tree.

"I go in search of God," answered the man. "I have a complaint to lodge with Him."

"Wait a moment, O traveler," begged the tree, "I, too, have a question for God.

"Please ask Him why I am dry both in summer and winter. Though I live by this wet river, my leaves do not turn green. Ask God how long I must suffer. Ask Him that for me, good friend," said the tree.

The man listened to the tree's complaint, promised to tell God, and continued once again upon his way.

Finally, the poor man reached the end of his journey. He found God seated beneath the ledge of a cliff.

"Good day," said the man as he approached God.

"Welcome, traveler," God returned his greeting. "Why have you journeyed so far? What is your trouble?"

"Well, I want to know why there is injustice in the world. Is it fair that I toil and labor from morn till night—and yet never seem to earn enough for a full stomach, while many who do not work half as hard as I live and eat as rich men do?"

"Go then," replied God. "I present you the Gift of Luck. Go find it and enjoy it to the end of your days."

"I have yet another complaint, my Lord," continued the man—and he proceeded to list the complaints and requests of the starved wolf, the beautiful maid, and the parched tree.

God gave appropriate answers to each of the three complaints, whereupon the poor man thanked Him and started on his way homeward.

Soon he came upon the dry, parched tree.

"What message did God have for me?" asked the tree.

"He said that beneath your trunk there lies a pot of gold which prevents the water from seeping up your trunk to your leaves. God said your branches will never turn green until the pot of gold is removed."

"Well, what are you waiting for, foolish man!" exclaimed the tree. "Dig up that pot of gold. It will make you rich—and permit me to turn green and live again!"

"Oh, no," protested the man. "I have no time to dig up a pot of gold. God has given me the Gift of Luck. I must hurry and search for it." And he hurried on his way.

Presently, he met the beautiful maid who was waiting for him. "Oh, kind friend, what message did God have for me?"

"God said that you will soon meet a kind man who will prove to be a good life's companion to you. No longer will you be lonely. Happiness and contentment will come to you," reported the poor man.

"In that case, what are you waiting for, foolish man?" exclaimed the maid. "Why don't you stay here and be my life's companion."

"Oh, no! I have no time to stay with you. God has given me the Gift of Luck. I must hurry and search for it." And the man hurried on his way.

Some distance away, the starving wolf impatiently awaited the man's coming, and hailed him with a shout.

"Well, what did God say? What message did He send to me?"

"Brother wolf, so many things have happened since I saw you last," said the man. "I hardly know where to begin. On my way to seek God, I met a beautiful maid who begged me to ask God the reason for her unhappiness. And I met a parched tree who wanted God to explain the dryness of its branches even though it stood by a wet river.

"I told God about these matters. He bade me tell the maid to seek a life's companion in order to find happiness. He bade me warn the tree about a pot of gold buried near its trunk which must be removed before the branches can receive nourishment from the earth.

"On my return, I brought God's answers to the maid and to the tree. The maid asked me to stay and be her life's companion, while the tree asked me to dig up the pot of gold.

"Of course, I had to refuse both since God gave me the Gift of Luck—and I must hurry along to search for it!"

"Ah-h-h, brother man, and what was God's reply to me?" asked the starving wolf.

"As for you," replied the man, "God said that you would remain hungry until you met a silly and foolish man whom you could eat up. Only then, said God, would your hunger be satisfied."

"Hmmmmmm," mused the wolf, "where in the world will I find a man more silly and stupid than you?"

And he ate up the foolish man.

Notes and Comments

As the Trickster tales demonstrated, the teller of folktales was well aware that Luck could be assisted by cleverness, duplicity, and sheer accident. Many undeserving tricksters such as Brer Rabbit, Anansi, and Hodja triumphed over enemies who had justice and right on their side. In the moral tale, however, the interest is in the principle of Luck itself and its relationship to mankind. Having studied many of these tales in Greece, Dawkins concludes:

> In these stories we see the various, often incompatible, ideas by which men try to explain why it is that one man is happy and successful, another poor and miserable. We are shown Destiny; we see in her house the personification of Luck, the luck of men, who distributes good or ill at random; we see the Will of God; and lastly we see in the answers to the traveller's questions, how each man can do much to improve his fortune. Logically, these ideas exclude one another; practically they are all present to some degree in the puzzled mind of man contemplating the mysteries of human life.

(*Modern Greek Folk Tales,* p. 458)

The modern preoccupation with attempting to explain the meaning of life is nothing new. Folktales have always concerned themselves with such apparent contradictions as the triumph of evil over good, or the rewarding of the undeserving, or the misfortunes of the poor.

Tale types 460A and the closely related 460B *The Journey in Search of Fortune* are based on the theme of a journey to find God (or Chance) who controls the destinies of men. While the seeker is on his journey, he encounters various unfortunates who ask him to question God about their fates as well. What is most interesting in the Armenian variant of these stories is that the poor man, the protagonist, does not understand what God tells him and thus misses his chance for the very thing he was seeking. Ironically, though his quest is successful, he fails utterly to comprehend the perspective of his own life in terms of what he wants and what he could have if he would just seize the opportunities available to him. Passing up both riches and love, he returns home in haste, seeking an intangible happiness. Unfortunately for him, the wolf understands perfectly and spares the man the misery of the rest of his life.

Although the main character of this story is called a "foolish man" on several occasions and although he is too preoccupied to see what should be obvious, he is not a fool in the sense of a simpleton or a noodle. He is a tragic representative of all those who will wake up at the end of their lives, only to discover that they have never lived at all. Thus, as Dawkins interprets the Greek and Mediterranean view of life, the outcome of the story suggests that "misfortune originates in failure to take advantage of opportunity."

A similar suggestion that Luck or God helps those who help themselves is made by Lloyd Alexander in his Chronicles of Prydain. In the fourth book, *Taran Wanderer,* he introduces a character called Llonio who impresses Taran by his apparent continual luck. Llonio's family can produce a meal and clothe themselves from assorted bits and pieces that they fish out of the river or find in the fields. Before Taran continues his journey to the Mirror of Llunet, he asks Llonio for the secret of his luck. Llonio explains:

> Why, my luck's no greater than yours or any man's. You need only sharpen your eyes to see your luck when it comes, and sharpen your wits to see what falls into your hands. (Ch. 17)

Dawkins has made an extensive study of the variants of Tale Type 460B in *Forty-Five Stories from the Dodekanese,* pp. 358–68 (#35).

Tale Types: 460A   The Journey to God to Receive Reward
          460B   The Journey in Search of Fortune

Principal Motifs:

H1263   Quest to God for fortune
H1291   Questions asked on way to other world
H1292   Answers found in other world to questions propounded on the way

Parallel Stories in:

Dawkins, *Forty-Five Stories,* #35 (major study and tale)
———, *More Greek,* #12
Megas, *Greece,* #46

55

The Old Man and His Grandson*

There was once a very old man, whose eyes had become dim, his ears dull of hearing, his knees trembled, and when he sat at table he could hardly hold the spoon, and spilt the broth upon the table-cloth or let it run out of his mouth. His son and his son's wife were disgusted at this, so the old grandfather at last had to sit in the corner behind the stove, and they gave him his food in an earthenware bowl, and not even enough of it. And he used to look towards the table with his eyes full of tears. Once, too, his trembling hands could not hold the bowl, and it fell to the ground and broke. The young wife scolded him, but he said nothing and only sighed. Then they bought him a wooden bowl for a few half-pence, out of which he had to eat.

They were once sitting thus when the little grandson of four years old began to gather together some bits of wood upon the ground. "What are you doing there?" asked the father. "I am making a little trough," answered the child, "for father and mother to eat out of when I am big."

The man and his wife looked at each other for a while, and presently began to cry. Then they took the old grandfather to the table, and hence-

---

*From *Grimms' Fairy Tales* by Jakob and Wilhelm Grimm (London: Routledge and Kegan Paul, 1948), #78.

forth always let him eat with them, and likewise said nothing if he did spill a little of anything.

Notes and Comments

This short tale, scarcely more than a motif, reflects the continuing concern in widely scattered communities about the role of the aged in societies they can no longer actively serve. Tale Type 980 is widely diffused in literary and oral formulations, variants having been found in countries as far afield as Brazil and Russia, Greece and Japan.

The two predominant versions of the type, 980A and 980B, differ only slightly. Tale Type 980A, for example, revolves around motif J121 where a man gives his father half a carpet to keep him warm and the grandson keeps the other half for the day when his father too will grow old. Tale Type 980B embraces those variants in which the grandparent is given a wooden drinking cup or similar utensil from which to eat his meals.

All stories embodying motifs J120–J125 concern wisdom learned from children who act from an ingenuous and open nature. The effectiveness of the story stems in large measure from the fact that the child does not intend to criticize his father when he imitates the cruel act he has just witnessed. Nevertheless, by the naive simplicity of his actions, he succeeds in shaming his parent into repentance.

The Christian commandment to "Honor thy father and thy mother" is perhaps easily overlooked in its abstract ethical perfection. Sharper focus for some is obtained when the commandment is translated into the down-to-earth terms of "Treat your old parent the way you would like your son, who is (by the way) watching you, to treat you in your old age." Robert Burns has spoken to the problem of the need "to see ourselves as others see us." The child here reflects the future in the most graphic way possible.

The folktale as always reflects the standards of the group, but it does not prescribe them. Neither does the practical folk ethic appear to have major cultural boundaries. A Korean variant of the same tale, "The Aged Father," puts the same problem in a different geographical and cultural setting; yet the crux remains the same. Korean society embraces the Confucian Five Principles—two of which are filial respect and veneration for elders. Nevertheless, the actions of the father in carrying the aged grandfather to the mountain in a basket to die are mirrored with the same ruthless clarity when the young grandson retrieves the discarded basket for the time when his father will need similar treatment.

While readers are often intrigued by the cultural differences reflected in tales from many parts of the world, it is instructive to bear in mind just how universal are human concerns when dealing with such ritualistic milestones as birth, marriage, and death.

Tale Type 980B   Wooden Drinking Cup for Old Man

Principal Motifs:

J121.1   Ungrateful son reproved by naive action of his own son
W154   Ingratitude

Parallel Stories in:

Briggs, *Dictionary,* B (2), p. 266 (summary)
Clouston, *Popular* 2: 372–77 (5 variants)
Crane, *Exempla,* p. 260, #288 (extensive references)
Grimm, #78
In-Sŏb, *Korea,* #82
Schmidt, *EMU*

I

Beginnings:

POURQUOI TALES

Less form here than content, with themes greatly reduced in scope and import from their more weighty mythological ancestors. A simple distinction between the myth and the pourquoi tale can rest upon the presence or absence of gods and goddesses. Pourquoi tales are primarily imaginative stories of how things might have happened if logic and fancy had intermingled in the very beginning.

56 *HOW THE MANX CAT LOST HER TAIL*   329
Motif A237.2—*Why animals lack tail*
Also known as *The Buried Tail, How the (Rabbit) (Bear) (Wolf) or Other Animal Lost His Tail*

57. *COMPAIR LAPIN AND MADAME CARENCRO*   332
Motif A2317.3—*Why buzzard is bald*
Also known as *The Baldhead of the Buzzard, Why Buzzards Have No Feathers on Their Head*

58. *WHY THE SEA IS SALT*   336
TT 565—*The Magic Mill*
Also known as *The Salt-Producing Mill, The Salty Sea and the Magic Mill*

59. *THE TORTOISE AND THE OSPREY*   342
TT 225A—*Tortoise Lets Self Be Carried by Eagle*
Also known as *Why Tortoise Has a Cracked
Shell*

56

How the Manx Cat Lost Her Tail*

W hen Noah was calling the animals into the Ark, there was one cat who was out mousing and took no notice when he was calling to her. She was a good mouser, but this time she had trouble to find a mouse and she took a notion that she wouldn't go into the Ark without one.

So at last, when Noah had all the animals safe inside, and he saw the rain beginning to fall, and no sign of her coming in, he said:

"Who's out is out, and who's in is in!" And with that he was just closing the door when the cat came running up, half drowned—that's why cats hate the water—and just squeezed in, in time. But Noah had slammed the door as she ran in and it cut off her tail, so she got in without it, and that is why Manx cats have no tails to this day. That cat said:

Bee bo bend it,
My tail's ended,
And I'll go to Mann
And get copper nails,
And mend it.

*From *Manx Fairy Tales* collected by Sophia Morrison (London: David Nutt, 1911), pp. 14–15.

Notes and Comments

Almost every culture tells a story of a great flood, and this catastrophic event is a natural point of departure for explanations of those unusual characteristics of some animals. All animals not on the Ark must surely have perished. And so the explanation of the extinction of the griffin (Motif A2234.4) is that he refused to go inside the Ark and was drowned. The problems of the unicorn (Motif A2214.3), on the other hand, seem to have stemmed from trouble on the Ark from which he was unceremoniously thrown, never to be seen again.

This short tale of the Manx cat who lost her tail combines many of the elements of legendary explanations of natural phenomena, including both the reason why all cats hate water and why one breed has no tail.

A certain fascination with the subject of tails in general is found in the pourquoi tale. In part, it is the simple fact that the presence of a tail quite often distinguishes men from animals. But additional contrasts between the tailed and the tailless have darker overtones in those stories about the devil and his forked tail. Also traditional are strange stories of mysterious Norwegian *huldre* folk from the otherworld who seem normal enough but who take great care not to have their cows' tails discovered beneath their dresses. No one can overlook "That," the solitary impet in "Tom Tit Tot," who keeps twirling his tail around his head just before he leaps out the window and disappears into the black region he inhabits.

Men do not have tails; animals do. Therefore, in folktales about animals, to have a large and bushy tail is noble and a sign of great beauty. Such "tragedies" as those found in Tale Type 2 *The Tail Fisher,* where a magnificent tail is lost or shortened, attempt to account for why the bear or the rabbit has a stumpy tail. As the poor animal stupidly sits on the ice fishing with his tail, innocently unaware of the misfortune that lies just ahead, we can only pity him if indeed the other animals in the kingdom are going to mock him because his tail now is quite short and stumpy. Who is to say what defines beauty as it exists in the eye of the animal beholder? Indeed, how do porcupines show affection? Perhaps the Devonshire proverb sums up one aspect of the whole question: "All's well that ends well, said the peacock as he looked at his tail." Whatever the answer, the Manx cat nevertheless walks through the Isle of Man as aloof as ever, perhaps all the more haughty for the distinction she claims as now being the only cat in the world who has no tail.

Principal Motif:

A2378.2   Why animals lack tail

Parallel Story in:

Young, *Manx,* pp. 29–39

Other Animals Lose Tails in:

Aesop, "The Fox Without A Tale"
Backus, *Georgia,* pp. 125–26
Belting, *Long-Tailed,* pp. 13–15 (bear), 29–33 (ground hog), 46–50 (possum)
Campbell, *West Highlands* 1:280–81 (wolf)
Dorson, *American Negro,* #11 (rabbit)
Harris, *Nights,* "Why Brother Bear Has No Tail"
———, *Remus,* "How Mr. Rabbit Lost His Fine Bushy Tail"
Hill, *Glooscap,* pp. 55–62
Jacobs, *More Celtic,* #46
Jones, *Scandinavian,* pp. 108–9 (bear)
Leach, *Mountains Up,* p. 69 (rabbit), 113–14 (tadpole)
MacMillan, *Glooskap's,* pp. 58–63 (rabbit)
———, *Canadian,* p. 60–65
Scheer, *Cherokee,* pp. 31–32 (ground hog), 75–79 (possum)
Smiley, *Virginia,* p. 361

57

Compair Lapin and Madame Carencro*

D o you know why buzzards are bald? No. Well, I am going to tell you.

Once upon a time Mme. Carencro was setting upon her nest on an oak-tree. Her husband was a good-for-nothing fellow, and she was always starving. At the foot of the tree there was a big hole in which a rabbit dwelt. Compair Lapin was large and fat, and every time Mme. Carencro saw him she wished to eat him. One day, while Compair Lapin was sleeping, she took some moss and bricks and closed the hole in the tree. Then Compair Lapin would not be able to get out and would die of hunger.

When Compair Lapin woke up and he found out that he was shut up in the hole, he begged Mme. Carencro to let him out, but she replied each time: "I am hungry and I must eat the flesh on your bones."

When Compair Lapin saw that it was of no use to beg, he stopped speaking, but Mme. Carencro was so glad she had caught Compair Lapin that she licked her lips when she thought of the good dinner she would make. As she did not hear Compair Lapin move, she thought he was dead, smothered, and she took away the moss and the bricks which closed the

---

*From *Louisiana Folk-Tales* collected and edited by Alcée Fortier, *Memoirs of the American Folk-Lore Society* 2, no. 6 (1895).

hole. She began to go down the opening, but Compair Lapin made one jump and got out. When he was at some distance he said: "You see, it is you who are caught, and not I."

He ran away and went to stay at the house of one of his friends, because he was afraid to go back into the oak-tree near Mme. Carencro. Some days later Mme. Carencro, who had forgotten Compair Lapin, went to take a walk with her children, who had all come out of their shells. They passed near the house of Compair Lapin's friend. Compair Lapin was glad, and he thought how he could take vengeance on Mme. Carencro. He ran into the kitchen, he took a large tin pan full of burning embers and hot ashes; and when Mme. Carencro and her children passed near the gallery, he threw down on them all that he had in the tin pan, in order to burn them. But you know that buzzards have thick feathers except on the top of their heads. They shook off the embers and ashes, but not quick enough to prevent the feathers on their heads to burn down to the skin.

This is why the buzzards are bald and never eat bones of rabbits.

Notes and Comments

Pourquoi stories about unusual animal characteristics do not exist for all creatures. Those animals that have captured the imagination of primitive peoples have often been distinguished by at least a hint of anthropomorphism. For example, baldness is equated with becoming old; loss of hair must therefore correlate with loss of youthful vitality or be a sign of an illness or infirmity. So it must be reasoned that long hair and elegant plumage are highly prized both in the animal and human world. Nothing else would seem to account for the appeal of hair-restoring elixir and countless "magic" ointments selling briskly over the counter in the modern drugstore. Certainly a hair fetish accounts for the prevalence of such traditional motifs as C949.2, "Baldness from breaking tabu," to say nothing of D2161.3.4, "Baldness magically cured," or even D1389.8 "Magic helmet prevents baldness."

Thus it is that pourquoi narrators have chosen to overlook the buzzard's obvious talent in aviation, focusing almost entirely on his prominently bald head. No one seems to tell stories about his remarkable ability to soar endlessly on air currents; no stories cite his important ecological role as a scavenger. No, when viewed at close range, that bald head is amazingly ugly, so ugly that it hardly seems possible that he should have been created that way on purpose. Surely the buzzard has been punished for something, or perhaps he crossed paths with some trickster along the way. If we can believe the traditional tales found primarily in primitive cultures, such a change did take place. These tales suggest that the buzzard once had a very fine feathered head and only later became bald.

In North American Indian tales the buzzard runs afoul of the Ojibwa trickster Nanibozhu who captures him, imprisons him until he is bald, and gloats, "There'll be no quills on your head forever." In Jamaica, Anansi and Johnny Crow cross swords over whether the crow has destroyed Anansi's web or is perhaps a better dancer. In revenge, Anansi, playing on the crow's love for food, invites the bird to dinner and pours boiling water on his head. Off go the feathers "wid hot pop." In a southern black tale, Brer Rabbit pushes Buzzard's head into a dish of hot hominy while all the others' eyes are closed during grace. In most of these black tales the feathers are pulled out or scalded off in either anger or jealousy. By contrast, some North American Indian myths give a more dignified account. In one Cherokee story the buzzard is making an effort to bring the light to the animal people by carrying a piece of the sun on his head. In a similar Hopi story, the sun has stopped halfway up the sky. Turkey tries first to push the sun up in place, but his head is burned and red to this day. Then Buzzard tries and keeps on pushing until his feathers are scorched away.

The reaction of these two cultures to the buzzard reflects the attitudes seen here in the stories. In the beliefs of the southern plantation blacks, the buzzard was an omen of death or a finder of thieves. If the thief had stolen meat, for example, hot sun, no refrigeration, and a buzzard on the roof were specific clues. For the Pueblo Indians, however, he is a "purifying and cleansing power" because of his scavenging habits. Leach in her *Dictionary* notes that buzzard feathers are used in exorcism by all the curers (I, p. 177). Such curative beliefs are shared by the plantation blacks who used to tie a bag of buzzard feathers around a baby's neck to ease the pains of teething. Ultimately:

> To drive someone crazy, Mississippi Negroes pick up the victim's foot-prints, put them in a gourd along with two buzzard feathers, and throw the gourd into running water at midnight. The person will go insane the next day.
>
> (Leach, *Dictionary,* I, p. 177)

Richard Dorson points out that many United States black tales of the buzzard becoming bald begin with the buzzard capturing some animal and imprisoning him. Then a verbal exchange takes place to determine the health and welfare of the prisoner. In one Michigan version an elaborate chant begins with the buzzard soaring overhead and singing:

Da-tum, da-tum, da-tum, dey,
I been sailing three or four days.

Fox in the hole says:

Da-tum, da-tum, da-tum day,
I been starving three or four days.

The buzzard can only conclude, "No, I ain't quite got him." When finally the voice in the hollow log doesn't answer back, Buzzard concludes the fox is dead. When he sticks his head inside, however, to pull his victim out, the fox grabs him by the head feathers and yanks them all out. (*Michigan,* pp. 41–42).

Whatever the case, whether the feathers are pulled out, scalded off, or burned away, the poor buzzard has been soaring around for the rest of time hunting for carrion with the most ugly bald head imaginable. In fact, Uncle Remus says, "They look so b'ar on der head an' neck that you wanter give 'um a piece o' rag fer to tie roun' it to keep um fum ketchin' cold."

Principal Motif:

A2317.3   Why buzzard is bald

Parallel Stories in:

Arkhurst, *Spider,* pp. 21–30
Backus, *Animal,* #5
Beckwith, *Jamaica Anansi,* #47
Courlander, *Hat-Shaking,* pp. 13–17 (Anansi), based on a story in Rattray, *Akan-Ashanti,* #32
Dorson, *Michigan,* pp. 41–42 (see for references)
Hampden, *Gypsy,* pp. 147–54
Skinner, *Ojibwa,* p. 282 (2 variants)

58

Why the Sea Is Salt*

Once upon a time, long, long ago, there were two brothers, the one rich and the other poor. When Christmas Eve came, the poor one had not a bite in the house, either of meat or bread; so he went to his brother, and begged him, in God's name, to give him something for Christmas Day. It was by no means the first time that the brother had been forced to give something to him, and he was not better pleased at being asked now than he generally was.

"If you will do what I ask you, you shall have a whole ham," said he. The poor one immediately thanked him, and promised this.

"Well, here is the ham, and now you must go straight to Dead Man's Hall," said the rich brother, throwing the ham to him.

"Well, I will do what I have promised," said the other, and he took the ham and set off. He went on and on for the livelong day, and at nightfall he came to a place where there was a bright light.

"I have no doubt this is the place," thought the man with the ham.

An old man with a long white beard was standing in the outhouse, chopping Yule logs.

*From *The Blue Fairy Book* edited by Andrew Lang (Philadelphia: MacRae Smith Co., 1926), pp. 156–160.

"Good-evening," said the man with the ham.

"Good-evening to you. Where are you going at this late hour?" said the man.

"I am going to Dead Man's Hall, if only I am in the right track," answered the poor man.

"Oh! yes, you are right enough, for it is here," said the old man. "When you get inside they will all want to buy your ham, for they don't get much meat to eat there: but you must not sell it unless you can get the hand-mill which stands behind the door for it. When you come out again I will teach you how to stop the hand-mill, which is useful for almost everything."

So the man with the ham thanked the other for his good advice, and rapped at the door.

When he got in, everything happened just as the old man had said it would: all the people, great and small, came round him like ants on an ant-hill, and each tried to outbid the other for the ham.

"By rights my old woman and I ought to have it for our Christmas dinner, but, since you have set your hearts upon it, I must just give it up to you," said the man. "But, if I sell it, I will have the hand-mill which is standing there behind the door."

At first they would not hear of this, and haggled and bargained with the man, but he stuck to what he had said, and the people were forced to give him the hand-mill. When the man came out again into the yard, he asked the old woodcutter how he was to stop the hand-mill, and when he had learnt that he thanked him and set off home with all the speed he could, but did not get there until after the clock had struck twelve on Christmas Eve.

"But where in the world have you been?" said the old woman. "Here I have sat waiting hour after hour, and have not even two sticks to lay across each other under the Christmas porridge-pot."

"Oh! I could not come before; I had something of importance to see about, and a long way to go, too; but now you shall just see!" said the man, and then he set the hand-mill on the table, and bade it first grind light, then a table-cloth, and then meat, and beer, and everything else that was good for a Christmas Eve's supper; and the mill ground all that he ordered. "Bless me!" said the old woman as one thing after another appeared; and she wanted to know where her husband had got the mill from, but he would not tell her that.

"Never mind where I got it; you can see that it is a good one, and the water that turns it will never freeze," said the man. So he ground meat and drink, and all kinds of good things, to last all Christmas-tide, and on the third day he invited all his friends to come to a feast.

Now when the rich brother saw all that there was at the banquet and in the house, he was both vexed and angry, for he grudged everything his brother had. "On Christmas Eve he was so poor that he came to me and begged for a trifle, for God's sake, and now he gives a feast as if he were both a count and a king!" thought he. "But, for heaven's sake, tell me where you got your riches from," said he to his brother.

"From behind the door," said he who owned the mill, for he did not choose to satisfy his brother on that point; but later in the evening, when he had taken a drop too much, he could not refrain from telling how he had come by the hand-mill. "There you see what has brought me all my wealth!" said he, and brought out the mill, and made it grind first one thing and then another. When the brother saw that he insisted on having the mill, and after a great deal of persuasion got it; but he had to give three hundred dollars for it, and the poor brother was to keep it till the haymaking was over, for he thought: "If I keep it as long as that, I can make it grind meat and drink that will last many a long year." During that time you may imagine that the mill did not grow rusty, and when hay-harvest came the rich brother got it, but the other had taken good care not to teach him how to stop it. It was evening when the rich man got the mill home, and in the morning he bade the old woman go out and spread the hay after the mowers, and he would attend to the house himself that day, he said.

So, when dinner-time drew near, he set the mill on the kitchen-table, and said: "Grind herrings and milk pottage, and do it both quickly and well."

So the mill began to grind herrings and milk pottage, and first all the dishes and tubs were filled, and then it came out all over the kitchen-floor. The man twisted and turned it, and did all he could to make the mill stop, but, howsoever he turned it and screwed it, the mill went on grinding, and in a short time the pottage rose so high that the man was like to be drowned. So he threw open the parlor-door, but it was not long before the mill had ground the parlor full too, and it was with difficulty and danger that the man could go through the stream of pottage and get hold of the door-latch. When he got the door open, he did not stay long in the room, but ran out, and the herrings and pottage came after him, and it streamed out over both farm and field. Now the old woman, who was out spreading the hay, began to think dinner was long in coming, and said to the women and the mowers: "Though the master does not call us home, we may as well go. It may be that he finds he is not good at making pottage, and I should do well to help him." So they began to straggle homewards, but when they had got a little way up the hill they met the herrings and pottage and bread, all pouring forth and winding about one over the other, and the man himself in front of the flood. "Would to heaven that each of you had a hundred stomachs! Take care that you are not drowned in the pottage!" he cried as he went by them as if Mischief were at his heels, down to where his brother dwelt. Then he begged him, for God's sake, to take the mill back again, and that in an instant, for, said he: "If it grind one hour more the whole district will be destroyed by herrings and pottage." But the brother would not take it until the other paid him three hundred dollars, and that he was obliged to do. Now the poor brother had both the money and the mill again. So it was not long before he had a farmhouse much finer than that in which his brother lived, but the mill ground him so much money that he covered it with plates of gold; and the farmhouse lay close by the seashore, so it shone and glittered far out to sea. Everyone who sailed by there now had to put in to visit the rich man in the gold farmhouse, and everyone wanted to see the wonderful mill, for the report of it spread far and wide, and there was no one who had not heard tell of it.

After a long, long time came also a skipper who wished to see the mill. He asked if it could make salt. "Yes, it could make salt," said he who owned it, and when the skipper heard that he wished with all his might and main to have the mill, let it cost what it might, for, he thought, if he had it, he would get off having to sail far away over the perilous sea for freights of salt. At first the man would not hear of parting with it, but the skipper begged and prayed, and at last the man sold it to him, and got many, many thousand dollars for it. When the skipper had got the mill on his back he did not long stay there, for he was so afraid that the man should change his mind, and he had no time to ask how he was to stop it grinding, but got on board his ship as fast as he could.

When he had gone a little way out to sea he took the mill on deck. "Grind salt, and grind both quickly and well," said the skipper. So the mill began to grind salt, till it spouted out like water, and when the skipper had got the ship filled he wanted to stop the mill, but, whichsoever way he turned it, and how much so ever he tried, it went on grinding, and the heap of salt grew higher and higher, until at last the ship sank. There lies the mill at the bottom of the sea, and still, day by day, it grinds on: and that is why the sea is salt.

Notes and Comments

This pourquoi tale is perhaps full of much more magic than any other tale to be found in this section or in any collection of etiological tales. It is included here because the tenacity of the explanation of why the sea is salt is equalled only by the pervasiveness of the briney stuff itself. Regardless of origin, culture, language, or details in the narration—the crux of the story is always the same. Somewhere, out there, under all that water, is a magic mill grinding and grinding and grinding—producing all the salt necessary to keep all the oceans filled with salt for all time.

The cast of characters of this explanatory tale usually includes two brothers, one rich and one poor. Essential to the plot is a little old man with a long beard, a beggar who is really a god, or even a talking cow, as well as an object of barter: a Christmas ham, an Easter lamb, a Japanese *manju* cake, or just an ordinary piece of meat. Exchanges are made in such awesome places as the devil's dam, Dead Man's Hall, or even Buddha's temple; exchanges are made with the Temptations, the little people, or merely goblins. The magic object received is most frequently a mill, but millstones, a gourd, and querns are also mentioned.

The central problem in the story has to do with exercising a certain amount of caution when dealing with anything magical. Turning on the mill or any other magic object is easy—turning it off is something else again, as Kwako found out in "The Do-All Ax." Much of the humor of the story occurs at this point in the plot, for trickery is punished and greed is rewarded with excess as the older brother gets much, much more than he asked for from a magic mill to which he was not entitled. Almost everyone laughs at the greedy rich brother flailing along in a river of fish and gravy originating in his kitchen and now threatening to engulf the town unless he can stop the mill. A cheer is bound to go up when the once-poor brother calmly says to the gravy-covered one, "Take you a chear and set down and we'll talk about that mill awhile" (Roberts, *Sang Branch,* p. 268).

The magic incantation to control the supernatural events appears in some versions of this tale. In the Kentucky mountain version mentioned above, the phrase is a simple one: "Hoky, spoky, foky, stop." (Cf. a similar incantation in the notes to "The King of the Cats" from an informant in the Ozarks.) In the Icelandic version the incantation is religiously significant:

> Grind neither malt nor salt;
> Grind in the name of the Lord.

Later when the older brother who has stolen the mill finds himself wanting to work the mill at sea, the mill refuses to start on his command. In a rage he shouts:

Bring, then, both malt and salt;
Grind in the name of the Devil.

The Costa Rican booby in "The Witches' Ride" or anyone familiar with incantations in folklore can anticipate the result and brace for the inevitable. But just in case there is any doubt of the outcome, one narrator suggests:

If you don't think that the mill is grindin' today in the sea, you taste of the sea water and see if it ain't salty.

(Roberts, *Sang Branch*, p. 269)

Tale Type 565 The Magic Mill

Principal Motifs:

D1601.21.1	Self-grinding salt mill
A1115.2	Why the sea is salt, magic salt-mill
D851	Magic object acquired by exchange
N825.2	Old man helper
D1651	Magic object obeys master alone

Parallel Stories in:

Arnason, *Icelandic*, II, pp. 12–21
Asbjørnsen, #2 (also in Rugoff, *Harvest*, pp. 672–76)
Belting, *Earth*, pp. 55–57
Briggs, *Dictionary*, A (1), p. 427 (summary)
Eberhard, *China*, #49
Grimm, #103
Haviland, *Norway*, pp. 30–44
Ikeda, *Type*, #565
Leach, *Mountains Up*, pp. 28–29
Megas, *Greece*, #36
Parsons, *Antilles*, 2, #50
Roberts, *Sang Branch*, #137
Seki, *Japan*, #39

59

The Tortoise and the Osprey*

"W hy can't I fly?" grumbled Kamba, the Tortoise. "Or climb trees? Or . . ."

"For the very good reason that you weren't meant to!" snapped the Tortoise's wife, who had heard all this before and strongly disapproved of her husband's adventurous ambitions.

"But, my dear," he explained, "think what Prestige it would give us!" Tortoise had no idea what "Prestige" meant but he thought it sounded grand and he knew he was safe in trying it on his wife. It ought to impress her.

It did not impress her.

"What's 'Prestige' and why do you want it?" she demanded suspiciously.

"Oh, er . . . er . . . I thought you'd like it, my dear," he stammered lamely.

"Then you thought wrong. I'm quite content with things as they are, and I haven't time to waste talking about prestiges and things of that sort. Prestige indeed!" Tortoise's wife snorted with contempt and bustled off to her cooking-pots.

---

*From *Where the Leopard Passes: A Book of African Folktales* by Geraldine Elliot (New York: Schocken Books, 1968), pp. 66–71. © 1949 by Geraldine Elliot. Reprinted by permission of A. Watkins, Inc., for Geraldine Elliot.

Kamba, the Tortoise, looked a little crushed, but only for a moment. The first few puffs of tobacco from his ancient pipe restored his confidence and before long he fell asleep in the hot sunshine, murmuring sadly to himself, "if only I could fly!"

The reason why Kamba yearned for this accomplishment was that he wished to visit his rich and noble friend, the Osprey. How the friendship came about it is hard to say, but no doubt the funny little Tortoise amused the Osprey who was a happy-go-lucky, kindhearted bird, and he often used to drop in at the Tortoises' for a smoke and a chat before returning to his own home in the tree-tops. And as he was leaving he would always ask, "When are you going to pay us a visit, Kamba?" And Kamba would hurriedly say, "Well, not *this* week, Osprey, old friend, I'm afraid I am much too busy. But I'll come as soon as I can."

Now if only Tortoise had been honest enough to explain that he had no means of getting to Osprey's home, all would have been well. But Kamba thought that Osprey would despise him if he were to say he could not fly, or climb trees or, in fact, do anything but crawl along the ground and that very slowly. So Tortoise went on hoping that he would find a way. The trouble was that he must find it soon. He could not put off the visit indefinitely, or Osprey would begin to wonder why. Then, too, there was the Chameleon who lived nearby who had guessed what was up and who now never missed an opportunity of jeering at Tortoise.

"Have you learnt to fly yet, Kamba?" he would call out. "Have you paid your call on Osprey?" And Tortoise did not know how to avoid him because he never saw him until he heard his voice.

It was the voice of the Chameleon that now roused him from his pleasant sleep.

"Pity you can't climb trees like me, isn't it, Kamba?" he was saying. He was disguised as a rock this morning and Tortoise had to look twice before he discovered him.

"It's a pity you've got such a long tongue!" retorted Kamba, and he moved off as fast as he could, found another sunny corner, and gave himself up to thought once more.

Suddenly an idea came to him. A brilliant idea! A splendid idea! Tortoise could hardly contain himself at the thought of it and crawled off at top speed to find his wife.

"What's the hurry?" she enquired as soon as she saw him.

"My dear, I have a wonderful idea! I think even you will be pleased with it," replied Tortoise and, as quickly as he could, he told her of his plan.

"H'm!" said Tortoise's wife. "It is not a bad idea . . . and it certainly would be polite to return the Osprey's many calls. And perhaps if you do, you will be more contented. Yes, I don't mind helping you this time. When do you expect Osprey to come here again?"

"I think he will come to-morrow," answered Tortoise. "So we must be prepared."

Sure enough, next morning the Osprey arrived, looking very fine and handsome. Tortoise's wife met him and said how sorry she was that her husband was out. He had had to go visiting, but he had left a present of tobacco for Osprey.

Osprey was delighted, politely said that it was very kind of Tortoise to have given him a present and added that he was sorry not to see him.

"I expect you will see him soon," said Kamba's wife, giving him a bundle of tobacco leaves. It was a very neat bundle, carefully tied up with twine. Osprey took it in his beak, spread his great wings and flew off.

Inside the bundle, of course, was Tortoise, and he was thinking to himself how well his plan had worked and how surprised and pleased Osprey would be to see him when he undid the tobacco leaves. But after a while Tortoise began to feel very hot and uncomfortable and he hoped that Osprey had not got much further to go. But it seemed that Osprey had. Tortoise became more and more unhappy. He decided he did not like flying, that he never would like flying. . . . At last, he could bear it no longer.

"Hi!" he called. "Put me down. I feel . . ."

He never finished his sentence for, at the sound of a voice coming from the middle of a bundle of tobacco leaves, Osprey opened his beak and let out a squawk of terror and his bundle dropped to the ground.

Luckily for Tortoise, Osprey had not been flying very high and the tobacco leaves helped to break his fall. Moreover, he landed on his back, where he had his hard shell to protect him, but it was a very bruised and shaken Tortoise who crept out of what had been the present-for-Osprey, and when he reached his home, he found that his shell was cracked in several places.

Tortoise's wife was not very sympathetic.

"Be thankful it wasn't worse," she said, when she had heard the sad story. "I never really approved of your foolish plan"—which wasn't quite true—"but now, perhaps, you'll be content to stay on the ground for the rest of your days," she finished up.

"Yes, my dear," said Tortoise humbly and crawled to his favorite place in the sun.

"Hullo!" said a clump of red aloes, in which Kamba eventually discovered the Chameleon. "I like your new shell. It *is* handsome with that criss-cross pattern on it."

Tortoise looked at Chameleon and saw that he was quite serious. He tried not to show his surprise as he answered in an off-hand manner, "It is smart, isn't it? I am so glad you like it. Good-bye" and he crept hurriedly back to his wife and told her what Chameleon had said.

"So you see," he chortled happily, "I think I've got Prestige after all!"

"Pouf!" said his wife. "I don't believe you know what it is!"

All this happened a very long time ago, and as Kamba was the father of all Tortoises, every one of them has criss-cross pattern cracks in his shell.

Notes and Comments

Pourquoi tales in general attempt to explain nature, the world around us, and the peculiarities and seeming incongruities that are merely part of the way things are. The fact that primitive cultures have spent more time contemplating the vagaries of natural phenomena than their more civilized counterparts does not necessarily indicate a predilection for the factual on either side. One group has simply chosen to observe, contemplate, and relate in narrative form some possible answers to questions that really have no answers. Who can say why the leopard is spotted and the zebra striped? Who can say why the chipmunk has three stripes instead of four spots?

Answers to such fascinating questions, however, are almost always assigned a reason that substitutes for a natural cause. Tortoise has a cracked shell simply because he tried to fly and shouldn't have. Seldom is there intervention in any of these events by divine or higher powers than the animals themselves. Most stories, too, seem to take place in a vague period of prehistory when men and beasts talked and lived as equals, and when natural laws were still being shaped.

A simple distinction exists between the pourquoi story and the myth. The pourquoi story is told because it is a good story; whether or not a person chooses to believe in that particular version of the rearrangement of nature is unimportant. Myths, on the other hand, deal with far weightier matters —the formation of the world, the arrangement of the land and water masses, and the relationship of the deities to man. A myth deals with the actions of the gods and is part of the body of sacred belief of a culture around which they structure their lives and actions. The pourquoi story is much less profound, although it too may have vestiges of a prevailing morality.

Thus stories explaining why the tortoise has cracks in his shell are on the surface rather simple stories, often funny, but sometimes serious or sad. And there remains an undercurrent of truth and morality in which the cheater is caught, the greedy punished, and the vain humbled.

The troubles of the tortoise almost always stem from his wanting to fly. In Greek mythology, this presumption had tragic results for the foolish Icarus and represented the great sin of *hubris*, or excessive pride. In the natural order of things for the Greeks, only the gods could fly, and man had no business imitating the gods with wax wings, no matter how cleverly they were constructed. In the primitive world, it is no less absurd for the aerodynamically unsuited tortoise to want to do that very thing for which he simply was not designed. Yet in almost all the tales he tries to fly, either by sticking some feathers on his back, by hiding in a bundle being presented to his friend the osprey or the vulture, or by holding on to a stick carried by two friendly egrets. In every case his pride gets the best of him, and he falls, cracking his shell. This is his gift (and warning) to all his descendants.

If flying is not his principal sin in all stories, then greed or unkindness becomes a substitute vice. In an American Indian tale, Tortoise taunts a woman grinding corn: "Old woman you are slow, you are slow, you are slow." She throws the grinding stone and cracks his shell. In a black American tale he is trying to keep all the world's wisdom to himself and falls trying to hang the wisdom pot in a high tree. In a West African tale he drinks too much wine, is late for the feast, and is caught outside the compound in the rain. When he is discovered later, the earthenware pot of wine on his back has caked together with the dust, and he has been creeping around with that shell on his back ever since.

Geraldine Elliot, as a folktale revisionist, represents much of what professional folklorists object to in versions rewritten for children. In a preface to another of her books, she indicates that she has spent a great deal of time in the huts of the Ngoni people listening to their stories. The selections in her book were told to her by one old Ngoni man who learned them from his grandmother. So far, so good. But then in a note from the editor, the extent of her revision is made obvious: "Her imagination has clothed them in her own speech, captivating all listeners, young and old." At that point, folklorists would be interested in the skeleton of the story, but would eternally regret having missed the flavor of the stories as told by the old Ngoni man in his own or translated words.

Tale Type 225A   Tortoise Lets Self Be Carried by Eagle

Principal Motifs:

A2312.1.1 Origin of cracks in tortoise's shell
A2214.5.1 Tortoise dropped by eagle; hence cracks in his shell
K1041   Borrowed feathers

Parallel Stories in:

Barker, *West Africa,* pp. 115–17
Belting, *Long-Tailed,* pp. 54–56
Ch'iu, *Chinese Fables,* p. 14
Courlander, *Olode,* pp. 72–76
———, *Terrapin's,* pp. 24–27
Eberhard, *China,* #5 (crab)
Ikeda, *Type,* #91, #225A
Scheer, *Cherokee,* pp. 65–68
Sherlock, *Iguana's,* pp. 53–67
Smith, *Ila-Speaking,* pp. 373–74

J

Noodles and Simpletons From All Over:

DROLL TALES

If there is the slightest possibility of a misunderstanding, the numskull will seize it gladly. Give him instructions and he either forgets them or follows them too literally, oblivious of the disastrous result. Given any chance to display their lack of wit, the country bumpkin, the absentminded professor, the henpecked husband—all stumble happily along, leaving chaos in their wake.

60. *LAZY JACK*   351
    TT 1696—*"What Should I Have Said (Done)?"*
    Also known as *The Right Instructions at the Wrong Time*

61. *THE STORY OF BRAVE KONG*   356
    TT 1640—*The Brave Tailor*
    Also known as *Seven at a Whack, Jack and the Varmints*

62. *BASTIANELO*   362
    TT 1450—*Clever Elsie*
    Also known as *What If the Knife Should Fall,*

The Husband Seeks Three People as Stupid as His Wife,
The Woman Draws the Beer

63. *THE MIRROR* 367

TT 1336A—*Man does not Recognize his own*
Reflection in the Water (Mirror)
Also known as *So That's the Hussy You've Been*
Seeing

64. *THE OLD WOMAN AND THE TRAMP* 370

TT 1548—*The Soup-stone*
Also known as *The Axe-Stew, Nail Broth, The Poor*
Man's Meal

65. *NOW I SHOULD LAUGH, IF I WERE NOT DEAD* 377

TT 1406—*The Merry Wives Wager*
TT 1313—*The Man Who Thought Himself Dead*

66. *THE PIG-HEADED WIFE* 381

TT 1365A—*Wife Falls into a Stream*
Also known as *The Obstinate Wife, Wife Floats*
Upstream, Cutting with the Knife or Scissors

60

*Lazy Jack**

O nce upon a time there was a boy whose name was Jack, and he lived with his mother on a dreary common. They were very poor, and the old woman got her living by spinning, but Jack was so lazy that he would do nothing but bask in the sun in the hot weather, and sit by the corner of the hearth in the winter time. His mother could not persuade him to do anything for her, and was obliged at last to tell him that if he did not begin to work for his porridge, she would turn him out to get his living as he could.

This threat at length roused Jack, and he went out and hired himself for the day to a neighboring farmer for a penny; but as he was coming home, never having had any money in his possession before, he lost it in passing over a brook. "You stupid boy," said his mother, "you should have put it in your pocket." "I'll do so another time," replied Jack.

The next day Jack went out again, and hired himself to a cow-keeper, who gave him a jar of milk for his day's work. Jack took the jar and put it into the large pocket of his jacket, spilling it all, long before he got home. "Dear me!" said the old woman; "you should have carried

*From *Popular Rhymes and Nursery Tales of England* collected by James Orchard Halliwell (London: John Russell Smith, 1849).

it on your head." "I'll do so another time," replied Jack.

The following day Jack hired himself again to a farmer, who agreed to give him a cream cheese for his services. In the evening, Jack took the cheese, and went home with it on his head. By the time he got home the cheese was completely spilt, part of it being lost, and part matted with his hair. "You stupid lout," said his mother, "you should have carried it very carefully in your hands." "I'll do so another time," replied Jack.

The day after this Jack again went out, and hired himself to a baker, who would give him nothing for his work but a large tomcat. Jack took the cat, and began carrying it very carefully in his hands, but in a short time pussy scratched him so much that he was compelled to let it go. When he got home, his mother said to him, "You silly fellow, you should have tied it with a string, and dragged it along after you." "I'll do so another time," said Jack.

The next day Jack hired himself to a butcher, who rewarded his labors by the handsome present of a shoulder of mutton. Jack took the mutton, tied it to a string, and trailed it along after him in the dirt, so that by the time he had got home the meat was completely spoilt. His mother was this time quite out of patience with him, for the next day was Sunday, and she was obliged to content herself with cabbage for her dinner. "You ninnyhammer," said she to her son, "you should have carried it on your shoulder." "I'll do so another time," replied Jack.

On the Monday Jack went once more, and hired himself to a cattle-keeper, who gave him a donkey for his trouble. Although Jack was very strong, he found some difficulty in hoisting the donkey on his shoulders, but at last he accomplished it, and began walking slowly home with his prize. Now it happened that in the course of his journey there lived a rich man with his only daughter, a beautiful girl, but unfortunately deaf and dumb; she had never laughed in her life, and the doctors said she would never recover till somebody made her laugh. Many tried without success, and at last the father, in despair, offered her in marriage to the first man who could make her laugh. This young lady happened to be looking out of the window, when Jack was passing with the donkey on his shoulders, the legs sticking up in the air; and the sight was so comical and strange, that she burst out into a great fit of laughter, and immediately recovered her speech and hearing. Her father was overjoyed, and fulfilled his promise by marrying her to Jack, who was thus made a rich gentleman. They lived in a large house, and Jack's mother lived with them in great happiness until she died.

Notes and Comments

The story of the silly son who spends all his energies muddling everything is so widespread as to be almost universal. Although he is often lazy, the silly son when forced to work is extraordinarily successful in creating confusion at every turn. The core of this tale type lies in the noodle's following his mother's instructions absolutely literally, even when it is patently unwise to do so. His antics prove him generally beyond redemption; his actions are absurd to the point of imbecility; and the fact that he sometimes wins the hand of the princess in the end is simply incredible, but true.

Yet despite his bumbling antics, there is something familiar about the noodle's human frailties, for who has not at some time followed instructions to the letter only to have things still go awry in spite of all precautions. Perhaps because of the universal nature of such experiences, this tale type has been found as far afield as Iceland and Mongolia.

Thompson in *The Folktale* (p. 15) suggests that this tale may go back to Chinese Buddhist sources, only to appear later in a number of Renaissance jest books before being collected in more than two hundred versions in Europe as well as in the Far East, Africa, and America.

Another group of tales centering around the disastrous results of following instructions to the letter are near relatives of Lazy Jack. In Type 1865 the noodle is told to add parsley to the soup; he then throws in the dog who just happens to be named Parsley. When advised to cast sheep's eyes at his sweetheart to win her affections, the noodle acts quite literally, buys some sheep's eyes from the butcher, and throws them at the astonished girl. Whatever the situation, the tales illustrate the folly of expecting good sense from a dullard, however judicious the instructions.

Nevertheless, the basic humor of the tale often lies not only in the noodle's following the right instructions at the wrong time but also in watching him bumble into favor with the king, marry the princess, and live happily ever after. When Type 1696 *"What Should I Have Said (Done)?"* is combined with Type 574 *Making the Princess Laugh,* as in the above tale, those of us who claim to be sane may begin to wonder whether madness does not after all have its method. Is it insane that he should leave us laughing while he goes off with the princess? If ignorance is bliss, then 'tis folly to be wise.

Lazy Jack has many cousins around the world. Jean-Sot (Foolish John) in France, Silly Mat in Norway, Guifa in Sicily, Xailoun in Arabia, Goose

Hans in Germany, Hone Kaha in Japan—all are blunderers whose antics are as familiar as the Simple Simon of the nursery rhyme:

> Simple Simon went a-fishing,
> For to catch a whale;
>
> All the water he had got
> Was in his mother's pail.

Tale Type 1696   "What Should I Have Said (Done)?"

Principal Motifs:

H341	Suitor test: Making the princess laugh
H341.3	Princess brought to laughter by foolish action of hero
J2450	Literal fool
J2461.1	Literal following of instructions about actions
J2461.1.1	Literal numskull drags [bacon] on string
L161	Lowly hero marries princess
T68	Princess offered as prize

Parallel Stories in:

Afanas'ev, pp. 334–36
Briggs, *Dictionary,* A (1), (5 variants)
Campbell, *Cloud Walking,* pp. 94–97
Chase, *Jack,* #9
Clouston, *Noodles,* pp. 123–26 (with notes)
Dorson, *Buying,* pp. 343–44
Foster, *Wit,* pp. 75–77 (dialect)
Grimm, #32, #143
Hartland, *English Fairy,* pp. 269–71 (from Halliwell, *Nursery,* pp. 37–38)
Hurston, *Mules,* pp. 115–16
Jacobs, *English,* #27
Kennedy, *Fireside,* pp. 30–33
———, *Legendary,* pp. 39–42
Marwick, *Orkney,* 172–73 (Scots dialect)
Massignon, *France,* #20
Megas, *Greece,* #67
Randolph, *Devil's,* pp. 72–73
Saucier, *Louisiana,* #22, #22a
Thompson, *One,* #98 (from Afanas'ev)
Walker, *Turkey* pp. 159–61

PICTURE BOOKS:

Epaminondas and his Auntie. Retold by Sara Cone Byrant and illustrated by Inez Hogan. New York: Houghton Mifflin, 1938.

Silly Simon. Retold by Molly Clark and illustrated by Eccles. New York: Follett, 1967.

Three Gay Tales From Grimm. Edited and illustrated by Wanda Gag. New York: Coward McCann, 1943.

Gormless Tom. John Greenway. Illustrated by Jan Palmer. Morristown, N. J.: Silver Burdett Co., 1968.

61

*The Story of Brave Kong**

O nce upon a time, long ago in the Kingdom of Cambodia, there lived a man called Kong, who had two wives. One was called Ahm and the other was called Kum.

One day, Kong set off with his wives to visit his younger brother in a far-off country. On the way there lived a fierce tiger, who had terrified people for miles around through his attacks on men and animals.

One day on their travels Kong and his two wives came to the thick forest, the haunt of this fierce tiger. Just as they entered the forest, the fierce tiger himself came bounding out at them, roaring loudly. Kong was terrified and ran to hide in the hollow trunk of a tree. He was quite ill and pale with fright, his hands shook and his knees knocked together. But Ahm and Kum, his two wives, stood their ground, seized some pieces of wood as cudgels and beat the tiger to death.

As soon as Kong saw that his wives had beaten the tiger to death, he ran out of the hollow tree trunk, took a huge stick himself and started to beat the dead tiger. His wives scolded Kong, saying: "What sort of a cowardly, lily-livered man is this, who comes to beat a tiger that somebody else has already killed?"

---

*From *Mr. Basket Knife and Other Khmer Folktales* translated by A. R. Milne (London: George Allen and Unwin Ltd., 1972), pp. 51–55. Reprinted by permission of the publisher.

But Kong would not accept this. "Nonsense," he replied, "the tiger was not dead. There is not a woman in the world who could beat a tiger to death. Everyone knows that only a man could kill a tiger." So saying, Kong tore down some creepers from the trees, tied up the tiger with them and slung the dead body from a pole. With the pole carried on the shoulders of his two wives, Kong set off towards his brother's country.

The people in his brother's country saw Kong coming with the tiger slung from a pole. They all came out to see the sight, saying: "However did you manage to kill this fierce tiger who used to catch and eat men and cattle for miles around?" Then Kong's two wives related what had happened and explained how, when the tiger had come bounding out, Kong had rushed to creep into a hollow tree trunk. "We two wives," they said, "beat the tiger to death." When Kong heard this he grew angry. "Oh no," he said, "there is not a woman anywhere strong or daring enough to kill a tiger; that is a man's job." And Kong started boasting to all the people around. "When the tiger came rushing out at us," he said, "I just took up a position like this and killed the tiger." And Kong demonstrated how he had done this. He put up his fists and stood like a boxer. All the people around were filled with admiration for Kong, who, from that day on, was always known as Brave Kong, and celebrated as the strong man who boxed a tiger to death.

The story spread far and wide and even got as far as the King, who sent for Brave Kong to make him an Officer, to lead the King's army into battle.

Not long after this, a war broke out, and the King's realm was invaded by an army from another Kingdom. The King at once sent for Brave Kong and appointed him to lead his force into battle. Brave Kong was very much afraid. He didn't know what to do; it was impossible to avoid going off to battle, because it was the King's order and he had a reputation as a brave man. He crept off home and lay down to sleep.

When his two wives came home, Brave Kong explained to them what had happened. "I am very frightened," said Brave Kong, "I don't know what to do." Ahm and Kum did their best to cheer him up. They made him get up and have a meal, take a bath and get ready his weapons to go out to battle. They practically had to push Brave Kong in to do obeisance to the King and say farewell to the Court before setting out for battle. At last, Brave Kong was ready and rode off on an elephant, sitting up on the elephant's head, with his two wives riding just behind him. The enormous army of soldiers marched off in formation with Kong in front.

When at last they got near the enemy, so that Brave Kong could see them quite clearly, he was very frightened indeed. He was so terrified that it made him sick. His arms and legs began to tremble with fear and knock against the elephant's head. Then the elephant, thinking that this knocking was a signal from his rider to go faster, broke into a run and would not stop. All the soldiers marching with Brave Kong followed suit.

When they saw Brave Kong make his elephant run, the enemy thought that he must be backed up by a very strong army and sure of victory. So the enemy broke ranks and scattered in all directions. Seeing his foes thus routed, Brave Kong began boasting loudly to all the officials and soldiers around him about his bravery and prowess. In fact, all the officials had, with their own eyes, seen Brave Kong being sick on the elephant's head and so they asked him: "General, why ever were you sick like that?" Brave Kong answered, "Well, if I had been ill in the middle of the battle and had got down from the elephant, I would surely have been cut down by the enemy, but I was far too busy directing the battle to get down, so I was just sick as I went along." When the officials and soldiers heard this they thought how devoted and clever Brave Kong was. If they had known the truth of the whole affair—that Brave Kong had simply been afraid—they would certainly have despised him very much; but, as it was, Brave Kong was the victor of the Army. He hastened back to make obeisance to the King and told him of all that had happened. The King was delighted at Brave Kong's version of events and loaded him with honors and awards, making him a high official of his Court. From that day on there was no stopping Brave Kong from boasting of his strength and prowess.

Some time after this, the King learned of a fierce crocodile which was troubling his people. This crocodile would seize any animals, or even men, going down to the river where he lived. No one dared to bathe in the waters or even to take out a boat. The King decided that something must be done to relieve the people, and so he sent for Brave Kong and ordered him to go out and catch this fierce crocodile. Brave Kong was again very frightened when he heard this but, of course, he did not dare to go against the Royal Command.

Brave Kong promised the King to do his bidding and then went off home to tell his wives what had happened. "Alas," said Brave Kong, "now the King has sent me to catch a very fierce crocodile from the river. This time I shall surely never come out alive; the crocodile will get me without fail. Before, I was on dry land; I could at least see. But this time I shall be in the water. Whatever shall I do to escape him? The King has ordered me into this affair and there is no getting out of it. The only thing to do is to jump into the water to catch the crocodile and let him get me first."

Brave Kong talked the matter over with his two wives. Finally, they decided to call all his relations together to prepare to go out with him and catch the crocodile. All the people in the country, both high and low, heard that Brave Kong was going off to catch this crocodile and so a huge crowd gathered at the river to watch.

When Brave Kong came down to the river he soon saw the crocodile which was floating, fast asleep, on the surface of the water, quite near the edge of the river. It happened that at that spot on the river bank a very large tree was growing. Its branches hung down over the water and one large forked bough reached right out over the surface of the river. Brave Kong looked all round and wondered what to do. He was terrified of falling into the water, when the crocodile would surely catch him. He jumped into the water, expecting the crocodile to kill him. The sudden noise of Brave Kong falling into the water roused the crocodile. He gave a great start as he awoke, rearing up his head, which stuck right in the fork of the bough which was hanging over the water. The crocodile was caught! He wriggled forward and he could not escape; he wriggled backward and he could not escape. Just then, Brave Kong, who had fallen deep into the river, rose to the surface and looked up to see the crocodile caught in the fork of the branches. He shouted out to his relations on the bank to bring a lance so that he could finish off the crocodile. This he quickly did.

All the people on the bank who had been watching thought that Brave Kong had jumped into the river on purpose and pushed the crocodile up from below into the fork of the tree.

Brave Kong himself, when he saw that the crocodile was dead, began boasting again, louder than ever. All the people sang his praises and it was soon reported back to the King that Brave Kong had shown great courage in killing the crocodile. The King loaded Brave Kong with all the honors and treasure at his command.

For many years after that, Brave Kong lived happily on his reputation for outstanding courage.

Notes and Comments

While some noodles have good fortune thrust upon them, others like "Brave Kong" (an ironic title) have the occasional good sense to capitalize on their luck, whether they deserve it or not. In the male-dominated Far Eastern world of Kong, no one even believes for a moment that his two wives had the strength and courage required to kill a tiger. After all, they should have been honored just to be allowed to carry such a noble trophy into the village. No, this lively Cambodian tale, despite its sexual bias, is typical of the tale type in which a sham hero profits from a series of lucky successes that boost his inflated and undeserved reputation among the gullible.

"The Story of Brave Kong" printed here is perhaps very close to its original source since many scholars feel that the tale itself is of oriental origin. Nevertheless, Tale Type 1640 is well known in Europe and America. In an analysis of 350 variants, Thompson concludes:

> This form of the story, popular in oral tradition all over Europe and the Near East, and known in many parts of both North and South America, seems to come from a jestbook of Montanus published in 1592, though the tale was mentioned several times in the century preceding.

(Folktale, p. 144)

The more familiar title of the tale is "The Brave Tailor," and the central character in many of the European versions is actually a tailor who is encouraged in his exploits by his family, although he has heretofore had relatively little experience in heroism. Sometimes such a hero is allowed to play a small part in arranging the "accidents" that seem to come his way; at other times he seems lucky merely to have escaped his predicament.

A favorite American version of this tale features a cowardly character who takes some hunters on a bear hunt. Having discovered a bear quite by accident, the noodle runs for his life through the front door of the hunting cabin where the hunters are waiting for him. The noodle, closely followed by the bear, manages to shout as he runs out the back door, "Here, hold this one while I bring you another."

The European and American heroic tests—killing a giant, capturing a bear, a unicorn, or a wild boar—are far removed from the oriental crocodile and the elephant charge. Nevertheless, the effect is always the same for our lucky hero. Despite his natural inclination to the contrary, he succeeds in becoming the greatest man in the kingdom, and there are few who have not heard of his bravery. Kong, had he been in the Western tradition, might have followed Lazy Jack's lead and married the princess, but Kong is already married—twice—and perhaps enough is enough.

Tale Type 1640   The Brave Tailor

Principal Motifs:

K1700   Deception through bluffing
K1951   Sham warrior
K1953.1   Coward boasts he has frightened [killed] a bear [tiger]

Parallel Stories in:

Campbell, *West Highlands* 2: #45
Carrière, *Missouri,* #67 (summary in English)
Carter, *Mountain White,* #6
Grimm, #20
Hyde, *Beside the Fire,* pp. 3–15
Jacobs, *English,* #19
———, *More English,* #58, #79 (variant)
Lang, *Blue Fairy,* pp. 337–45
Massignon, *France,* #4
Parsons, *Bahamas,* #82
Roberts, *South,* #62b
Thompson, *One,* #94 (Grimm)

PICTURE BOOKS:

Sixty at a Blow. Illustrated by Christine Price. New York: E. P. Dutton and Co., 1968.
The Valiant Tailor. Illustrated by Kurt Werth. New York: Viking Press, 1965.

62

Bastianelo[*]

Once upon a time there was a husband and wife who had a son. This son grew up, and said one day to his mother: "Do you know, mother, I would like to marry!" "Very well, marry! whom do you want to take?" He answered: "I want the gardener's daughter." "She is a good girl; take her; I am willing." So he went, and asked for the girl, and her parents gave her to him. They were married, and when they were in the midst of the dinner, the wine gave out. The husband said: "There is no more wine!" The bride, to show that she was a good housekeeper, said: "I will go and get some." She took the bottles and went to the cellar, turned the cock, and began to think: "Suppose I should have a son, and we should call him Bastianelo, and he should die. Oh! how grieved I should be! oh! how grieved I should be!" And thereupon she began to weep and weep; and meanwhile the wine was running all over the cellar.

When they saw that the bride did not return, the mother said: "I will go and see what the matter is." So she went into the cellar, and saw the bride, with the bottle in her hand, and weeping, while the wine was running over the cellar. "What is the matter with you, that you are weeping?" "Ah!

[*]From *Italian Popular Tales* by Thomas Crane (Boston: Houghton, Mifflin and Co., 1885), pp. 279–82.

my mother, I was thinking that if I had a son, and should name him Bastianelo, and he should die, oh! how I should grieve! oh! how I should grieve!" The mother, too, began to weep, and weep, and weep; and meanwhile the wine was running over the cellar.

When the people at the table saw that no one brought the wine, the groom's father said: "I will go and see what is the matter. Certainly something wrong has happened to the bride." He went and saw the whole cellar full of wine, and the mother and bride weeping. "What is the matter?" he said; "has anything wrong happened to you?" "No," said the bride, "but I was thinking that if I had a son and should call him Bastianelo, and he should die, oh! how I should grieve! oh! how I should grieve!" Then he, too, began to weep, and all three wept; and meanwhile the wine was running over the cellar.

When the groom saw that neither the bride, nor the mother, nor the father came back, he said: "Now I will go and see what the matter is that no one returns." He went into the cellar and saw all the wine running over the cellar. He hastened and stopped the cask, and then asked: "What is the matter, that you are all weeping, and have let the wine run all over the cellar?" Then the bride said: "I was thinking that if I had a son and called him Bastianelo and he should die, oh! how I should grieve! oh! how I should grieve!" Then the groom said: "You stupid fools! are you weeping at this, and letting all the wine run into the cellar? Have you nothing else to think of? It shall never be said that I remained with you! I will roam about the world, and until I find three fools greater than you I will not return home."

He had a bread-cake made, took a bottle of wine, a sausage, and some linen, and made a bundle, which he put on a stick and carried over his shoulder. He journeyed and journeyed, but found no fool. At last he said, worn out: "I must turn back, for I see I cannot find a greater fool than my wife." He did not know what to do, whether to go on or to turn back. "Oh!" he said, "it is better to try and go a little farther." So he went on and shortly he saw a man in his shirt-sleeves at a well, all wet with perspiration and water. "What are you doing, sir, that you are so covered with water and in such a sweat?" "Oh! let me alone," the man answered, "for I have been here a long time drawing water to fill this pail and I cannot fill it." "What are you drawing the water in?" he asked him. "In this sieve," he said. "What are you thinking about, to draw water in that sieve? Just wait!" He went to a house near by, and borrowed a bucket, with which he returned to the well and filled the pail. "Thank you, good man, God knows how long I should have had to remain here!" "Here is one who is a greater fool than my wife."

He continued his journey and after a time he saw at a distance a man in his shirt who was jumping down from a tree. He drew near, and saw a woman under the same tree holding a pair of breeches. He asked them what they were doing, and they said that they had been there a long time, and that the man was trying on those breeches and did not know how to get into them. "I have jumped, and jumped," said the man, "until I am tired out and I cannot imagine how to get into those breeches." "Oh!" said the traveller, "you might stay here as long as you wished, for you would never get into them in this way. Come down and lean against the tree." Then he took his legs and put them in the breeches, and after he had put them on, he said: "Is that right?" "Very good, bless you; for if it had not been for you, God knows how long I should have had to jump." Then the traveller said to himself: "I have seen two greater fools than my wife."

Then he went his way and as he approached a city he heard a great noise. When he drew near he asked what it was, and was told it was a marriage, and that it was the custom in that city for the brides to enter the city gate on horseback, and that there was a great discussion on this occasion between the groom and the owner of the horse, for the bride was tall and the horse high, and they could not get through the gate; so that they must either cut off the bride's head or the horse's legs. The groom did not wish his bride's head cut off, and the owner of the horse did not wish his horse's legs cut off, and hence this disturbance. Then the traveller said: "Just wait," and came up to the bride and gave her a slap that made her lower her head, and then he gave the horse a kick, and so they passed through the gate and entered the city. The groom and the owner of the horse asked the traveller what he wanted, for he had saved the groom his bride, and the owner of the horse his horse. He answered that he did not wish anything and said to himself: "Two and one make three! that is enough; now I will go home." He did so and said to his wife: "Here I am, my wife; I have seen three greater fools than you; now let us remain in peace and think about nothing else." They renewed the wedding and always remained in peace. After a time the wife had a son whom they named Bastianelo, and Bastianelo did not die, but still lives with his father and mother.

Notes and Comments

Sometimes a wife or a sweetheart can be so silly that there seems little hope of settling down comfortably with her. The Italian husband in "Bastianelo" learns that things may not be quite as bad as they seem. "Bastianelo," like most humorous tales about wives, has had a place in jest books and was included by Basile in the *Pentamerone,* but it has remained in oral form and can be found throughout the world, though its origins have been traced to India and Ceylon.

Like so many noodle stories "Bastianelo" is an example of the clustering of independent types to form an episodic plot. In the simple German form, Elsie goes to draw beer, and when all the household has joined her in soggy lamentations, the suitor comes down to find out where they are. When he hears Elsie's fears, he congratulates his bride-to-be on being very clever to think things through (Tale Type 1450). In a common English variant, the suitor departs in a huff to seek three persons as stupid as Elsie (Tale Type 1384). During his searches he may encounter a man jumping into his trousers, both legs at once (Tale Type 1286); or some fools trying to rescue the reflection of the moon in a pond where they think it has fallen (Tale Type 1335A); or another fool trying to carry sunlight into a windowless house in a wheelbarrow (Tale Type 1245). Thus, the story of Clever Elsie may be found independently, or it may be the convenient introduction to a continuing noodle tale.

Two familiar motifs are omitted from this Italian variant: J1904.1 "Cow taken to the roof to graze" (included in Section B in Tale 8) and J2161.2 "Man's head cut off so that a shirt sewn together at the neck will fit." But the principal motif, J2063 "Distress over imagined troubles of unborn child" is found in all versions. This inclusion undoubtedly reflects the anxieties parents feel about the future of their children. The breeches motif is also popular, probably because the wearing of trousers, or something like them, is well-nigh universal.

The tale of Clever Elsie's fears is a favorite all around the world. William Clouston heard one version in which a man was seen with a horse and cart. In the cart was a cow that was discovered to have been stolen. The townsfolk condemned not only the man to death but also his horse for dragging the cart. Such stories accelerate the search of the suitor for three persons more stupid than Elsie and bring the tale to a suitable conclusion while delighting the listeners with a string of noodle anecdotes.

The basic plot of the beer in the cellar and Elsie's imagined fears has one slight variation in a Gaelic version. In that story a young husband buys a cradle for his child, although he and his wife do not have a child. One day the husband happens to throw something in the cradle, at which time his wife bursts into tears, sobbing, "Oh, if he had been there, he had been killed." This outburst is sufficient to send the young husband out of the house in search of three greater noodles.

It is satisfying to relate that the man's search for three greater fools is always successful, and he returns as Tom does in the Ozark tale "There's Bigger Fools than Tildy":

> So then he turned round and went right back where he started from. Tildy was still worried about the butcher knife a-falling on the baby, but Tom says, "Never mind, honey, because everything will be all right." And pretty soon him and Tildy got married and they lived happy ever after.

> (*Devil's*, p. 51)

Tale Types:

1286 Jumping into the Breeches
1450 Clever Elsie
1384 The Husband Seeks Three People as Stupid as His Wife

Principal Motifs:

H1312.1 Quest for three persons as stupid as his wife
J2063   Distress over imagined troubles of unborn child
J2161.1 Jumping into breeches
J2198   Bewailing a calamity that has not occurred

Parallel Stories in:

Asbjørnsen, #24
Campbell, *West Highlands* 2: #20, #48
Christiansen, *Norway*, #77
Clouston, *Noodles*, pp. 191–204 (7 variants)
Dorson, *Buying*, pp. 132–33
Gardner, *Schoharie*, pp. 163–72 (references)
Grimm, #34
Jacobs, *English*, #2
Kennedy, *Fireside*, pp. 9–14
Massignon, *France*, #38
Parsons, *Sea Islands*, #87
Randolph, *Devil's*, pp. 49–51
Ranke, *Germany*, #76

63

The Mirror*

Wang the Third was a stupid man. One day his wife wanted him to buy her a wooden comb and, being afraid that he would forget it, she pointed at the narrow moon crescent in the sky and said, "Buy me a wooden comb, but it must be just like the moon in the sky."

A few days later, the moon shone full and round in the sky. Wang the Third remembered what his wife had told him and, since his purchase was to be as round as the moon, he bought a round mirror and took it home.

The moment his wife looked in it, she stamped on the ground, fled back to her parents' house, and said to her mother, "My husband has taken a concubine."

The mother-in-law looked into the mirror and said with a sigh, "If only he had chosen a young woman! Why did he take such a hideous old hag?"

Later they brought the case before the district judge. When he saw the mirror, he said, "How dare you people, when you have a quarrel, dress up just like me! It's unbelievable."

*From *Folktales of China* edited by Wolfram Eberhard (Chicago: University of Chicago Press, 1965), p. 179. Reprinted with permission of the publisher. Text from P'ing-hu in Chekiang Province. *Lou Tse-K'uang, Ch'iao-nü,* pp. 88–89.

Notes and Comments

Tale Type 1336A and Motif J17951.7, "Man does not recognize his own reflection in the water (mirror)," are found chiefly in Asia and eastern Europe, though English and American versions exist. The full tale, consisting of three parts, is widely distributed in Japan where fifteen variants have been located.

In the complete tale, a noodle discovers a mirror and thinks his reflection is a picture of an ancestor. Next, his wife sees her reflection and jumps to the conclusion that her husband has a mistress. In the third part, often omitted in Anglo-American variants, a third noodle looks into the mirror and comes to an equally absurd conclusion. Thus, in one Japanese version, the quarreling couple comes before a nun who looks into the mirror and pronounces all to be well since the alleged mistress has now taken holy orders.

Sometimes the couple asks for a magistrate's help, but even he seldom has the answer. A Korean variant has a magistrate who believes the image he sees is his replacement and fears a political plot. Interestingly enough, this variant includes an extra part in which a bright young official solves the problem and explains the nature of mirrors to the bewildered noodles.

In the Anglo-American tradition of a two-part tale, there is a cowboy version in which the wife ends the story by smashing the mirror over her husband's head and screaming, "So that's the sour-faced hussy you've been chasing, is it?" Her English counterpart, in a variant collected by Edward Wilson from Westmorland, concludes, "That's the bloomin' old geyser he's been knocking about wi', is it?"

One longer version collected by Lafcadio Hearn in Japan has a completely serious tone in the midst of the misunderstanding. A dying mother bequeaths the mirror to her daughter saying that each time the daughter looks into it she will see her mother watching over her. When the father sees the daughter looking at the mirror so often, he is deeply moved. Ikeda in *A Type and Motif Index of Japanese Folk-Literature* points out that a *Noh* play, *Matsuyama Kagami,* is based on this legend.

If it is to be any mitigation of the foolishness of the characters in the story, it should be pointed out that mirrors were once quite rare and greatly prized.

Tale Type 1336A   Man does not Recognize His own Reflection in the Water (Mirror)

Principal Motifs:

J1791.7   Man does not recognize his own reflection in the water [mirror]
J1795   Image in mirror mistaken for picture
J1795.2(B)   Man finds mirror, thinks it is picture of grandfather; wife thinks it is picture of husband's new girlfriend.

Parallel Stories in:

Briggs, *Dictionary,* A (2), p. 84
———, *England,* #77
Dorson, *Buying,* pp. 81–82
Hearn, *Japanese,* pp. 46–52
Randolph, *Turtle,* pp. 62–64, 197–98 (references)
Seki, *Japan,* #55
Thorp, *Pardner,* p. 209
Wilson, *English Folk-Tales,* #14

64

The Old Woman and the Tramp*

There was once a tramp, who went plodding his way through a forest. The distance between the houses was so great that he had little hope of finding a shelter before the night set in. But all of a sudden he saw some lights between the trees. He then discovered a cottage, where there was a fire burning on the hearth. How nice it would be to roast oneself before that fire, and to get a bite of something, he thought; and so he dragged himself towards the cottage.

Just then an old woman came towards him.

"Good evening, and well met!" said the tramp.

"Good evening," said the woman. "Where do you come from?"

"South of the sun, and east of the moon," said the tramp; "and now I am on the way home again, for I have been all over the world with the exception of this parish," he said.

"You must be a great traveller, then," said the woman. "What may be your business here?"

"Oh, I want a shelter for the night," he said.

"I thought as much," said the woman; "but you may as well get away

*From *Fairy Tales from the Swedish* by Nils G. Djurklo, translated by H. L. Braekstad (New York: Frederick Stokes Co., 1901), pp. 33–41.

from here at once, for my husband is not at home, and my place is not an inn," she said.

"My good woman," said the tramp, "you must not be so cross and hard-hearted, for we are both human beings, and should help one another, it is written."

"Help one another?" said the woman, "help? Did you ever hear such a thing? Who'll help me, do you think? I haven't got a morsel in the house! No, you'll have to look for quarters elsewhere," she said.

But the tramp was like the rest of his kind; he did not consider himself beaten at the first rebuff. Although the old woman grumbled and complained as much as she could, he was just as persistent as ever, and went on begging and praying like a starved dog, until at last she gave in, and he got permission to lie on the floor for the night.

That was very kind, he thought, and he thanked her for it.

"Better on the floor without sleep, than suffer cold in the forest deep," he said; for he was a merry fellow, this tramp, and was always ready with a rhyme.

When he came into the room he could see that the woman was not so badly off as she had pretended; but she was a greedy and stingy woman of the worst sort, and was always complaining and grumbling.

He now made himself very agreeable, of course, and asked her in his most insinuating manner for something to eat.

"Where am I to get it from?" said the woman. "I haven't tasted a morsel myself the whole day."

But the tramp was a cunning fellow, he was.

"Poor old granny, you must be starving," he said. "Well, well, I suppose I shall have to ask you to have something with me, then."

"Have something with you!" said the woman. "You don't look as if you could ask any one to have anything! What have you got to offer one, I should like to know?"

"He who far and wide does roam sees many things not known at home; and he who many things has seen has wits about him and senses keen," said the tramp. "Better dead than lose one's head! Lend me a pot, grannie!"

The old woman now became very inquisitive, as you may guess, and so she let him have a pot.

He filled it with water and put it on the fire, and then he blew with all his might till the fire was burning fiercely all round it. Then he took a four-inch nail from his pocket, turned it three times in his hand and put it into the pot.

The woman stared with all her might.

"What's this going to be?" she asked.

"Nail broth," said the tramp, and began to stir the water with the porridge stick.

"Nail broth?" asked the woman.

"Yes, nail broth," said the tramp.

The old woman had seen and heard a good deal in her time, but that anybody could have made broth with a nail, well, she had never heard the like before.

"That's something for poor people to know," she said, "and I should like to learn how to make it."

"That which is not worth having, will always go a-begging," said the tramp.

But if she wanted to learn how to make it she had only to watch him, he said, and went on stirring the broth.

The old woman squatted on the ground, her hands clasping her knees, and her eyes following his hand as he stirred the broth.

"This generally makes good broth," he said; "but this time it will very likely be rather thin, for I have been making broth the whole week with the same nail. If one only had a handful of sifted oatmeal to put in, that would make it all right," he said. "But what one has to go without, it's no use thinking more about," and so he stirred the broth again.

"Well, I think I have a scrap of flour somewhere," said the old woman, and went out to fetch some, and it was both good and fine.

The tramp began putting the flour into the broth, and went on stirring, while the woman sat staring now at him and then at the pot until her eyes nearly burst their sockets.

"This broth would be good enough for company," he said, putting in one handful of flour after an other. "If I had only a bit of salted beef and a few potatoes to put in, it would be fit for gentlefolks, however particular they might be," he said. "But what one has to go without, it's no use thinking more about."

When the old woman really began to think it over, she thought she had some potatoes, and perhaps a bit of beef as well; and these she gave the tramp, who went on stirring, while she sat and stared as hard as ever.

"This will be grand enough for the best in the land," he said.

"Well, I never!" said the woman; "and just fancy—all with a nail!"

He was really a wonderful man, that tramp! He could do more than drink a sup and turn the tankard up, he could.

"If one had only a little barley and a drop of milk, we could ask the king himself to have some of it," he said; "for this is what he has every blessed evening—that I know, for I have been in service under the king's cook" he said.

"Dear me! Ask the king to have some! Well, I never!" exclaimed the woman, slapping her knees. She was quite awestruck at the tramp and his grand connections.

"But what one has to go without, it's no use thinking more about," said the tramp.

And then she remembered she had a little barley; and as for milk, well, she wasn't quite out of that, she said, for her best cow had just calved. And then she went to fetch both the one and the other.

The tramp went on stirring, and the woman sat staring, one moment at him and the next at the pot.

Then all at once the tramp took out the nail.

"Now it's ready, and now we'll have a real good feast," he said. "But to this kind of soup the king and the queen always take a dram or two, and one sandwich at least. And then they always have a cloth on the table when they eat," he said. "But what one has to go without, it's no use thinking more about."

But by this time the old woman herself had begun to feel quite grand and fine, I can tell you; and if that was all that was wanted to make it just as the king had it, she thought it would be nice to have it just the same way for once, and play at being king and queen with the tramp. She went straight to a cupboard and brought out the brandy bottle, dram glasses, butter and cheese, smoked beef and veal, until at last the table looked as if it were decked out for company.

Never in her life had the old woman had such a grand feast, and never had she tasted such broth, and just fancy, made only with a nail!

She was in such a good and merry humor at having learnt such an economical way of making broth that she did not know how to make enough of the tramp who had taught her such a useful thing.

So they ate and drank, and drank and ate, until they became both tired and sleepy.

The tramp was now going to lie down on the floor. But that would never do, thought the old woman; no, that was impossible. "Such a grand person must have a bed to lie in," she said.

He did not need much pressing. "It's just like the sweet Christmas time," he said, "and a nicer woman I never came across. Ah, well! Happy are they who meet with such good people," said he; and he lay down on the bed and went asleep.

And next morning when he woke the first thing he got was coffee and a dram.

When he was going the old woman gave him a bright dollar piece.

"And thanks, many thanks, for what you have taught me," she said.

"Now I shall live in comfort, since I have learnt how to make broth with a nail."

"Well, it isn't very difficult, if one only has something good to add to it," said the tramp as he went his way.

The woman stood at the door staring after him.

"Such people don't grow on every bush," she said.

Notes and Comments

Much of the attraction of this tale lies in the way the reader is at first deceived into believing that the tramp's sufferings have addled his brains. Surely no one can make soup from a stone (or a nail)? But the tramp is no ordinary noodle, and it is particularly satisfying to find the tables turned in such a way that the real noodle is unaware of the deception practiced upon her. The old woman thanks her benefactor for conjuring up a soup for which she has supplied *all* the useful ingredients.

"The Old Woman and the Tramp" is a Swedish variant of a tale that is well known in the Scandinavian countries and in their neighbor to the east, Russia. Elizabethan jest books have preserved the texts, and some English, French, and American versions have been collected.

This anecdote can be extended, shortened, or given a different ending, according to the narrator's inclinations. In a French version, a missionary uses a stone from the fireplace as the soup stone. At the end of the tale, he is busily looking for two more stones to give it just the right flavor. In a Russian variant, a soldier uses his ax as the initial ingredient. When the old woman asks him when he will eat his ax too, he replies that it is not quite tender enough but should be just right by dinner time. In this particular version, the old woman dupe does not even share the soup she has so unwittingly made. Although deception by using a soup stone or nail is the most popular motif, similar impositions are practiced upon unsuspecting noodles in a variety of amusing ways.

Randolph reports an Ozark tale in which a tramp asks first for a piece of thread, then some cloth to make a patch for his old britches, then some new britches instead of his old torn ones, and finally some food for his stomach so that the new britches won't be too big for him. Dorson reports a similar ruse with a slightly different twist in his New England story of the traveler who first asks the landlady for a few small potatoes to eat with his cold meat, and then wants a little cold meat to eat with his nicely roasted potatoes.

All these stories relate to those tales in which a seemingly innocent hero profits from either the greed or the gullibility of his victims. A Jamaican tale has a purchaser who, always anxious to get something for nothing, eagerly buys an alleged soup-making pot (Motif K112.2.1) with the ingredients already in it. Other motifs deal with sale of pseudo-magic cake tree (K112.3) in a Korean tale, as well as the equally phony sale of an alleged bill-paying hat (K111.2) in a tale from the Philippines. Such tales seem limited only by the inventiveness of the hero or the human frailty of his victim.

Several fine picture books of "The Old Woman and the Tramp" tale have been published. One of the best is Marcia Brown's *Stone Soup* which captures in gay and earthy colors the spirit of a French variant in which three soldiers trick greedy villagers into sharing with others less fortunate than themselves. This book, a runner-up for the Caldecott Medal, is an excellent starting place for dramatizing the tale. From her illustrations Weston Woods has produced a filmstrip complete with recording.

Tale Type 1548   The Soup-stone

Principal Motif:

K112.2   "Soup stone" sold

Parallel Stories in:

Briggs, *Dictionary,* A (2), pp. 94–95
Dorson, *Jonathan,* p. 226
Prato, *Quelques Contes,* #3, #4 (in French)
Randolph, *Turtle,* pp. 147–48

PLAY:

The Pot of Broth. William Butler Yeats. 1 act.

PICTURE BOOKS:

Nail Soup. Nada Curcija-Prodanovic. Illustrated by Joan Kiddell-Monroe in *Yugoslav Folktales.* New York: Henry Walck, 1957.
Nail Soup. Retold by Harve Zemach and illustrated by Margot Zemach. New York: Follett, 1964.

Stone Soup: An Old Tale. Retold and illustrated by Marcia Brown. New York: Charles Scribner's Sons, 1947.

"Stone Soup in Bohemia." James Morris. Illustrated by Pauline Baynes (in *The Upstairs Donkey and Other Stolen Stories*). New York: Pantheon Books, 1961.

"*Stone Stew.*" I. G. Edmonds. Illustrated by Sean Morrison (in *Trickster Tales*). Philadelphia: J. B. Lippincott Co., 1966.

65

Now I Should Laugh, If I Were Not Dead*

O nce two married women had a dispute about which of their
husbands was the biggest fool. At last they agreed to try if they
were as foolish as they seemed to be. One of the women then played this
trick. When her husband came home from his work, she took a spinning-
wheel and carders, and sitting down, began to card and spin, but neither
the farmer nor anyone else saw any wool in her hands. Her husband
observing this, asked if she was mad to scrape the teazles together and spin
the wheel, without having the wool, and prayed her to tell what this meant.
She said it was scarcely to be expected that he should see what she was
doing, for it was a kind of linen too fine to be seen with the eye. Of this she
was going to make him clothes. He thought this a very good explanation,
and wondered much at how clever his good wife was, and was not a little
glad in looking forward to the joy and pride he would feel in having on these
marvellous clothes. When his wife had spun, as she said, enough for the
clothes, she set up the loom, and wove the stuff. Her husband used, now
and then, to visit her, wondering at the skill of his good lady. She was much
amused at all this, and made haste to carry out the trick well. She took the

*From *Icelandic Legends* collected by Jón Arnason, translated by George Powell and Eiríkr
Magnússon (London: Longmans, Green, and Co., 1866), II: 627–30.

cloth from the loom, when it was finished, and first washed and fulled it, and last, sat down to work, cutting it and sewing the clothes out of it. When she had finished all this, she bade her husband come and try the clothes on, but did not dare let him put them on alone, wherefore she would help him. So she made believe to dress him in his fine clothes, and although the poor man was in reality naked, yet he firmly believed that it was all his own mistake, and thought his clever wife had made him these wondrous-fine clothes, and so glad he was at this, that he could not help jumping about for joy.

Now we turn to the other wife. When her husband came home from his work, she asked him why in the world he was up, and going about upon his feet. The man was startled at this question, and said: "Why on earth do you ask this?" She persuaded him that he was very ill, and told him he had better go to bed. He believed this, and went to bed as soon as he could. When some time had passed, the wife said she would do the last services for him. He asked why, and prayed her by all means not to do so. She said: "Why do you behave like a fool; don't you know that you died this morning? I am going, at once, to have your coffin made." Now the poor man, believing this to be true, rested thus till he was put into his coffin. His wife then appointed a day for the burial, and hired six coffin-carriers, and asked the other couple to follow her dear husband to his grave. She had a window made in one side of the coffin, so that her husband might see all that passed round him. When the hour came for removing the coffin, the naked man came there, thinking that everybody would admire his delicate clothes. But far from it; although the coffin-bearers were in a sad mood, yet nobody could help laughing when they saw this naked fool. And when the man in the coffin caught a glance of him, he cried out as loud as he could: "Now I should laugh, if I were not dead!" The burial was put off, and the man let out of the coffin.

Now it came out that these women had thus tricked their husbands, and they got for it a public whipping at a parish court.

Notes and Comments

Here is the silliest of noodles—the man who doubts the evidence of his senses. It is a tale that has a wide currency throughout Europe, especially in Hungary, the Middle East, and the Far East.

The particular story printed here is from Iceland and is made up of two types: 1406 *The Merry Wives' Wager,* and 1313 *The Man Who Thought*

Himself Dead. Each of the tales is found independently in extended versions as well as in combinations.

The basic story, that of the wager of the two wives, lends itself to the greatest variation. In order to prove the stupidity of their respective husbands, the wives resort to all kinds of tricks and deceptions. One wife, after employing all the usual tricks, convinces her noodle husband that he is a dog and should therefore bark. In some versions, the merry wife will convince her husband that his house has moved during his absence and that what he thought was his house is in fact an inn. Such tricks abound in literature; in Shakespeare's *Taming of the Shrew* Christopher Sly is persuaded that he is a prince recovering from insanity. In Oliver Goldsmith's *She Stoops to Conquer* Young Marlow is convinced that Mr. Hardcastle's house is an inn.

The motif that seems to have had the greatest variation beyond the wager tale has to do with the husband who does not recognize himself or else believes that he is dead. Such tales seem to draw on a strong philosophical undercurrent, questioning the very nature of existence itself. When one noodle wakes up and finds himself covered with tar and feathers and a fish net, he wonders whether he can indeed really be himself. He resolves the question by going to his own house and asking if he is at home. When the spouse who has perpetrated the trick answers affirmatively, the noodle can but decide that all is not as he had thought, that he is not really himself, and that existence is at best a transitory matter.

Husbands who are ultimately convinced that they are really dead have a somewhat more complex problem since they have to endure the rigors of a funeral and the procession. Some noodles have their deaths predicted by a passerby who gives a warning: "If you keep on sawing that way, the branch will fall and you will break your neck." When the inevitable accident occurs, the noodle is convinced that the warning must be accurate and that he is truly dead. His problem is that his friends and villagers seem even more noodlelike than himself, and when they can't even manage to carry the coffin home on the right road or when they mistake his house for another's house, he is forced to raise up in his casket and set things right. Clearly, the noodle story of the man who thinks himself dead is either the silliest noodle or the most profound of all, for the questions of identity and existence are perhaps the only really serious ones to be encountered.

The other part of the wager in this tale, that of the wife who sets out to convince her husband that the "cloth" she is weaving is really too fine for him to see, or else can't be seen by any man who has been lying to his wife, has its best known literary treatment in Hans Christian Andersen's "The Emperor's New Clothes." This version of the folktale became a skill-

·fully written tongue-in-cheek satire aimed at the pompous incompetents who made Andersen suffer in his early impoverished years.

Tale Types:

1406 The Merry Wives' Wager
1313 The Man Who Thought Himself Dead

Principal Motifs:

J2301	Gullible husband
J2311.0.1	Wife makes her husband believe that he is dead
J2312	Naked person made to believe that he is clothed
K1545	Wives wager as to who can best fool her husband

Parallel Stories in:

TT1313: Boucher, *Moondaughter,* pp. 88–90
Clouston, *Noodles,* pp. 160–63 (reprinted in Foster, *Wit,* pp. 103–4)
Walker, *Turkey,* pp. 228–29

TT1406: Chase, *Grandfather,* #18
Christiansen, *Norway,* #76
Noy, Israel, #69

66

The Pig-Headed Wife*

W hen Matti married Liisa, he thought she was the pleasantest woman in the world. But it wasn't long before Liisa began to show her real character. Headstrong as a goat she was, and as fair set on having her own way.

Matti had been brought up to know that a husband should be the head of his family, so he tried to make his wife obey. But this didn't work with Liisa. It just made her all the more stubborn and pig-headed. Every time that Matti asked her to do one thing, she was bound to do the opposite, and work as he would he generally got her own way in the end.

Matti was a patient sort of man, and he put up with her ways as best he could, though his friends were ready enough to make fun of him for being henpecked. And so they managed to jog along fairly well.

But one year as harvest time came round, Matti thought to himself, "Here am I, a jolly goodhearted fellow, that likes a bit of company. If only I had a pleasant sort of wife, now, it would be a fine thing to invite all our friends to the house and have a nice dinner and drink and a good time. But it's no good thinking of it, for as sure as I propose a feast, Liisa will declare a fast."

---

*From *Tales From a Finnish Tupa* by James Cloyd Bowman and Margery Bianco (Chicago: Albert Whitman & Co., 1936), pp. 201–4. Copyright © 1936, 1964 by Albert Whitman & Company.

And then a happy thought struck him.

"I'll see if I can't get the better of Liisa, all the same. I'll let on I want to be quiet, and then she'll be all for having the house full of guests."

So a few days later he said, "The harvest holidays will be here soon, but don't you go making any sweet cakes this year. We're too poor for that sort of thing."

"Poor! What are you talking about?" Liisa snapped. "We've never had more than we have this year. I'm certainly going to bake a cake, and a good big one too."

"It works," thought Matti. "It works!" But all he said was, "Well, if you make a cake, we won't need a pudding too. We mustn't be wasteful."

"Wasteful, indeed!" Liisa grumbled. "We shall have a pudding, and a big pudding!"

Matti pretended to sigh, and rolled his eyes. "Pudding's bad enough, but if you take it in your head to serve stuffed pig again, we'll be ruined!"

"You'll kill our best pig," quoth Liisa, "and let's hear no more about it."

"But wine, Liisa," Matti went on. "Promise me you won't open a single bottle. We've barely enough to last us through the winter as it is."

Liisa stamped her foot. "Are you crazy, man? Who ever heard of stuffed pig without wine! We'll not only have wine, but I'll buy coffee too. I'll teach you to call me extravagant by the time I'm through with you!"

"Oh, dear, oh, dear," Matti sighed. "If you're going to invite a lot of guests, on top of everything else, that'll be the end of it. We can't possibly have guests."

"And have all the food spoil with no one to eat it, I suppose?" jeered Liisa. "Guests we'll have, and what's more, you'll sit at the head of the table, whether you like it or not."

"Well, at any rate I'll drink no wine myself," said Matti, growing bolder. "If I don't drink the others won't, and I tell you we'll need that wine to pull us through the winter."

Liisa turned on him, furious. "You'll drink with your guests as a host should, till every bottle is empty. There! Now will you be quiet?"

When the day arrived the guests came, and great was the feasting. They shouted and sang round the table, and Matti himself made more noise than any of his friends. So much so, that long before the feast was over Liisa began to suspect he had played a trick on her. It made her furious to see him so jolly and carefree.

As time went on she grew more and more contrary, until there was no living with her. Now it happened one day in the spring, when all the streams were high, that Matti and Liisa were crossing the wooden bridge over the little river which separated two of their meadows. Matti crossed first, and noticing that the boards were badly rotted, he called out without thinking, "Look where you step, Liisa! The plank is rotten there. Go lightly or you'll break through."

"Step lightly!" shouted Liisa. "I'll do as—"

But for once Liisa didn't finish what she had to say. She jumped with all her weight on the rotted timbers and fell plop into the swollen stream.

Matti scratched his head for a moment; then he started running upstream as fast as he could go.

Two fishermen along the bank saw him and called, "What's the matter, my man? Why are you running upstream so fast?"

"My wife fell in the river," Matti panted, "and I'm afraid she's drowned."

"You're crazy," said the fishermen. "Anyone in his right mind would search downstream, not up!"

"Ah," said Matti, "but you don't know my Liisa! All her life she's been so pig-headed that even when she's dead she'd be bound to go against the current!"

Notes and Comments

Aarne/Thompson divides the stories about obstinate wives into various categories. Type 1365A *Wife Falls into a Stream* is the story we have reprinted here. The humor of the tale lies in the husband's conviction that his wife is so obstinate that even while drowning she will go against the current. A second type that is equally well known deals with 1365B *Cutting with the Knife or the Scissors.* Here a domestic argument about whether a knife or scissors has been used concludes with the wife sinking under the water while still making the sign of the scissors with her index and third finger. Other categories include arguments about who shall eat the third egg, whose hair is in the soup, whether rats or minks have made the holes in the floor, and so on. Finally, in an eleventh subcategory, 1365K, Thompson lists a tale complimentary to wives, *The Obstinate Husband,* but only the French-Canadians seem to be fond of this version.

Possible variations of the "falling into the stream" stories center around establishing conclusively that the wife is indeed obstinate. This problem is rapidly solved in a Hodja tale by choosing for drowning the most obstinate of all traditional figures—a mother-in-law. The heroine in our Finnish story, however, is a victim of an elaborate scheme of reverse psychology in which her own character flaw finally proves her undoing. The number of examples of the wife's perversity during the preparation of the harvest party is sufficient evidence for the good man's actions in looking for the corpse upstream.

Study has shown that traditional anecdotes survive with great tenacity but not always in a recognizable tale type form. Many are mere capsule versions of the original story with perhaps only the punch line or principal point of humor retained. In a New York version, the setting is a river baptism, the cast of characters is a group of Baptists, and the entire story is compressed into a shout by the son as his father is immersed in the river: "Don't let loose of him; but if you do happen to let him go, look for him upstream—he's too damn contrary to go down" (Thompson, *Boots,* p. 170).

The second type of obstinate wife story is that dealing with the argument about the scissors. In some stories the argument centers around whether something has been cut with the scissors or the knife. In an Italian variant, a tailor's wife tells her husband that a pair of scissors is responsible for a pile of broken dishes in the kitchen. The enraged husband demands a more rational answer and gradually lowers his wife down the well. As the water closes over her head, she raises her hand and signs "scissors."

The common themes in both these story types are the obstinacy of the wife and her subsequent drowning in the river or well, though there are a few versions in which the wife is strangled and buried. Even in the grave, however, she is obstinate, two fingers protruding from the earth, fingers spread apart, scissors fashion.

Tale Type 1365A   Wife Falls Into a Stream

Principal Motifs:

T255   The obstinate wife or husband
T255.2   The obstinate wife sought for upstream

Parallel Stories in:

Barnham, *Khoja,* p. 191
Boggs, *North Carolina,* p. 306
Brown, *Scissors,* #1
Courlander, *Fire,* pp. 35–39
Crane, *Italian,* #96
Dorson, *Buying,* p. 84
———, *Jonathan,* p. 230
Halpert, *Wellerism,* p. 75 (references given)
Hazlitt, *Shakespeare Jest* III, "Mother Bunches Merriments," p. 27
Wilson, *Humorous,* #2 (reprinted in Briggs, *Dictionary,* A (2), pp. 47–48, and
     Briggs, *England,* #75)

Appendix I:
Folktales in the Elementary Classroom

Approaches to using the folktale in the elementary classroom will be as varied as the creativity and the background of the individual teacher. But whether the object of the unit is to expose children to many different kinds of tales or to study one in depth, the result is almost guaranteed to be both productive and enjoyable. The suggestions below are intended as points of departure for any teacher in those broad areas where folktales can make a contribution to classroom creativity at the elementary level.

Folktales and Reading

1. *The Basal Readers:* The elementary school teacher has a wealth of traditional material at his disposal. Publishers of basal readers have recognized the appeal of folktales because of their strong plots and clear themes. Today Anansi and Jack are almost as well known as Dick and Jane in some areas. Thus the reading period in the morning can come alive in the afternoon in the form of an adjunct activity of art, drama, or related background study.

2. *Remedial Readers:* The Dolch First Readers are typical of many "high interest/low vocabulary" readers that depend heavily on traditional

385

folktales to entice slow readers. Prepared by Edward and Marguerite Dolch (University of Illinois) and published by Garrard (Champaign, Illinois), these readers present tales using the Dolch 95 Commonest Nouns and the 110–220 words of their Basic Sight Words List. On an average, these books present approximately one new word per page beyond the basic word lists.

Two versions of "The Hare and the Hedgehog," both rewritten versions, will give an idea of the broad appeal of tales made possible by different retellings. The Dolch controlled vocabulary version is simplicity itself:

> One morning Mr. Hedgehog went for a walk. The sun was out and the birds were singing. Mr. Hedgehog said, "I think that I shall go and see how my cabbages are growing." (Dolch, *Animal Tales,* p. 49)

In the hands of a literary storyteller like Walter de la Mare (#25 in the text), the same beginning becomes:

> Early one Sunday morning, when the cowslips or paigles were showing their first honey-sweet buds in the meadows and the brook was in bloom, a hedgehog came to his little door to look out at the weather. He stood with arms a-kimbo, whistling a tune to himself—a tune no better and no worse than the tunes hedgehogs usually whistle to themselves on fine Sunday mornings. And as he whistled the notion came into his head that, before turning in and while his wife was washing the children, he might take a little walk into the fields.

In either version the excitement of the race and the trick played on the hare remains the central point of the story.

The purpose of such high interest/controlled vocabulary stories such as those in the Dolch readers is to encourage independent reading as soon as possible. Such easy-to-read stories are staple fare at the Reading Club at Highland Park Elementary in Austin, Texas, a highly acclaimed project using parent volunteers on a one-to-one basis with students who have various learning disabilities. The reading club augments the work of the classroom teacher by providing a wide variety of stimulating materials that encourage the development of reading skills through practice. Books like the Dolch readers are only one part of the extensive remedial program, but they represent a very important use of the folktale in the elementary school.

3. *Quiet Time Reading:* Perhaps the most obvious use of folktales in the very early grades is in sharing and listening groups after lunch or during quiet time. Folktales are the stories to turn to when an action-filled plot is needed to hold the attention of wiggly ones after lunch. Whether a teacher is best at telling the tales or reading them aloud will soon become clear. It

may be cold comfort to hear, but it is the teller's skill and not the tales that is on trial. These traditional tales have held the interest of children (and adults) for thousands of years. The successful storyteller must practice, practice, and increase his repertory to ensure the success of those magic times that begin "Once upon a time."

Folktales and Social Studies

When the geographic method of selecting folktales is used, folktales become an integral part of each social studies unit. Almost every elementary library will have long lists of Folktales of Africa, Folktales of Samoa, or Folktales of whatever country is being studied.

Such units can range from merely reading a few tales that enhance the "flavor" of the countries being studied to reading entire units devoted to folklore. Clague Middle School in Ann Arbor, Michigan, put on a full-dress storytelling program for classmates and parents at the conclusion of a three-week unit on African and Afro-American folktales. The entire class dressed in multicolored African robes and dashikis and decorated the stage with carved African masks. While one group of boys accompanied on the "talking drums," individual *griots* (pronounced gree-oh) told their stories. Leaping up in the middle of the audience in true griot fashion, one boy began:

GRIOT: A Story—a story!
LISTENERS: Let it come, let it go!
GRIOT: Now, what I am going to tell you didn't happen in my part of
             the forest, but it did happen in a part of the forest far, far away.

When he had finished his tale, another of the boys explained, "When the African people gather around a fire under the big trees to hear stories, it is the custom to begin this way." He also explained that the *griot* in African culture is the "vessel of history" and an important member of the court of the king or chief. "The *griot* keeps all the records of his people in his head and is called upon to recite them at court or ceremonial occasions," he added. Then several other stories were presented which called for audience participation and response. Together with the drums, costumes, scenery, and drama, the folktales transported many children as far into the continent of Africa as they might ever go on a summer afternoon.

Folklore and English

1. *The Comparative Paper.* One fourth-grade textbook, *The World of Language* (Follett), edited by Muriel Crosby, begins an entire section on theme and variation by looking at illustrations in art, music, poetry, and prose. For example, the theme of a storm is presented first in paintings and photographs, and then in a poem by Sandburg and prose by Laura Ingalls Wilder. Students are asked to try their hand at writing poems about a storm or drawing pictures of a story to the accompaniment of recorded "storm" music. Finally, students are presented with an example of several different versions of a folktale, also in the context of different forms of theme and variation. Students are asked to point out differences and similarities in the stories and finally to "describe the theme that runs through all the stories."

Using this material as a springboard, a brief comparative folktale unit was taught to Mrs. Susan Browne's fourth-grade class at Highland Park in Austin. The children were told three or four plot summaries of the Cinderella story and asked to read "Little Burnt Face," or "The Indian Cinderella" (Tale #4.) They were then asked to answer the following questions:

1. How is this Indian Cinderella similar to the other Cinderella stories you have read or heard in class? Make a list of the similarities you can find in all "Cinderella" stories. Using this list, state in one or two sentences the theme that runs through all the stories.

2. Make a list of the differences in the stories. You may want to make this list in the form of a chart. Some of the main topics might include the number of sisters in each story, the different names given to Cinderella, and the places where she meets the prince. Think of as many topics as you can.

	Names	Heroes	Magic by
JAPANESE	Crimson Dish	Prince	
RUSSIAN	Hearth Cat	Prince	Doves
APPALACHIAN	Ash Pot	Prince	Old witch woman
INDIAN	not named	Warrior	Warrior's sister
ENGLISH	Cinderella	Prince	Fairy Godmother

Some of the answers were: "The Indian Cinderella is similar to other Cinderella stories because the two main characters are a handsome important person of means looking for someone to be his wife, and a young sweet beautiful girl of humble origins who's living a life of hardships with people who don't care about her. With the help of a little magic they find each other and live happily after" (Mark, age 10); Kent, also 10: "The heroine is always ragged and a nothing"; and Rob: "In all the stories there is a heroine who is abused by jealous people. Then by magic she turns from rags to riches and meets a handsome hero and they live happily ever after." Rob's chart of the differences was most complete, and is given below (pp. 388–89).

After exploring the idea of theme and variation with the Cinderella stories, the class turned to a more elaborate project of comparison. This time the Rumpelstiltskin tales were chosen. Since we have a comparative paper example of this tale type in Chapter 5, we thought it might be intriguing to see how elementary school children fared with the same material. This particular class had just been studying the structure of the narrative, so they were all familiar with such terms as plot, character, rising action, and climax. They had also been doing exercises in their reading class in defining the theme of a story. Most of the children were able to begin their writing with "The theme of the story is. . . ." The concept of theme and variation was new to them, however, but all of them were able to see that the four different stories ("Duffy and the Devil" from Cornwall, Grimm's "Rumpelstiltskin," Jacobs's "Tom Tit Tot," and two recently printed Norwegian versions of "St. Olav, the Master Builder") were really only variations of a basic "Rumpelstiltskin" plot. The following instructions (p. 390), therefore, became almost self-explanatory, at least for the upper reading groups.

Where she meets hero	Test	Villains
theater	best poem	2 sisters
ball	foot to fit in glass slipper	1 stepmother 2 stepsisters
meeting	foot to fit in shoe	1 employer and her daughters
tent	see invisible warrior	2 sisters
ball	foot to fit in glass slipper	1 stepmother and 2 stepsisters

HOW TO WRITE A COMPARATIVE FOLKTALE PAPER
—FOURTH GRADE

1. Think of a good title, but make sure it contains the name of the tales you are going to study.

2. Paragraph #1 should contain the following:
   a. One sentence that tells what the tales are about
   b. One sentence that lists the complete titles of the three tales you have read for this paper.

3. Paragraph #2 should contain the following:
   a. Something about the plot *similarities* of all three tales. Think of them in the order of:
      1) An Impossible Task
      2) A Bargain with a Supernatural Helper
      3) The Helper Defeated.
   b. Something about *differences* you discovered in the stories.

4. Paragraph #3 should contain the following:
   Comments about any details you especially liked or found unusual. Examples you might choose are:
   a. How the heroines and helpers looked or acted
   b. How the heroine got into trouble
   c. How the helper's name is overheard
   d. How the helper behaves after his name is discovered
   e. Any details in the tales that tell you which country the story happened in.
   You may use as many of these suggested topics as you like, but be sure to give one good example from each of the three stories each time.

5. Paragraph #4 should end with a brief sentence about what you understand about "theme and variation" in a folktale, now that you have written your first comparative folktale paper.

   P. S. The secret to the whole paper is to use lots of examples!

Any adult faint hearts who may have trembled in despair over their own comparative paper assignment should read the following paper carefully. It is reprinted in its entirety with only minor changes in spelling and punctuation so that mechanics will not detract from a marvelously clear understanding and insight into theme and variation in a folktale.

RUMPELSTILTSKIN, ST. OLAV, THE MASTER BUILDER, AND TOM TIT TOT: A STUDY OF THE MAGIC OF THE NAME
by Carlos Solé, Age 9

The theme of all the "Rumpelstiltskin" stories is the same. An impet helps someone who has an impossible task but the person with the impossible task finds out the helper's name and makes him so angry that the impet ends up killing himself or totally disappearing. For example, in "St. Olav" a troll was putting up the spire. St. Olav said the troll's name, so the troll got so angry he plunged from the tower and killed himself. In "Tom Tit Tot" a girl guesses the impet's name (Tom Tit Tot's) and he flies into the dark. The most interesting differences are how people get in trouble. In "Rumpelstiltskin" the king is greedy and the impet will take the Queen's child if she can't guess his name. In "Tom Tit Tot" the girl likes to eat, have nice dresses and company, and Tom Tit Tot will take the girl away if she can't guess his name. In "St. Olav" St. Olav likes to build churches and the payment to the troll is the sun because it is cold in Norway and the summers are very short over there. The tales I have read are "St. Olav the Master Builder," "Rumpelstiltskin," and "Tom Tit Tot."

The similarities are that there is an impossible task. In "Tom" the task is to spin five skeins in a day in the last month of the year. In "St. Olav" it is to put the spire on the tower. In "Rumpelstiltskin" the girl has to spin hay into gold. In "Tom" the girl bargains with a little black thing, in "Rumpelstiltskin" with a little man, and in "St. Olav," St. Olav bargains with a troll. In all the stories the helpers come in magic form. In "Tom" the helper gets too confident that the girl does not know his name because she says two names that are wrong, but on the third try, she says it. In "St. Olav" the troll does not know that St. Olav knows his name, but when the troll is putting on the spire, St. Olav yells his name, and in "Rumpelstiltskin" the girl guesses his name at the end.

The plot differences are that in "Tom" the girl's mother gets her in trouble. She tells the king that her daughter spun five skeins not to embarrass her daughter. The girl could lose her head if she did not spin five skeins a day later. In "Rumpelstiltskin" her (the girl's) father gets his daughter in trouble so he can higher his position by having the girl marry the king, yet she could lose her life. St. Olav gets himself in trouble not because he wants to raise his position but to finish the church, and St. Olav won't lose anything. There are variations about the helpers. For example, in "St. Olav," the helper is just a troll who lives in a mountain. In "Tom" there is a little black thing that lives in a chalk pit. In "Rumpelstiltskin" it is a ridiculous little man who lives in a little house on a mountain top. The only thing they have in common is that they are mean and given to great anger. There are also similarities among the heroines. For example, the heroines in "Rumpelstiltskin" and "Tom" get in trouble because of their parents. Yet they never tell the truth about themselves. Once they are in trouble they sit back and cry helplessly and also lie to their husbands by making them believe things which they cannot do. St. Olav just gets in trouble by himself and never lies. They all get out of trouble in similar ways. For example, in "Tom" the girl finds out the impet's name from the king. The miller's daughter finds out from a messenger. St. Olav finds out when he sails past Ladehammeren. In short, they find out through sheer luck.

We know that the story takes place in different countries. For example, in "St. Olav" there is mention of several Norwegian towns. In "Tom" an English dialect is used. In "Rumpelstiltskin," Rumpelstiltskin is a German name. In "St. Olav" and "Rumpelstiltskin" the impet dies once his name is known. In "Tom" he flies into the dark.

In all the three stories the character takes on an impossible task, finds himself at the mercy of a cruel helper, and is finally released by magic. In these folk tales it is the magic of the name. This is the theme of these tales but there are different versions because people live in different parts of the world, want different things and speak different languages.

It is only fair to say that Carlos's paper clearly represents the top end of the spectrum of a fourth-grade class, but other ways of handling the comparison paper were equally interesting. With many children, the variety of titles was imaginative. Samples ranged from "The Name of the Game is My Name" and "Rumpelstiltskin—A Story of a Queen Who Gets Tangled Up" to "A Study of Folktales With a 'Guess the Name' Theme." The theme of the stories was readily identified and expressed in a variety of ways. Rob decided that "the theme that runs through all three stories is that the main character must guess the name of a magic helper," while Gavin concluded rather independently that "the theme of the Rumpelstiltskin stories is that little people can do big jobs." Missy was more concise: "The theme of the stories is about guessing names."

In dealing with the plot similarities, the children had very little difficulty. The instructions had given them the outline of the story, and all children seemed to be able to move sequentially through all three stories, scene by scene. Much emphasis was placed on the "deal" with the helper, though not one child used the term "bargain." Rob said: "In all these stories a girl is assigned an impossible task by an important man. Because she is trapped, she makes a deal with a magic helper." Missy ticks off in 1-2-3 fashion all the similarities she found: "A similarity in these stories was the impossible task of guessing the names. Another one was the deal with an impet or troll or a manikin. And another one was the helpers all getting very mad."

Though plot differences are not numerous in the stories, Gavin noticed that "in the story 'St. Olav' the plot differs from the other Rumpelstiltskin stories in that there is not a heroine given an impossible task." Rob, one of the few students who used the oral version of "Duffy and the Devil" as his source, had a bit more material to work with. He comments on the "danger of dying" in "Rumpelstiltskin" and "Tom Tit Tot," a threat that is absent in "Duffy." He also points out the "surprise ending" in "Duffy": "After the devil leaves, all the clothes he has made disappear. In the other stories the things the magic helpers make stay with the people."

Comments from all the children about the variations in narrative embellishments were by far the most interesting. Notice that Carlos is aware of some social tension in topic 4b when he talks about the girl being in trouble because her father or someone else wants to "higher his position." Also he is observant enough to remark: "Yet they never tell the truth about themselves and also lie to their husbands by making them believe things which they cannot do." All the boys seemed to share a certain derision for the seemingly helpless girl in her very real predicament. Gavin's characterization of the heroine in "Tom Tit Tot" as "a cry-baby, greedy, and dumb" was typical of many reactions.

It was most interesting to see that the children had an instinctive feel for local color in each of the stories. Gavin handled the whole geography question with aplomb:

The reason I can tell that the story "St. Olav" is from Norway is because it says "in the Bringsaas mountains in Seljord." The reason I know that "Tom Tit Tot" is an English story is because of the way they talk. The reason I know that "Rumpelstiltskin" is a German tale is because of the manikin's name which sounds German to me.

Their conclusions in these papers were both interesting and heartening. Mark could see that "the theme of comparative folktales remains the same, but it is presented differently—different characters, different places, and different things to do." Rob felt that "many countries have the 'Rumpelstiltskin' story. They all have the same basic theme but small variations throughout the folktale make it more interesting. If it had no variations it would be the same old story all over the world." Carlos perhaps has the last word when he sees that "there are different versions because people live in different parts of the world, want different things and speak different languages."

2. *Folktales and Literature.* Obviously, folktales ought to be presented somewhere in the curriculum as a legitimate form of oral literature. At Highland Park Elementary School, such units are the norm rather than the exception. According to Librarian Carolyn Hart, almost every teacher past the second grade has a one- to three-week unit on folktales every year. These units have made such a demand on the traditional tale section of the library that the librarian has had to coordinate classes throughout the year, even though this most adequate thirteen-thousand-volume elementary library has almost three hundred folktale books available. In the opinion of this very active and experienced librarian, a background in folktales is as essential to understanding literature as is mythology or any other genre. She sees folktales as an important element in any child's cultural heritage, an element that he must have in order to understand the allusions and references he will encounter in literature and life. As an enthusiastic supporter of the importance of folktales in the curriculum, she offers her library display cases to a continuing cycle of the wonderful objects discussed below.

Folktales and Art

Just as no storyteller can ever tell a story exactly the same way twice, so neither will any child imagine and illustrate any folktale in exactly the same way. But moving from the many-colored many-spangled imagination of a child to his crayon pictures, his finger-painted outlines, his wonderfully original concepts of the funny and magical creatures of folktales is a delight for any teacher or parent.

Artwork is only limited by the art technique of the teacher, certainly not by the imagination of the children. In the Highland Park Library, mobiles revolve endlessly as the three billy goats gruff chase a many-headed cardboard troll through the breeze and Anansi (as a large black blob of yarn) spins his tales of capturing the bees in the calabash and trapping the wood fairy with the sticky gum-baby.

On the display shelves simple shoe box dioramas can become the most imaginative scenes of terror and hilarity, complete with toothpick figures, paper scenery, and much Elmer's school glue. More elaborate scenes are constructed with papier-mâché, the ubiquitous colored clay, and even a few sugar-cubed castles.

The Highland Park librarian likes every child to have the opportunity to try his hand at illustrating a book, and a folktale is as good a point of departure for a third grader as it is for many a Caldecott winner. Inexpensive lamination or spiral binding of such creations makes them all the more special for their creators and preserves their magic so that other children may look and enjoy them for many years to come.

Folktales and Creative Dramatics

There is a wealth of source material for classroom dramatics to be found among traditional folktales. One kindergarten class was the feature story in the neighborhood section of the local Austin, Texas, papers when they presented their version of "Stone Soup," combining the dramatization of the tale, complete with stingy old woman and crafty soldiers, with a delicious pot of wonderfully aromatic soup which they then shared with the audience and each other. One carefully washed stone, a sneaky bouillon cube (the teacher wouldn't say), some vegetables, noodles, seasonings, and a lot of imagination produced a meal fit for the king, or more importantly, the school principal.

Dramatization of "Henny Penny" by the slow reading group of a second-grade class was equally successful and boosted the self-confidence of those readers who needed the most encouragement. Taking the text directly from the basal reader, this group carried the major thrust of the narration while the rest of the class, dressed in improvised paper costumes, portrayed the large cast of panicky animals.

Simple stage props such as chairs stacked in an improvised bridge became the scene of a first-grade encounter with the dreadful troll in the

"Three Billy Goats Gruff." Paper horns and curly white paper beards made the billy goats so fierce that even the large paper-plate eyeballs of the troll seemed to bulge as he scampered away to safety on the other side of the classroom.

Folktales lend themselves equally well to puppet shows. A simple barrier will hide the young puppeteers as they work their own puppets made of sundry materials such as paper bags, old socks, and pieces of felt. The teacher need only be able to divide the folktale into its proper dramatic scenes to ensure the smooth flow of the performance, for the action-packed plot will do the rest. Silhouettes on the overhead projector can also be a medium for the drama, and shadow boxing can take on a literal meaning as a cut-out Jack chases a monstrous giant across the black-and-white screen of the projector.

A more elaborate staging for any drama can be attempted, of course, such as one where a folktale was used in conjunction with choral verse and fable recitations. This performance was for an assembly program and was entitled "Scenes of Wind and Weather." The drama began with poems about the sun, wind, and rain. The choral group kept the rhythm of the rain poem by tapping on the floor with rubber boots. The "curtain" signaling the end of the poetry section turned out to be a barrier of opened umbrellas which shielded the antiphonal group as it exited.

The scene quickly shifted to the other side of the stage where a beautiful young child dressed in many layers of streaming yellow crepe paper came out to argue with her friend the Wind, equally splendid in gray crepe paper, about their relative strengths. The fable of "The Sun and the Wind" was then enacted. The unwary traveler first drew his coat tighter and tighter as the Wind tried to make him take it off. Then as the smiling Sun began to beam brightly upon him, the traveler shed his coat, removed his sweater, and finally mopped his brow with an enormous spotted handkerchief.

The Sun remained smiling in triumph until the appearance of the North Wind, howling from the wings and swirling overhead a long piece of cheesecloth as he blew himself lustily across the stage, signaling the beginning of the folktale "The Lad Who Went to the North Wind" (Tale #1). As the lad confronted him and demanded recompense for his supper which had been blown away, the fierce North Wind swirled his cheesecloth vapor trail round and round as offstage a tin sheet was hammered to simulate thunder.

The scenery for this production was simple but effective. To give the illusion of distance and height, the North Wind was perched atop a high stool on a raised platform. Down below, a simple cabin was sketched by a table and some chairs. There the hero's patient mother waited for his return.

The third scene was set in the Inn, a dwelling suggested only by a bed under which to hide the magic objects until they are either stolen or put to use punishing the thieving innkeeper. All the rest was magic and illusion, such as has been spun by other tellers of this tale for centuries.

Folktales and the Library

One highly successful program at Highland Park has been a storytelling project growing out of the library program. Under the direction of the librarian, some selected fourth and fifth graders who needed to improve their ability to speak in front of a group were given stories that they memorized and practiced telling with a partner. In some cases they prepared illustrations on poster board to go with the story. When each member of the storytelling team had gathered his confidence, he began to tell his tale to small groups of kindergarteners coming to the library for story time. Sometimes one partner told the story while the other showed the pictures. On other occasions the story might be told half and half by each or in dialogue.

The primary result of the project was that the fourth and fifth graders, using familiar material carefully rehearsed and well prepared, developed confidence in their ability to speak before a group. In addition the kindergarteners were treated to some delightful stories, and their enthusiastic reactions to the tales did more for the self-image of the storytellers than any amount of reinforcement from a teacher could possibly have.

Folktales and Creative Writing

Creative short story writers must first understand thoroughly the nature of the narrative and then have the opportunity to practice their imaginative skills. A study of the inner workings of the folktale can become a marvelous device to illustrate the structural aspects of literature. Plot is seen more easily when it is as direct and clear-cut as it is in folktales. Conflict is easy to identify; rising action plateaus are often underlined by triplification; and the climax of the story is always conclusive and full of impact. From such basic analysis, it is easy to move on to more complex narratives where developing characterizations give an added complexity not found in folktales.

Creative writing assignments growing out of such a study can be wholly imaginative or can be some form of extrapolation of a familiar

folktale. The etiological tales blend easily into the assignment of some
original "Just So Stories" about how or why some fanciful animal came to
be. A postplot extrapolation of "Mollie Whuppie" would certainly produce
a dramatic encounter when the thrice-tricked giant *does* run into Mollie
Whuppie later, now that she's a queen and perhaps a mother herself.
Certainly examining "Mollie Whuppie" from the giant's point of view
would require a good understanding of the story and sympathy for the
bumbling creature who loses both his worldly possessions and the children
he loves in his ogreish fashion.

Other kinds of rewritings ranging from the "fractured folktales" told
in modern slang to the lyric musings of a poem about a visit to fairyland
or the loss of a magic wish can be both effective and fun. In most such
instances, the folktale is merely a vehicle for the task at hand, and the end
product is a creative writing assignment and certainly not an "improved"
folktale. A careful distinction should be made between a traditional folktale
carefully preserved in time and a modern short story inspired by a folktale
plot.

The Folktale Unit

Finally, the study of folktales as a legitimate form of oral literature
should be a part of the elementary curriculum. It is our hope that with the
reference material available in *World Folktales* plus a thorough understanding of the nature of traditional material after working through the comparative paper, any teacher will be prepared to add a fascinating unit on folktales
to his own curriculum at all grade levels.

The list of the suggestions on using the folktale in the elementary
classroom presented here is only a sampling of ideas, a mere beginning of
those units that will occur to you in your own classroom. For the most part,
we have tried to limit our suggestions to those examples that were part of
the curriculum in a single elementary school observed over a short period
of time in order to demonstrate just how much impact traditional material
will have on your own teaching. We are grateful to Highland Park Elementary School in Austin, Texas, for allowing us the freedom to roam the halls,
borrow individual classes, interview teachers and children, and soak up
some of the excitement that can be found in a really first-rate elementary
school where folklore is an integral part of the school curriculum.

Appendix II:
Folktales in the College Classroom

The content and scope of folktales themselves vary as widely as the interest and ability of individual college students, and we have found from years of experience that the more specific the assignment of the comparison paper, the more rewarding the results. Therefore, we provide here an example of the kind of written instructions we have given students semester after semester. Because the comparative paper has been such a useful teaching tool, we have never regretted our attempts to be specific, even at the risk of overstating the obvious.

We have found it necessary through the years to give directions for researching the paper as well as for writing it. The objectives of each section of the paper have also been useful in identifying relevant purposes for this method of study. Finally, the sample worksheet and sample paper have been worth more than the traditional "thousand words" when dealing with students, but they are reprinted here merely as examples and guidelines for the nature and scope of the comparative paper to be expected from college students.

The Comparison Paper—
Overview and Objectives

The comparison paper will contain the following sections:

I.   Introduction of the Tale Type Studied and Variants Surveyed

Objectives: To become familiar with the scholarly indexes of traditional narrative. To learn how to use the tools of comparative folktale research.

II. History and Brief Background of the Tale

Objectives: To become familiar with the standard scholarly study of the folktale in English. To become aware of the kinds of information early folktale scholars found interesting. To develop some concept of the geographical diversity of the folktale in general.

III. Comparison of Four Tale Variants

Objectives: To study one tale in depth from various cultures. To gain insight into the nature of the folk process as it relates to narrative. To appreciate the stylistic variation, formulaic patterns, narrator mannerisms, geographic and cultural influences and differences. To understand how motifs and tale types assemble and reassemble with quiltlike precision.

IV. Bibliography

Objective: To give adequate information about where tales are found so that others may read them for themselves.

Directions for Researching the Comparative Paper

1. Choose a tale with the following characteristics:
   a. A plot that you find particularly attractive
   b. A tale with sufficient parallel versions
   c. A tale with a broad geographic range to offer you interesting variation.

2. Determine the above qualities of a tale by consulting the following three sources:
   a. The annotations in this book

b. Baughman, *Motif Index/North America* (described in detail in Part One, p. 9)

c. Aarne/Thompson *Tale Type Index* (also in Part One).

3. Identify the skeletal structure of your tale in the following two ways:

a. Check the Aarne/Thompson *Tale Type Index* to see whether or not he gives a detailed analysis of the tale. If so, he will have assigned Roman numerals to all the major divisions of the tale. These numerals form an outline for the study of the plot of the tale.

b. If Aarne/Thompson has not done your outline for you, then you are on your own. You must read enough versions of your tale in order to draw your own conclusions as to where the major "scenes" of the story take place. If you were directing the folktale as a play, for example, where would you let down the curtain as a signal that you had completed that section of the plot? The answer to those stage directions will equal the outline of the major skeletal sections of your paper. Remember that formula tales will need special treatment because their similarities may well depend on structure and not narrative content.

NOTE TO THE WEARY

Keep in mind that entries in indexes of whatever kind are highly abbreviated; that not everyone in the world speaks English; that not all contributions to an international index will be in English; that not all the most useful books are in the average college library (even on reserve); and that thousands before you have mastered the art of using these scholarly tools and have been pleased with the paper they have written.

NOTE TO THE OVERENTHUSIASTIC

Try to aim for a compromise between tales that vary widely and are really interesting, and tales that are sufficiently kin one to the other to be able to deal with them in such a short paper. The entire folktale field is fascinating to study, but you must finish the paper this semester.

Directions for Writing the Comparison Paper

TITLE

The title should indicate some key feature of the story as well as tell which tale type you are studying.

INTRODUCTORY PARAGRAPH

Instructions for this section of the paper are very specific for two reasons:

1. Getting started is always the hardest part of any paper; if you can get through paragraph one, then paragraph two is easier. By the time you reach paragraph three, you have momentum.

2. Much of the information you present in the introductory paragraph is absolutely essential to an understanding of everything else you will talk about in the paper. You must be as clear and to the point as possible. A chance to exercise your own creativity will come after you have taken care of these preliminary details.

sentence #1: Make a general statement that summarizes the entire tale by focusing on its most important element. A big heavy door still turns on some rather small hinges: your job is to locate those hinges essential to your tale type, and focus, finally, on the absolute, most important one.

sentence #2: Make a specific statement about one part of the tale that strikes you as particularly noteworthy or interesting OR one part that differs widely from variant to variant. If you are careful with your sentence, you can even give a few examples to spark the interest of the reader.

sentence #3: List all the variants you will be discussing in the paper in some form that is both simple and clear. In the comparative section of the paper you will be referring to these stories many times by name, and you must specify them clearly in the simplest form possible. *Suggestions:* Try to pick tales from different countries so that you may refer to them as "the French tale," "the German tale," and so on. If that is not possible and you select two tales from one country, then you must resort to Roman numerals such as French I, French II. Perhaps best of all is some form of short title combined with the country of origin, for example, "the Scottish 'Whuppity Stoorie.' "

HISTORY AND BACKGROUND

Discuss in a rather full Paragraph #2 the general history, geographic spread, and literary influences of the tale you are studying. You will find such information in the following places:

1. Stith Thompson, *The Folktale*—the standard reference work on the folktale in English. If he discusses your tale at all, you must take note of it.

2. Notes and comments in this book.

3. Notes and comments in the annotations of other texts where you find your particular variant.

Documentation and proper footnoting here are essential. Obviously you have not devoted a lifetime to the study of this tale, but others have. By drawing on their insights and experience, you will give authority to your own generalizations and reassure the reader that you have in fact worked hand in hand with the masters in the field. Remember: the phrase "according to . . ." is a simple way of avoiding the dangers of plagiarism. You may wish to consult a handbook for proper footnote style, or you may choose to follow our simplified example in the sample paper.

STRUCTURAL (PLOT) VARIATION

The number of paragraphs needed to deal comprehensively with this section of your paper depends on how many major plot elements you have in the tale you select for comparison. To find out how many sections you have, call upon the Aarne/Thompson *Tale Type Index.* If your story has an extensive plot, Aarne/Thompson will have assigned Roman numerals for each element and your work is laid out for you. For example, the first element in Tale Type 500 of our sample paper is listed as "I. The Impossible Task." Therefore, in order to be considered a variation of Tale Type 500 and a cousin to Rumpelstiltskin, all tales in that category must have an impossible task, be it spinning straw into gold or finding the needle in the haystack.

On the other hand, if your story is not a long one, Thompson may not have assigned a Roman numeral outline for it. In that case you will need to construct your own plot outline and perhaps consider using more than four variants for comparison.

Special attention is needed in this section. By following the outline of major elements in Aarne/Thompson together with the work sheet to be described below, you will avoid the most horrible pitfall of the comparison paper—that one dreadful thing guaranteed to destroy all your comparative efforts, that one fatal mistake that turns the beauty of scholarship into the cut-and-paste babble of a parrot.

At all costs you must avoid the sequential summary—the mindless retelling, in summary form, of the entire tale, a sort of inventory of everything you found of interest in one tale, and then turning to the next tale, listing another set of interesting facts, and so on. You simply must go into all the boxes at once, sort out all the blue-spotted apples or the Roman numeral I "Impossible Task" sections and discuss them *across the board* in all four variants before you go on to any mention whatever of Roman numeral II "Bargain with the Helper."

Having carefully avoided this major pitfall, you should construct the kind of chart printed on pp. 406–07. Virtues of such a worksheet are infinite, but some of them might be listed so you won't be tempted to skip this step. A work sheet will help 1) establish the basic divisions of the tale; 2) separate the essential structure from the very interesting but for the moment unessential narrative elaborations; 3) keep you in the mainstream of your plot and avoid the murky eddies of subplots, and 4) remind you of the major skeletal variations in the plot so that you won't have to go back and check out the same book three times. The sample worksheet will serve as a model, encourage you to think and analyze, and remind you not to waste time by avoiding this step.

NARRATIVE EMBELLISHMENTS

In this final section you are free to select those parts of the tale that vary most noticeably and talk about them in detail. If you will look at the sample paper, you will notice that it has taken less than two pages to write down all the essentials. You have had to be very specific, very concise, and very efficient. Now you may turn to the embellishments of the individual narrator and deal with the cultural clothes each puts on the rather bony and rigid skeleton you have just finished describing.

Some of the elements of narrative technique that you may want to consider are the following:

1. Formulaic expressions: beginnings and endings, incantations, and triplification
2. Description of major characters and motivation—why do they do what they do? how did they get into the situation in the first place?
3. Examples of local color and dialect

4. Geographic, historic, and cultural differences
5. Evidence of the folk narrative process:
   a. Adding other tale types
   b. Adding other motifs
   c. Forgetting essential details or sequence
6. Songs and verses.

Your only rules here are to group like ideas together—when you talk about formulaic beginnings, talk about all of them together. The danger of the sequential summary is not so great in this section, but it is still a threat.

A final note on narrative technique refers to your own writing. In all cases use the historical present tense when talking about the tales. For example, "Cinderella *sits* in the ashes." It is her lot in life, and if you read the same tale twenty years later, she will still be sitting there. When words are immortalized on a page, they never change. Therefore, Cinderella never *"sat"* in the ashes once she made her way onto the printed page.

What's in a Name: A Comparison of Tale Type 500 (Sample Comparison Paper)

In Tale Type 500 *The Name of the Helper,* the heroine is faced with the problem of discovering the secret name of a supernatural being who has helped her complete an impossible task. Although "Rumpelstiltskin" is perhaps the best known of the secret names, other names include "Tom Tit Tot," "Gilitrutt," "Rompetailtailskin," "Winterkolbe," "Trwtyn-Tratyn," and "Perifool." The following variants of Tale Type 500 will be discussed in this paper: "Rumpelstiltskin" from the Grimm brothers' collection; "Duffy and the Devil," a long English tale from Cornwall; "Whuppity Stoorie" from Scotland; and "Rampelstampeldam," a black version from the Sea Islands off the South Carolina coast.

According to Stith Thompson in *The Folktale* (p. 48), Tale Type 500 is most heavily distributed in Ireland, Germany, Denmark, and Finland, but it is also found throughout the British Isles. Katharine Briggs says that the English tale "Duffy and the Devil" was often presented in dramatic form and "would last a long winter's night" (*Dictionary,* p. 220).

The basic elements of this tale deal with: I. An Impossible Task; II. A Bargain with the Helper; and III. The Helper Overcome. The impossible task is generally imposed because of a false boast made either by the girl's

TALE TYPE 500: THE NAME OF THE HELPER*
(A Tabular Analysis of Four Major Variants)

	"RUMPELSTILTSKIN" GERMANY (Grimm, #55)	"DUFFY AND THE DEVIL" ENGLAND (Cornwall) (from Hunt, Romances)	"WHUPPITY STOORIE" SCOTLAND (from Chambers, Popular Rhymes)	"RAMSTAMPELDAM" AMERICA (South Carolina) (from Parsons, "Sea Islands")
I. Impossible Task				
	H914 b. Miller boasts daughter can spin straw into gold (cf. Type 501)	H915 a. Duffy claims to be the best spinner in parish (cf Type 501)	[No boasting. Goodwife is in despair because her sow is dying.]	H383.2.1 b. [No boasting.] Girl to spin gold as condition of marrying king.
II. Bargain with Helper				
	M242 a. A manikin agrees to help the daughter	M242 a. Devil agrees to help girl	M242 a. Fairy agrees to help goodwife by curing her pig	M242 a. Dwarf agrees to help girl
	S211 c. but she must give her first child to, him	d. but she must give herself to him	c. but she must give up her son	c. but she must give up first child
	H521 e. if she cannot guess his name in three days	H521 e. if she cannot guess his name at the end of three years	H521 e. if she cannot guess her name within three days	H521 e. if she cannot guess his name in three days
	D2183 H1092 He spins the straw into gold	G303.9.8.1 He spins yarn into stockings, though there is always a "stitch down"	[No spinning test]	D2183 He spins a room full of gold

III. The Helper Overcome

	G284 Witch promises to assist Duffy overcome devil		
N475 a. Messenger sent by queen overhears manikin's name by accident	**N475 a.** Duffy's husband overhears devil's name at witches' sabbat	**N475 a.** Goodwife hears fairy singing her name as she spins	**N475 a.** Queen's maid overhears dwarf in hut singing his name
C432.1 b. Queen pronounces Rumpelstiltskin's name; he tears himself in two	**C432.1 b.** Duffy pronounces Terrytop's name and he vanishes The devil's spinning comes unravelled	**C432.1 b.** Goodwife pronounces Whuppity Stoorie's name; fairy runs off as though witches were after her	**C432.1 b.** Queen pronounces Ramstampeldam; he stamps foot and runs off "wid one laig"

*Motifs from Thompson's *Motif Index*; subdivisions (indicated by lower-case letters) from Thompson's *Tale-Type Index*.

mother or by the maiden herself. Extraordinary spinning is usually the impossible task: the Grimm tale involves spinning straw into gold while in the English story Duffy is given a whole room of fleeces to turn into yarn. The black variant, "Ramstampeldam," omits the boast and says without elaboration that the girl must fill a room with gold if she is to marry the king. Only "Whuppity Stoorie" demands no spinning or gold: the impossible task here is to cure the goodwife's pig which is dying.

The second major division of the tale is "The Bargain with the Helper." The helper may be a manikin, devil, fairy, or dwarf. He completes the impossible tasks and strikes a bargain with the woman who has no choice other than to promise either herself or her first child to the supernatural creature unless she can discover his name within a set period of time. By the end of the second section, the task is accomplished, the heroine saved from her immediate disaster, and the race to discover the name in time is on.

The third major division of Tale Type 500, consisting of two parts, is "The Helper Overcome." First, the name of the helper is overheard by an eavesdropper or the woman herself while the little impet is chanting a rhyme or verse in secret glee. Second, the woman pronounces the creature's name; this gives her power over him and releases her from the bargain. The helper's subsequent enraged exit is one of the more dramatic moments in traditional literature.

While these structural elements remain relatively fixed, narrative embellishments reflect individual and cultural influence. Triplification, for example, is strong in all four tales. The maiden is given three attempts, three days, or three years, to guess the helper's name. Grimm's tale employs the number three more than any other. "Rumpelstiltskin" spins three reels (three turns each) and fills three rooms with gold. He allows three days for the girl to discover his name, and when the queen guesses his name, it is on the third day at the third attempt. In each variant the helper's name is guessed on the third attempt of the third try.

Tale Type 500 is not only dramatic, it is one of the liveliest of tales, and part of the jauntiness of the tale comes from the verses and chants found there. Almost all known variants contain a song by the helper in which he reveals his name, gloating over his victim's inability to discover it:

> Little kens our good dame at hame
> That Whuppity Stoorie is my name.

So sings the green fairy at the bottom of a hollow as she sits spinning near the spring. In the German "Rumpelstiltskin," the little man jumps around the fire near a high mountain singing:

> Today I bake, tomorrow brew,
> The next I'll have the young Queen's child.
> Ha! glad am I that no one knew
> That Rumpelstiltskin I am styled.

In the English tale amidst the swirling frenzy of the witches' sabbath, the queer little man dressed in black, his long forked tail now both prominent and obvious as he holds it high and twirls it around, drinks a bit too much blackjack cider and lets slip the famous name:

> Duffy, my lady, you'll never know—what?—
> That my name is Terrytop, Terrytop—top!

Descriptions of the major female character range from a rather full treatment in the English tale to the virtual absence of detail in the black "Ramstampeldam." In "Duffy and the Devil" we are told that our heroine is a "lazy hussy" who spends

> all her time courseying and courranting with the boys! she will never stay in to boil the porridge, knit the stockings, or spin the yarn!

The goodwife of "Whuppity Stoorie," on the other hand, faces a serious problem. Her husband went off to the fair one day and was taken by the press gang near Kittlerumpit. The widow, left with a small son, has pinned all her hopes on a successful farrowing by her sow only to discover the poor animal lying on her back in no condition to give birth. Little is told of the circumstances of the young girl in "Rumpelstiltskin"; she is a victim of a proud father who feels it necessary to brag to the king "in order to make himself appear important." The character of the poor lady in "Ramstampeldam" is reduced to a single pronoun, though we gather her marriage depends on her successfully passing the spinning test.

Variations in the nature of the supernatural helper are equally wide. In "Duffy and the Devil," his satanic majesty appears in response to Duffy's invitation: "The devil may spin and knit . . . for what I care." At that moment there appears:

> a queer-looking little man with a remarkable pair of eyes which seemed to send out flashes of light. . . . He was dressed in black and moved towards Duffy with a jaunty air, knocking something against the floor at every step he took.

The manikin of Grimm's tale and the dwarf of the South Carolina variant are not described in any detail, the former being "quite a ridiculous little man" and the latter merely an old dwarf. More colorful, but equally dangerous, is the fairy of the Scots "Whuppity Stoorie" who is "dressed in green with a white apron, a black velvet hood, a steeple-crowned beaver hat, and a long walking staff, as tall as herself." She is, however, endowed with extraordinary healing powers as she transfixes the sow with a stare, utters an incantation:

> Pitter, patter
> Haly water,

and annoints the animal with a special oil. The pig jumps up with a grunt and runs to her breakfast.

Most supernatural helpers react violently when cheated of their prizes. Only in "Duffy and the Devil" does the helper behave with dignity, promising Duffy that the pleasure of her company has only been postponed. More typical is the line from the black variant "Ramstampeldam":

> de ol' man got so mad, he stamped his foot, went t'rough de floor, pop his laig off, ran off wid one laig,

an ending clearly influenced by Grimm's "Rumpelstiltskin":

> the little man . . . plunged his right foot so deep into the earth that his whole leg went in; and then in a rage he pulled his left leg so hard with both hands that he tore himself in two.

The conclusion of the Scottish "Whuppity Stoorie" is scarcely less dramatic:

> The fairy lept high in the air, as though blown up by gunpowder, and rushed screaming down the brae as though witches had been after her.

Examples of dialect and local color are found in all the tales. Dialect is particularly evident in the Scottish tale where the well-dressed fairy comes "up the brae . . . amaist like a leddy"; where the goodwife crouches "down among the gorse" as she overhears the green fairy spinning; and when the fairy abruptly comes to the point of the bargain with the goodwife: "What will ye gie me gin I cure her?"

Local color is prominent in the setting of the longer "Duffy and the Devil," for the story occurs in cider-making time. Squire Lovel spends much of his time hunting in new stockings

Through brambles and furze in all sorts of weather;
His old shanks were as sound as if bound up in leather.

He wanders through such places as "past the Pipers, and through the Dawnse Main into the downs, . . . from Trove to Trevider . . . and finally into the Fugoe Hole," a traditional Cornish setting for the witches' sabbath, a grim place in which hares often take refuge and are never seen again.

Certain geographical and cultural differences are revealed in the retellings. For example, European versions have a great deal of the supernatural. In "Duffy and the Devil" the devil comes in response to Duffy's summons, attends a sabbath during which he twirls a long forked tail, and disappears in fire and smoke when cheated of his prize. The fairy of "Whuppity Stoorie" comes uninvited but with magic foreknowledge of the goodwife's problem. She acknowledges that she is bound by fairy laws not to take the child for three days.

In the South Carolina variant, however, much of the supernatural has been lost in the journey to the New World. The dwarf does produce three rooms of gold and he must have had supernatural powers, but the narrator does not specify them. The dwarf's main concern is not to get the soul of a child for the devil, but to have a companion in his loneliness:

Tomorrow I'll be de happiest man in de worl', because I'll have company. I'll have a little baby wid me.

When his name is revealed, he is properly furious but does not accuse the queen of learning it from the devil as his European counterpart, Rumpelstiltskin, does.

Evidence of the folk narrative process occurs in the long English version where the story of the witches' sabbath has been interpolated. This version, we are informed in the introduction, is the product of professional narrators who have added "such things as they fancied would increase the interest of the story to the listeners." The story is a leisurely retelling designed for the amusement of an audience on a long winter night. It contains many elements that are interesting in themselves, though they are not part of the original tale. The additions are a professional teller's way of lengthening a short tale to while away a long evening.

This comparison of four variants of Tale Type 500 reveals the folktale process in action. Cultural and geographic differences may embellish the tale, but they do not alter its basic structure. Rather, the accretions reflect cultural change. The tale retains its vitality, evidence that folktales still exist, telling of magic beings, supernatural events, and enchanted objects.

Tales Compared:

1. "Rumpelstiltskin." From *Grimm's Fairy Tales,* translated by Margaret Hunt (London: Routledge and Kegan Paul, 1948), pp. 264–68.

2. "Duffy and the Devil." From Robert Hunt, *Popular Romances of the West of England,* 2nd edition (London: John Camden Hotten, 1871), pp. 239–47.

3. "Whuppity Stoorie." From Robert Chambers, *Popular Rhymes of Scotland* (Edinburgh, 1890), pp. 72–76.

4. "Ramstampeldam." From Elsie Parsons, *Folklore of the Sea Islands, South Carolina,* Memoirs of the American Folk-Lore Society 16 (Cambridge, Mass.: American Folk-Lore Society, 1923): 23–24.

(End of Sample Comparion Paper)

Appendix III:
Popular Title Index

Tales are often known only by titles. Two hundred of these "popular" titles are here cross-referenced to the tales in this collection, indicating whether a similar tale under a different title is included.

TITLE	TALE
Advice is Better that Wages	53
Aiken Drum	17
And This Sheep Jumped Over the Fence	40a
The Animals in Night Quarters	23
Apprentice and the Ghost	5
The Axe-Stew	64
The Bald Head of the Buzzard	57
The Bear Went Over the Mountain	40b
The Big Black Toe	30
Blowing the House In	24
The Brave Girl and the Giant	6
Brave Kong	43
The Brave Tailor	43, 61
The Bremen Town Musicians	23

Brer Rabbit's Harvest Time Tricks   44
A Brer Rabbit Trick   44
The Bumblebee in the Bag   41
The Buried Tail   56
By the Hair of my Chinny-Chin-Chin   24

The Cat Witch's Paw   28
The Cauld Lad of Hilton   17
Caught in Fairy Land   15
Chicken Licken   37
Chickie Birdie   37
The Child is Father of the Man   55
The Children and the Ogre   6
Chunk o' Meat   30
Cinderella and the Strong Wind   4
Clever Elsie   62
Cleverness and Gullibility   46, 49
The Clever Peasant Girl   13
Cooperation Always Wins   50
The Corpse and the Shroud   31
The Count of Carabas   3
The Crescent and the Wolf Child   32
Cricket   9
The Crop Division   44
Cutting with Knife or Scissors   66

Dancing Past Midnight   34
Dead Man as Helper   29
The Demon with the Matted Hair (Jatakas)   42
The Devil and the Fiddler   34
Devil Leaves at Mention of God's Name   34
Doctor Know-All   9
The Doughnut   39
Duffy and the Devil   14

The Enchanted Prince   7
Endless Tales—And this Sheep Jumped Over the Fence   40a
The Extraordinary Companions   50

A Fairy History   15
The Fairy Master   18

Fairy Shows his Treasure   16
The Fairy's Magic Ointment   18
The Fat Cat   35
The Fat Goat and the Troll   22
The Fleeing Pancake   39
Flight from the Witch   27
Following the Witch   26
The Fox Eats his Fellow-Lodger   41
The Frog King   7
The Frog Prince   7

The Girl as Helper in the Hero's Flight   27
Going to Squintum's   41
Good is Always Repaid with Evil   52
Good Guys Always Finish Last   52
A Good Trick Today is Bad Luck Tomorrow   21
Goody, My Neighbor   28
The Gum Baby   42

Happiness is Often Close at Hand   54
Hare and Tortoise Race   25
The Helpers   50
Henny Penny   37
A Hero Meets a Troop of Fairies   20
Hog in the Cadillac   47
Hogs in the Mud; Sheep in the Air   49
Hospitality Rewarded   51
How the (Rabbit) (Bear) (Wolf) or Other Animal Lost
   His Tail   56
How to Dig the Well   45
How to Fell the Oak   45
How to Marry the Princess   45
Husband Seeks Three People as Stupid as His Wife   62
Husband Who Was to Mind the House   8

"Imagine That, A Talking Yam!"   36
Iron Henry   7

Jack and the Varmints   61
Jack the Giant Killer   43
John and Marster and the Stolen Meat   47

The Journey-Cake Ho!   39
Journey in Search of Fortune   54
The Journey to God to Receive Reward   54

The Kind and the Unkind Girls   2
The King and the Abbot   11
King of the Cats is Dead   33
The King's Tasks   45

The Lad Who Went to the North Wind   1
Laying a Brownie   17
The Leprechauns and their Tricks   16
Let Them What Knows Tell Them What Don't Know   48
Little Burnt Face   4
The Look-Alike Relatives   25
Lucky Hans   10

Magic Incantations   26
The Magic Mill   58
Magician and the Pupil   5
Mak and the Sheep   47
The Man from the Gallows   30
The Man Does Not Recognize his own Reflection in
   the Water (Mirror)   63
The Man Who Does his Wife's Work   8
The Man Who Thought Himself Dead   65
The Maori Fairy Host   20
The Master Cat   3
The Merry Wives' Wager   65
The Most Precious Thing in the World   13
Mother Holle   2
The Mouse Regains its Tail   38
My Eyes are Dim, I Cannot See   40b

Nail Broth   64
The Name of the Helper   14
The New Suit   16
No Need for the Parson   48
A Nut Hits the Cock's Head   37

Obstinate Wife   66
The Ogre Kills his own Children   6

Old Gallymander	2
The Old Woman and Her Pig	38
One Fine Day	38
The Parson Has No Need to Preach	48
The Peasant and the Corpse	31
Perifool	14
Pig in the Cradle	47
The Poor Man's Meal	64
The Profitable Exchange	41
Puss in Boots	3
Race Between Hedgehog and Hare	25
Race Won by Deception	25
The Ram and the Pig Who Went into the Woods	23
Ramstampeldam	14
Return for Tools	46
A Riddle Story	13
The Ride to the Witches' Sabbath	26
The Right Instructions at the Wrong Time	60
Rounds	40b
The Saint's Visit	51
The Salt-Producing Mill	58
The Salty Sea and the Magic Mill	58
The Sausage on the Nose	51
The Seal Wife and Her Skin	19
The Seal Woman	19
The Servant's Good Counsels	53
Seven at a Whack	43, 61
Sharing the Crops	44
The Shepherd Substituting for the Priest Answers the King's Questions	11
The Silkie of Skule Skerry	19
The Silver Toe	30
Six Go Through the World	50
So That's The Hussy You've Been Seeing	63
Some Animals Never Learn	21
Soul Released from Torment	29
The Soup Stone	64
Sorcerer's Apprentice	5
Staying in the Haunted House	29

Suzy Truth is Dead 33
A Swallowing Story 35
A Swapping Story 10

The Table, the Ass, and the Stick 1
The Tail Fisher 56
The Tale of the Tails 49
Talking Horse and Dog 36
Taming of the Shrew 12
The Tarbaby and the Rabbit 42
Teeny Tiny 30
Tell Puss thy Catten 33
The Theft of Fish 21
This is the House that Jack Built 38
Three Little Pigs 24
Three Spinning Women by the Spring 2
The Tiger, the Brahmin and the Jackal 52
Titeliture 14
Tom Tildrum's Dead 33
Tom Tit Tot 14
Tools for a Horse Thief 46
Tops and Bottoms 44
Tortoise Lets Self be Carried By Eagle 59
Tricking the Gringo 46
Troll Under the Bridge 22
The Troll Who Was Cut Open 35

The Ungrateful Serpent Returned to Captivity 52

The Vampire 31
Visits to Fairy Land 18

Wager on the Faithful Wife 10
Wait for the Fat Goat 22
Wee Bannock 39
The Werewolf Husband 32
What if the Knife Should Fall 62
"What Should I Have Said (Done)" 60
Why Animals Lack Tails 56
Why Buzzard is Bald 57
Why Tortoise Has a Cracked Shell 59

Wife Falls into a Stream 66
Wife Floats Upstream 66
The Wily Coyote 46
Wise Through Experience 53
The Wishes 51
The Witch That Was Hurt 28
The Wolf-Changeling 32
The Woman Draws the Beer 62
The Wooden Bowl for the Aged 55
Wooden Drinking Cup for Old Man 55

"You Haven't Carried the Saddle" 12
"You've Got the Old Coon Now" 9

Appendix IV:
Index of Motifs

This index catalogues all the motifs discovered in each tale type in this collection. The motif numbers are from Stith Thompson's *Motif Index of Folk Literature* and Baughman's *Type and Motif-Index of the Folktales of England and North America*. The reader can tell at a glance if a motif is found in any of the sixty-six tales in the collection.

Motif		Tale
	A. MYTHOLOGICAL MOTIFS	
A1115.2	Why the sea is salt, magic salt-mill	58
A2214.5.1	Tortoise dropped by eagle; hence cracks in his shell	59
A2312.1.1	Origin of cracks in tortoise's shell	59
A2317.3	Why buzzard is bald	57
A2378.2	Why animals lack tail	56
A2433.5.3	Haunts of spider	42
A2762.1	Why aspens leaves tremble	4

B. ANIMALS

B103.0.3	Gold-producing ram	1
B210.2	Talking animal or object refuses to talk on demand	36
B211.1.7	Speaking dog	36
B211.7.2	Speaking toad	7
B241.2.3	King of cats	33
B296	Animals go a-journeying	23
B342	Cat leaves house when report is made of death of one of his companions	33
B394	Cow grateful for being milked	2
B401	Helpful horse	2
B412	Helpful sheep	2
B435.1	Helpful fox	3
B580	Animal helps man to wealth and greatness	3
B582.1.1	Animal wins wife for his master (Puss in Boots)	3
B651.8	Marriage to seal in human form	19
B655	Marriage to amphibia in human form	7

C. TABU

C31.10	Tabu: giving garment back to supernatural wife	19
C211.1	Tabu: eating in fairyland	15
C322	Tabu: looking into a bag	41
C337	Tabu: looking up a chimney	2
C432.1	Guessing name of supernatural creature gives power over him	14
C631	Tabu: breaking Sabbath	34
C631.6	Tabu: playing music on the Sabbath	34

D. MAGIC

D113.1.1	Werewolf	32
D327.2	Transformation: seal to person	19
D395	Transformation: frog to person	7
D671	Transformation flight	27
D672	Obstacle flight	27

D721.3	Disenchantment by destroying skin	7
D789.6.1	Disenchantment by speaking proper words	32
D793	Disenchantment made permanent	32
D806	Magic object effective only when exact instructions for its use are followed	5
D851	Magic object acquired by exchange	58
D861	Magic object stolen	1
D881.2	Recovery of magic object by use of magic cudgel	1
D950.2	Magic oak tree	45
D1045	Magic beer	16
D1254	Magic stick	1
D1401.1	Magic club beats person	1
D1472.1.8	Magic table cloth supplies food and drink	1
D1581	Task performed by use of magic object	45
D1601.14	Self chopping axe	5, 45
D1601.21.1	Self-grinding salt mill	58
D1610	Magic speaking object	36
D1651	Magic object obeys master alone	58
D1681	Charm incorrectly uttered will not work	26
D1711.0.1	Magician's apprentice	5
D1761.0.2	Limited number of wishes granted	51
D1981	Certain persons invisible	4
D2083.1	Cows magically made dry	28
D2183	Magic spinning usually performed by supernatural helper	14

E. DEAD

E31	Limbs of the dead voluntarily reassemble and revive	29
E235.4.1	Return from dead to punish theft of golden arm from grave	30
E251	Vampire. Corpse which comes from grave at night and sucks blood	31
E251.1	Vampire's power overcome	31
E251.3	Deeds of vampire	31
E352	Dead returns to restore stolen goods	29

E371.4(B)	Ghost of man returns to point out buried treasure	29
E373.1	Money received from ghost as reward for bravery	29
E442	Ghosts laid by piercing grave (corpse) with stake	31
E451.5.1	Money must be distributed to beggars so that ghost may be laid	29
E459.3	Ghost laid when wishes are acceded to	29
E592.2	Ghost carries coffin on back	31

F. MARVELS

F167.8	Otherworld creatures unacquainted with fire	20
F200.1	Pixies	15
F211	Fairyland under a hollow knoll	20
F233.6	Fairies fair (fine, white)	20
F233.8	Fairies as brown and hairy	17
F235.4.1	Fairies made visible through use of ointment	18
F239.4.3	Fairies are tiny	20
F244.2	Fairy shows hiding place of treasure in return for freedom	16
F251.2	Fairies as souls of the departed	15
F320	Fairies carry people away to fairyland	15
F372	Fairy take human nurse to attend fairy child	18
F376	Mortal as servant in fairyland	15, 18
F377	Supernatural lapse of time in fairyland	15, 18
F378.0.1	Mortal expelled from fairyland for breaking tabu	18
F378.2	Tabu: bathing or touching water in lake in fairyland	18
F378.6	Tabu: using fairy bathwater, soap or ointment on oneself while bathing fairy child	18
F378.7(B)	Tabu: eating while with fairies	15
F381.3	Fairy leaves when he is given clothes	17
F382.4	Opening Holy Bible in presence of fairies nullifies their spells	17

F385.1	Fairy spell averted by turning coat [glove]	15
F451.0.1	Luchrupáin (leprechauns) (as fairies)	16
F482	Brownie	17
F482.5.4	Helpful deeds of brownie or other household spirit	17
F482.5.4c(B)	Brownie does farmwork for owner	17
F600	Persons with extraordinary powers	50
F601.5	Extraordinary companions are brothers	50
F641	Person of remarkable hearing	50
F715.1.1	River issues from nut	45
F982.2	Four cats carry coffin	33
F990	Inanimate objects act as if living	36

G. OGRES

G84	Fee fi fo fum	6
G204	Girl in service of witch	27
G224.1	Witch's charm opposite of Christian	26
G242.1	Witch flies through the air on broomstick	26
G242.7	Person flying with witches makes mistake and falls	26
G243	Witches' Sabbath	26
G248	Witches feast on rich food and drink	26
G252	Witch in form of cat (toad) has hand cut off; recognized next morning by missing hand	28
G272.4	Fires burnt in street to ward off witches	32
G272.11	Horseshoe hung up as protection against witches	32
G272.12	Straws as protection against witch	32
G273.1	Witch powerless when one makes the sign of the cross	32
G273.4	Witch powerless to cross stream	27
G303.3.1.2	Devil as well-dressed gentleman	34
G303.3.4.6	Devil in the shape of a stone	32
G303.4.4	Devil has claws	34
G303.4.1.6	Devil has horns	34
G303.9.4.7	Devil tempts girl	34
G303.10.4.5	Devil dances with maid and puts his claws through her hands	34

G303.16.2.2	Person saved from devil by prayer to Virgin	34
G303.16.3	Devil's power avoided by the cross	34
G303.16.8	Devil leaves at the mention of God's name	34
G303.16.11.2	Devil prevented from revenge by pious priest	34
G303.16.14.1	Priest chases devil away	34
G303.17.2.5	Devil retreats into Hell amid thunder and lightning	34
G303.17.2.9	Devil disappears in carriage drawn by four [one] horse	34
G519.1	Ogre's wife killed through other tricks	6
G610.2	Stealing from ogre to help friendly king	6

H. TESTS

H335	Tasks assigned suitor	45
H341	Suitor test: making the princess laugh	60
H341.3	Princess brought to laughter by foolish action of hero	60
H386	Bride test: obedience	12
H512	Guessing with life as wager	14
H521	Test: Guessing unknown propounder's name	14
H540.3	King propounds riddles	11
H632.1	What is the swiftest? Thought	13
H633.1	What is the sweetest? Sleep	13
H682.1	Riddle: How far is it from earth to heaven?	11
H1021.8	Task: spinning gold	14
H1023.1.2	Task: hatching eggs immediately; counter task: sowing seeds and bringing in crop next morning	13
H1053.3	Task: coming neither on horse nor on foot (comes with one leg on animal's back, one on ground)	13
H1054.1	Task: coming neither naked nor clad (comes clothed in net or the like)	13
H1057	Task: coming neither by day nor by night (comes at twilight)	13

H1092	Task: spinning impossible amount in one night	14
H1263	Quest to God for fortune	54
H1291	Questions asked on way to other world	54
H1292	Answer found in other world to questions propounded on the way	54
H1312.1	Quest for three persons as stupid as his wife	62
H1411.1	Fear test: staying in haunted house where corpse drops piecemeal down the chimney	29

J. THE WISE AND THE FOOLISH

J21	Counsels proved wise by experience	53
J21.2	Do not act when angry	53
J21.3	Do not go where an old man has a young wife	53
J21.5	Do not leave the highway	53
J121.1	Ungrateful son reproved by naive action of his own son	55
J163.4	Good counsels bought	53
J1115.6	Clever peasant	11
J1172.3	Ungrateful animal returned to captivity	52
J1191.1	*Reductio ad absurdum:* the decision about the colt	13
J1545.4	The exiled wife's dearest possession	13
J1786.1	Man costumed as demon thought to be devil; thieves flee	26
J1791.7	Man does not recognize his own reflection in the water [mirror]	63
J1795	Image in mirror mistaken for picture	63
J1795.2(B)	Man finds mirror, thinks it is picture of grandfather; wife thinks it is picture of husband's new girlfriend*	63
J1810	Physical phenomena misunderstood	37
J1904.1	Cow taken on roof to graze	8
J2063	Distress over imagined troubles of unborn child	62
J2071	Three foolish wishes	51

J2075	The transferred wish	51
J2075.2	Two transferred wishes used unwisely	51
J2081.1	Foolish bargain; horse for cow, cow for hog, etc., finally nothing left	10
J2132.2	Numskull ties the rope to his leg as the cow grazes on the roof	8
J2161.1	Jumping into breeches	62
J2176	Fool lets wine [milk] run in the cellar [kitchen]	8
J2198	Bewailing a calamity that has not occurred	62
J2301	Gullible husband	65
J2311.0.1	Wife makes her husband believe that he is dead	65
J2312	Naked person made to believe that he is clothed	65
J2355.1	Fool loses magic objects by talking about them	1
J2411.4	Imitation of magician unsuccessful; person does self injury	5
J2431	A man undertakes to do his wife's work; all goes wrong	8
J2450	Literal fool	60
J2461.1	Literal following of instructions about actions	60
J2461.1.1	Literal numskull drags [bacon] on string	60

K. DECEPTIONS

K11.1	Race won by deception: relative helpers	25
K111	Pseudo-magic treasure-producing object sold	49
K112.1	Alleged self-cooking kettle sold	49
K112.2	"Soup stone" sold	64
K171.1	Deceptive crop division: above the ground, below the ground	44
K251.1	The eaten grain and the cock as damages	41
K330.1	Man gulled into giving up his clothes	46
K335.1.4.1	Animals cry out; frighten robbers	23
K341.6	Shoes dropped to distract owner's attention	21

K341.8.1	Trickster pretends to ride home for tools to perform tricks	46
K371.1	Trickster throws fish out of wagon	21
K401	Blame for theft fastened on dupe	21
K404.1	Tails in the ground	49
K406	Stolen animal disguised as person so that they may escape detection	47
K406.2	Stolen sheep dressed as baby in cradle	47
K525.6	Escape leaving dog as substitute	41
K526	Captor's bag filled with animals or objects while captives escape	6, 41
K553.2	Wait for the fat goat	22
K741	Capture by tarbaby	42
K842	Dupe persuaded to take prisoner's place in sack; killed	6
K1026	Dupe imitates trickster's theft and is caught	21
K1041	Borrowed feathers	59
K1161	Animals hidden in various parts of a house attack owner with their characteristic powers	23
K1545	Wives wager as to who can best fool her husband	65
K1611	Substituted caps cause ogre to kill his own children	6
K1700	Deception through bluffing	43, 61
K1911.3.3.2	False bride fails when magician tests her	4
K1951	Sham warrior	43, 61
K1953.1	Coward boasts he has frightened [killed] a bear [tiger]	3, 61
K1954.1	Helpful cat [fox] borrows measure for his master's money	3
K1956.2	Sham wise man hides something and is rewarded for finding it	9
K2212	Treacherous sister	4

L. REVERSAL OF FORTUNE

L10	Victorious youngest son	45
L52	Abused youngest daughter	4
L55	Stepdaughter heroine	27
L102	Unpromising heroine	4

L161   Lowly hero marries princess   60
L162   Lowly heroine marries prince   4

N. CHANCE AND FATE

N11   Wager on wife's complacency   10
N475   Secret name overheard by eavesdropper   14
N538   Treasure pointed out by supernatural
            creature (fairy, etc.)   16
N611.1   Criminal accidentally detected: "That is
            the first"—sham wise man   9
N688   What is in the dish: "Poor Crab".   9
N825.2   Old man helper   58

Q. REWARDS AND PUNISHMENTS

Q223.6.4.(B) Punishment for dancing on Sunday   34
Q386.1   Devil punishes girl who loves to dance   34
Q469.3   Punishment: grinding up in a mill   2

S. UNNATURAL CRUELTY

S211   Child sold (promised) to devil (ogre)   14

T. SEX

T68   Princess offered as a prize   45, 60
T251.2.3   Wife becomes obedient on seeing husband
            slay a recalcitrant horse   12
T255   The obstinate wife or husband   66
T255.2   The obstinate wife sought for upstream   66

W. TRAITS OF CHARACTER

W154   Ingratitude   55
W154.2.1   Rescued animal threatens rescuer   52

X. HUMOR

X452   The parson has no need to preach   48
X600   Humor concerning races or nations   46

Z. MISCELLANEOUS GROUPS OF MOTIFS

Z11	Endless tales	40a
Z17	Rounds	40b
Z33.1	The fleeing pancake	39
Z33.2	The fat cat	35
Z41	The old woman and her pig	38
Z41.4	The mouse regains its tail	38
Z47	Series of trick exchanges	41
Z81	Blowing the house in	24

Appendix V:
Index of Tale Types

Tale type numbers are here cross-referenced with the tales included in this book. The tale type numbers are from Aarne-Thompson's *Types of the Folktale,* and the migratory legend types are from Christiansen's *Migratory Legends.*

TYPE	TITLE	TALE
1	The Theft of Fish	21
113A	King of the Cats Is Dead	33
122E	Wait for the Fat Goat	22
124	Blowing the House In	24
130	The Animals in Night Quarters	23
155	The Ungrateful Serpent Returned to Captivity	52
170	The Fox Eats his Fellow Lodger	41
175	The Tarbaby and the Rabbit	42
225A	Tortoise Lets self Be Carried by Eagle	59
275A	Hare and Tortoise Race: Sleeping Hare	25
313H	Flight From the Witch	27
325*	Apprentice and Ghost	5

---

*A subdivision of 325

326A	Soul Released from Torment	29
327	The Children and the Ogre	6
363	The Vampire	31
366	The Man from the Gallows	30
440	The Frog King or Iron Henry	7
460A	The Journey to God to Receive Reward	54
460B	The Journey in Search of Fortune	54
480	The Spinning-Women by the Spring, The Kind and Unkind Girls	2
500	The Name of the Helper	14
510A	Cinderella	4
513	The Extraordinary Companions	50
545B	Puss in Boots	3
563	The Table, the Ass, and the Stick	1
565	The Magic Mill	58
577	The King's Tasks	45
750A	The Wishes	51
817	Devil Leaves at Mention of God's Name	34
875	The Clever Peasant Girl	13
901	Taming of the Shrew	12
910B	The Servant's Good Counsels	53
922	The Shepherd Substituting for the Priest Answers the King's Questions	11
980B	Wooden Drinking Cup for Old Man	55
1004	Hogs in the Mud; Sheep in the Air	49
1030	The Crop Division	44
1074	Race Won by Deception: Relative Helpers	25
1119	The Ogre Kills his Own Children	6
1286	Jumping into the Breeches	62
1313	The Man who Thought Himself Dead	65
1336A	Man does not Recognize his own Reflection in the Water (Mirror)	63
1365A	Wife Falls Into a Stream	66
1384	The Husband Hunts Three Persons as Stupid as his Wife	62
1406	The Merry Wives Wager	65
1408	The Man who Does his Wife's Work	8
1415	Lucky Hans	10
1450	Clever Elsie	62
1525M	Mak and the Sheep	47
1539	Cleverness and Gullibility	46, 49

1542A	Return for Tools	46
1548	The Soup-stone	64
1640	The Brave Tailor	43, 61
1641	Doctor Know-All	9
1655	The Profitable Exchange	41
1696	"What Should I Have Said (Done)?"	60
1705	Talking Horse and Dog	36
1826	The Parson has no Need to Preach	48
2025	The Fleeing Pancake	39
2027	The Fat Cat	35
2028	The Troll (Wolf) who was Cut Open	35
2033	A Nut Hits the Cock's Head	37
2034	The Mouse Regains its Tail	38
2300	Endless Tales	40
2320	Rounds	40

MIGRATORY LEGENDS

3045	Following the Witch	26
3055	The Witch that Was Hurt	28
4005	The Werewolf Husband	32
4075	Visits to Fairyland	18
4077**	Caught in Fairyland	15
4080	The Seal Woman	19
5071**	The Fairy Master	18
6070B	The King of the Cats	33
7015	The New Suit	17

TALES WITH NO TYPE

F244.2	The Field of Boliauns	16
	Te Kenawa and the Fairies	20
	Compair Lapin and Madame Carencro	57
	How the Manx Cat Lost Her Tail	56

**Briggs' Additional Types

Selected Bibliography

Full bibliographical references to the works cited in the annotations are given here. The short form used in the Notes and Comments is indicated by italics. In addition, the following journal and series abbreviations are used.

CFQ—California Folklore Quarterly
FL—Folklore
FLJ—Folklore Journal
FL Record—Folklore Record
HFB—Hoosier Folklore Bulletin
JAF—Journal of American Folklore
MAFLS—Memoirs of the American Folklore Society
MF—Midwest Folklore
NYFQ—New York Folklore Quarterly
PMLA—Publications of the Modern Language Association
PTFLS—Publications of the Texas Folklore Society
SFQ—Southern Folklore Quarterly
TFSB—Texas Folklore Society Bulletin
WF—Western Folklore

ADAMS, ADRIENNE. The *Shoemaker* and the Elves. New York: Charles Scribner's Sons, 1960.

ADDY, SIDNEY O. *Household* Tales with Other Traditional Remains. London: D. Nutt, 1895.

AFANAS'EV, ALEKSANDR. Russian Fairy Tales. Translated by Norbert Guterman, illustrated by A. Alexeiff. New York: Pantheon Books, 1945.

AIKEN, RILEY. *"Pack Load* of Mexican Tales," PTFLS 12 (1935): 1–87.

———. "Six Tales from *Mexico,"* PTFLS 27 (1957): 78–95.

ALDERSON, WILLIAM L. "Two *Circular* Formula Tales," WF 11 (1952): 288.

ALEXANDER, LLOYD. Taran Wanderer. New York: Holt, Rinehart and Winston, 1967.

ALLSOP, FRED W. Folklore of Romantic *Arkansas.* 2 vols. New York: Grolier Society, 1931.

ANDERSEN, HANS CHRISTIAN. Danish Fairy Legends and Tales. Translated by Caroline Peachey. London: Henry G. Bohn, 1861.

———. The Emperor's New Clothes. Illustrated by Erik Blegvad. New York: Harcourt, Brace, and World, 1959.

———. What the Good Man Does is Always Right. New York: Dial Press, 1968.

ARBER, EDWARD, ed. History of *Reynard* the Fox Translated and Printed by William Caxton, June 1481. London: Constable and Co., 1899.

ARKHURST, JOYCE COOPER. The Adventures of *Spider.* West African Folk Tales illustrated by Jerry Pinkney. Boston: Little Brown and Co., 1964.

ARNASON, JON. *Icelandic* Legends. Translated by George Powell and Eirikr Magnusson. 2 vols. Second series. London: Longmans, Green and Co., 1866.

ARNOTT, KATHLEEN. *African Myths* and Legends. Illustrated by Joan Kiddell-Monroe. New York: Henry Z. Walck, 1963.

ARTZYBASHEFF, BORIS. Seven Simeons. New York: Viking Press, 1937.

ASBJØRNSEN, PETER CHRISTEN. Popular Tales from the Norse. Translated by George Webbe Dasent. 2d ed. Edinburgh: Edmonston and Douglas, 1859.

———. Tales from the *Fjeld.* Illustrated by Moyr Smith. New York: George Putnam's Sons, 1908.

ATWELL, M. *EMU* Archive. Ypsilanti, Michigan (1971): Eastern Michigan University.

AUSUBEL, NATHAN. Treasury of *Jewish* Folklore. New York: Crown Publishers, 1948.

BACKUS, EMMA M. *"Animal* Tales from North Carolina," JAF 11 (1898): 284–92.

———. "Negro Tales from *Georgia,"* JAF 25 (1912): 125–36.

BARBEAU, MARIUS. *"Anecdotes* Populaires du Canada," JAF 33 (1920): 173–297.

———. *"Contes Populaires* Canadiens 7th series," JAF 53 (1940): 89–190.

BARKER, WILLIAM H. *West African* Folk-Tales. Northbrook, Illinois: Metro Books, Inc., 1972 (originally published in 1917.)

BARNHAM, HENRY D. The *Khoja.* New York: D. Appleton and Company, 1924.

BASILE, GIOVANNI. Il *Pentamerone:* or The Tale of Tales. Translated by Sir Richard Burton. New York: Horace Liveright, 1927.

BAUGHMAN, ERNEST W. *Type* and Motif-Index of the Folktales of England and North America. Indiana University Folklore Series no. 20. The Hague: Mouton and Co., 1966.

BECKWITH, MARTHA. *Jamaica Anansi* Stories. MAFLS 17 (1924).

BELTING, NATALIA. *Earth* Is On a Fish's Back. Illustrated by Esta Nesbitt. New York: Holt, Rinehart and Winston, 1965.

———. The *Long-Tailed* Bear and Other Indian Legends. Illustrated Louis F. Cary. New York: Bobbs-Merrill, 1961.

BERGEN, FANNIE. *"Johnny-Cake,"* JAF 2 (1889): 60–63.

BISHOP, CLAIRE H. Five Chinese Brothers. Illustrated by Kurt Wiese. New York: Coward-McCann, 1938.

BOAS, FRANZ. "Notes on *Mexican* Folk-Lore," JAF 25 (1912): 204–60.

BOGGS, RALPH STEELE. *"North Carolina* White Folktales and Riddles," JAF 47 (1934): 289–328.

———. *Three Golden* Oranges and Other Spanish Folk Tales. Illustrated by Emma Brock. New York: Longmans, Green and Co., 1936.

BOLTE, JOHANNES and POLÍVKA, GEORG. *(BP)* Anmerkungen zu den Kinder-Und Hausmarchen der Bruder Grimm. 5 vols. Hildesheim: Georg Olms, 1963.

BORSKI, LUCIA, and MILLER, KATE. The Jolly Tailor and Other Fairy Tales. Illustrated by Kazimir Klepacki. New York: Longmans, Green and Co., 1928.

BOTKIN, BENJAMIN, ed. Lay My *Burden* Down: A Folk History of Slavery. Chicago: University of Chicago Press, 1945.

———. A Treasury of *American* Folklore. New York: Crown Publishers, 1944.

———. A Treasury of *Southern* Folklore. New York: Crown Publishers, 1949.

BOUCHER, ALAN. Mead *Moondaughter* and Other Icelandic Folk Tales. London: Rupert Hart-Davis, 1967.

BOWMAN, JAMES CLOYD, and BIANCO, MARGERY. Tales from a Finnish *Tupa*. Translated by Aili Kolehmainen, illustrated by Laura Bannon. Chicago: Albert Whitman and Co., 1936.

BRANDT, KATRIN. Elves and the Shoemaker. New York: Follett, 1967.

BREWER, JOHN MASON. *American Negro* Folklore. Chicago: Quadrangle Books, 1968.

———. *"John Tales,"* PTFLS 21 (1946): 81–104.

———. *"Juneteenth,"* PTFLS 10 (1932): 9–54.

———. *"Juneteenth," PTFLS 26* (1954): 55–66.

BREWSTER, H. POMEROY. "The *House* that Jack Built," JAF 2 (1899): 209–12.

BRIGGS, KATHARINE M. A *Dictionary* of British Folk—Tales in the English Language. 4 vols. London: Routledge and Kegan Paul, 1970–71.

———. The *Fairies* in Tradition and Literature. London: Routledge and Kegan Paul, 1967.

———, and TONGUE, RUTH. Folktales of *England.* Folktales of the World Series. Chicago: University of Chicago Press, 1965.

BROWN, CHARLES EDWARDS. "Wisconsin Versions of *'Scissors'* " HFB 2,2 (1943): 46–47.

BROWN, MARCIA. Cinderella; or Little Glass Slipper. New York: Charles Scribner's Sons, 1954.

———. Puss in Boots. New York: Charles Scribner's Sons, 1952.

———. Stone Soup: An Old Tale. New York: Charles Scribner's Sons, 1947.

———. Three Billy Goats Gruff. New York: Harcourt, Brace and World, 1957.

BRUNVAND, JAN HAROLD. Folklore: A Study and Research *Guide.* New York: St. Martin's Press, 1976.

———. "Folktales by Mail from *Bond,* Kentucky," Kentucky Folklore Record 6 (1960): 69–76.

———. The *Study* of American Folklore: An Introduction. New York: W. W. Norton, 1968.

BRYANT, MARGARET. "Folklore from *Edgerfield County,* South Carolina," SFQ 12 (1948): 197–209.

BRYANT, SARA CONE. *How* to Tell Stories to Children. Boston: Houghton Mifflin and Co., 1905.

———. Epaminondas and His Auntie. Illustrated by Inez Hogan. New York: Houghton Mifflin, 1938.

BURLINGAME, EUGENE. The Grateful *Elephant* and Other Stories Translated from the Pali. New Haven: Yale University Press, 1923.

BURNE, CHARLOTTE. *"Two* Folk-Tales," FLJ 2 (1884): 20–23.

BURTON, WILLIAM F. P. The *Magic Drum:* Tales from Central Africa. Illustrated by Palph Thompson. New York: Criterion Books, 1962.

C, D. *"Dildrum,* King of Cats," Notes and Queries, 2d. series 10 (1860): 463–64.

CAMPBELL, JOHN. Popular Tales of the *West Highlands.* 4 vols. London: Alexander Gardner, 1890–93.

CAMPBELL, MARIE. Tales from the *Cloud Walking* Country. Bloomington, Indiana: Indiana University Press, 1958.

CARRIÈRE, JOSEPH M. Tales from the French Folk-Lore of *Missouri.* Northwestern University Studies in the Humanities, no. 1. Evanston, Illinois: Northwestern University Press, 1937.

CARTER, ISABEL G. *"Mountain White* Folk-Lore: Tales from the Southern Blue Ridge," JAF 38 (1925): 340–74.

CH'IU, KATHY. *Chinese Fables.* Mount Vernon, New York: Peter Pauper Press, 1967.

CHAMBERS, ROBERT. *Popular Rhymes* of Scotland. Edinburgh: William Hunter, 1826 (also subsequent editions).

CHASE, RICHARD. *American Folk* Tales and Songs etc. Drawings by Joshua Tolford. New York: New American Library, 1956.

———. *Grandfather* Tales: American English Folk Tales. Illustrated by Berkeley Williams Jr. Cambridge, Mass.: Houghton Mifflin Co., 1948.

———. "Jack and the Three Sillies" (recording).

———. The *Jack* Tales. Illustrated by Berkely Williams. Cambridge, Mass.: Houghton Mifflin, Co., 1943.

CHILD, CLARENCE G. The Second Shepherd's Play, Everyman, and Other Early Plays. Boston: Houghton Mifflin, 1910.

CHILD, FRANCIS JAMES. English and Scottish Popular Ballads *(Child Ballad)*. 5 vols. New York: Dover, 1965. Reprints 1st. ed. 1882–98.

CHRISTIANSEN, REIDAR. Folktales of *Norway*. Folktales of the World Series. Chicago: University of Chicago Press, 1964.

———. The *Migratory Legends*. Folklore Fellows Communications #175. Helsinki, 1958.

CLARK, MOLLY. Silly Simon. Illustrated by Eccles. New York: Follett, 1967.

CLAUDEL, CALVIN. "Four Tales from the French Folklore of *Louisiana,*" SFQ 9 (1945): 191–208.

CLEARE, W. T. "Four Folk-Tales from *Fortune Island,* Bahamas," JAF 30 (1917): 228–29.

CLEMENS, SAMUEL LANGHORN. *How to Tell a Story and Other Essays.* New York: Harper and Brothers, 1897.

CLODD, EDWARD. "The *Philosophy* of Rumpelstiltskin," FLJ 7 (1889): 135–63.

———. *Tom Tit Tot,* an Essay on Savage Philosophy in Folk-Tale. London: Duckworth and Company, 1898.

CLOUSTON, WILLIAM A. The Book of *Noodles:* Stories of Simpletons, or Fools and their Follies. London: Elliot E. Stock, 1888.

———. *Popular* Tales and Fictions, their Migrations and Transformations. 2 vols. Edinburgh: W. Blackwood and Sons, 1887.

CONANT, L. "*English* Folk-Tales in America," JAF 8 (1895): 143–44.

COURLANDER, HAROLD. Cow-*Tail* Switch and Other West African Stories. Illustrated by Madye Lee Chastain. New York: Henry Holt and Co., 1947.

———. The *Fire* on the Mountain and Other Ethiopian Stories. Illustrated by Robert W. Kane. New York: Henry Holt and Co., 1950.

———. The *Hat-Shaking* Dance and Other Tales from Ghana. Illustrated by Enrico Arno. New York: Harcourt, Brace and World. 1957.

———. *Olode* the Hunter and Other Tales from Nigeria. Illustrated by Enrico Arno. New York: Harcourt, Brace and World, 1968.

———. *Terrapin's* Pot of Sense. Illustrated by Elton Fax. New York: Henry Holt and Co., 1957

COWELL, E. B. The *Jataka;* or, Stories of the Buddha's Former Births. 6 vols. London: Luzac and Co., 1957. (Originally published 1895–1905)

COX, JOHN H. "*Negro Tales* from West Virginia," JAF 47 (1934): 341–57.

———. "The *Witch Bridle,*" SFQ 7 (1943): 203–9.

COX, MARIAN. *Cinderella:* 345 Variants. London: David Nutt, 1893.

CRANE, THOMAS F., ed. Jacobus: *Exempla* or Illustrative Stories from the Sermones Vulgares of Jacques de Vitry. London: David Nutt, 1890.

———. *Italian* Popular Tales. Boston: Houghton, Mifflin and Co., 1885.

CROKER, THOMAS C. *Fairy Legends* and Traditions of the South of Ireland. 3 vols in 1. New York: Lemma Publishing Corp, 1971.

CROSBY, MURIEL, ed. The World of Language, Book Four. Chicago: Follett Educational Corporation, 1970.

ĆURČIJA-PRODANOVIĆ, NADA. *Yugoslav Folktales.* Illustrated by Joan Kiddell-Monroe. London: Oxford University Press, 1957.

CURTIN, JEREMIAH. *Myths and Folk-Lore* of Ireland. Boston: Little, Brown, and Co., 1917.

CUSHING, FRANK H. *Zuni* Folk Tales. New York: G. P. Putnam's Sons, 1901.

DAWKINS, R. M. *Forty-Five Stories* from the Dodekanese. Cambridge: University Press, 1950.

———. *Modern Greek* Folktales. Oxford: Clarendon Press, 1953.

———. *More Greek* Folktales. Oxford: Clarendon Press, 1955.

DEGH, LINDA. Folktales and *Society:* Story-Telling in a Hungarian Peasant Community. Translated by Emily Schossberger. Bloomington: Indiana University Press 1969.

———. Folktales of *Hungary.* Folktales of the World Series. Chicago: University of Chicago Press, 1965.

DE LA MARE, WALTER JOHN. Come Hither: A Collection of Rhymes and Poems for the Young of All Ages. Illustrated by Alec Buckels. London: Constable and Co., 1923.

———. Peacock Pie: A Book of Rhymes. London: Constable and Co., 1913.

———. Songs of Childhood. London: Longmans, Green and Co., 1902.

———. The Three Mulla Mulgars. London: Duckworth and Co., 1910.

———. *Told Again.* New York: Alfred Knopf, 1927.

DELARUE, PAUL. *Borzoi* Book of French Folk Tales. Translated by Augustin Fife. New York: Alfred Knopf, 1956.

DJURKLO, NILS G. Fairy Tales from the *Swedish.* Translated by H. L. Braekstad. New York: Frederick Stokes Co., 1901.

DOBIE, BERTHA MCKEE. "Tales and Rhymes of a *Texas Household,"* PTFLS 6 (1927): 23–71.

DOLCH, EDWARD, and MARGUERITE P. DOLCH. *Animal Stories in Basic Vocabulary.* Champaign, Ill.: Garrard, 1952.

DORSON, RICHARD. *American Folklore* and the Historian. Chicago: University of Chicago, 1971.

———. *American Negro* Folktales. Greenwich, Conn.: Fawcett Publications, 1970.

———. *Bloodstoppers* and Bearwalkers: Folk Traditions of the Upper Penninsula. Cambridge, Mass.: Harvard University Press, 1952.

———. *Buying* the Wind: Regional Folklore of the United States. Chicago: University of Chicago Press, 1964.

———. *"Comic Indian* Anecdotes," SFQ 10 (1946): 113–28.

———. Folktales Told Around the *World.* Chicago: University of Chicago Press, 1975.

———. *Jonathan* Draws the Long Bow. Cambridge, Mass.: Harvard University Press, 1946.

————. Negro Folktales in *Michigan.* Westport, Conn.: Greenwood Press, 1974.

————. *"Negro Tales,"* WF 13 (1954): 77–97.

————. "Negro Tales, Mary *Richardson,"* MF6, 1 (1956): 5–26.

EASTMAN, MARY H. Index to Fairy Tales, Myths and Legends, 2d ed. Boston: F. W. Faxon Co., 1926 (Supplements 1937, 1952).

EBERHARD, WOLFRAM. Folktales of *China* rev. ed. Chicago: University of Chicago Press, 1965.

EDDINS, A. W. *"Brazos* Bottom Philosophy," PTFLS 9 (1931): 153–64.

————. *"Negro* Tales and Jokes," PTFLS 26 (1954): 50–66.

EDMONDS, I. G. *Trickster Tales.* New York: J. P. Lippincott Co., 1966.

ELLIOT, GERALDINE. Where the *Leopard* Passes. New York: Schocken Books, 1968 (ca. 1949).

EMENEAU, M. B. "Studies in the Folktales of *India:* II The Old Woman and Her Pig," JAF 56 (1943): 272–88.

EMMONS, MARTHA. *"Cats* and the Occult," PTFLS 11 (1933): 94–100.

————. "Confidences from Old *Nacogdoches,"* PTFLS 7 (1928): 119–34.

ESPINOSA, AURELIO M. "New *Classification* of the Fundamental Elements of the Tar Baby Story on the Basis of 267 Versions," JAF 56 (1943): 31–37.

ESPINOSA, PORTO-RICAN. See Mason, *Porto-Rican.*

————. *"Pueblo Indian* Folk Tales," JAF 49 (1936): 69–133.

————. "Notes on the Origin and History of the *Tar-Baby* Story," JAF 43 (1930): 129–209.

FANSLER, DEAN. *Filipino* Popular Tales. Hatboro, Pa.: Folklore Associates, 1965. (Originally in MAFLS 12)

FAUSET, ARTHUR HUFF. "Folklore from *Nova Scotia,"* MAFLS 24 (1931).

————. *"Negro* FolkTales from the South," JAF 40 (1927): 213–303.

FELDMANN, SUSAN. The *Storytelling* Stone: Myths and Tales of the American Indians. New York: Dell Publishing, 1965.

FILLMORE, PARKER. Mighty Mikko. New York: Harcourt, Brace and Co., 1922.

————. Shepherd's *Nosegay:* Stories from Finland and Czechoslovakia. Illustrated by Enrico Arno. New York: Harcourt, Brace and World, 1958.

FISCHER, HANS. Puss in Boots. New York: Harcourt, Brace and World, 1959.

"Folk-Lore Scrapbook," JAF 10 (1897): 240–41.

FODOR, NANDOR. "Lycanthropy as a Psychic Mechanism," JAF 58 (1945): 310–316.

FORTIER, ALCÉE, ed. *Louisiana* Folk-Tales. MAFLS 2 (1895).

FOSTER, JAMES R. Great Folktales of *Wit* and Humor. New York: Harper and Brothers, 1955.

FROBENIUS, LEO. *African Genesis.* New York: Stackpole Sons, 1937.

GAG, WANDA. Gone is Gone. New York: Coward-McCann, 1935.

———. Three Gay Tales From Grimm. New York: Coward McCann, 1943.

GALDONE, PAUL. The Old Woman and Her Pig. New York: McGraw Hill, 1960.

GARDNER, EMELYN. Folklore From the *Schoharie* Hills, New York. Ann Arbor: University of Michigan Press, 1937.

GARNER, ALAN. *Elidor.* New York: Henry Z. Walck, 1965.

GASTER, MOSES. *Ma'Ash Book of Jewish Tales and Legends.* Philadelphia: Jewish Publication Society of America, 1934.

GILCHRIST, A. G. "The *Bone,*" FL 50 (1939): 378–79.

Gingerbread Boy. *St. Nicholas* Magazine (May 1875): 448–49.

GOLDSTONE, HERBERT. *"From Uncle Remus* to Mark Twain," SFQ 18 (1954): 242–43

GRAHAME, KENNETH. The Wind in the Willows. New York: Charles Scribner, 1908.

GREENWAY, JOHN. Gormless Tom. Illustrated by Jan Palmer. Morristown, New Jersey: Silver Burdett Co., 1968.

GRIERSON, ELIZABETH. Children's Tales from the Scottish Ballads. London: Adam and Charles Black, 1906.

GRIMM, JAKOB, and GRIMM, WILHELM. Grimms' Fairy Tales. Illustrated by Josef Scharl. London: Routledge and Kegan Paul, 1948.

———. Kinder-und Hausmärchen, 1812.

GROOME, F. HINDES, ed. *"Notes* and Queries," Ipswich Journal 15 (January, 1878).

GRUNDTVIG, SVEND H. *Danish* Fairy Tales. Translated by Gustav Hein. London: George Harrap and Co., 1914.

HALEY, GAIL E. A Story a Story. New York: Atheneum, 1970.

HALLIWELL, JAMES O. Popular Rhymes and *Nursery* Tales of England. London: Bodley Head, 1970. (Originally published 1849)

HALPERT, HERBERT. *"City Jests,"* HFB 2 (1943): 19–20.

———. "Folktales From Indiana University Students," HFB 1 (1942): 85–97

———. "Folktale and *Wellerism—*A Note," SFQ 7 (1943): 75–76.

———. *"Indiana Folktales,"* HFB 1 (1942): 3–34.

———. *"Indiana Storyteller,"* HFB 1 (1942): 43–61.

HAMPDEN, JOHN. The *Gypsy* Fiddle and Other Tales Told by the Gypsies. Illustrated by Robin Jacques. New York: World Publishing Co., 1969.

HAND, WAYLAND D. *Humaniora:* Essays in Literature, Folklore, Bibliography, Honoring Archer Taylor. Locust Valley, New York: J. J. Augustin, 1960.

HARLAND, JOHN WILKINSON, T. T. *Lancashire* Legends, Traditions, Pageants, Sports etc. London: George Routledge and Sons, 1873.

HARRIS, JOEL CHANDLER. *Nights* with Uncle Remus; Myths and Legends of the Old Plantation. Boston: Houghton Mifflin and Co., 1889.

———. Uncle *Remus,* His Songs and His Sayings. Illustrated by A. B. Frost. New York: D. Appleton and Co., 1898.

―――. *Told* By Uncle Remus: New Stories of the Old Plantation. New York: McClure Philips Co. 1905.

HARRIS, STANLEY. "Stories of *Ranch* People," PTFLS 30 (1961): 173–77.

HARTLAND, EDWIN S. *English Fairy* and Folk Tales. London: Walter Scott Ltd., n.d.

HAVILAND, VIRGINIA. Favorite Fairy Tales Told in *Norway.* Illustrated by Leonard Weisgard. Boston: Little Brown and Co., 1961.

HAZLITT, WILLIAM CAREW. *Shakespeare Jest Books.* London: Willis and Sotheran, 1864.

HEARN, LAFCADIO. *Japanese* Fairy Tales. Mount Vernon, New York: Peter Pauper Press, n.d.

HERRICK, ROBERT. *Hesperides.* Menston, England: Scholar Press, 1969.

HERRTAGE, SIDNEY, ed. Early English Versions of the *Gesta Romanorum.* London: Kegan Paul, Trench and Trubner and Co., 1879.

HILL, KAY. *Glooscap* and His Magic. New York: Dodd, Mead and Co., 1963.

HOFFMANN, DAN G. "Half a Dozen *Repeating Games,*" NYFQ 4 (1948): 207–12.

HOFFMANN, FELIX. Four Clever Brothers. New York: Harcourt, Brace and World, 1967.

―――. The Wolf and the Seven Kids. New York: Harcourt, Brace and World, 1959.

HOGROGIAN, NONNY. One Fine Day. New York: Macmillan, 1971.

HOKE, HELEN. *Witches,* Witches, Witches. Illustrated by W. R. Lohse. New York: Franklin Watts, 1958.

HUDSON, ARTHUR P. "Some *Versions* of 'The King of the Cats'," SFQ 17, no. 4 (1953): 225–31.

HUNT, ROBERT. *Popular Romances* of the West of England. 1st and 2d series in one volume. London: John C. Hotten, 1871.

HURSTON, ZORA N. *Mules* and Men. Philadelphia: J. B. Lippincott Co., 1935.

HYDE, DOUGLAS. *Beside the Fire.* London: David Nutt, 1910.

IKEDA, HIROKO. A *Type* and Motif Index of Japanese Folk-Literature. FF Communications 209. Helsinki, 1971.

IM, BANG. *Korean* Folktales: Imps, Ghosts, and Fairies. London: J. M. Dent, 1913.

IN-SŎB, ZŎNG. Folktales from *Korea.* London: Routledge and Kegan Paul, 1952.

IRELAND, NORMA. *Index* to Fairy Tales 1949–72. Westwood, Mass.: F. W. Faxon Co., 1973.

JACOBS, JOSEPH. *Celtic* Fairy Tales. Illustrated by John D. Batten. London: D. Nutt, 1892.

―――. *English* Fairy Tales. Illustrated by John D. Batten. 3rd. ed. New York: G. P. Putnam's Sons, 1898.

―――. *Europa's* Fairy Book. Illustrated by John D. Batten. London: G. P. Putnam's Sons, 1916.

———. The Fables of *Aesop.* Illustrated by Richard Heighway. New York: Schocken Books, 1966.

———. *Indian* Fairy Tales. Illustrated by John D. Batten. London: David Nutt, 1892.

———. Molly Whuppie. Illustrated by Pelagie Doane. New York: Oxford University Press, n.d.

———. *More Celtic* Fairy Tales. Illustrated John D. Batten. London: David Nutt, 1894.

———. *More English* Fairy Tales. Illustrated by John D. Batten. London: David Nutt, 1894.

———. The Three Wishes. Illustrated by Paul Galdone. New York: McGraw Hill, 1961.

JANSEN, WILLIAM H. "Tales from a *Steel Town,* Part 2," HFB 1 (1942): 78–81.

JOHNSON, CLIFTON. "Travels of a Fox," Outlook 57, no. 11 (November 13, 1897): 689–90.

———. *What They Say* in New England and Other American Folklore. New York: Columbia University Press, 1963.

JONES, GWYN. *Scandinavian* Legends and Folktales. Illustrated by Joan Kiddell-Monroe. New York: Henry Z. Walck, 1956.

JONES, LOUIS C. "The *Devil* in York State," NYFQ 8 (1952): 5–19.

JONES, THOMAS GWYNN. *Welsh* Folklore and Folk-Custom. London: Methuen and Co., 1930.

JONES, W. HENRY. The Folk-Tales of the *Magyars.* London: E. Stock, 1889. (PFLS 13, 1886)

KEIGHTLEY, THOMAS. The *Fairy Mythology.* London: H. G. Bohn, 1850. (Republished New York: AMS, 1968.

KELSEY, ALICE. Once the *Hodja.* Illustrated by Frank Dobias. New York: McKay, 1964 (ca. 1943).

KENNEDY, PATRICK. "*End* of the World," Dublin University Magazine, January 1867, pp. 8–9.

———. *Fireside* Stories of Ireland. Dublin: McGlashan and Gill, 1875.

———. *Legendary* Fictions of the Irish Celts. London: Macmillan and Co., 1866.

KENT, JACK. The Fat Cat. New York: Parents' Magazine Press, 1971.

KENT, MARGERY. Fairy Tales from *Turkey.* London: George Routledge and Sons, 1946.

KIRN, ANN. Beeswax Catches a Thief. New York: W. W. Norton, 1968.

KITTREDGE, GEORGE LYMAN. *English Folk-Tales* in America," JAF 3 (1890): 291–92.

———. *Witchcraft* in Old and New England. Cambridge, Mass.: Harvard University Press, 1929.

LALIBERTE, KATHRYN. "Toad Witch." Ypsilanti, Michigan, The Eastern Michigan University Folklore Archive, 1973.

———. "*Contes* Populaires Canadiens," JAF 44 (1931): 225–94.

LANCTÔT, GUSTAVE. "*Fables*, Contes et Formules," JAF 29 (1916): 141–51.

LANG, ANDREW. "At the Sign of the *Ship*," Longman's Magazine, July 1889, pp. 327–36.

———. The *Blue* Fairy Book. Illustrated by Manning DeV. Lee. Philadelphia: Macrae Smith Co., 1926.

———. The *Green* Fairy Book. Illustrated by H. J. Ford. London: Longmans, Green and Co., 1906. (7th impression)

LANGSTAFF, JOHN. Swapping Boy. Illustrated by Beth and Joe Krush. New York: Harcourt, Brace and World, 1960.

LASKOWSKI, REV. CORNELIUS. "*Polish* Tales of the Supernatural Collected in Albany, New York," NYFQ 10 (1954): 165–75.

LEACH, MARIA. Funk and Wagnalls Standard *Dictionary* of Folklore, Mythology, and Legend. 2 vols. New York: Funk and Wagnalls Co., 1949–50.

———. How the People Sang the *Mountains Up*. New York: Viking Press, 1967.

LEATHER, ELLA MARY. Folk-Lore of *Herefordshire*. Hereford: Jakeman and Carver, 1912.

LEWIS, C. S. The Lion, the Witch and the Wardrobe. Illustrated by Pauline Baynes. New York: Macmillian Co., 1950.

LOWRIMORE, BURTON. "*Six California* Tales," CFQ 4 (1945): 154–57.

MACCURDY, RAYMOND R. "*Spanish* Folklore from St. Bernard Parish, Louisiana: 3 Folktales," SFQ 16 (1952): 227–50.

MACMANUS, SEUMAS. *Donegal* Fairy Stories. Illustrated by Frank Verbeck. New York: Doubleday Page and Co., 1916.

MACMILLAN, CYRUS. *Canadian* Wonder Tales. London: John Lane, 1920.

———. *Glooskap's* Country and Other Indian Tales. New York: Henry Walck, 1962.

MAGNUS, LEONARD. *Russian* Folk-Tales. London: Kegan Paul, Trench, Trubner and Co., 1915.

MARRIOT, ALICE. *Winter-Telling* Stories. New York: Thomas Y. Crowell, 1969.

MARWICK, ERNEST W. The Folklore of *Orkney* and Shetland. New Jersey: Rowman and Littlefield, 1975.

MASON, J., and ESPINOSA, AURELIO. "*Porto-Rican* Folklore," JAF 34 (1931): 143–208.

MASSIGNON, GENEVIÈVE. Folktales of *France*. Folktales of the World Series. Chicago: University of Chicago Press, 1968.

MASTERS, ANTHONY. The Natural History of the Vampire. New York: G. P. Putnam's Sons, 1972.

MCALLISTER, J. GILBERT. "*Kiowa-Apache* Tales," PTFLS 22 (1949): 1–141.

———. "*Indian Tales:* Kiowa-Apache Tales," PTFLS 26 (1954): 1–11.

MCCLOSKEY, ROBERT. Burt Dow, Deep Water Man. New York: Viking Press, 1963.

MCINTOSH, DAVID S. "You Haven't Packed the *Saddle*," Illinois FL 1 (October 1947): 17–19.

MEGAS, GEORGIOS. Folktales of *Greece.* Folktales of the World Series. Chicago: University of Chicago Press, 1970.

MILLER, ELAINE. Mexican Folk Narrative from the *Los Angeles* Area. MAFLS 56 (1973).

MILNE, A. R., trans. *Mr Basket Knife* and Other Khmer Folktales. London: George Allen and Unwin, 1972.

MOHAN, BEVERLY. *Punia* and the King of Sharks. Illustrated by Don Bolognese. Chicago: Follett, 1964.

MONTRESOR, BENI. Cinderella. New York: Alfred Knopf, 1965.

MORRIS, JAMES. The Upstairs Donkey and Other Stolen Stories. Illustrated by Pauline Baynes. New York: Pantheon Books, 1961.

MORRISON, SOPHIA. *Manx* Fairy Tales. London: David Nutt, 1911.

MUSICK, RUTH A. *Green Hills* of Magic. Lexington, Kentucky: University of Kentucky Press, 1970.

NESS, EVALINE. Long, Broad, and Quick Eye. New York: Charles Scribner's Sons, 1969.

NESTRICK, NOVA. The Gingerbread Boy. Illustrated by Bonnie and Bill Rutherford and Eulalie. New York: Platt and Munk, 1961.

NEWALL, WILLIAM. "The *Passover* Song of the Kid and an Equivalent from New England," JAF 18 (1905): 33–48.

NICHOLS, LYDIA R. "An Old English *Nursery* Tale," JAF 13 (1900): 228–29.

NORTON, MARY. The Borrowers. New York: Harcourt, Brace and World, 1953.

NOY, DOV. Folktales of *Israel.* Folktales of the World Series. Chicago: University of Chicago Press, 1963.

OPIE, IONA, and OPIE, PETER. The Classic Fairy Tales. London: Oxford University Press, 1974.

ORBELL, MARGARET. *Maori* Folktales. New York: Humanities Press, 1968.

OSMA, LUPE DE. Witches' Ride and Other Tales from Costa Rica. New York: William Morrow and Co., 1957.

O'SUILLEABHAIN, SEAN. A *Handbook* of Irish Folklore. Hatboro, Pa.: Folklore Associates Inc., 1963.

O'SULLIVAN, SEAN. The *Folklore* of Ireland. Illustrated by John Skelton. New York: Hastings House, 1974.

———. Folktales of *Ireland.* Folktales of the World Series. Chicago: University of Chicago Press, 1966.

OWEN, MARY. "*Coyote* and Little Pig," JAF 15 (1902): 63–65.

PANCHATANTRA. See Ryder, *Panchatantra.*

PAREDES, AMERICO. Folktales of *Mexico.* Folktales of the World Series. Chicago: University of Chicago Press, 1970.

PARSONS, ELSIE CLEWS. "Folk-Lore from *Aiken,* S. C.," JAF 34 (1921): 1–39.

———. "Folk-Lore of the *Antilles,* French and English," MAFLS 26 (1933–43).

————. "Folk-Lore from the *Cape Verde* Islands," MAFLS 15 (1923).

————. "Tales from *Guilford County,* North Carolina," JAF 30 (1917): 168–208.

————. "Folktales of Andros Island, *Bahamas,*" MAFLS 13 (1918).

————. "Folk-Lore of the *Sea Islands* S. C.," MAFLS 16 (1923).

————. *"Zapoteca* and Spanish Tales of Mitla, Oaxaca," JAF 45 (1932): 277–317.

PAVEL, FRANCES. Elves and the Shoemaker. Illustrated by Joyce H. Hewitt. New York: Holt, Rinehart and Winston, 1961.

PEDROSO, CONSIGLIERI. *Portuguese* Folk-Tales. London: Folk-Lore Society, 1882. (PFLS, #9.)

PERCY, THOMAS. *Reliques* of Ancient English Poetry. 3 vols. London: L. A. Lewis, 1839.

PERRAULT, CHARLES. *Fairy Tales* of Charles Perrault. Translated by Geoffrey Brereton. Harmondsworth, Middlesex, Eng.: Penguin Books, 1957.

————. Popular Tales. Edited by Andrew Lang. Oxford: Clarendon Press, 1888.

PINO-SAAVEDRA, YOLANDO. Folktales of *Chile.* Folktales of the World Series. Chicago: University of Chicago Press, 1968.

PORTER, ENID. The Folklore of *East Anglia.* Illustrated by Gay John Galsworthy. Totowa, N. J.: Rowman and Littlefield, 1974.

PRATO, STANISLAS. *"Quelques Contes* littéraires dans la tradition populaire," Revue des traditions populaires 4 (1889): 167–78.

PRICE, CHRISTINE. Sixty at a Blow. New York: E. P. Dutton and Co., 1968.

PROTTER, ERIC, and PROTTER, NANCY. *Celtic* Folk and Fairy Tales. Illustrated by Charles Keeping. New York: Duell, Sloan and Pearce, 1966.

PUCKETT, NEWBELL N. *Folk Beliefs* of the Southern Negro. New Jersey: Patterson Smith, 1968.

R., L. "The Legend of *Titty Tod,*" Atheneum, January 2, 1847, p. 18.

RALSTON, WILLIAM. *Russian* Folk-Tales. London: Smith, Elder and Co., 1873.

RAMSAY, ALLAN. Tales from *Turkey.* London: Simpkin, Marshall, Hamilton, Kent and Co., 1914.

RANDOLPH, VANCE. *Devil's* Pretty Daughter and Other Ozark Folk Tales. Illustrated by Glen Rounds. New York: Columbia University Press, 1955.

————. *"Missouri* Folktales," MF 2 (1952): 77–90.

————. Ozark Superstitions. New York: Columbia University Press, 1947.

————. Sticks in the *Knapsack,* and Other Ozark Folk Tales. Illustrated by Glen Rounds. New York: Columbia University Press, 1958.

————. *"Tales from Missouri,"* MF 6 (1956): 38–49.

————. The Talking *Turtle* and Other Ozark Folk Tales. Illustrated by Glen Rounds. New York: Columbia University Press, 1957.

————. Who Blow'd Up the *Church House?* and Other Ozark Folk Tales. Illustrated by Glen Rounds. New York: Columbia University Press, 1952.

RANKE, KURT. Folktales of *Germany.* Folktales of the World Series. Chicago: University of Chicago Press, 1966.

RANSOME, ARTHUR. The Fool of the World and the Flying Ship. Illustrated by Uri Shulevitz. New York: Farrar, Strass, Giroux, 1968.

———. *Old Peter's* Russian Tales. London: Thomas Nelson, 1968.

RATTRAY, ROBERT S. *Akan-Ashanti* Folk-Tales. Oxford: Clarendon Press, 1930.

REAVER, J. RUSSELL. *"Four Lithuanian-*American Folk Tales," SFQ 12 (1948): 259–65.

———. *"Lithuanian* Tales from Illinois," SFQ 14 (1950): 160–68.

REED, ALEXANDER. Treasury of *Maori* Folklore. Wellington, New Zealand: A.H. & A.W. Reed, 1963..

REY, HANS A. Curious George. Boston: Houghton Mifflin, 1941.

REYNARD THE FOX. See Arber, Edward.

REZWIN, MAX. *Sick Jokes,* Grim Cartoons, and Bloody Marys. New York: Citadel Press, 1958.

ROBE, STANLEY L. *"Basque* Tales from Eastern Oregon," WF 12 (1953): 153–57.

———. Mexican Tales and Legends from *Los Altos,* Berkeley: University of California Press, 1970.

ROBERTS, LEONARD. "The *Cante Fable* in Eastern Kentucky," MF 6 (Summer 1956): 69–88.

———. *Sang Branch* Settlers: Folksongs and Tales of a Kentucky Mountain Family. Austin, Texas: University of Texas Press, 1974. MAFLS 61.

———. *South* from Hell-fer-Sartin. Berea, Ky.: Council of Southern Mountains Inc., 1964.

ROBERTS, WARREN. Tale of the *Kind and Unkind* Girls. Berlin: W. de Gruyter, 1958.

ROCHE, A. K. The *Clever Turtle.* Englewood Cliffs, N. J.: Prentice Hall, 1969.

ROCKWELL, ANNE. The Monkey's Whiskers. New York: Parent's Magazine Press, 1971.

ROOTH, ANNA B. The *Cinderella Cycle.* Lund, Sweden: Gleerup, 1951.

ROSE, E. H. *"Quebec* Folklore Notes, IV," FL 25 (1914): 251–52.

RUGOFF, MILTON A. A *Harvest* of World Folk Tales. Illustrated by Joseph Low. New York: Viking Press, 1949.

RYDER, ARTHUR. The *Panchatantra.* Chicago: University of Chicago Press, 1925.

SAUCIER, CORINNE L. Folk Tales from French *Louisiana.* New York: Exposition Press, 1962.

SAWYER, RUTH. Journey Cake Ho! Illustrated by Robert McCloskey. New York: Viking Press, 1953.

SCHEER, GEORGE F., ed. *Cherokee* Animal Tales. Illustrated by Robert Frankenberg. New York: Holiday House Inc., 1968.

SCHMIDT, DOROTHY. *EMU* Archive. Ypsilanti, Mich.: Eastern Michigan University.

Second Shepherds' Play. See Child, Second

SEKI, KEIGO. Folktales of *Japan.* Folktales of the World Series. Chicago: University of Chicago Press, 1963.

SELLERS, CHARLES. Tales from the Lands of Nuts and Grapes. London: Field and
    Tuer, Leadenhall Press, 1888.
SHEDLOCK, MARIE L. *Eastern Stories* and Legends. New York: E. P. Dutton and
    Co., 1920.
SHERLOCK, PHILIP M. *Anansi* the Spider Man: Jamaican Folk Tales. Illustrated by
    Marcia Brown. New York: Thomas Y. Crowell, 1954.
————, *Iguana's* Tail: Crick, Crack Stories from the Caribbean. New York:
    Thomas Y. Crowell, 1969.
SIMPSON, JACQUELINE. *Icelandic* Folktales and Legends. Berkeley: University of
    California Press, 1972.
————. The Folklore of *Sussex.* Illustrated by Gay John Galsworthy. London:
    Batsford, 1973.
SKINNER, ALANSON. "Plains *Ojibwa* Tales," JAF 32 (1919): 280–305.
SMALL, ERNEST. Baba Yaga. Illustrated by Blair Lent. Boston: Houghton Mifflin,
    1966.
SMILEY, PORTIA. "Folk-Lore from *Virginia,* South Carolina, Georgia, Alabama and
    Florida," JAF 32 (1919): 357–83.
SMITH, EDWIN W. The *Ila-Speaking* Peoples of Northern Rhodesia. 2 vols. London:
    Macmillan and Co., 1920.
SMITH, KIRBY F. "An Historical Study of the *Werwolf* in Literature," PMLA 9
    (1894): 1–42.
SMYSER, H. M. "*Analogues* to the Mak Story," JAF 47 (1934): 378–80.
SPEERS, MARY W. "*Notes* and Queries," JAF 25 (1912): 284–86.
STIMSON, ANNA. "Cries of *Defiance* and Derision and Rhythmic Chants of West
    Side New York City," JAF 58 (1945): 124–29.
STRAPAROLA. See Waters, *Nights*
STROUP, THOMAS B. "*Analogues* to the Mak Story," JAF 47 (1934): 380–81.
————. "Another Southern Analogue to the *Mak* Story," SFQ 3 (1939):
    5–6.
SUMMERS, MONTAGUE. The *Werewolf.* London: Kegan Paul, Trench, Trubner and
    Co., 1933.

TASHJIAN, VIRGINIA. Once There Was and Was Not: Armenian Tales Retold.
    Boston: Little, Brown and Co., 1966.
TAYLOR, ARCHER. "Review of Liungman's *Varifron* Kommer Vara Sagor," JAF 67
    (1954): 92–94.
THOMAS, LOWELL. *Tall Stories,* the Rise and Triumph of the Great American
    Whopper. Illustrated by Herb Roth. New York: Funk and Wagnalls Co.,
    1931.
THOMPSON, HAROLD. Body, *Boots,* and Britches. Philadelphia: J. B. Lippincott,
    1940.
THOMPSON, STITH. The *Folktale.* New York: Dryden Press, 1951.
————. *Motif Index* of Folk-Literature. 6 vols., rev. and enlarged ed. Bloomington,
    Ind.: Indiana University Press, 1955–58.

————. *One* Hundred Favorite Folktales. Bloomington: Indiana University Press, 1968.

————. The *Types* of the Folktale: A Classification and Bibliography. 2d. rev. ed. Folk Lore Fellows Communications #184. 1961.

THOMSON, DAVID. The *People* of the Sea. New York: John Day, 1955.

THORNE-THOMPSON, GUDRUN. Gudbrand on the Hillside. Recording.

THORP, NATHAN HOWARD. *Pardner* of the Wind. Caldwell, Idaho: Caxton Printers, 1945.

TOLKIEN, JOHN R. R. The Hobbit; or, There and Back Again. London: Allen and Unwin, 1937.

TOOR, FRANCES. A Treasury of *Mexican* Folkways. Illustrated by Carlos Merida. New York: Crown Publishers, 1947.

URE, JEAN. *Romanian* Folktales. New York: Franklin Watts, 1960.

WALKER, WARREN and UYSAL, AHMET. Tales Alive in *Turkey.* Cambridge, Mass.: Harvard University Press, 1966.

WALLACE, PAUL. Baptiste *Larocque:* Legends of French Canada. Toronto: Mussen Book Co., 1927.

WALLRICH, WILLIAM J. *"Spanish-American* Devil Lore in Southern Colorado," WF 9 (1950): 50–55.

WATERS, WILLIAM G. The *Nights* of Straparola. 2 vols. Illustrated by E. R. Hughes. London: Lawrence and Bullen, 1894.

WERTH, KURT. Lazy Jack New York: Viking, 1970.

————. The Valiant Tailor. New York: Viking Press, 1965.

WESSELSKI, ALBERT. Der *Hodscha* Nasreddin. 2 vols. Weimar: A. Duncker, 1911.

WHEELER, HOWARD. "Tales from *Jalisco* Mexico," MAFLS 35: (1943).

WHITING, B. J. "An Analogue to the *Mak* Story," Speculum 7 (1932): 552.

WHITING, JULIA D. *"English Folk-*Tales in America," JAF 2 (1889): 213–18.

WHITNEY, THOMAS. Vasilisa the Beautiful. Illustrated by Nonny Hogrogian. New York: Macmillan, 1970.

WIESNER, WILLIAM. Happy Go Lucky. New York: Seabury Press, 1970.

WIGGIN, KATE. Tales of *Laughter.* Garden City, N.Y.: Doubleday, Page and Co., 1923.

WILDER, LAURA INGALLS. On the Banks of Plum Creek. New York: Harper 1953.

WILKINSON, BARRY. Puss in Boots. New York: World Publishing., 1969.

WILSON, E. M. "Some *Humorous* English Folk Tales," Folklore 49 (1938): 182–192.

————. "Some Humorous English *Folk-Tales,* Pt.2," Folklore 49 (1938): 277–86.

WITHERS, CARL. I Saw a *Rocket* Walk a Mile. New York: Holt, Rinehart and Winston, 1965.

WRITERS PROJECT, GEORGIA. *Drums* and Shadows. Westport, Conn.: Greenwood Press, 1973. (originally published 1940)

YATES, DORA E. A Book of *Gypsy* Folk-Tales. London: Phoenix House, 1948.

YEATS, WILLIAM BUTLER. The Pot of Broth.

YOUNG, BLANCHE C. How the *Manx* Cat Lost its Tail and Other Manx Stories. New York: David McKay Co., Inc. 1959.

ZEMACH, HARVE. Nail Soup. Illustrated by Margot Zemach. New York: Follett, 1964.

ZIEGLER, ELSIE. Folklore: An Annotated Bibliography and Index to Single Editions. Westwood, Mass.: F. W. Faxon Co, 1973.